# THE
# FEMALE
# COMPLAINT

LAUREN BERLANT

# THE

# FEMALE

# COMPLAINT

*The Unfinished Business of Sentimentality*

*in American Culture*

DUKE UNIVERSITY PRESS

DURHAM AND LONDON   2008

© 2008 Duke University Press
All rights reserved.
Printed in the United States of America on acid-free paper ∞
Designed by Heather Hensley
Typeset in Monotype Fournier by Achorn International
Library of Congress Cataloging-in-Publication Data appear
on the last printed page of this book.

# CONTENTS

# PREFACE

Previous versions of this preface narrated how emotionally thorny it was to write this book. I wrote of myself and of women in my particular family—from Lena and Sadie to Mara and Cindy—who entered femaleness at different historical moments and yet whose styles of being in femininity have contained uncanny similarities. As you can imagine, such resonances raised intensities of attachment, love, protectiveness, gratitude, disappointment, despair, anger, and resentment that created obstacles to lithesome storytelling.

Then a friend not from the humanities asked me, "Why are you airing your personal business here? Isn't your knowledge the point?" Right, I responded—well, in the humanities we try to foreground what motivates and shapes our knowledge, and a personal story can telegraph a perspective efficiently and humanly. I wasn't happy with this somewhat canned response, although I also believe it. Yet the autobiographical isn't the personal. This nonintuitive phrase is a major presupposition of *The Female Complaint*. In the contemporary consumer public, and in the *longue durée* that I'm tracking, all sorts of narratives are read as autobiographies of collective experience. The personal is the general. Publics presume intimacy.

But how can I call "intimate" a public constituted by strangers who consume common texts and things? By "intimate public" I do not mean a public sphere organized by autobiographical confession and chest-baring, although there is often a significant amount of first-person narrative in an intimate public. What makes a public sphere intimate is an expectation that the consumers of its particular stuff *already* share a worldview and emotional knowledge that they have derived from a broadly common historical experience. A certain circularity structures an intimate public, therefore: its consumer participants are perceived to be marked by a commonly lived history; its narratives and things are deemed expressive of that history while also shaping its conventions of belonging; and, expressing the sensational, embodied experience of living as a certain kind of being in the world, it promises also to provide a better experience of social belonging—partly through participation in the relevant commodity culture, and partly because of its revelations about how people can live. So if, from a theoretical standpoint, an intimate public is a space of mediation in which the personal is refracted through the general, what's salient for its consumers is that it is a place of recognition and reflection. In an intimate public sphere emotional contact, of a sort, is made.

In other words, an intimate public is an achievement. Whether linked to women or other nondominant people, it flourishes as a porous, affective scene of identification among strangers that promises a certain experience of belonging and provides a complex of consolation, confirmation, discipline, and discussion about how to live as an *x*. One may have chosen freely to identify as an *x*; one may be marked by traditional taxonomies—those details matter, but not to the general operation of the public sense that some qualities or experience are held in common. The intimate public provides anchors for realistic, critical assessment of the way things are and provides material that foments enduring, resisting, overcoming, and enjoying being an *x*. To be all of these things to all of these people, though, the intimate public's relation to the political and to politics is extremely uneven and complex. This book tracks the "bargaining" with power and desire in which members of intimate publics always seem to be engaging.

*The Female Complaint* tells a story about the emergence and conventions of the first mass cultural intimate public in the United States. This "women's culture" is distinguished by a view that the people marked by femininity already have something in common and are in need of a conversation that feels intimate, revelatory, and a relief even when it is mediated by commodities, even when it is written by strangers who might not be women, and even when its particular stories are about women who seem, on the face of it, vastly different from each other and from any particular reader.

Women have long come to "women's culture" to experience versions of personal life that are made up by other people claiming to derive their stories from other women's real lives, and who knows? The consumers of "women's culture" do not always need its material to be true empirically—so much of it is marked as fantasy and expressed in extreme genres tending to hyperbole and grandiosity, which are forms of realism when social suffering is the a priori of experience, seen historically and across a wide variety of locations. But the commodities of women's intimate public sphere implicitly claim to sanction perspectives derived broadly from women's experience. The contents are TBA.

This presumption that there is a structure of relevancy, address, and absorption enables the consumers of "women's culture" to feel that their emotional lives are already shared and have already been raised to a degree of general significance while remaining true to what's personal. The domain of detail is always being negotiated, debated, and taken personally. This means that people participate in it who may share nothing of the particular worlds being represented in a given magazine, book, film, or soap opera venue. But even when people speak out against the terms the intimate public sets out as normative, they are still participating in the promise of belonging that it represents insofar as they are trying to recalibrate whose experience it can absorb so that they can feel included in the mass intimacy that has promised to include them.

One of the main jobs of the minoritized arts that circulate through mass culture is to tell identifying consumers that "you are not alone (in your struggles, desires, pleasures)": this is something we know but never tire of hearing confirmed, because aloneness is one of the affective experiences of being collectively, structurally unprivileged. This is barely a paradox. You experience taxonomic saturation ("labels") personally, but they are not about *you* personally. They are bigger than the both of us. What gets uttered is a collective story about the personal that is not organized by the singular autobiography. In "What Is a Minor Literature?" Deleuze and Guattari argue that one's identification with any material marked by a "minor" voice performs one's attachment to being generic, to being a member of a population that has been marked out as having collective qualities that are apprehensible in individuals. They also suggest that there are no simply personal voices for the minoritized author: the singular materials of a specific life are readable only as particulars that are exemplary not of the individual's life but of that *kind* of life. So consumption of "women's culture" would be, in this view, which is also my view, a way of experiencing one's own story as part of something social, even if one's singular relation to that belonging is extremely limited, episodic, ambivalent, rejecting, or mediated by random encounters with relevantly marked texts.

The works of "women's culture" enact a fantasy that my life is not just mine, but an experience understood by other women, even when it is not shared by many or any. Commodified genres of intimacy, such as Oprahesque chat shows and "chick lit," circulate among strangers, enabling insider self-help talk such as "girl talk" to flourish in an intimate public. These genres claim to reflect a kernel of common experience and provide frames for encountering the impacts of living as a woman in the world. Sentimentality and complaint are two ends of this commercial convention, with feminism as a kind of nosy neighbor. In the book I call women's culture "juxtapolitical" because, like most mass-mediated nondominant communities, that of feminine realist-sentimentality thrives in *proximity* to the political, occasionally crossing over in political alliance, even more occasionally doing some politics, but most often not, acting as a critical chorus that sees the expression of emotional response and conceptual recalibration as achievement enough. The strange and widespread phenomenon of publics ambivalent about politics is one of the main concerns of this book.

*The Female Complaint* constitutes the second stage of my "national sentimentality" project, flanked by *The Anatomy of National Fantasy* on one side and *The Queen of America Goes to Washington City* on the other. This series charts the emergence of the U.S. political sphere as an affective space, a space of attachment and identification that is not saturated merely by ideological or cognitive content but is also an important sustainer of people's desires for reciprocity with the world. Publics are affective insofar as they don't just respond to material interests but magnetize optimism about living and being connected to strangers in a kind of nebulous *communitas*. This book focuses on the ways a variety of nonprivileged subjects circulate through intimate publics to engender kinds of insider recognition and cultural self-development that, while denigrated in the privileged publics of the United States, provide an experience of social belonging in proximity to the technologies that make the nation itself a site of affective investment and emotional identification. (To readers who do think that women in the United States are subordinated no longer, here is another view. In modern liberal democratic societies, most inequality is partial, contradictory, and contested: it is often more informal [in behavior] than formal [law or policy]. Yet these complex conditions are not so complicated that their negative impacts are unpredictable. Disrespect for women is not unpredictable *enough*. It is more often affectively sensed or experienced in episodes than objective and dramatically fixable. Popular culture is terrible at dealing with mixed bags and mixed feelings when the register is ideological and the topic is intimate, and women remain the default managers of the intimate. Even if social negativity and antagonism are intricate and uneven and not merely top-down, the social field is still shaped powerfully by them.)

In *The Anatomy of National Fantasy* the law and the spaces of everyday life provide overlapping contexts for tracking the development of official and intimate publics in the early U.S. period: sometimes "the people" are authoritarian and identify with the law's strict discipline of its most vulnerable people *and at the same time* they develop their own networks of sympathy and recognition that create alternative spaces of survival and solidarity. This contradiction never bothers anyone: intimate publics, politically and institutionally mediated, but also emerging from shared spaces of the reproduction of life, thrive *because of* the extreme amount of contradiction they absorb about the range of possible, plausible responses to conditions of unfairness. Just as people are politically incoherent, so too are intimate publics and bodies politic: remember, national sentimentality is not about being right or logical but about maintaining an affective transaction with a world whose terms of recognition and reciprocity are being constantly struggled over and fine-tuned.

The last chapter of *Anatomy* opens up into the world of *The Female Complaint*, showing how Hawthorne's concept of a public was shaped by the sentimental focus on feminine suffering and conventions of reparative compassion. *The Female Complaint* then goes on to argue that starting in the 1830s an intimate public sphere of femininity constituted the first subcultural, mass-mediated, market population of relatively politically disenfranchised people in the United States. The intimate public branched off from, without entirely becoming antagonistic toward, the political scene of inequality that organized women as a subaltern population. Strategies for new improvisations and adaptations around women's suffering, emotional expertise, and practical agency became the main register for the sentimental publicity associated with this nondominant population. Even arguments about what the vote meant for women turned on how women feel and how that feeling produces knowledge that shapes what is politically possible. Popular and feminist melodramas repeat variations on this domain of feeling, where the question of the desire for and cost of feminine conventionality keeps being replayed in conventional texts. *The Queen of America* takes up this genealogy of public intimacy, tracking the development of a dominant public sphere organized around suffering and other intimate topics in the United States. What was a minor register of survival aesthetics has also become a predominant way even for elites to orchestrate a claim that their social discomfort amounts to evidence of injustice to them. Meanwhile, the fear and prospect of mass or live political activity by bodies politic permeates all of the books in this trilogy. The displacement of politics to the realm of feeling both opens a scene for the analysis of the operations of injustice in lived democracy and shows the obstacles to social change that emerge when politics becomes privatized.

At the same time, the fact that political feeling has a history of mediation means that its conventions can change. The optimism of this book, and there's not much of it, is located in the centrality of aesthetics and pedagogy to shaping fantasies, identifications, and attachments to particular identities and life narratives. The frustration accompanying that optimism has to do with the difficulty of inducing structural transformation out of shifts in collective feeling.

I owe many thanks to many people for talking about this material with me. Much appreciation goes to the wonderful graduate students and colleagues at the University of Chicago who have made a real intellectual difference to this project. Some deserve special mention for their willingness to be pedagogical: Zarena Aslami, Sam Baker, Homi Bhabha, Jim Chandler, Kris Cohen, Bradin Cormack, Jackie Cooper, Eva Fernandez, Beth Freeman, Elaine Hadley, Miriam Hansen, Beth Helsinger, Nancy Henry, Michelle Jensen, Arthur Knight, Hana Layson, Adam Lowenstein, Mark Miller, Alison Landsberg, Debbie Nelson, Jay Schleusener, Laurie Shannon, Emily Shelton, Allison Smith, Mary Lass Stewart, Jackie Stewart, Dana Seitler, Xiomara Santamarina, and Neda Ulaby. Also, from other schools are Dana Luciano and Jaime Hovey. I hope that you will recognize your impact here. In the too many years since this project emerged I have been lucky to have many great assistants: Meagan Shein, Beatriz Santiago-Muñoz, Gayle Liles, Suchitra Gururaj, Dina Mannino, Courtney Carson, Ryan Singel, Heather Bliven, Andrew Johnston, and Mary Hudgens. For the last few years Christa Robbins has provided sharp and creative bibliographical gathering, along with Rachel Furnari, who saw these thoughts and this production through to the end with fabulous acuteness, frankness, and grace. I am extremely indebted and grateful to them.

I have given a zillion talks from this project, and each chapter names the interlocutors that I can remember (sigh). I am thankful for fellowship and research support at the University of Pittsburgh, the Bain Center at Berkeley, the library at the University of Texas, Austin, the Lilly Library, the Library of Congress (thanks again, Madeline!), the UCLA and USC film archives, and the Clark and Brandeis libraries. Excerpts from *Show Boat* were used by permission of the Edna Ferber Literary Trust and Hammerstein Properties LLC, all rights reserved. I would like also to thank Duke University Press for permission to republish a revised version of "Poor Eliza" and "Uncle Sam Needs a Wife"; and Verso for permission to republish a revised version of "The Compulsion to Repeat Femininity." Thanks also to the great Heather Hensley, Courtney Berger, Katharine Baker, and Fred Kameny at Duke University Press for their wise editorial guidance. And thanks to the proofreaders: Kris Cohen, Eleanor Hyun, Michelle Menzies, and Gerard Cohen-Vrignaud.

For salutary influence on the project over the years I am very grateful to Jonathan Arac, Nina Baym, Rob Corber, Ann Cvetkovich, Cathy Davidson, Lee Edelman, Julie Ellison, June Howard, Claudia Johnson, Carol Kay, Laura Kipnis, Michael Moon, José Muñoz, Andy Parker, Don Pease, Mary

Poovey, Shirley Samuels, David Scobey, Eric Smoodin, Hortense Spillers, Jackie Stacey, Bill Warner, Michael Warner, Linda Williams, Candace Vogler, and Ken Wissoker. Each person deserves chocolate and a paragraph about the vital intellectual and emotional work he or she provided and I received. Special thanks go to Al Ravitz. Tom Stillinger and Roger Rouse introduced an especial amount of sense into my sentences, if not into me: I have been very lucky.

Then, there are the excellent friends and collaborators whose ongoing conversations and commitment produce vitalizing folds of space and time that mime what better worlds might be like—the Late Liberalism Group (Candace Vogler, Bradin Cormack, Elaine Hadley, Mark Miller, and Patchen Markell) and Feel Tank Chicago (Mary Patten, Debbie Gould, Rebecca Zorach, and Vanalyne Green); Sara Ahmed, Mandy Berry, Ann Cvetkovich, Lee Edelman, Sarah Franklin, Celia Lury, Neville Hoad, Susie Orbach, Claire Pentecost, Roger Rouse, Bev Skeggs, Jackie Stacey, Katie Stewart, and Lorelei Sontag. These people keep my head above water while pushing me beyond myself. Is that a possible sentence? My gratitude abounds.

Finally, I dedicate *The Female Complaint* to Geoff Eley, my great colleague and friend, whose critical acumen and political passion have helped my writing so much and who inspired me at key moments not to become a case study subject for this book. And to my housemates Ian and Puck I am grateful to have nothing to say of complaint and something happy to say about fun and love.

**INTRODUCTION**    Intimacy, Publicity, and Femininity

> Every normal female yearns
> to be a luminous person.
> FANNIE HURST

Everyone knows what the female complaint is: women live for love, and love is the gift that keeps on taking.[1] Of course that's a simplifying phrase: but it's not false, just partial. In the contemporary world of U.S. women's popular culture the bitter vigilance of the intimately disappointed takes up a lot of space: *The Bitch in the House*; *The Bride Stripped Bare*; and *Are Men Necessary?* among many others.[2] These hard-edged titles, however, conceal the tender fantasies of a better good life that the books also express. They market what is sensational about the complaint, speaking from a pretense to skewer an open secret that has been opened and skewered, in U.S. popular culture, since at least the 1830s. Fusing feminine rage and feminist rage, each has its own style of hailing the wounded to testify, to judge, to yearn, and to think beyond the norms of sexual difference, a little.

These books manifest the latest developments in what this book calls the mode of "the female complaint." They foreground witnessing and explaining women's disappointment in the tenuous relation of romantic fantasy to lived intimacy. Critical, they are also senti-mental, and therefore ambivalent: they trust affective knowledge and irratio-nal assurance more than the truths of any ideology; they associate femininity with the pleasures, burdens, and virtues of emotional expertise and track its methods in different situations; they focus on the sacrifice of women's emo-tional labor to a variety of kinds of callousness, incompetence, and structural inequity; they catalog strategies of bargaining, adaptation, and flouting the rules. But in popular culture ambivalence is seen as the failure of a relation, the opposite of happiness, rather than as an inevitable condition of intimate attachment and a pleasure in its own right (as evidenced in the affection-ate ironies toward personality of the situation comedy and the thrilling re-encounter with pleasure, foreboding, and disappointment familiar to fans of the soap opera and the melodrama).[3] The complaint genres of "women's culture," therefore, tend to foreground a view of power that blames flawed men and bad ideologies for women's intimate suffering, all the while main-taining some fidelity to the world of distinction and desire that produced such disappointment in the first place. They also provide tremendous pleasure in their vigilance toward recording how other women manage. One might say that it's a space of disappointment, but not disenchantment.

*The Female Complaint* focuses on what has evolved and shifted around but not changed profoundly in the history of public-sphere femininity in the United States—a love affair with conventionality. It emerges from a desire to understand what keeps people attached to disaffirming scenarios of ne-cessity and optimism in their personal and political lives.[4] It argues that the unfinished business of sentimentality—that "tomorrow is another day" in which fantasies of the good life *can* be lived[5]—collaborates with a sentimen-tal account of the social world as an affective space where people ought to be legitimated because they have feelings and because there is an intelligence in what they feel that *knows* something about the world that, if it were listened to, could make things better.

This very general sense of confidence in the critical intelligence of affect, emotion, and good intention produces an orientation toward agency that is focused on ongoing adaptation, adjustment, improvisation, and developing wiles for surviving, thriving, and transcending the world as it presents itself. It is not usually expressed in or addressed to the political register: as I indi-cated in the preface, generally intimate publics such as this one operate in aesthetic worlds that are juxtapolitical, flourishing in proximity to the political because the political is deemed an elsewhere managed by elites who are interested in reproducing the conditions of their objective superiority, not in the well-being of ordinary people or life-worlds. As the first half of this book argues in some detail, even when women sentimentalists turn to politics, it is not usually because they view politics as a resource for living but because they see it as a degraded space and a threat to happiness and justice that needs reforming so that better living can take place.[6]

Each chapter of the book looks at a different permutation of the space of permission to thrive that this particular women's intimate public stands for, for its participants: permission to live small but to feel large; to live large but to want what is normal too; to be critical without detaching from disappointing and dangerous worlds and objects of desire. Over more than a century and a half of publication and circulation, the motivating engine of this scene has been the aesthetically expressed desire to be *somebody* in a world where the default is being nobody or, worse, being presumptively *all wrong*: the intimate public legitimates qualities, ways of being, and entire lives that have otherwise been deemed puny or discarded. It creates *situations* where those qualities can appear as luminous.

Thus to love conventionality is not only to love something that constrains someone or some condition of possibility: it is another way of talking about negotiating belonging to a world. To love a thing is not only to embrace its most banal iconic forms, but to work those forms so that individuals and populations can breathe and thrive in them or in proximity to them.[7] The convention is not only a *mere* placeholder for what could be richer in an underdeveloped social imaginary, but it is also sometimes a profound placeholder that provides an affective confirmation of the idea of a shared confirming imaginary in advance of inhabiting a material world in which that feeling can actually be lived. In short, this affair is not an assignation with inauthenticity. In popular culture, when conventionality is not being called a homogenizing threat to people's sovereignty and singularity it is seen as a true expression of something both deep and simple in the human. By "conventionality" I span the term's normative and aesthetic senses and claim that the mass mediation of desires in women's genres constructs a deep affinity between them.[8]

This is to say that, in the scene of this particular public, femininity is a genre with deep affinities to the genres associated with femininity. In this book, a genre is an aesthetic structure of affective expectation, an institution or formation that absorbs all kinds of small variations or modifications while promising that the persons transacting with it will experience the pleasure of encountering what they expected, with details varying the theme. It mediates what is singular, in the details, and general about the subject.[9] It is a form of aesthetic expectation with porous boundaries allowing complex audience identifications: it locates real life in the affective capacity to bracket many kinds of structural and historical antagonism on behalf of finding a way to connect with the feeling of belonging to a larger world, however aesthetically mediated.[10]

To call an identity like a sexual identity a genre is to think about it as something repeated, detailed, and stretched while retaining its intelligibility, its capacity to remain readable or audible across the field of all its variations. For femininity to be a genre *like* an aesthetic one means that it is a structure of conventional expectation that people rely on to provide certain kinds of affective intensities and assurances. (This is to say that what we have called the "performativity" of personality usually produces variations *within* a conventional expectation of self- and world- continuity, rather than mainly providing dramas of potentially frame-breaking alternativity.[11]) Even the prospects of failure that haunt the performance of identity and genre are conventional: the power of a generic performance always involves moments of potential collapse that threaten the contract that genre makes with the viewer to fulfill experiential expectations. But those blockages or surprises are usually *part of* the convention and not a transgression of it, or anything radical. They make its conventionality interesting and rich, even.

The status of minor or inconsequential details and swerves from the usual is a major topic of this book, as women's culture always contains episodes of refusal and creative contravention to feminine normativity, even as it holds tightly to some versions of the imaginable conventional good life in love. Does this mean that its aim is to neutralize dissent, to protect the givens of ordinary life? Those two conserving aims are readily available, but they are not the whole story. Does this mean that the emphasis on convention secretly aims at making people sick of convention, releasing energies of radical critique toward substantial social change? Sometimes, in middlebrow texts, this is a motive (see chapter 6, on Dorothy Parker), but not usually: middlebrow

*femininity as genre* [handwritten marginal note]

THESIS [handwritten note]

popular genres are about the management of ambivalence, and not the destruction of pleasures or power.[12] My claim is that the gender-marked texts of women's popular culture cultivate fantasies of vague belonging as an alleviation of what is hard to manage in the lived real—social antagonisms, exploitation, compromised intimacies, the attrition of life. Utopianism is in the air, but one of the main utopias is normativity itself, here a felt condition of general belonging and an aspirational site of rest and recognition in and by a social world.

*normativity*

*normativity as utopia*

## Intimate Publics

"Women's culture" is one of many flourishing intimate publics in the United States. An intimate public operates when a market opens up to a bloc of consumers, claiming to circulate texts and things that express those people's particular core interests and desires. When this kind of "culture of circulation" takes hold, participants in the intimate public *feel* as though it expresses what is common among them, a subjective likeness that seems to emanate from their history and their ongoing attachments and actions.[13] Their participation seems to confirm the sense that even before there was a market addressed to them, there existed a world of strangers who would be emotionally literate in each other's experience of power, intimacy, desire, and discontent, with all that entails: varieties of suffering and fantasies of transcendence; longing for reciprocity with other humans and the world; irrational and rational attachments to the way things are; special styles of ferocity and refusal; and a creative will to survive that attends to everyday situations while imagining conditions of flourishing within and beyond them.

"Women's culture" was the first such mass-marketed intimate public in the United States of significant scale.[14] As a market domain where a set of problems associated with managing femininity is expressed and worked through incessantly, women's culture solicits belonging via modes of sentimental realism that span fantasy and experience and claim a certain emotional generality among women, even though the stories that circulate demonstrate diverse historical locations of the readers and the audience, especially of class and race. In all cases, it flourishes by circulating as an already felt need, a sense of emotional continuity among women who identify with the expectation that, as women, they will manage personal life and lubricate emotional worlds.

This commodity world and the ideology of normative, generic-but-unique femininity trains women to expect to be recognizable by other members of this intimate public, even if they reject or feel ambivalent about its dominant terms.

For example, this book argues that embedded in the often sweetly motivated and solidaristic activity of the intimate public of femininity is a white universalist paternalism, sometimes dressed as maternalism. As long as they have had a public sphere, bourgeois white women writers have mobilized fantasies of what black and working-class interiority based on suffering must feel like in order to find a language for their own more privileged suffering at the hands of other women, men, and callous institutions.[15] As we will see especially in "Poor Eliza," *Show Boat*, and *Imitation of Life*, in many instances melodramatic conventions that locate the human in a universal capacity to suffer and romantic conventions of individual historical acts of compassion and transcendence are adapted to imagine a nonhierarchical social world that is postracist and "at heart" democratic because good intentions and love flourish in it. Yet the mechanisms of this fantasy of generality through emotional likeness in the domain of pain are both very complex and not complex enough. Compassionate liberalism is, at best, a kind of sandpaper on the surface of the racist monument whose structural and economic solidity endures: in the intimate sphere of femininity a kind of soft supremacy rooted in compassion and coercive identification wants to dissolve all that structure through the work of good intentionality, while busily exoticizing and diminishing the inconvenient and the noncompliant. Hazel Carby, Paula Bennett, Laura Wexler, many others, and I have elsewhere noted that these aesthetic and ideological norms produced ambivalent responses from nonwhite, immigrant, and working-class literary writers writing in the United States, responses both critical and attached to the idea of a conversation among women.[16] Insofar as these writers were writing from *within* a sphere of address and demanding revision of its terms of recognition they were writing as critical members of an intimate public to demand its reorganization.

But most people who feel held by the intimacy of a public would not recognize this part of the description: intimate spheres *feel* like ethical places based on the sense of capacious emotional continuity they circulate, which seems to derive from an ongoing potential for relief from the hard, cold world. Indeed the offer of the simplicity of the feeling of rich continuity with a vaguely defined set of like others is often the central affective magnet of an intimate public.

Indeed, "women's culture" survives as a recognizable thing in the United States not just because markets revitalize it constantly in all media; not just because the U.S. social field is so saturated by normative heterofemininity; and not just because the intimate sphere provides a convenient register in which to debate and obscure larger knots of social attachment and antagonism: it survives also because its central fantasy, and the one this book elaborates, is the constantly emplotted desire of a complex person to rework the details of her history to become a vague or simpler version of herself, usually in the vicinity of a love plot. If she cannot achieve this condition of generality through the standard marital and reproductive modes of building reciprocity with the world or having "a life" that adds up to something, she does it through gestures, episodes, and other forms of fantasy improvisation, perhaps with less conventional objects, so long as she can feel in a general sense that she has known the feeling of love and carries the memory of having been affectively recognized and emotionally important. The complexities and stresses of lives managed under all of the vectors of subordination that we know about produces a vast market in such moments of felt simplicity. But because those fantasies of translation are in relation to what is hard about surviving, there is nothing simple about them or the astounding amount of creativity they absorb in the course of the ordinary reproduction of life.

To market normalcy not as a lifestyle achievement but as a feeling of aspirational generality within an intimate public might be to describe the dissemination of a feeling we *could* call imminently political or democratic, if it were, and when it is. But to do this we would not need the language of an intimate public—"counterpublic" would do. Counterpublic theory, associated with Nancy Fraser and Michael Warner, has joined the terms "subculture" and "minor culture" in our critical attempts to address the public mediation and ongoing life of dominated social populations.[17] Are all groups who take pleasure in their identifications with themselves counterpublics? The counterpublic model tends to over-enmesh a mess of different things: a group's being nondominant; being historically subordinated; being distinct; having cultivated cultural specificity; being alternative; and being in an antagonistic relation to a dominant paradigm. But these positions and processes are not the same, and it is worth paying attention to that so that we can understand how it is possible for publics to be overdetermined and also organized differently from each other.

Fraser distinguishes "weak" from "strong" publics to differentiate those that address themselves toward cultural flourishing from those that address questions of structural inequality mediated by the state and related institutions.[18] The strong public is strong because it organizes its sense of belonging in a conventionally political register, whereas the weak public is not focused by or aspirationally mimetic of a civic orientation. In her lexicon, an intimate public would function mainly as a weak public: but this taxonomy underdescribes the dynamics of indirection and mediation that characterize even strong publics, while bracketing the difficult question of what kinds of views can be said to constitute the circulated "opinion" that produces civil society as a force in institutional political life. Can absorption in affective and emotional transactions that take place at home, on the street, and between intimates and strangers be deemed irrelevant to civil society unless they are somehow addressed to institutions? What is the relation between feeling detached and being detached from the political, between feeling invested and exercising agency? The unclear line between these positions is manifest in the liberal sentimental imaginary of women's culture tracked in this book's first half, which follows adaptations of the *Uncle Tom's Cabin* tradition.

The problem at hand is of naming what appears when a collectivity is historically created by biopower, class antagonism, nationalism, imperialism, and/or the law and, at the same time, is engendered by an ongoing social life mediated by capital and organized by all kinds of pleasure (from personal consumption to active community membership to being "a regular" somewhere). Intimate publics elaborate themselves through a commodity culture; have an osmotic relation to many modes of life; and are organized by fantasies of transcending, dissolving, or refunctioning the obstacles that shape their historical conditions. But most nondominant collective public activity is not as saturated by the taxonomies of the political sphere as the counterpublic concept would suggest.

Biopower has indeed reorganized individuals into populations deemed incompetent to the privileges of citizenship—political, cultural, and/or social.

It produces fields of historical commonality that are at once specifically related to events (this bomb, that rape, this war, that police encounter, this epidemic, that moral panic) and to what it was like back in the day. As chapter 4, *Uncle Sam Needs a Wife*, argues, no population has ever erased the history of its social negativity from its ongoing social meaning. There are elaborations, amnesias, shifts, new potentials constantly released in the activity of living, but historical wounds always remain available for reopening. Nonetheless, ongoing and developing social practices and mobile identifications within a field of belonging generate diverse kinds of absorption in the activity of the reproduction of life—not just at work, but in domains of the pleasures.

In other words, distinct social populations, made so by law, science, religion, social conventions, and intellectuals, do not function at a level of theoretical coherence, even if a violent, simplifying force shaped their historical formation. Fantasies and practices of social belonging operate imprecisely, in interaction with complicated and contradictory environments of living. People live their fantasies incoherently too, in uneven practices of attachment and attention. Michael Moon has made a crucial contribution to this line of thought by pointing out that even conventional identity often lurks in the semi-public and semi-explicit spaces of consciousness and of the built world.[19] Additionally, to desire belonging to the normal world, the world as it appears, is at root a fantasy of a sense of continuity, a sense of being generally okay; it is a desire to be in proximity to okayness, without passing some test to prove it. In this version of the desire, the subject desires not to feel responsible for inhabiting or policing most social distinctions.

How should we calibrate this with what we also know about the discipline of normativity, which is that a hygienic, morally constrained version of the aspirational good life is always available as an instrument of moral trumping in the political public sphere? The vagueness of the affective fantasy of the normal requires activation of what Sedgwick calls "the privilege of unknowing" the social costs to others of a general sense of personal freedom.[20] One support for the privilege of unknowing is the desire to identify daily life as the space where living really takes place, and to see ordinary life as a scene of constant bargaining, dodging, strategizing, making claims, and moving under the radar. Plus, being vague can be a defense, a response to the attrition wrought by the pressures of living. These zones and practices are not scenes

*the desire to be normal v the discipline of normativity)*

vagueness — unknowing

of constant crisis but part of the *casualness* of identity. They are an effect of the ways agency is mediated and delegated in mass society. In focusing on the dynamics of lived structure as they manifest themselves in sentimental bargaining, each chapter of this book tells a story about living shiftingly among this cluster of forces.

The concept of the "intimate public" thus carries the fortitude of common sense or a vernacular sense of belonging to a community, with all the undefinedness that implies. A public is intimate when it foregrounds affective and emotional attachments located in fantasies of the common, the everyday, and a sense of ordinariness, a space where the social world is rich with anonymity and local recognitions, and where challenging and banal conditions of life take place in proximity to the attentions of power but also squarely in the radar of a recognition that can be provided by other humans. It is textually mediated: as Miriam Hansen has argued, modern publics required stylistic strategies and modes of narration to absorb viewers into textually constructed positions of general subjectivity that also served the historical convergence of social and economic objectives.[21] Juxta (*iuxta*, in Greek) means "near": more often than not, though, in mass society, what counts as collectivity has been a loosely organized, market-structured juxtapolitical sphere of people attached to each other by a *sense* that there is a common emotional world available to those individuals who have been marked by the historical burden of being harshly treated in a generic way and who have more than survived social negativity by making an aesthetic and spiritual scene that generates *relief from the political*. The "women's culture" concept grows from such a sense of lateral identification: it sees collective sociality routed in revelations of what is personal, regardless of how what is personal has itself been threaded through mediating institutions and social hierarchy. It marks out the nonpolitical situation of most ordinary life as it is lived as a space of continuity and optimism and social self-cultivation. If it were political, it would be democratic.[22]

Ironically, in the United States the denigration of the political sphere that has always marked mass politics increasingly utilizes these proximate or "juxtapolitical" sites as resources for providing and maintaining the experience of collectivity that also, sometimes, constitutes the body politic; intimate publics can provide alibis for politicians who claim to be members of every community *except* the political one. There are lots of ways of inhabiting these intimate publics: a tiny point of identification can open up a field of fantasy and de-isolation, of vague continuity, or of ambivalence. All of these energies of attachment can indeed become mobilized as counterpublicity but usually aren't. Politics requires active antagonism, which threatens the *sense* in consensus: this is why, in an intimate public, the political sphere is more often seen as a field of threat, chaos, degradation, or retraumatization than a condition of possibility.

Addressing femininity from the perspective of the mediated fantasies that magnetize many different kinds of women to the scene of suffering, sacrifice, survival, criticism, and sometimes sublimity that has historically provided the narrative of women's culture thus shows us something about the operation of mass-mediated identity—that is, how it manages to sublimate singularity on behalf of maintaining proximity to a vague prospect of social belonging via the generic or conventional plot that isolates an identity as the desired relay from weakness to strength, aloneness to sociability, abandonment to recognition, and solitary agency to reciprocity. In this book we encounter these fantasies of emplacement, exchange, and transcendence for women in conventional narratives, fantasies, and ideologies of fulfillment. These alternative scenes of love—of projection, displacement, attachment, and belonging—operate in concert, though sometimes in competition: the couple/family form, the nation, and capitalism. For the writers of these narratives both the nation and capital have two special kinds of function. One function is institutional, in their disciplinary organization of materialized or lived life. The other function is to serve not as sources of reciprocity or justice, but as magnetizing forms for *fantasies* of reciprocity and justice whose very impersonality and constitution in an ongoing near future is a source of relief and optimism. This is why, in the pamphlets, novels, and films to follow, even when critical observations about the gap between lived and fantasy life survive the sifting through generic conventionality, political critique tends to appear mainly in episodes that don't matter narratively, or in resistant movements, phrases, or timbres.

Joan Copjec argues, nonetheless, that the perspective of feminine aesthetic sentimentality reveals and confronts the absence of ethical foundations in the world; Paula Bennett insists that women's culture's edge was much less blunted than what I've suggested.[23] But from what I can tell, the feminine literary figures whom these scholars describe are defined so much by their desires for there to be a ground to stand on in the world as it exists that they remain, on the whole, committed to the normative permission of feminine fantasy as a ground—despite everything. The ground of mass normative fantasy is wobbly, a scene of bargaining for survival and jockeying for supremacy: but the cohabitation of critique, conventionality, and the commodity produces more movement within a space than toward being or wanting to be beyond it. This jerky aesthetics negotiates constantly the significant difference between fantasizing fulfillment, witnessing disappointment, and engendering transformative events. Tears and the varieties of mourning, melancholia, satire, and bargaining that respond to disappointment are gestures that define living as responsiveness to the urgencies of the ongoing moment, as a scene of heroism and pragmatism authorized by fantasy. A commitment to this mediation distracts from having to confront the potential for events to induce breaks. When politics is serious, it risks a loss of the ground of living in which people have come to know their competencies and their desires: fantasy, in contrast, is a zone of stop-loss, a demand for the ongoing present to be the scene of lived fulfillment.

To catch the drift of modern mass-mediated femininity in the United States we will look at the relation of social to aesthetic conventionality; of repetition to imitation; of adaptation to transformation; of ineloquence to expressivity. We will see women generate an affective and intimate public sphere that seeks to harness the power of emotion to change what is structural in the world. We will see a culture of "true feeling" emerge that sanctifies suffering as a relay to universality in a way that includes women in the universal while attaching the universal more fully to a generally lived experience; we will see commodities help to distribute and to enable the building of this intimate public of femininity, whose core is to witness women's lives in a conflation of extremity and ordinariness that constitutes the struggle to master a social situation rife with contradictions about desire, suffering, and fantasies of amelioration; and we will ask how transformed subjectivity can make and change worlds.

The example of the intimate public organized by affect and emotion also forces questions about the centrality of economies of suffering to mass capitalist aesthetics, and the relation between the aesthetic pleasures in extremity and the redeployment and banalization of violence and ordinary inequality. Why and how do specific kinds of collective but individually experienced pain get turned into modern forms of entertainment? How do we come to terms with the use of aesthetic conventions of excess (in melodrama, satire, comedy, romance) in processes of national cultural normativity and critique, especially insofar as these genres are depended on to express the true suffering and true desires of ordinary persons? How are different types of person and kinds of population hailed by the universalist icon of the person who loves, suffers, and desires to survive the obstacles that bind her or him to history? How are structural antagonisms refracted in the intimate anxieties of emplotted love, here mediated by conventions of addressing conventionality? What are the political consequences of a commoditized relation among subjects who are defined not as actors in history but as persons who shop and feel?

Mass-mediated popular culture is always generating more opportunities for fomenting a sense of focused belonging to an evolving world in this intensely connected yet mediated way. But the market frames belonging to an intimate public as a condition of possibility mainly for those who can pass as conventional within its limited terms. Belonging to an intimate public is therefore a condition of feeling general within a set of porous constraints, and of feeling held or sustained by an evolving sense of experience that confirms some homogeneity and elaborates social distinctions.

## Love: Repeat after Me

The female complaint *is* a discourse of disappointment. But where love is concerned, disappointment is a partner of fulfillment, not an opposite. Each is central to the absorbing anxiety that gets animated by having an object of desire—anxiety being, after all, the affective copy of ambivalence, where we work out conflicting inclinations toward what kinds of closeness and distance we want, think we want, and can bear our object to have.[24] Think of the frequent moments in the life of a relationship when you experience frustrated sovereignty, needing to feel free to be vague, wrong, opaque, distracted, withholding, or irresponsible at the same time as you need your intimate to remain open, unsuspicious, clear, and caring, as well as alive with the capacity to surprise you (but not too much!). Love demands an imbalancing act. This section lays out some of the psychoanalytic frames for what follows, which saturate the writing without usually being its explicit idiom. In advance of the cases, this may seem bizarre, since being overwhelmed by the specific historical and lived detail of the everyday is the sense that the chapters follow: but amid the scene of historical enunciation of the texts and their remakes, psychoanalytic formalism stands as training in thinking about the drive to become unhistorical, to become general through repetition into convention.

This double-time of the double-take so deeply inscribed in love leads Jacques Lacan to argue that "love is giving something one doesn't have to someone who doesn't want it"[25]: but by this he doesn't mean that one could choose otherwise.[26] His logic goes like this: you, the lover, assert that you love while demanding that your love object (the woman, in Lacan's symbolization) provide for you the surreal combination of ego recognition and idealization that you require in order to give love in the first place. This is why, when someone says, "I have so much love to give" he or she means that under the right circumstances he or she would return what was given to him or her. But circumstances are never just right; they are always just being righted. Therefore to Lacan love and melancholy are like "this," anxiously tangling the ongoing pleasures of desire, projection, and disappointment, and hauntingly aligned with the paradoxical certitudes of ecstasy (loss of self-control, or *jouissance*) and misery (absolute loss of the other and therefore of access to one's own idealized ego). By *pleasures* I mean the self-confirmation one receives by repeating the dynamics of an affective scene—something does not have to feel good viscerally for it to be a pleasure.[27] The loss of pleasure, then, can be defined as the insufferable interruption of a repetition with which a lover has identified the optimism of a fundamental attachment.[28]

In this view, love is a formal promise and an aspiration to try and try again to intend to be faithful to an enduring project of projection, mirroring, and repetition.[29] It is a fidelity to a form that only exists in its recurrence. While the conventions of romantic love identify it as an unmistakable feeling (except when it isn't and has to be revealed), love is a binding relation to time, not a steady state of object desire; it involves a need for events both of grandiose and credible ego confirmation; and it is a form of repetitive attachment that attracts to itself many affects and emotions all at once, usually in a jumble—but figuratively or ideologically they are all of a piece.[30] "Passion is no less real for the fact that it is repetition," writes Zelda Fitzgerald.[31] Modern lovers are defined by their desire to remain in proximity to the clarity—not simplicity—of the form of love; the form of love is an intention—not a compulsion—to repeat being attached. The intention to repeat is what gets expressed in wanting to "have a future together" or to be someone's "intended." This is why the sideways gaze, the held breath, the mumbled phrase, or the strange piece of paper can so disconcert the dynamics of an attachment. This is how intimates who repulse each other can remain coupled when it is no longer fun. They ride the wave of love's phantasmatic contract with imminent mutual transparency, simultaneity, and completion all too well.[32]

Love is the gift that keeps on *giving* when people can rely on re-experiencing their intimates' fundamental sympathy with the project of repetition and recognition, no small feat since the terms of that sympathy are constantly shifting internally just as they are renegotiated in the world. This explains the fetishistic optimism of romantic love about "tomorrow," as in "tomorrow is another day" when there will be opportunities to try again. Love is the gift that keeps on *taking* for the same reason: the search for mirroring (desire) demands constant improvisation (anxiety) and taking of accounts (disappointment). But let us not think that the complaint carries the force of devastating critique, even as it manifests the ruthlessness of emotional measurement. As I argue in the opening to this chapter, the fantasy dictum that love *ought to be* the gift that keeps on *giving* is a fundamental commitment of female complaint rhetoric. The position of the depressive realist who sees that love is nonetheless the gift that keeps on taking is the source of complaint epistemology.

In the ideology of romantic love, the successful negotiation of these projections and flows is called "reciprocity." In the universe of companionate intimacy that emerged during the consolidation of so-called middle-class cultural values in the American and English Victorian periods, when romantic love became elevated over economic interest as the normative motivator of long-term couplings, reciprocity emerged as central to what counts as care and carelessness.[33] Reciprocity is a morally laden, actuarial, and at the same time lovely, fantasy-based concept of what mutuality in love might actually be like: mutuality is a tableau, reciprocity a practice. These are not psycho-analytically rich enough concepts—in fact psychoanalytic accounts from many schools of thought equate reciprocity and mutuality while providing very little analysis of their specific enactments apart from that of the maternal gaze or maternal/caretaking constancy and the patterns that extend from that formation.[34] (See chapter 5, on *Now, Voyager,* for more on this.)

But in the archive of women's culture, questions about what counts as emotional reciprocity matter tremendously. Which acts are commensurate? When do intentions matter? How ought lovers to track the relation of local acts to long-term practices? What is the status of the ordinary event in the project of collaborative, intimate life-making? From the nineteenth century on, we witness in women's culture's stories the many kinds of bargaining women do to stay in proximity to the work of love at the heart of normative femininity, the utopian and pathetic impulses behind this bargaining, and its costs and pleasures, including the tragicomic pleasures of the love plot's incompleteness up to and often beyond death. Women's will, aggression, abjection, and fatalism concerning the demand for reciprocity constitute the driving forces of these narratives. It is also worth noting that, according to Jacqueline Rose, anxiety is the core affect of femininity, which operates un-der an imperative never to fail to stop working on itself.[35]

Take, for example, Lydia Davis's recent book of prose episodes, *Almost No Memory.* The title story refers to a piece about a "certain woman" writer who takes notes on her reading and notes on her notes, but who is then con-signed to living among her notebooks because she has almost no memory and must retrieve herself from them, as though she is not the author of what she has written.[36]

And so she knew by this that these notebooks truly had a great deal to do with her, though it was hard for her to understand, and troubled her to try to understand, just how they had to do with her, how much they were of her and how much they were outside her and not of her, as they sat there on the shelf, being what she knew but did not know, being what she had read but did not remember reading, being what she had thought but did not now think, or remember thinking, or if she remembered, then did not know whether she was thinking it now or whether she had only once thought it, or understand why she had had a thought once and then years later the same thought, or a thought once and then never that same thought again.[37]

The tight rhythms of Davis's piece, organized breathlessly by long sentences containing phrases parsed by commas, perform rhetorical realism in the workspace of ordinary life lived as so much crisis reactivity. (In the sentimental mise-en-scène all texts are docudramas, their realism intensified into a kind of soft surrealism that constitutes a command and a demand for the real to show up and be adequate to fantasy.) Davis's woman finds that she has cramped her "sharp consciousness" into pages and pages of phrases containing insights she has almost no capacity to remember, learn from, or work through. I am extrapolating here, as the woman gives no details about herself apart from the work of keeping up with herself through work: its very separateness from the labor of the reproduction of the unarchived life feels desperately hermetic, as the notebooks' wisdom archive is the place where she catches up with herself only to lose herself in fragments once again.

Generally, the women in *Almost No Memory* lament this cramped existence, turning into cedar trees that "group together in a corner of the graveyard and moan in the high wind"; fulfilling their femininity by being reactive to men and children; being emotionally central to intimates while querying the value of the bargains they've struck with these ongoing intimacies.[38] Their main fascination is in watching themselves shuttle between emotional generosity and resentment at the demands for emotional service by children and lovers to whom they are attached.[39] Says one woman, "I am trying to learn that this playful man who teases me is the same as that serious man talking money to me so seriously he does not even see me anymore and that patient man offering me advice in times of trouble."[40] She loves the patient man and wants to protect him from her resentment of the serious man, but the patient man is accidentally wounded when she speaks her bitter words to the aspect of him who is her "enemy": in other words, she is always too emotionally competent, overreactive, in the moment. She cannot respond to a whole person: her duty or habit is to be emotionally mimetic minute to minute. She feels a failure not because she has not developed emotional competence but because she has overdeveloped it. Her feminine anxiety to demonstrate excellent emotionality bars her capacity to see a lover more complexly, over time. Her knowledge can only produce happiness in knowledge itself, in the products of its "sharp observation": because different knowledge styles dissolve the very bonds of intimacy that lovers' misrecognitions also generate, she keeps from falling apart by shifting between hypervigilance and inattention. This enables her to remain close not to her lover but to the situation of love and the promise of exchange, which is the low bar of reciprocity figured here in Davis's formalism.

Over and over in Davis's work, a woman's self-consciously writerly eloquence and keen insight lead to descriptions of what does *not* change despite the woman's frantic aspirational activity toward making emotional simultaneity. As Jacques Derrida's "The Law of Genre" would have predicted, Davis's point is to show that somehow the accumulation of knowledge leads to an *unraveling* for the writer/speaker and yet this unraveling, which ought to produce madness, is actually ordinary feminine consciousness. It turns out that even unraveling has its genres. The tightness of Davis's phrases belies the fraying of the emotional condition her narrators try to maintain by creating emotional harmonies that are in tune, at least, with themselves. But because they do not censor or defend themselves against the minute-to-minute anxieties of emotional adequation, they also perform the impossibility of reliable intersubjectivity across individuals and the fields of habitation zoned by laws and norms.[41] In this sense the repetition of laws and norms becomes the only intersubjectivity or practical reciprocity her couples can experience.

Davis's exposition of feminine undoing as a condition of normative feminine competence provides us with patterns that warrant further attention. There is likely to be a tension between the rhetorical or aesthetic representation of accumulated emotional experience (as in a plot) and the surfacing of sexual conventionality as a process, topic, and seeming inevitability in a text. In Davis's particular brand of avant-garde narrative, performances of feminine fraying align with the reader's capacity to make the sense the narrator can no longer surround, mentally or emotionally. Usually, though, in narratives of feminine expressivity, the load of detail eventuates not in disaster but in the emergence or agency of *genre* to provide the logic of rescue or amelioration. Blockage is central to any genre's successful execution: the threat that *x* might *not* happen (love in a love plot, poetic justice in a thriller, death in a tragedy) allows absorbing but not shocking anxieties to be stimulated and vanquished. How else would narratives represent femininity as what does not or must not change fundamentally, if the whole thrust of a narrative were to invest its specific details with meaningful instability and transformative potential? In women's culture, normative femininity and aesthetic conventionality constitute the real central couple, with the love plot as the vehicle for and object of desire. Spivak's description of the "concept/metaphor" that is simultaneously descriptive and transformative is useful here[42]: in the texts of women's intimate public, however, femininity is a concept/metaphor for *not* changing, but adapting, propping the play of surface against a stubborn demand to remain in proximity to the promise.

Thus the complaint is often a half-truth in the guise of a whole one, hyperbole projected out of a consciousness that observes struggle and registers the failure of the desired world without wanting to break with the conditions of that struggle. Sometimes the motive for the bargaining relation of critique to defense performs a fear of throwing the whole norm of femininity and heterosexual romance into a crisis; sometimes the fear is of something more abstract, of entering the abyss of not knowing what another kind of life could be. Sometimes it expresses dissatisfaction with another set of social injustices and nonreciprocities (between mothers and children, between states and citizens, between labor and value). Often, it is a combination of these, appearing in the artwork propped on each other, and not theorized. But insofar as the intimate public of femininity registers this field of crisis as a crisis for femininity, the question will be phrased in the idiom of love.

For a woman committed to romantic fantasies of love as reciprocity to break with the normative emotional bargains is to threaten her participation in the good life that seems to unfold from desire and to be maintained by ordinary emotional labor. The sentimental bargain of femininity is, after all, that the emotional service economy serves both intimates and the woman herself, who receives her own value back not only in the labor of recognition she performs but in the sensual spectacle of its impacts. In this discursive field the emotional labor of women places them at the center of the *story* of what counts as life, regardless of what lives women actually live: the conjuncture of family and romance so structures the emergence of modern sexuality, with its conflation of sexual and emotional truths, and in that nexus femininity marks the scene of the reproduction of life as a project. It is the project of femininity—whatever place in the wide variety of kinds of life women take up—to be proximate to this story of emotional centrality. The circularity of the feminine project will not escape you, therefore: it is a perfect form, a sphere infused with activities of ongoing circuits of attachment that can at the same time look like and feel like a zero.

### Sentimentality: Love, Then Repeat

As the preface suggested, the intimate public of femininity has always conjoined the very act of consumption to a powerful hunger to know and adapt the ways other people survive being oppressed by life. The therapeutic intensity of this drive is so conventional to sentimentality it comprises a story that barely needs to be told, a promise of aesthetic recognition and redemption whose consumption is its own reward. Such an economy is an important part of the sense of belonging an intimate public provides: the cliché and the convention represent "insider knowledge." It would be easy to dismiss the social productivity of this kind of reward, as it associates subjective confirmation with fundamental changes of the sort the privileged rarely want to risk. But the mechanism of sentimental saturation of the intimate sphere with materials and signs of consumer citizenship has been crucial to what Mark Seltzer has called the "pathological public sphere" of the contemporary United States, which Karen Halttunen locates in the sensationalism of the late nineteenth and the early twentieth century.[43] The *Uncle Tom* genealogy is notable precisely because its sensationalism was a politically powerful suturing device of a bourgeois revolutionary aesthetic. The contradictions evoked by that phrase will be played out variously throughout each chapter: what links them is the centrality of affective intensity and emotional bargaining amid structural inequity, and the elaboration and management of ambivalent attachments to the world as such, the *as-suchness* of the world.[44]

I have been speaking of conventions, of stereotypes, and forms, the diacritics of congealed feeling that characterize the cultural scene of sentimentality: behind this is a desire to see the sentimental itself as a form—a dynamic pattern—not just a content with scenic themes, like that of weeping, sacrifice, and sanctified death. As when a refrigerator is opened by a person hungry for something other than food, the turn to sentimental rhetoric at moments of social anxiety constitutes a generic wish for an unconflicted world, one wherein structural inequities, not emotions and intimacies, are epiphenomenal.[45] In this imaginary world the sentimental subject is connected to others who share the same sense that the world is out of joint, without necessarily having the same view of the reasons or solutions: historically, the sentimental intervention has tended to involve mobilizing a fantasy scene of collective desire, instruction, and identification that endures within the contingencies of the everyday. The politico-sentimental therefore exists paradoxically: it seeks out the monumental time of emotional recognition, a sphere of dreaming and memory, and translates that sense into an imaginary realm of possible acting, where agency is somehow unconstrained by the normative conventions of the real as it presents itself; and it holds the real accountable to what affective justice fantasy has constructed.

This is to say that where sentimental ideology is, so will there be a will to separate and compartmentalize fundamental psychically felt social ambivalences, so that a sense of potentiality can be experienced enduringly, motivatingly, and even utopianly. The downside is that, often, all of the forces in play can seem formally equivalent. For example, the critique of patriarchal familialism that sentimental texts constantly put forth can be used to argue against the normativity of the family; at the same time, the sacred discourse of family values also sustained within this domain works to preserve the fantasy of the family as a space of sociability in which flow, intimacy, and identification across difference can bridge life across generations and model intimate sociability for the social generally. Likewise, at the same time that bourgeois nationalism promotes a sentimental attachment among strangers that is routed through the form of the nation, it also abjures the sentimental when the idiom of certain claims is inconvenient. (Sentimentalists talk about the emotional costs of injustice, not the material ones; the personal impacts of *not* changing, not the structural benefits of continuity.) Arguments for rationality and individual affective and appetitive self-management in the everyday have also been used to build and to critique identity discourses associated with historically subordinated U.S. populations;[46] at the same time sentimental rhetoric is mobilized to describe everything from the timeless psychic unity of citizens possessing a national identity to the fragility of normal culture itself when faced with challenges to it.[47] Meanwhile, social progressives have for over a century represented the ordinary effects of structural suffering in tactically sentimental ways—modes of testimony, witnessing, visual documentation about the personal impact of structural subordination—to critique the racist/patriarchal/capitalist world; now that same world has assimilated those genres to describe the psychic effects of feminism/multiculturalism on those who once felt truly free, nationally speaking.

What conclusions can we reach from this jumble of ambitions to use and refuse sentimentality in the political sphere? That politics, mediated by publics, demands expressive assurance, while political subjectivity is, nonetheless, incoherent; that ideological incoherence or attachment to contradictory ethics and ways of life is not a failure but a condition of mass belonging; that ambivalent critique produces domains (such as intimate publics) to one side of politics that flourish insofar as they can allow the circulation of the open secrets of insecurity and instability without those revelations and spectacles engendering transformative or strongly resistant action in the idiom of political agency as it is usually regarded. Tracking mass-mediated norms of belonging in the affective register and conventions of engendering emotional solidarities helps us to understand the reproduction of normative life amid serious doubts about the probability that anyone, except the lucky, will be able to forge durable relations of reciprocity among intimates or strangers; such fractures produce the complaint as a register not merely of a stuckness but of the conditions of bargaining that allow people to maintain both their critical knowledge and their attachments to what disappoints.

So, in the nineteenth-century history and legacy of liberal national sentimentality we see that at moments of crisis persons violate the zones of privacy that give them privilege and protection in order to fix something social that feels threatening.[48] They become public on behalf of privacy and imagine that their rupture of individuality by collective action is temporary and will be reversed once the national world is safe, once again, for a return to personal life. Sentimental politics in that idiom works on behalf of its eradication. This horizon of autoerasure constitutes the dream-work of sentiment and the culture industry that supports it, and in the heritage of sentimentality the nationally supported taxonomies—involving race, gender, class, and regional hierarchies in particular—still largely govern the horizon of failure and possibility sentimental authors and readers construct. (This material is covered in chapters 1–4, with chapter 4 as the transitional study.) During the twentieth century, this publicity on behalf of affective and emotional privacy was added to and changed by the emergence of psychoanalysis and popular self-help psychologies, as well as by feminism among the bourgeoisie. These new idioms of understanding the shaping force of sexual subjectivity to human functioning produce more desperation around the impossibility of maintaining personal life as a stable, safe space. Therefore the affective range of sentimentality itself expands in these chapters to include narrations of depression, anxiety, and what Sedgwick calls *perversia*, those veerings of the sexual drive to find bearable terms of reciprocity in invented forms, nonce practices, or just adequate objects, rather than holding out for entire ways of life. (This is the material of chapters 4 through the final "Overture/Aperture.")[49]

On Method and Ambivalence

This book emerges in a terrible time: of vast and burgeoning global economic inequality, environmental destruction, and state antinomianism of the usual and unusual sorts; when distinctions between authoritarian and democratic motives, movements, and aims are profoundly unstable and contested: it is a time like any other modern time, but with its own bleak fractures. But this is a book about early twentieth-century fictions and their filmic adaptations, whose main gaze is at the United States, at white women, at liberal hetero-femininity, fantasy, and love. The women who wrote and who populate the books and films adapted from these books about affective and emotional adaptation are often economically and culturally privileged, heirs at the intersection of two traditions, of genteel sentimentality and progressive solidarity. Fannie Hurst reported from the Russian Revolution and wrote diet books; Dorothy Parker reported the anti-Franco struggles in Spain and left her estate to Martin Luther King, while writing countless variations on the story of thwarted feminine heterosexuality; Edna Ferber fought tirelessly against fascist anti-Semitism in the United States, before doing so was a patriotic act, while also writing sprawling liberal patriotic historical novels of the United States such as *Come and Get It* and *Giant*; Olive Higgins Prouty wrote about posttraumatic stress disorder in World War I and wrote a suffrage novel, too, while also producing two classic melodramas, *Stella Dallas* and *Now, Voyager*. All of these women were frank about their politics and their sentimentality: they were all critics and sustainers of fantasy as a mode of disappointment management or adaptation and of interruption of the realism of the present. They wrote fictions as well as journalism, produced analyses of fantasy in its relation to the lived real.

In a sense, my position is very like theirs. Why bother writing, publishing, or reading a book about fictions now? How can a focus on the juxtapolitical interfere with the reproduction of the present, as enumerated above? How can thinking about genres mediating survival and fantasies of transcendence deal with the pressures of the attrition of life for most people? Is it possible that the engagements of such a project can say something about why things do not change, or open up some vistas that do not reproduce the ordinary and extraordinary violence and carelessness whose thriving in the face of counterknowledge and political action mainly produces, in me, fantasies of more direct action and head-butting against power? As Ferber asks of *Show Boat* in the shadows of World War II (see chapter 2), I have asked myself this question many times: When does one have the ethical room for indirection?

In the public mode of sentimentality ordinary lives articulate with fantasies of being "somebody." The intimate publics of capitalist culture articulate historically subordinated populations with individuals' fantasies of becoming somebody to each other, in that vague and porous sense I outlined earlier. What makes this project worth doing is its attempt to understand what it means to flourish as a public on the condition that the register of importance in its negotiation of the process of survival *not* be in the idiom of politics, or valued in the elitist terms of value that mark capitalist culture. For too long the only importance a counterpublic has had to intellectuals is its convertibility to politics. The urgency of the scholarship has led to conventional distortions in the moral and political analysis of subculture, a concept that has been rightly critiqued for its tendency to homogenize members without having a *concept* of homogeneity as a desire. Even the world of postsubculture studies, largely back-room, dance-floor, and flash-mob based, has wanted to make transgression and resistance the values against which the data were measured. In this book the work of critical distance in the context of the reproduction of life focuses on scenes of ordinary survival, not transgression, on disappointment, not refusal, to derive the register of critique. Here, ordinary restlessness appears as a symptom of ambivalence about aspirational normativity and not a pointer toward unrealized revolution. It seeks to understand the flourishing of the social to one side of the political as something other than a failure to be politics.

I first conceived this book in the late 1980s as a way of helping to elaborate what I had learned from *The Anatomy of National Fantasy*, that publics were not just structural effects but also affective spaces whose shapes, logics, and procedures were not identical to the intellectual and political history of public life that Hawthorne was also telling. My aim then became to tell the long story of U.S. women's culture as a sphere of intimacy with a complex relation to nationality or political metaculture.[50] My plan was to track novels that had become adapted into melodramas, often more than once, by the Hollywood culture industry: *Imitation of Life*; *Now, Voyager*; and *Show Boat*. I assumed I would have chapters on *Gone with the Wind* and *Stella Dallas* too (especially after that execrable remake appeared in 1990), along with multiple chapters on lesser-known novels by the same authors that had been multiply adapted, Fannie Hurst's *Back Street* and *Humoresque* and Edna Ferber's *Cimarron* and *Giant* in particular (the latter has not yet been remade but it is always being cited and seemed irresistible). I also wanted to say something of the authors' biographies because publicity around their lives was central to the marketing of their novels as "good" literature, and because the archives offer up amazing material. Above all I wanted to use the story of feminine publicity after 1837 (the first year of *Godey's Lady's Book*) to tell what happened as cities and mass culture became conjoined sites for the production of social belonging in the United States that did not always remediate the collective sense that was building through the political sphere.

I also expected to turn the question of mass cultural genre to the scene of political theory, having noted that both genre and normative identities traffic in the liberal imaginary of universal emotion as the place where the body politic can find its unity even when its political institutions are not adequate and even when the social field is rife with all sorts of antagonism. That book project had me visiting every relevant library and film archive in the United States as well as reading in the history of liberal political theory to get a sense of what the terms of emotional universalism actually were at a given moment.[51] To tell the story of the twentieth century through the adaptation of novels and short stories into film was to see a broad story of femininity as a red thread throughout countless changes. Much of this aim persists in what follows.

But then, out of a sense of political urgency, I interrupted this project to formulate and write the essays that became *The Queen of America*, which tracks how the logic of intimate publicity became a tool of power, while not obliterating entirely the association of the intimate public with political subordination. In fact, the title chapter of *The Queen of America*, on Frances Ellen Watkins Harper, was originally destined for this book, which needs a chapter on black women's intimate publics and their complex interactions with white feminine presumptiveness, but because it became a chapter on Anita Hill and the pedagogy of failed teaching I decided to put it there.[52] Then I fell ill. Then I got better. As I made my way back to *The Female Complaint* I felt some great pleasure and relief in not having to tell the whole eighteenth- and nineteenth-century story of national sentimentality—Paula Bennett's *Poets in the Public Sphere*, Julia Stern's *The Plight of Feeling*, Julie Ellison's *Cato's Tears*, Elizabeth Barnes's *States of Sympathy*, and Lori Merish's *Sentimental Materialism* extended and reshaped expertly the precedents established by Philip Fisher, Ann Douglas, Jane Tompkins, Nina Baym, and Cathy Davidson, which had themselves been contested and expanded by my own generation's collection, Shirley Samuels's *The Culture of Sentiment*. That anthology grew into many important historicizing works of literary and cultural criticism around sentimentality and femininity as politically contradictory forces of institution and subjectivity building, as this chapter has already attested.

Much remains to be said about the particular authors of whom I am writing as well as of the twentieth-century activity of feminine sentimentality as it continues into the present. But I no longer felt required to write a literary or cultural *history* of it. Now, this is a project more focused on the concept and operation of intimate publics, and on their aesthetic conventions of generalization and transcendence, a project focused more on affect and emotion than on anyone's material practices. It is strongly informed by feminist and queer cultural studies, by the Frankfurt school from Habermas to Adorno and Jameson, by Lacanian and object relations psychoanalysis, especially that of Christopher Bollas, by critical race theory, following Fanon and Spillers, and by writers following Foucault and Deleuze, especially Giorgio Agamben. It is strongly informed by my own idiosyncratic training as a close reader who wants to understand how a certain phrase or sentence got to seem meaningful when it seemed to me, after all, to be a placeholder for a set of intensities and aims that had not really yet found their full expressive form.

But this is also a project about why collectivities abjure politics in their imaginaries of the better good life. I have suggested that academic progressives tend only to respect and take seriously what is convertible to their vision of politics. But since most collective life takes place to one side of or under the radar of politics—and not just because people are trained to be passive, to delegate their political agency to institutional representatives, and to misunderstand action in consumer terms—it seems important to understand what is absorbing in the defensive, inventive, and adaptive activity of getting by, along with the great refusals to go through power to attain legitimacy. In a sentimental worldview, people's "interests" are less in changing the world than in not being defeated by it, and meanwhile finding satisfaction in minor pleasures and major fantasies. To see how the creative energy of living has gotten taken up in intimate spheres that promote such absorption is really what shapes this book's relation to the social tragedy of the attrition of life in which such folds of potentiality are enjoyed.

## The Chapters

Each chapter of this book tracks the marriage of aesthetic conventions and subjective conventionality as detailed in women's intimate public. Profoundly overdetermined dissatisfactions, desires for change, and commitments to some aspects of imaginable intimacy come into contact within and are remediated by normative conventions of intimacy, which make the problem of imagining life outside women's terms feel often like a threat to everything importantly imaginable about the endurance of the subject in the life-world of love, even if she is unhappy at the moment. The texts of women's intimate public worry about what it means to live within the institutions of intimacy, across all kinds of domestic, laboring, cosmopolitan, rural, and political spaces, but they worry even more about what it would mean not to be framed by them. The threatening consequence of being outside of that story is named by one of the most popular U.S. melodramas of the twentieth century's second half: *Imitation of Life*.

Just as this book has two beginnings, the preface and the introduction, so too it has two closings, a coda and an overture/aperture. The introductions lay out the affectivity and materiality of the intimate public from slightly different perspectives—moving from the personally to the impersonally intimate. The two closing pieces focus on the problem of normativity and formalism from two angles, investigating related but distinct problems for femininity after feminism and then for analysts of the affective-aesthetic elaboration of power and belonging as such. In between, the chapters cluster into two parts. The first three chapters move from sentimentality as a public form of intimate sociality where love's aura of authenticity and claim for recognition shape sentimental stories about democracy; the second cluster, chapters 5 through 7, looks at sentimentality as a therapeutic mode that organizes even the feminist-inflected fantasy of what being normal might be like, if it could only be achieved and enjoyed unambivalently. Chapter 4, "Uncle Sam Needs a Wife," is a hinge chapter, marking the transition from political to subjective happiness as the material for belonging.

More precisely, chapter 1, "Poor Eliza," tracks the politico-aesthetic aspects of compassionate emotion in *Uncle Tom's Cabin*'s continual adaptation. It establishes the novel's status as a master sign or supertext, whose reiteration in the twentieth century articulates an array of distinct and often conflicting desires about the execution of cultural difference through spectacles of subaltern pain and their alleviation. The textual span reaches from Stowe to *Beloved*, with Shirley Temple, James Baldwin, and *The Bridges of Madison County* in between. In this chapter, what releases people from their singular history into generality is the offer of affective communication itself as evidence for the universal potential of sentimental conventions, with their offer of absorptive emotional worlds that operate by better rules.

Chapter 2, "Pax Americana: The Case of *Show Boat*," follows revisions to Edna Ferber's novel on stage and screen. It looks particularly at the logic of adaptation that produces commoditized love as the optimism of modernity that might finally effectively drown out the haunting legacies of slavery in the body, the appetites, the law, and nature itself. Here love, performance, and entertainment are the vehicles of becoming general and American. Here adaptation works not only in the revisions or remakes; it is thematized *within* the texts as an operation on freeing memory from its constitutive traumas. Detailing the uneven distribution of amnesias and memory across different scenes of privilege provides the analytic energy of this chapter; so does the spectacle of modernity as itself an amnesia machine dressed in memory's garb.

Chapter 3, "National Brands, National Body: *Imitation of Life*," develops the south-to-north route of national sentimentality by beginning where *Show Boat* ends, in the space of racialized performance in the north. This chapter develops a notion of prosthetic subjectivity and prosthetic bodies as vehicles for self-generalization, or leaving history behind through identification with celebrity (a topos throughout the book, to the very end). To identify with someone in mass society is not necessarily to want to be them or to have them, but to be freed from being who you were, with all of its burdensome historical determinations. To see an identification as a departure from rather than an imitation of might seem ironic in a chapter on imitating life, but the imitators turn out all to have chosen bad objects in their flights from their historical (racial, classed, sexual, and gendered) unfreedom. This chapter also tracks the white liberal exploitation of black pain as a source of white supremacy: white supremacy, here, is not protected by a split between personal and structural relations, as in *Show Boat*, but in the class and intergenerational trajectory of the women in this novel and these films, in the conscription of fantasy by racist law and social norms, and by the availability of a fantasy of sexuality as a relief from structural subordination that never quite fulfills its promise.

Chapter 4, "*Uncle Sam Needs a Wife*: Citizenship and Denegation," tells the other side of the story, using the long history of expanded suffrage in the United States to talk about politics as therapy culture for political depression. It focuses on juxtapolitical activity among consumers throughout the twentieth century, consumers who, depressed by the political, do not see it as a resource for its own reformulation or theirs. It looks at citizenship training manuals and the deaths of Princess Diana and John F. Kennedy Jr. as ways of understanding the endurance of mass optimism for intimate belonging that wants to sublate the universality of bare life (political meaninglessness) into juxtapolitical fantasies of collective and simultaneous social mourning for the political.

Chapter 5, "Remembering Love, Forgetting Everything Else: *Now, Voyager*," leaves behind the fantasy of nationality as the name for the space of vague generality that might absorb anyone and engages fully the flourishing forms of conventionality under the radar of public scrutiny that this classic melodrama dramatizes. This chapter puts forth a concept of "the enabling cliché" to describe the therapeutic episteme of U.S. mass-mediated popular culture and of culture generally as a solution to the problem of the burden of bearing a personality in a nonreciprocal and unjust world. *Now, Voyager* was written by Olive Higgins Prouty in 1941. The chapter looks at different mid-century psychoanalytic traditions as they played out in Prouty's life, works, and the film of the novel; it resituates the question of desire from the maternal plot on which most people focus to the fantasy of playing house that Charlotte maintains as she shifts from the sexual style of white Brahmin aristocracy to the miscegenated norms of mass cultural pleasure.

Chapter 6, " 'It's Not the Tragedies That Kill Us, It's the Messes': Femininity, Formalism, and Dorothy Parker," takes the previous chapter's focus on cliché and femininity and extends it to poetic form. Its title could have been "The Economic Problem of Masochism," the essay by Freud that shapes this chapter's pursuit of form as an aftereffect of affective patterns and the rise and fall of psychic intensities. It elaborates a concept of the loved object as a placeholder form. It also considers the middlebrow location of so much female complaint literature and film, and the centrality of middlebrow disavowals of sentimentality to Parker's investment in the rationality of aesthetic form, as evidenced in her couples, couplets, stories, and her Academy Award winning screenplay for *A Star Is Born*.

Chapter 7, the coda, is called "The Compulsion to Repeat Femininity: *Landscape for a Good Woman* and *The Life and Loves of a She-Devil*." This chapter plays out the late twentieth-century interaction of sentimental and feminist female complaint in Carolyn Steedman's *Landscape for a Good Woman* and Fay Weldon's *The Life and Loves of a She-Devil* (this has been made into a film starring the brilliant female complainer Roseanne Barr, but the chapter does not track the unfinished business of sentimentality that Barr's story keeps linked to feminism). Steedman's autobiography introduces the class dimensions of feminine affective attachments to fantasies congealed in the consumption of *things*. The novel plays out fantasies that a feminist femininity could serve to emancipate women from the means of sexual and economic *production*. But both heroines' feminism does not detach them from their sentimentality: they end wishing for a break they cannot instantiate. Both provide a tragi-comic confirmation, offering a view of what it would be like to share the goods of a sexually and economically emancipated life only to end, again, in the closed shop of sentimental fantasy.

Unfinished Business

Each chapter closes with an opening, a segment of "unfinished business." (So does the book: its final chapter, "Overture/Aperture," is organized around one more adaptation—*Showboat 1988—the Remake* [1977].) These segments point to unpredicted destinies of material in the chapter that precedes them. I won't describe the swerves each chapter segment performs here, but I will identify their purpose in the book as a whole.

This was a depressing book to write because it is a case study in what happens when a capitalist culture effectively markets conventionality as the source and solution to the problem of living in worlds that are economically, legally, and normatively not on the side of almost anyone's survival, let alone flourishing. Nonetheless, flourishing happens. For many people, sentimentality and the fantasy of a better proximate world so close that one can experience it affectively without being able to live it objectively produces art that does, that transports people somewhere into a *situation* for a minute. The next book in this sequence, *Cruel Optimism*, will focus more precisely on the terror of detaching, even when the object of sentimental assurance turns out to be a bad object. In *The Female Complaint*, the emphasis is on the process of bargaining with what there is. Here, the sections that focus on sentimentality's unfinished business resonate as critical pedagogies in the ongoing work of making better good lives within a space of belonging that is problematic and virtual but no less affectively sustaining for all that. They show that events are never exhausted, and that most revision and adaptation *is* the activity of making change take place, even if it is also usually the opposite of that, and a mirage. This is one reason why politically engaged people write criticism, to vitalize and shape the potential event within any concept or scene. The unfinished business of sentimentality mostly profits people other than the ones it solicits to do more business. But it also teaches that endings can be made into openings.

THE SPECTRE OF A FIRST LOVE
—HAUNTING A WOMAN'S HEART!
Can marriage erase the memory of
romantic moments with another man?

UNIVERSAL PICTURES presents

*Irene Dunne*
*Robert Montgomery*
in
**UNFINISHED
BUSINESS**
with
*Preston Foster*

Eugene Pallette    Esther Dale
Walter Catlett    June Clyde
Dick Foran    Samuel S. Hinds

Produced and Directed by
**GREGORY
LA CAVA**
With all the grand comedy
of his "MY MAN GODFREY"
... all the poignant drama of
his "STAGE DOOR"...all the
heart-lifting romance of his
"PRIMROSE PATH"...!

SCREEN PLAY BY EUGENE THACKREY

# POOR ELIZA

> Sentimentality, the ostentatious parading of
> excessive and spurious emotion, is the mark of
> dishonesty, the inability to feel; the wet eyes
> of the sentimentalist betray his aversion to
> experience, his fear of life, his arid heart; and
> it is always, therefore, the signal of secret and
> violent inhumanity, the mask of cruelty.
> JAMES BALDWIN, "EVERYBODY'S PROTEST
> NOVEL"

"The Small House of Uncle Thomas"

Rodgers's and Hammerstein's *The King and I* is a rare instance of classic Americana whose scenario is not in America. Atypical for its time (1949), the lavish musical is set during an imperial crisis in relations between Britain and Siam, which involves a variety of military and economic intrigues but focuses on a culturalist politics.[1] Opening with the arrival of Anna Leonowens in Siam, the play recalls that Britain exported a civilizing pedagogy as part of its imperial strategy: Leonowens is imported "to bring to Siam what is good in Western culture."[2] Her teachings include respect for "science" and for anti-despotism in the political and palatial spheres.

Yet to describe *The King and I* this way neglects the sensuous spirit of the play: the spectacle and songbook continuously overwhelm the story, displaying the king's visibly smooth and muscular body, the palace's surface of shining metal and richly colored fabric, the women's and children's adorable exoticism, and the intensities of erotic and familial life in the world of the palace. Haunted by the love plot that never happens between the Siamese "King" (Mongut) and the British "I" (Leonowens), the play's story nonetheless uses the tragi-comic conventions of "the war between the sexes" to express political and cultural antagonisms that also appear here in stereotypic drag as national tragedy and imperial farce.

The scene of this war is the passing into modernity of Siam, for which the king has prepared by insisting that the elite of his nation develop economic, technological, and rational literacy in the ways of the West. Eventually he learns from Leonowens, however, that to be modern requires something more than a cultivated mind—it wants an educated heart. But the king's heart breaks and he dies when he is unable to follow Siam into the moment in which the nation becomes a state of feeling as opposed to a regime of power. As the play proffers the abject image of the king's waning virility and pompous philosophizing it sets up a series of organizing antinomies by which the audience can measure the king's and the nation's progress, including West and East, barbarism and civilization, the vulgar and the refined, the vernacular and the literary, the student and the teacher, the brutish and the feminine. Above all is the king's attempt to develop an organ of *compassion* as opposed to ideology or what the play calls *philosophy*. These changes are achieved aesthetically (in the play) and subjectively (by the characters) by a romance with a constellated third term: sentimentality, intimacy, democracy, America.

The unfinished business of sentimentality that this chapter tracks involves its political component, one that develops *within political thought* a discourse of ethics that, paradoxically, denigrates the political and claims superiority to it. This mode of sentimentality takes up the Enlightenment project of cultivating the soul of the subject toward a visceral capacity to embody, recognize, and sanction virtue, and it expands it into the collective activity of compassionate cosmopolitanism, which places affective recognition at the center of what binds strangers to each other.[3] Yet sentimentality's universalist rhetoric gains its authority not in the political domain, but near it, against it, and above it: sentimental culture entails a proximate alternative community of individuals sanctified by recognizing the authority of true feeling—authentic, virtuous, compassionate—at the core of a just world.[4]

The culture of true feeling has no inevitable political ideology. It does not always liberalize society, forcing politics to gain a higher ethical footing by dismantling structural inequalities or expanding the formal terms of citizenship.[5] Its core pedagogy has been to develop a notion of social obligation based on the citizen's capacity for suffering and trauma. This structure has been deployed mainly among the culturally privileged to humanize those subjects who have been excluded from the formal and capaciously social aspects of citizenship, embedded seemingly intractably on the bottom of class, racial, ethnic, and sexual hierarchies. As a force for the conversion of the politically privileged, sentimental politics has had powerfully transformative effects on which subordinate populations are recognized as candidates for inclusion in the body politic. But as Baldwin asserts, the humanization strategies of sentimentality always traffic in cliché, the reproduction of a person as a thing, and thus indulge in the confirmation of the marginal subject's embodiment of *inhumanity* on the way to providing the privileged with heroic occasions of recognition, rescue, and inclusion.[6] In this view, sentimentality from the top down softens risks to the conditions of privilege by making obligations to action mainly ameliorative, a matter not of changing the fundamental terms that organize power, but of following the elevated claims of vigilant sensitivity, virtue, and conscience.

The commodities of "women's culture," the first identity-marked mass cultural discourse in the United States, notably advanced these paradoxes of liberal sentiment, expressing a complex of desires as though they were a single claim. Primarily, "women's" texts are gendering machines, locating the ideality of femininity in fantasies of unconflicted subjectivity in an intimate world organized by a sense of emotional recognition, reciprocity, and self-mastery, traits that are deemed the conditions for the survival of femininity if not of actual humans, whose material survival and sense of alterity represents the realist counterpoint to the modes of feminine sentimental fantasy that these works also develop. The axis of sentimental *political* practice involves expanding this scene of the feminine soul's communion with a nimbus of abstract others to include a desire to build pain alliances from all imaginable positions in U.S. hierarchies of value: sentimental politics from the feminine position renders scenes and stories of structural injustice in the terms of a putatively nonideological nexus of vulnerability wherein a threat to the survival of individual lives is said also to exemplify and express conflicts in national life.

Thus while these emotions are normative (ranked according to culturally dominant virtues) in terms of the performance of femininity there are also affective components that invest any local drama of compassionate attachment with a sense of import beyond the scene of its animation, even if the personal-scale drama provides the register in which the collective scene is encountered. The expansion from the personal to more abstract domains constitutes the scene of judgment and critique. Emotional justice on the small scale figures the pre-experience of its resolution on the larger.

The main paradox here too lies in the centrality of cliché and stereotype to the establishment of the expanded terms of the human. Sentimental politics bridges fantasy and realism precisely insofar as the blatantly artificial register of conventional troping stands as the textual performance of universality itself. In "women's culture," stereotype and cliché bridge the complexity of the singular life and a conventional dialectic between a particular *type* of subject of true feeling and the general world that must absorb the claims of that subject.

The conjuncture of politics and mass norms of affective investment thereby raises aesthetic questions about the conventions with which exemplary relations have been posited between narratives of the experience and redemptiveness of personal suffering and the collective circumstances in which these plots are articulated as political. The archive of this essay— *Uncle Tom's Cabin* and a set of related works such as *The King and I*, *Dimples*, *The Bridges of Madison County*, and *Beloved*—inhabits many positions within the domain of the politico-sentimental aesthetic and enables us to understand the ways its conventional forms and ideologies of feeling have influenced the construction and valuation of subjects, types, and publics since the mid-nineteenth century in the United States. More than that, it provides a foundation for talking about the ambivalence even antisentimental artists express and perform in bargaining with rather than repudiating the sentimental contract: the normativity of emotional humanism and sentimental utopias is that strong, saturating the modern imaginary field with its vague definition of the human.[7] Other more historicist scholarship has catalogued every refunctioning of *Uncle Tom's Cabin* (although the list keeps expanding):[8] the aim of this chapter and the two chapters that follow is to set forth a model for encountering the politics of suffering and trauma at the heart of mass-mediated publicity in the United States that locates the tradition in this early intimate public. The *Uncle Tom* genealogy always stages the contradictions of liberal culture as lived in the body, in relations of production, and in fantasies of the better good life; sentimental in its attachments, melodramatic, gothic, and comic in its genres, but realist in its desire to remake the world, it always reanimates questions about the ethics of emotional universalism or sentimental politics in the United States.

Anyone who has seen *The King and I* will know that my title, "Poor Eliza," derives from the scene in which Tuptim, a sexual slave in the king's palace, stages a dramatic adaptation of what she calls *The Small House of Uncle Thomas*. The occasion is a dinner party at which the king is trying to convince the British ambassador of his own and Siam's sophistication, of Siam's worthiness to be considered a peer nation in political, economic, and cultural terms. Tuptim's play provides the "native" entertainment. However, her motives in performing *Uncle Tom* are different from the king's: most broadly, she cares not to reflect the nation's glory, but to use this as an opportunity to speak to the only sympathetic public she will ever have. The adaptation of *Uncle Tom's Cabin* is a performance of her belief in the power of Western, liberal compassion and a refusal to adapt to immoral power: it is also simply desperate.

Tuptim's specific complaint is that the king has decreed that she become his currently most favored "wife." She is thereby denied access to her true love, Lun Tha, and is a prisoner in the king's harem as well as a slave to his sexual will. Tuptim's hope to build a life around consensual love in a conjugal family rather than live with the authoritarian rules of royal sexuality merges the historical novel's traditional deployment of the love plot to play out political dramas with a contemporary Cold War-ish espousal of healthy heterosexuality as an emblem of "democratic" individual freedoms in a "modern" capitalist society.[9] Yet *Uncle Tom's Cabin* is far more than a commercial for U.S.-style democracy in *The King and I*.

In the autobiographical text by Anna Leonowens and its fictionalization by Margaret Landon, there are no royal performances of *Uncle Tom's Cabin*. In *The King and I*, the novel's citation touches on the aspect of Stowe's pedagogy that exhorts the nation to embrace the progressive urgencies of a revolutionary historical moment in order to preserve its ambition to be good as well as great. The citation of *Uncle Tom* here also figures the centrality of the aesthetic to mass national politics as that space of projection for unimagined or nondominant trajectories of national life. Just as the novel puts forth characters who model virtue for the individual reader, its example has become a truism, a monument to the claim that inspired art can produce a transformative environment toward which the fallen social world can aspire.

Thus it is not surprising that very different projections onto the novel's iconicity as a sign of national optimism are put into play in *The King and I*. For the king, the novel's presence at court is indeed a sign of Siam's modernity: a foreign text translated, an American text appropriated and mastered, a politics consumed that proves the achieved enlightenment of Siamese consciousness. Tuptim's decision to stage the book appears to the king as merely an equivalent act to the other preparations he makes for the event, such as learning Western table manners and clothing styles to augment the "scientific" knowledge he has cobbled together. Beyond this, however, the king's linkage with *Uncle Tom's Cabin* has already been established through his strong identification with the rationality and wit of "President Lingkong," whom he has been trying to enlist in a plan to bring elephants to the United States so that the North might win the Civil War.

Lincoln's presence in *The King and I* represents a horizon of possible development for the king, whose voice and body are otherwise staged through a kind of generic Asiatic bronzeface, his body exposed and his vernacular enjoyed in what a U.S. audience would recognize as minstrel fashion, further highlighting the paradoxical differences and linkages between "their" kind of slavery and "ours." The king's attraction to Lincoln's great and simple wisdom implicitly enables him to imagine saving Siam with similar aplomb at its own time of radical transition. Yet this self-understanding is a joke the play plays on the king. He comprehends the relation between wisdom, greatness, and the abolition of slavery, but he never recognizes the sexual slavery of the harem as relevant to these issues. His speeches about "Lingkong" are staged as funny and stupid, even though the self-misunderstanding he reveals through them has visibly violent effects. But the king's aspiration to be the American president is nowhere quarreled with in the play.

Tuptim's identification with *Uncle Tom's Cabin* also mixes up the personal and the political, but she configures their zones of overlap in distinct and incommensurate ways. One has to do with authorship as a figure of citizenship. "Harriet Beecher Stowa" represents to the slave the unthinkable possibility that a woman can be sovereign, circulate in public, and write a book, especially one that challenges the patriarchal national regime that forces her to do sexual hard labor. Authorship produces the form of public sphere disembodiment that mimes freedom in citizenship and predicts the intimate world of emotionally like strangers. But Tuptim also identifies with "poor Eliza," whose story inspires her own subsequent flight from the palace: as Lincoln is an emblem for the king, Eliza models for Tuptim the need for the slave's courage to invalidate morally unjust law. The story itself authorizes breaking the law and becoming therefore inhuman in a way that releases the gothic's intensified aesthetic, Buddha's spiritual superpower, and superhuman, antinomian energy. Like Eliza, Tuptim breaks the law that has broken itself by escaping to a new space and putting her body on the line to bridge the authoritarian world in which she lives and the emancipated world of freedom to love to which she seeks transport.

Usually the citation of the *Uncle Tom* form involves questions about whether intimacy between and among races is possible in the United States: these questions are frequently played out through love plots where heterosexual intimacy and gender norms are also deemed fragile. This casts heterosexual difference and the conventional hierarchies of value associated with it in the United States as vaguely analogous to the scene of African and Anglo-American racial difference, wherein visible corporeal distinctiveness is explained incoherently as an emanation of species and cultural differences. *The King and I* supplements these conventions and reveals their embeddedness in economic and imperial relations by having the king and Tuptim imaginatively enter the War between the States through Lincoln and Stowe: where they are concerned, the activity of citation marks a desire for identification and translation across nations, lexicons, and systems of hierarchy. It also marks the mobility of categories of privilege and subordination—for example, the king is imperially vulnerable but sexually strong, while Leonowens's lines of privilege are the inverse. For both figures, identification across radically different worlds involves a serious ambition to act courageously, to learn to become something radically different from what one is. But the will to appropriate and inhabit difference to explicate and transform the scene of one's own desire necessarily involves distortion, mistranslation, and misrecognition. This is why, in *The King and I* and *Uncle Tom's Cabin* as well as many other texts of sentimental politics, the play between various matrices of taxonomic "difference" produces comedy amid calamity, making a sort of slapstick of survival, along with working in the register of melodrama, because the conjuncture of extreme violence and the ordinary forces the ordinary realist sense of scale out the door and instates exaggerated modes as the new realism, the realism wrought from the absurd demands of power, contradictions of human attachment in scenes of inequality, and just the strangeness of difference itself. The centrality of melodrama and comedy in sentimental publics expresses a desire for a new vernacular, a new realism to be established in the dominant public: it speaks to the thinness of common sense. Processes of vernacularization are always struggles over the consensual terms in which nondominant ordinariness is expressed.[10]

The political tradition of sentimentality ultimately equates the vernacular with the human: in its imaginary, crises of the heart and of the body's dignity produce events that can topple great nations and other patriarchal institutions if an effective and redemptive linkage can be constructed between the privileged and the socially abject. The vehicle for this is intimate publicity. *Uncle Tom's Cabin* is a resource people come to when they want to comment on the political optimism for which the novel stands about the transformation of unjust social institutions through the production of new mentalities. The novel's very citation is a sign that an aesthetic work can be so powerful as to transform the privileged people who read it into identifying against the ways they understand their own interests. In so doing the text of sentimental politics figures a radical challenge to the bodies and body politic hailed by it. The artwork is shown to be as potentially powerful as a nation or any world-saturating system: it makes and remakes subjects.

Yet the forces of distortion in the world of feeling politics that the citation of *Uncle Tom* puts into play are as likely to justify ongoing forms of domination as they are to give form and language to impulses toward resistance.[11] In *The King and I*, as in many melodramas, the soundtrack tells this story first, and then the plot follows. Frustrated by the king's imperiousness, Leonowens begins to think of him as a barbarian. But his head wife, Lady Thiang, sings to her: the king "will not always say/What you would have him say,/But now and then he'll do/Something wonderful."[12] Because he believes in his "dreams" and makes himself vulnerable through that belief, he is, it is suggested, revolutionary and heroic—and worth loving. He is, in that sense, like a woman, and indeed his patriarchal authoritarianism is increasingly revealed as mere bluster. As a result, the king takes on the sacred aura of a sentimental heroine, complete with sacrificial death.

This plot turn marks a classic moment of politico-sentimental pedagogy. Although he is a tyrant, the king's story demands sympathy, and then compassion, from the women who surround him. Here they become stand-in figures for the audience, witnessing his death as a process of dramatic detheatricalization. As the play progresses and the king is "humanized" by feeling and therefore put less on display as a body, the narrative loses focus on the systemic violence of the king's acts. Violence must be taken offstage tactically in order to produce startling and transformative lines of emotional continuity—but here, compassion is directed toward the dominated and mainly toward the pain of the privileged for being enslaved by a system of barbarous power in which he is destined, somehow, to be caught.

*The King and I* then performs something general about the contradictions that are deliberately or inevitably animated by politically motivated deployments of sentimental rhetoric. Here is what is paradigmatic: when sentimentality meets politics personal stories tell of structural effects, but in so doing they risk thwarting the very attempt to perform rhetorically a scene of pain that must be soothed politically. Because the ideology of true feeling cannot admit the non-universality of pain, its cases of vulnerability and suffering can become all jumbled together into a scene of the generally human, and the ethical imperative toward social transformation is replaced by a passive and vaguely civic-minded ideal of compassion. The political as a place of acts oriented toward publicness becomes replaced by a world of private thoughts, leanings, and gestures projected out as an intimate public of private individuals inhabiting their own affective changes. Suffering, in this personal/public context, becomes answered by sacrifice or survival, which is, then, recoded as the achievement of justice or liberty. Meanwhile, we usually lose the original impulse behind sentimental politics, which is to see the individual effects of mass social violence as *different* from the causes, which are impersonal and depersonalizing.

So far, I have focused on the ways *The King and I* typifies sentimental conventions of textual projection and identification as they have developed since the mid-nineteenth century. This political pedagogy is based on a conjuncture of fixed taxonomies and labile emotions, a strategy that humanizes structures of violence by enacting them through narratives that demonstrate the universality of suffering and the transformative potentials of compassionate love. Two other ways of entering the rhetorical conventions of true feeling in the U.S. political sphere also contribute to the play's typically sentimental embodying of the structural: its relation to the feminine, and to femininity as a way of living; and its relation to capitalist culture, both at the juncture where abstract relations of value are extracted, projected onto, and represented by particular kinds of subaltern body, and at the place where the sovereignty and sociality of the commodity form (the mirror of the stereotype) are positioned as the solution to the experience of social negativity or isolatedness.[13]

In Margaret Landon's fictional retelling of Anna Leonowens's books on the court at Siam (Landon's work *Anna and the King of Siam* is the source of the musical) a similar domino theory of the *Uncle Tom's Cabin* effect is put forward: female authorship leads to female sexual dignity via women's identification across distinctions in racial, class, linguistic, national, and sexual location. But in Landon's text, the narrative that moves from the end of slavery to the beginning of democratic modernity exists apart from any love plot. In the historical texts it is not Tuptim who resists through Stowe (Tuptim does have illicit love but she is executed for it[14]). The king's senior wife, Son Klin, brings Stowe into Siam and adopts Stowe as her own epistolary persona.

According to Leonowens and Landon, Son Klin desires not to escape to another man, but rather seeks to identify her way out of her isolation through homosocial sentimentality. *Sentimentality is her scene of adultery.* Son Klin desires to imagine a world where women and kings will violate their privilege, just for a second, to make a fundamental structural shift in the modes of rule that dominate her and her world; she imagines that the sovereign classes might be converted not by principled argument, but by being convinced to honor what ought to be their feelings of grief and shame at the scandalous social violences they have been perfectly willing to see as ordinary, or necessary, or hardwired into the system they administer. In this relation to the transformative environment of true feeling about pain, she too is a typical sentimental subject. She is not fictional, but she is transformed by the utopia of fictional fantasy into a new kind of person.

Stowe-style sentimentality enabled Son Klin to identify against the privilege of her own position with respect to that of other women in the king's domain. But she could do nothing expressly political about this, apart from learning how powerful affective pedagogy can be. Likewise, in the Rodgers and Hammerstein play, relations of domination are made almost prepolitical, translated into a tactical difference between happy people who know true love and unhappy people who are not civilized enough for it. "Poor Eliza" is placed on spectacular display by Tuptim so that the structural conditions of a genericized subaltern unhappiness might be revealed and empathized with in a way that brings the feeling of a just and happy world into being long before its structural translation in the political sphere has been achieved or concretely imagined.

Yet *The King and I*, as it speaks through *The Small House of Uncle Thomas*, marks the space between the real and the fantasy nation by adapting the sentimental rhetoric of sacrifice to its particular locale. In *The Small House of Uncle Thomas*, the vehicle for the transformation of the nation into a zone fit for jubilation is neither Christ nor Lincoln, but Buddha. Tuptim's Buddha is not identical to the unambiguous Christian savior of Stowe's novel: feeling virtuous that he has saved Eliza and her baby, the Broadway Buddha actually extracts payment for his deed by sacrificing little Eva. Tuptim: "It is Buddha's wish that Eva come to him and thank him personally for saving of Eliza and baby. And so she die, and go to arms of Buddha."[15] Here and throughout *The King and I*, the play foregrounds the sacrificial costs to women of critical-sentimental ideology at the same time that it endorses the association of virtuous feeling and proper femininity as the foundation of a good world.[16] Protestant Christianity absorbs an ahistorical Buddhism as the West absorbs the East, women absorb men, whites absorb nonwhite and non-Western-originating populations in the universality of suffering that separates the good agents from the bad.

In this, as in so many other ways, the play reproduces conventions of sentimental bargaining between a realist critique and a variety of alibis that amount, in essence, to a recommitment ceremony to two intimate spheres, the heterosexual one and the feminine one. Heteronormativity thrives on the relation of these two nonidentical, punctually antagonistic domains of identification and experience. Its genres of pain and suffering simultaneously provide pedagogy in proper femininity, valorization of racially and sexually hegemonic normality, and a critical distance on the intimate scenes they represent as the ground of experience.

### The Unfinished Business of Sentimentality

The adaptations of *Uncle Tom's Cabin* vary quite a bit in what gets included and emphasized: different moments of comedy and pathos are differently foregrounded in its many recurrences. But the place of "Poor Eliza" in this ongoing story is striking: almost every adaptation of the novel involves an elaborate dramatic staging of the scene in which Eliza crosses the Ohio River riding rafts of ice. In the novel this event takes less than two pages. It emblematizes powerfully the will to survive so central to the scene of women's culture, lifting feminine agency out of the attenuations of the everyday toward a form of sovereignty beyond the materiality of power. Electrified by the awesome power of the mother to harness her own sublimity to the natural sublime, Eliza transforms into a species of superpersonhood.

Even in its very syntax the spectacle of Eliza seems to rise out of history and the text, flashing into the present of the writing and the reading simultaneously:

A thousand lives seemed to be concentrated in that one moment to Eliza. Her room opened by a side door to the river. She caught her child, and sprang down the steps towards it. The trader caught a full glimpse of her just as she was disappearing down the bank; and throwing himself from his horse, and calling loudly on Sam and Andy, he was after her like a hound after a deer. In that dizzy moment her feet to her scarce seemed to touch the ground, and a moment brought her to the water's edge. Right on behind they came; and, nerved with strength such as God gives only to the desperate, with one wild cry and flying leap, she vaulted sheer over the turbid current by the shore, on to the raft of ice beyond. It was a desperate leap—impossible to anything but madness and despair; and Haley, Sam, and Andy, instinctively cried out, and lifted up their hands, as she did it.

The huge green fragment of ice on which she alighted pitched and creaked as her weight came on it, but she staid there not a moment. With wild cries and desperate energy she leaped to another and still another cake; stumbling—leaping—slipping—springing upwards again! Her shoes are gone—her stockings cut from her feet—while blood marked every step; but she saw nothing, felt nothing, till dimly, as in a dream, she saw the Ohio side, and a man helping her up the bank.[17]

More than any scene in the adaptations of *Uncle Tom's Cabin* this one remains unadulterated—elaborated, embellished, naturalized, or made artificial and iconic—but almost never written out of the text, as the death of Uncle Tom frequently is, or reversed, as both Tom's and Eva's deaths sometimes are. Eliza's crossing recurs even when the story is rendered comic, as in "Felix the Cat in Uncle Tom's Crabbin" (1927), where, as Felix flees Simon Legree by jumping into an ice truck, the intertitle card reads "Felix substitutes for Eliza crossing the ice!"

Why does the bridge over troubled waters that Eliza's sublimity makes survive the continuous transformations of the supertext of *Uncle Tom's Cabin*? The dramaturgic and cinematic history shows that if its main purpose is to solicit audience identification with the overwhelming power of the mother's will to survive (figured in the paragraphs above by the imitative bodily responses of Haley, Andy, and Sam), the tacit purpose of the adaptations seems to have been to generate awe at the technological capacities of the play or the film. Edison's silent version, for example, makes you merge awe at the woman's power in the face of danger she endures for freedom, love, and family with the techno-aesthetic power of a new entertainment medium to reframe the real, to generate surplus pleasure and surplus pain at the visualized spectacle of the sublime object of sentimentality. Here moral victory and economic survival in plots about vulnerable, desiring, dominated, and powerful women merge with consumer pedagogy: and the act of enraptured consumption becomes inextricable from the moral act of identification.

In the many scenes of spectatorship and transformation embedded in this act merge witnessing and identifying with pain; consuming and deriving pleasure and moral self-satisfaction; and imagining that these impulses will lead, somehow, to changing the world. This ideological, aesthetic, national, and capitalist cluster is at the center of the death-driven, pain-saturated, therapy-seeking, and unevenly radical discourse of protest that *Uncle Tom's Cabin* generates as a central mental and material contradiction of modern American sentimental modes. Additionally, the capacity to generate awe at the bridge into which Eliza makes nature becomes a sign of personal, cultural, and national modernity, both ideologically and aesthetically. Reading back from the end, we see her passing from the intensities of slavery (it is not a passing to "freedom" until she reaches Canada, thanks to the 1850 Compromise's compromise of the concept of a nonslave state) as a shift from the regional to the national, the archaic to the modern. I will turn to two specific later citations of this moment: here I want to focus on the way the scene bridges the testifying moral function of suffering—which is the condition that authorizes the reader to imagine changing the world—and the commoditized world of aesthetic pleasure, distraction, and instruction that capitalist culture provides.

### Adorable Liberal Racism: Shirley Temple's *Dimples*

By the phrase "unfinished business" I mean to designate the specific conjuncture of adaptation, commodification, and affect that distinguishes this modern, politically inflected modality of expression. I also mean, here, to describe the way the semiotic substance of sentimentality has been used not only to hardwire the history of slavery into the forms of privileging affect that have long distinguished modes of pain, pleasure, identity, and identification in the U.S. culture industry, but also to see specifically how these habits of emotional quotation redraw the meanings of U.S. history, in two ways. First, as Ann Douglas and many after her have demonstrated, sentimentality performs a desire for change lubricated by emotional compliance, and in the United States the definitions of power, personhood, and consent that construe the scene of value in the political public sphere, such that any account of sentimentality has to be an account of change and of an ideology of change, which would include some explanations of what gets to count as historic change, and what kinds of activities fall out of the dominant definitions. Second, the redeployment of sentiment has generated its own archive of gestures, structures, and identities of emotion, prostheses, and modes of commentary that come to signify a metaculture, a place where "adaptation" itself, as a form of domination, fantasy, and necessity, is consented to and worked out.

That sentimentality always designates the activity of a transition and an ideology of adaptation to necessity means that the signs of surplus enjoyment, surplus pain, or sublimity, made on behalf of the sentimental subject for whom authors reimagine the real world, will link the overwhelming pressures to survive everyday life and the overwhelming desires to inhabit an imaginary space of transcendent identity whose mirror of the quotidian allows the utopian and the practical to meet intimately, and in a text you can buy that will give you an experience you can not, at this time, elsewhere have. We might call this aesthetics of remediation a space of deliberate *dis*-interpellation or self-misrecognition because, in order to benefit from the therapeutic promises of sentimental discourse, you must imagine yourself with someone else's stress, pain, or humiliated identity; the possibility that through the identification with alterity you will never be the same remains the radical threat and the great promise of this affective aesthetic.

On publication, *Uncle Tom's Cabin* immediately generated an entire industry of domestic objects and toys that appeared to turn the fascinating text of pain and survival into new kinds of pedagogical pleasure involving play about slavery. Thomas Gossett reports that "the novel inspired a whole new industry of souvenirs of its leading characters. Enterprising manufacturers hurriedly produced candles, toys, figurines, and games based upon it. One of the games had players compete with one another in reuniting members of slave families."[18]

That this competition for control of the zeitgeist of national modernity became an after-dinner pastime in bourgeois America of the 1850s does not diminish the importance of *Uncle Tom's Cabin* as a figure for the power of a commodity to shock its consumers into a contemporary crisis of knowledge and national power; its capacity to shock has indeed become a continually revived beacon of what the collaboration of capitalism and aesthetics might do to change the course of history, the practices of power, the wounds of dominated identity, or the transformative effects of fantasy. Its referential status as both a hallowed democratic treasure and a bit of banal Americana has everything to do with the way it unsettles the normative distances that protect a sense of privacy within the public sphere. The toy form of the novel brings politics into the home much as the novel form did, but this time the consciousness it produces must be shared and noncontroversial, requiring a group consensus conventional to melodrama about what winning would mean, where evil resides, and how to read the moral meaning of different deaths.[19]

The aesthetic and public reverberations of the novel, which helped to establish it as the proprietor of a semiotic field of fantasy identifications, were most powerfully registered in the American theater. Here, Stowe's almost Nietzschean concern that the aversive content of contemporary American life must be registered in the dramatic spectacle of images that burn conscientious feelings into the shocked souls of consenting readers became available to the mediations of embodied spectacle. At the same time, the very conventionality of the citation can make it light, casual, a state of emergency habitually returned to, as though the sublime spectacle of the transformed soul were equivalent to the destabilization of the responsive audience. This is to say that, exemplifying the power to recast and to change the world, the supertext of *Uncle Tom's Cabin* is itself a technology that retemporalizes specific historical crises, producing planes of detailed historicism and, simultaneously, displacement toward figural achronicity in scenes that fulfill the dictates of sentimental feeling to materialize a world that does not exist yet while making the very performances of displacement prompts for aesthetic pleasure.

As many scholars have noted, this tendency of the sentimental to proliferate itself in memorial forms from toys to sequels characterized *Uncle Tom's Cabin* from the start. George Aiken's stage melodrama of 1852 initiated hundreds of popular adaptations; more than ten feature films (and many more if you count partial productions such as in *Dimples* and *The King and I*) have been made of *Uncle Tom's Cabin*, along with more than a few cartoons and reappearances in print. The historical disarticulation, born of Protestant typological and allegorical modes, and the technological displacement, born of mass-mediated capacities to intensify spectacle, are repeated in the episodic appearance of genres of extreme affect as well. I have noted that *Uncle Tom's Cabin*'s own realism is propped on gothic and comic episodes (Cassie's deployment of haunting figuration; Sam's and Andy's vernacular hijinks; and many narrative asides), as though the violence that the text forces you to witness requires performative spectacle itself to register trauma throughout the range of aesthetic response—at the same time as absurdity provides, let's face it, entertainment and relief.

Central to this range of desired impacts is the presence of slave music to signify the scale of the surrealism of the ordinary slave encounter with power.[20] For example, from the 1903 Thomas A. Edison/Edwin S. Porter adaptation onward, slaves are constantly depicted while dancing. But their dance has an elastic meaning, signifying either slave humanity—dance as the only cultural production and site of pleasure the slaves own—or the greatest imaginable abjection to the master culture—as when slaves dance on the auction block, or as when little Harry dances his way into the slave trader Haley's heart in Pollard's production of 1927.[21]

The import of dance, music, and performance to the scene of spectacular identification in the *Uncle Tom* archive became another bridge between the personal and public narratives of political pain that became an entertainment industry in the years after *Uncle Tom* changed the ways people saw the potential for fiction's efficacy as evidence for radical thinking. The black/white, slave/free, south/north formulas put into play by the "period" narrative paradoxically provide an achronic image of national taxonomy itself, onto which other forms of cultural domination become mapped. In the *Uncle Tom* form race and nation figure monumentally, in tragic/utopian time, a space of time wherein meanings are set apart from their circulation in the everyday while becoming a vernacular citation with extraordinary referential stability.

A most spectacular example of the mass cultural process by which historical specificity is (mis)translated, via the *Uncle Tom* form, into the unchanging space of sentiment hovering around history was produced in 1936, when Shirley Temple, as ethereal as Eva and as comic as Topsy, took on the form in *Dimples*. As with all of Temple's juvenile films, *Dimples* plays out personal and public catastrophes that have preceded the narrative, which seeks to deliver Temple and her intimates from the bad fate they portend. In the classic mode of the historical romance, the redemption of the heroine would be incomplete if her world were not redeemed with her: *Dimples* is multiply framed by narratives of crisis and cultural struggle that indicate instability in the domains of the metropole, the nation, and Temple's particular audience. The film opens with this preamble: "Little old New York was neither old nor little in 1850 . . . it was a metropolis of half a million, in which decent folks were beginning to tolerate the theater and young radicals argued against so respectable an institution as slavery."

The theatrical, abolitionist, and youthful rebellions against stale parental proprieties, on the verge of an imminently grand national modernity: this constellation of reverberating changes distinguishes the sentimental genealogy of the *Uncle Tom* form. Yet the story *Dimples* mainly tells is of a white child who sells herself to a childless white woman, for $5,000. "Dimples" (Temple) does this in order to keep her con artist grandfather out of jail—not for conning someone, but for being conned by men who convince him to "invest" in an ersatz watch thought to have been Napoleon's, a sentimental gift from Josephine. The Professor (Frank Morgan) is vulnerable to this con both because he is vulnerable to love and because the "Appleby" family of which he is the surviving patriarch is said to have discriminating tastes. These contradictions make him potentially educable in the terms of sentimental pedagogy, but just barely. Prior to the con, in the depths of the depression, The Professor makes a living by training Dimples and her friends to sing and dance on the street while he picks the pockets of the audience.

Indeed the film opens amid a performance of theirs, moving from a close-up of the adorable Temple singing with a mixed-race group of street urchins to the exposure of The Professor as a scoundrel and a thief. The loyal Dimples cannot believe that he could be so venal because he is an "aristocrat." Like the king in *The King and I*, Dimples has only a partial, vernacular, and innocent understanding of the social form she so admires. At the same time the film emphasizes in such a joke the quotation marks it places around the aura of democratic cosmopolitan equality implied by the ironic national progress narrative it also offers: the popular fetishism of aristocratic taste is also parodied in Stepin Fetchit's performance as The Professor's "valet," since there is neither money nor food, and they live together in a hovel. Fetchit takes a lot of awful verbal abuse, but The Professor, of course, is soundly revealed as the bigger fool. This too displays the sentimentalist's ambivalence about class society. In a system that wallpapers structural inequality with jokes about the wealthy and cultured who live and dabble among the poor while valorizing the pseudo-democratic aura of class-mixed cosmopolitan consumption of the popular pleasures, the aristocratic figure continues to be deferred to and protected, an adorable archaic old generation. Adorableness provides an alibi for all sorts of injustice in *Dimples*.

As with *The King and I*, *Dimples*'s motives for citing *Uncle Tom* involve a reframing of what the bourgeoisie enjoys—the spatial experience of a distinction between "the public and the private." The cinematic image inevitably violates the fantasy of these bounded territories, which thematically hold only when no surprising exchanges take place between the home and the world, which is to say never, or at most off-screen. In a time of financial straits, all spaces are permeable by all people. Aristocrats are lonely and nonreproductive and bring in street urchins to revitalize the wealthy's wasting energies, and on the streets everyone scavenges in slapstick and tragic ways. Only the decent and respectable middle classes have the discipline to organize a nonchaotic metropolitan life and thus here represent the fulfillment of a national utopian promise: when they go to the theater, it is an Arnoldian experience, dedicated to pleasure and instruction. Since in *Dimples* the theater stands for the public sphere, popular culture generally is the space where identifications as respectable members of normative society can be made by anyone of any social position: the inclusive affects produced by the consumption of these commoditized identifications are implicitly foundational for national democracy.

The generic and ideological traces of politico-sentimentality are everywhere in the film. The opening crisis of the genteel Professor's economic malfeasance (shades of *The Wide, Wide World*) locates the film in that space between feminism and conservative femininity in which the female complaint resides: but here the complaint is barely audible, as when Dimples says to her future owner, the dowager Caroline Drew, "Sometimes I wonder whether men are worth all the trouble they give us." The film then spends the rest of its time showing that they aren't, but ultimately it doesn't matter, once *Uncle Tom's Cabin* translates the racially, economically, and sexually incommensurate audience into a shared mass of empathetic feeling. These intimacies are mirrored by the way the play of *Uncle Tom's Cabin* is interpellated into the film. In the mirror that the play implicitly claims to provide, the national and domestic divisions of slavery are dissolved by the vulnerability of virtuous citizens of all ranks; and meanwhile, the double transformation of history into a novel and the novel into a theatrical commodity brings into being a way of reading that turns any audience into properly sentimental citizens.

In *Dimples*, the play of *Uncle Tom's Cabin* is staged straight, in a way, with a blackface Uncle Tom and Topsy, and Temple ethereal in Little Eva's deathbed scene: but throughout it is a slapstick situation, with police running across the stage, and The Professor, disguised as Uncle Tom to hide from the police, following the "real" fake Uncle Tom on stage, leading to a standard comic double-take. Nonetheless, these hilarities and exaggerations provide an even more powerful negative frame for the uninterrupted sentimental auratic of the narrative proper. Crises from every aspect of the entire plot are resolved through these particular tears, except, of course, for the racial and sexual ones, which have nothing to do with any agency being exhibited onscreen.

Thus the critique of value *Dimples* offers is not primarily a sexual, racial, or economic one: it ends up being a critique of bad people, with plots organized by crises of living racial, economic, and sexual hierarchy providing a pseudoclarifying ruse for less visible crises of social relation. The film's big questions engage the relative value of a capitalism that sustains aristocratic rankings and mentalities versus one in which class mobility makes plausible the fantasy of everyday democratic experience. The film makes no bones about its democratic affiliation: it is against families and lineages, and for consumer identifications, which is to say the middle class, which must reinvent the family. There are no mothers in the film, no Eliza at all, and therefore no one to save the child; nor are there fathers. Each major adult woman is an idiot, an evil, authoritarian, or narrow-minded dominatrix, while men are ineffectual at best. The play disinherits the familial grounding of sentimentality, replacing it with the intimacy of consumers who have had the same moving experiences watching the play. Women cry and men clear their throats.

The argument the film makes for market democracy situates its plot in the difference between two kinds of acting: acting on the legitimate stage, which performs sentimental pedagogy to congeal the passive liberalism of the ascending middle classes, and acting on the street, in which kids simply entertain the mix of people who pass them by, making no pretense to educate or to appeal to higher values. When these two plots mix and produce the dramatic spectacle of Shirley Temple playing Eva, *Dimples* cites *Uncle Tom's Cabin* to link methods of survival on the street and in the parlor to an aesthetic that translates the static status hierarchies of rank, race, and gender into the mobile and labile improvisations of democracy, which the film takes enormous pleasure in at every moment. One such improvisation occurs in the moment after the play when, victorious in making the elite meet the street on behalf of completing the family form broken up by the depression of 1850, the first minstrel show ever performed in the north is supposedly staged in the film's last moments, with Dimples fronting a mixed-race chorus of men in blackface singing the song "Miss Dixiana" and dancing like Bill Robinson, as though the South had already, by 1850, been reduced to the region of minor, archaic, and uncanny culture the North has used as its plaything and exteriorized bad conscience ever since. To become anachronistic is to be available for adorableness; white economic supremacy, which was the violent support for a rank society, turns into entertainment, a style of a bygone pleasure now rescued from its context of production.

If the representation of this set of different historical stresses weren't entertaining enough, one more contemporary motor for the anachronistic deployment of the *Uncle Tom* form in *Dimples* must not be elided: the depression. Right after the caption appears describing the film's location in a radical double movement of modern aesthetics and modern race politics in the film's opening shot, the camera pans to a sign that says "Vote Pierce for President! He'll get us out of the depression by 1852!" Charles Eckert has argued that Shirley Temple, and the industry of commodity likenesses she generated, was a crucial ideological form for displacing and overcoming labor itself from the scene of national fantasy that needed revitalizing again, given the devastating effects the Great Depression had had on the modern American ideology of world expansion, of the nation's political, economic, and cultural imperialism.[22] All of the Shirley Temple films of the early 1930s figure her exteriority with respect to the conventional forms of the family, of bourgeois security, and of money, and all of them place her sympathies and tactical victories squarely on the sides of marginal cultures, exterior to the glamour practices and aspirations of the metropolitan north. She came to represent a mass fantasy of victory over the Depression, helping to return a spectacular and ordinary pleasure to thinking about surviving an impossible everyday life as a general experience of precarity, where there was no assurance of food, shelter, and the health and dignity of Americans regardless of one's position in status hierarchies. This is the trace she brings to Toni Morrison's *The Bluest Eye*, too: at the same time her iconic face suffers and seems unconstrained by economy, emanating magical perpetuity and invulnerability. Thus the depression of 1850 here too stands as a story about overcoming history, a story about slavery, poverty, gender domination, and rank. Only entertainment culture is set up as the economic and affective foundation of democracy, as it is a healthy enough economic machine to displace the blues, to diminish the difference between the play money and the real thing, to put food on every table and a dimple in every cheek; it stands in for the project a contemporary America should once again desire to undergo.

Here, as elsewhere, the citation of the *Uncle Tom* form both enacts and displaces the jeremiad, with its political critique made in the language of power; it aspires to transfigure the public sphere via the force of congealed mass feeling and builds a bridge toward bringing into representation new realms of freedom, by making a virtue of theatergoing. As long as the sentimental social problem play is consumed, it implies, virtue will generally prevail. The pleasure of being morally elevated by consumption is added to by the episodic comfort food of the archaic adorable Dixie song, slightly sexy dancing and singing, and other kinds of delighted (but not enlightened) consumer distraction. None of this is taken that seriously in *Dimples*: it means to be escapist. If personhood is defined there by its vulnerability to humiliation, its victories are, at best, personal ones. Consumers can work on the space of diminished agency that individualized worlds of intimacy provide; meanwhile, the moral work of entertainment culture is to encounter the scene of national trauma and to have the right feelings about what is wrong in it, so that the light, frothy remains of the violent history can be consumed as a meringue, a dessert made of air and sugar and just a few broken eggs.

This Is (Not) a Story to Pass On

In the genealogy we have been tracking, sentimental modes are tactically appropriated to produce political worlds and citizen-subjects who are regulated by the natural justice that is generated by suffering and trauma. But the *Uncle Tom* form has also engendered a parallel universe of textual resistance—to the *Uncle Tom* form itself. First and foremost, this constellation of dissident texts refuses to reproduce the fascinated pleasure/violence response so spectacularly hardwired into the white and U.S.-identified memory of slavery, even when that memory is used reparatively to express white guilt or national apology. The use of the *Uncle Tom* form against its fundamental claims involves a refusal to elevate the ethic of personal sacrifice, suffering, and mourning over a politically "interested" will to socially transformative action; and it repudiates a tendency to use self-exonerating rhetorical distractions such as slapstick, romance, or tragedy to draw a self-critical boundary between an "enlightened" present and an unfortunate past.

An author's or a text's refusal to reproduce the sublimation of subaltern struggles into conventions of emotional satisfaction and redemptive fantasy might be called "countersentimental," a resistant strain within the sentimental domain. Plots in this mode often remain compelled by the ideal of a "one people" that can absorb all difference and struggle into a sponge of true feeling. That metacultural ideal of liberal empathy is so embedded in the horizon of ethico-political fantasy that alternative models—for example, those that do not track justice in terms of subjective measures—can seem inhuman, hollow, and irrelevant to the ways people experience optimism and powerlessness in ordinary life.

Countersentimental narratives are lacerated by ambivalence: they struggle with their own attachment to the promise of a sense of unconflictedness, intimacy, and collective belonging with which the U.S. sentimental tradition gifts its citizens and occupants, whether or not they are politically exhausted, cynically extended, or just plain diffident. Tableaux of effective domestic pedagogy, moral praxis, and sheer peace dominate narratives that exemplify concepts of justice and freedom in tales of personal destiny wherein people, in the end, "feel right." The question becomes how to deprivatize politics and dissociate the display of suffering from the incitement to justice without merely demonizing the fantasy state liberalism proposes.

What distinguishes these critical texts are the startling ways they struggle to encounter the *Uncle Tom* form without reproducing it, declining to pay the inheritance tax. The countersentimental does not involve the aesthetic destruction of the contract sentimentality makes between its texts and readers, that proper reading will lead to more virtuous, compassionate feeling and therefore to a better self. What changes is the place of repetition in this contract, a crisis frequently thematized in formal aesthetic and generational terms. In its traditional and political modalities, the sentimental promises that in a just world *an expressive consensus would already exist* about what constitutes material uplift, amelioration, emancipation, and those other horizons toward which empathy directs itself. Identification with suffering, the ethical response to the sentimental plot, leads to some version of a mimetic repetition in the audience and thus to a generally held view about what transformations would bring the good life into being.

The presumption that the terms of consent are transhistorical, translocal, and transdifferential because true feeling is shared explains in part why emotions, especially painful ones, are so central to the world-building aspects of sentimental alliance. Countersentimental texts withdraw from the contract that presumes consent with the conventionally desired outcomes of identification and compassion. What about the democratic pleasures of anonymity and alterity, let alone sovereign individuality? Is sentimentality ultimately antisovereign, a discipline of the body toward assuming universal response? Such desires as those for a *felt* unconflictedness might well motivate the sacrifice of surprising thought on behalf of the emotional normativity of the sentimental world, as though there is not a political economy to the meaning of emotions that bridge inequalities, such as compassion and love.

What, if anything, can be built from diverse knowledges and experiences of the pain of nondominant peoples? How can one desire to refuse the enmeshment of one's story about the humiliations of history with the conventions of narrative suffering while being true to the facts and affects of ordinary subordination? Disinheriting without disavowing requires foregrounding ambivalence, as we will see. More than a critique of human empathic attachment as such, the countersentimental modality challenges the place literature and storytelling have come to stand for in the normalization of gestures of emotional humanism in the United States across a span of almost two centuries.

Three moments in this genealogy, which differ as much from each other as from the credulous citation of *Uncle Tom's Cabin* we saw in *The King and I* and *Dimples*, will mark here some potential within the archive that counters the repetitive compulsions of sentimentality. I cite these resistances and refusals not to side with claims about the immoral "aridity" of sentimental politics but to provide evidence of the kinds of ambivalence that the "liberal paternalism" of sentimentality engenders in those whom its aesthetic has spoken about, to, and for in ways that completely confuse definitions of the human and the inhuman.[23]

This essay begins with a famous passage from James Baldwin's "Everybody's Protest Novel," a much cited essay about *Uncle Tom's Cabin* that is rarely read in the strong sense because the powerful language of rageful truth telling it uses would want to shame in advance any desire to make claims for the tactical efficacy of suffering and mourning in the struggle to transform the United States into a counterracist nation. Baldwin's claim is that associating the human with the suffering actually limits the human to a mode of absolute passivity that, ethically, cannot embody the human in its fullness.

Baldwin's engagement with Stowe in this essay comes amid a general wave of protest novels, social problem films, and film noir in the United States after World War II: *Gentleman's Agreement*, *The Postman Always Rings Twice*, *The Best Years of Our Lives*. Works like these, he says, "emerge for what they are: a mirror of our confusion, dishonesty, panic, trapped and immobilized in the sunlit prison of the American dream."[24] They cut the complexity of human motives and self-understanding "down to size" by preferring "a lie more palatable than the truth" about the social and material effects the liberal pedagogy of optimism has, or doesn't have, on "man's" capacity to produce a world of authentic truth, justice, and freedom.[25]

"Truth" is the central keyword for Baldwin. He defines it as "a devotion to the human being, his freedom and fulfillment: freedom which cannot be legislated, fulfillment which cannot be charted."[26] Stowe's totalitarian religiosity, in contrast, her insistence that subjects "bargain" for heavenly redemption with their own physical and spiritual mortification, sanctions the fundamental abjection of all persons, especially the black ones who wear the dark night of the soul out where all can see it. Additionally, Baldwin argues that *Uncle Tom's Cabin* instantiates a tradition of locating the destiny of the nation in a false model of the individual soul, one imagined as free of ambivalence, aggression, or contradiction. In contrast, by advocating for the "human being" he means to repudiate stock identities as such, arguing that the stark simplicity of the icon, type, or cliché confirms the very fantasies and institutions against which the sentimental is ostensibly being mobilized. This national/liberal refusal of complexity is what he elsewhere calls "the price of the ticket" for membership in the American dream: as the *Uncle Tom* films suggest, whites need blacks to "dance" for them so that they might continue disavowing the costs or ghosts of whiteness, which involve religious traditions of self-loathing and cultural traditions confusing happiness with analgesia.[27]

The conventional reading of "Everybody's Protest Novel" sees it as a violent rejection of the sentimental.[28] Sentimentality is associated with the feminine (*Little Women*), with hollow and dishonest uses of feeling (*Uncle Tom's Cabin*), and with an aversion to the real pain that real experience brings. "Causes, as we know, are notoriously bloodthirsty," he writes: the politico-sentimental novel uses suffering vampirically to simplify the subject, thereby making the injunction to compassion safe for the consumer of the suffering spectacle.[29]

But it turns out that there is more to the story. In "Everybody's Protest Novel" Baldwin bewails the sentimentality of Richard Wright's *Native Son* too, because Bigger Thomas is not the homeopathic other to Uncle Tom after all, but one of his "children,"[30] the heir to his negative legacy. Both Tom and Thomas live in a simple relation to violence and die only knowing slightly more than they did before they were sacrificed to a white ideal of the soul's simple purity, its emptiness. This addiction to the formula of redemption through violent simplification persists with a "terrible power" and not just for the privileged classes: it constitutes minoritized U.S. populations as inhuman through attachment to the most hateful objectified, cartoon-like versions of their identities; it provokes the shamed subcultures of America to imitate the stereotypical image.

For Baldwin, the pleasure of the stereotype and the narratives of dominant and revolutionary violence waged on its behalf constituted his fundamental experience of white privilege. Yet his narrative of his own cultural formation, *The Devil Finds Work*, opens with a stunning revelation about the place of *Uncle Tom's Cabin* in his childhood:

I had read *Uncle Tom's Cabin* compulsively, the book in one hand, the newest baby on my hipbone. I was trying to find out something, sensing something in the book of some immense import for me: which, however, I knew I did not really understand. My mother got scared. She hid the book. The last time she hid it, she hid it on the highest shelf above the bathtub. I was somewhere around seven or eight. God knows how I did it, but I somehow climbed up and dragged the book down. Then my mother, as she puts it, "didn't hide it anymore," and, indeed, from that moment, though in fear and trembling, began to let me go.[31]

The narrative of self-development Baldwin tells here is linked to familial separation and reading against the grain. Baldwin has the sentimental education he is meant to have (the memory of a mother's protection), and at the same time he uses the protest novel to develop personal sovereignty and political consciousness. As he tells the story, *A Tale of Two Cities* soon joined Stowe's novel in Baldwin's childhood imaginary. The characters were his "friends," he writes, and in many senses—his bridge to another world.

This other world was affectively complex. First, the aesthetic otherworld of novelistic revolutionary history constituted a realm of pleasure and beauty outside of the family and bodily intimacy generally: the introduction of Baldwin's aesthetic self-education comes right after a long description of his physical and general repulsiveness to his father, who beat and taunted him, he says, not because they had no genetic relation, but alternately because he was so ugly and just because he was a child and therefore a general "burden."[32] Second, these novels introduced Baldwin to the language of "revolution" everywhere saturating his contemporary political world—from the Spanish Civil War to U.S. labor agitation. But, he wrote, "I could not see where I fit in this formulation, and I did not see where blacks fit."[33] The revolutionary historical novel opens up an incoherent set of attachments for Baldwin: an image of white racist submission, the sovereign creativity of the artist, the potential relation of art to revolution, the pleasures of feeling transformed by absorption in an alternative aesthetic space as a way of pre-experiencing a material world that had not yet come into being. This is the sentimental-political aesthetic. Baldwin learns about intimacy with strangers through this aesthetic connection to revolutionary shifts: experiencing a political and affective need to write black people into the story, he abjures the form of the protest novel but maintains the promise of its refusal to be bound by the normatively real.

For Baldwin, the narratives and forms of mass culture provide schooling in alternative worlds: its powerful texts do not bind him to the woundedness of his relegation to the inhuman, but provide the conditions to read as a utopian, a mapmaker for new conventions of expression and beyond. The revolution in the aesthetic sphere of feeling Baldwin senses as a positive legacy of politico-sentimental aesthetics resurfaces all of the time: Jared Diamond's *Collapse: How Societies Choose to Fail or Succeed*, Larry Kramer's *The Normal Heart*, Rachel Carson's *Silent Spring*, Marjory Douglas's *The Everglades*, Upton Sinclair's *The Jungle*, and Herman Melville's *White-Jacket* are among many books now analogized to *Uncle Tom's Cabin* to demonstrate "the ability of literature to engage with and have an impact on the social world."[34]

"Impact" is usually measured in the overlappingly normative domains of subjectivity, the nation, and the market when *Uncle Tom's Cabin* is the ancestor evoked. For example, the blockbuster novel of the 1990s, Robert Waller's *The Bridges of Madison County*, traverses the general realm of sexual and ethno-national difference in the conventional terms of domestic melodrama and feminine crisis. Frank Rich, writing in the *New York Times Magazine*, was the first to suggest that the bestseller would best be understood as the *Uncle Tom's Cabin* of the 1990s, although the novel makes no internal claim to such a genealogy.[35] But its placement there by Rich is not fundamentally thematic: it concerns the effects the novel has on its readers, who read into it a text of liberation from the silences around a quotidian death-in-life—here, of heterosexual intimacy, for *Bridges* is a female complaint. The imminent social change that citation of the *Uncle Tom* form always heralds was also accompanied by its other historic legacy, a commodity cluster (a cookbook, the novel, a CD, a calendar, coffee-table books of photographs of Madison County, parodies, and other paraphernalia).[36] But Rich's animation of this genealogy is not merely an instance of the farce wrought by tragedy's repetition. *The Bridges of Madison County* too resists the sentimental reiteration whose conventions make it intelligible and marketable, and in a number of ways.

*Bridges* is both *Uncle Tom's Cabin* and *The Key to Uncle Tom's Cabin* rolled into one. A text that can only be described as ersatz—pseudo-novel,

-biography, -diary, and so on—it nonetheless uses these variously realist genres to pronounce its authenticity. Like the lovers themselves, the novel claims to be the vanishing point of all that is redeemable in history. The author, Robert James Waller, writes in his framing narrative that he wants to take up the decay and failure of possibility that currently casts history as a record of small and big deaths (of persons, souls, and cultures); he wants to help modern persons be something other than tourists visiting the museums and the unlivable landscapes of their own lives. He wants to represent how to reimagine the sublime encounter between the time and space of the nation and the overwhelming difficulties of everyday life for men and women whose modalities of action, abstraction, violence, and desire within normal life progressively empty them out, rather than add up to a well-lived life. But *Bridges* is installed in the genealogy of *Uncle Tom's Cabin* not only because Waller wants to emancipate individuals and nations from the enervating and death-filled present they are generating. He also wants to give his readers the aesthetic tools—through an idiosyncratic model of the photograph—to help them read their lives as evidence for an uninevitable future. As with Baldwin's work, this countersentimental text repudiates the compulsion to repeat normative forms of personhood across generations and refuses to disavow the aggression at the heart of intimacy's institutions but sanctifies a kind of revolution. Love is the emancipating vehicle for this new knowledge. This version of love has a new concept of the archive.

*Bridges* attempts this by telling of a four-day love affair that takes place starting "on a hot dry Monday in August 1965," of the revolution in feeling that followed, and of the archival and autobiographical inheritance the woman, Francesca Johnson, left her children, which we, the readers of the novel, now inherit also and have the responsibility, presumably, to revive as something like a collective project. Robert James Waller is transformed by the writing of *The Bridges of Madison County*, he tells us, in this particular way:

> Preparing and writing this book has altered my world view, transformed the way I think, and most of all, reduced my level of cynicism about what is possible in the arena of human relationships. Coming to know Francesca Johnson and Robert Kincaid as I have through my research, I find the

boundaries of such relationships can be extended farther than I previously thought. Perhaps you will have the same experience in reading this story. That will not be easy. In an increasingly callous world, we all exist with our own carapaces of scabbed-over sensibilities. Where great passion leaves off and mawkishness begins, I'm not sure. But our tendency to scoff at the possibility of the former and to label genuine and profound feelings as maudlin makes it difficult to enter the realm of gentleness required to understand the story of Francesca Johnson and Robert Kincaid. I know I had to overcome that tendency initially before I could begin writing.[37]

Now the story of *The Bridges of Madison County* might best be understood, as so many politico-sentimental texts are, as involving the construction of a revolutionary transformation of world and personal history. The text wants to make vital, sensual experience out of the linkage between the person and the world; this involves a kind of a wild juxtaposition of incommensurate knowledges, of things that must be represented as crucial to living, but according to very different scales. For example, *Bridges* involves the telling of world history through an impossible encounter between modernity and two people, brought into what Stowe calls "living dramatic reality" through a vital emblem that shocks or displaces.[38] The male protagonist, Robert Kincaid, is a photographer who travels around finding the lost moments at which nature and human life meet up strangely, and so he works for *National Geographic*, allowing with some sadness the magazine to banalize what he thinks is the ordinary sublimity of organic human and natural existence. The female protagonist, Francesca Johnson, is also a world traveler, an Italian woman whose dreams of a lush life become, wrongly it turns out, condensed in what she calls "the sweet promise of America." She marries a soldier after World War II and comes to live in Iowa. But when the photographer and the farm wife meet, they realize that their tourist lives have been not ends, but events in the providential path directed toward their meeting. The radical rupture of self-understanding the lovers make makes it possible to reinvent history as the occluded pasts become possible futures, entirely changing the knowledge and desire archives of these persons. From the moment Kincaid and Johnson meet they re-historicize, telling the stories of where they have been, reading their meeting as an event produced by all the evolutionary and civilizational activity of the world, making all of their knowledge into memories of love, and thereby sanctifying their knowledge, censoring any enigma or uncertainty that might threaten its truth. Instantly they generate artifacts, traces: a note saved, jewelry exchanged, photographs taken; and later, after they part, the *National Geographic* where Kincaid publishes his photographs of Madison County, the cameras he leaves to Francesca on his death, the few letters they exchange. It is as though they create a commodity cluster about themselves for themselves, just as the sentimental text engenders its own spinoffs in the world. *Bridges* is like a medieval love book, an archive of techniques for performing and commemorating love's elevation of ordinariness to profound and world-historical uniqueness. This process involves more than the mere exchange of things made radiant by proximity to the lover; it involves the transformation of love into evidence that can be inherited: an archive of photographs, a diary, and a special box to hold everything close.

Yet when Francesca dies and leaves to her middle-aged children this box and a captioning letter that retells the novel's story, she makes it impossible for her progeny to receive the story as something from *her*: the mother they knew is not the woman who writes to them; their inheritance is a disinheritance, for they are now forced to make living up as they go along. The children bring the archive to the novel's narrator and again, the story is retold. The narrator, who describes himself as a researcher, is also transformed by the material he finds: he turns the box into a book and leaves it to his readers, hoping that they "will have the same experience in reading this story" that he has had, an experience of entering the archive of love to unlearn what they think they know about love's impossibility and to relinquish their feeling of superiority to its "maudlin," sentimental story. Through this repeated process of autoarchiving the narrator seeks to teach his readers how to reclaim their neglected desire to be in a living story, which is a story worth telling. It is a genealogy of love that leads to you, specifies your participation in the world, makes you unique as it makes you collective, and extends you into the future as something unimaginable to you now. This does not mean that to live you have to fall in love—it means that at least you have to inherit somebody else's story, be changed by what you unlearn from it, and then pass it on as a goad to someone else's unlearning, in the mode of privatized revolution, a cherry bomb in a can. That is to say that the experienced disjuncture between personal life and history enables the children to reinvent modernity for themselves, which means to transform radically the affectively distorted and muted body living in a world of violence and shame into a newly unscabbed genealogical body of affect and knowledge that will now inhabit not a death-driven nation or a familial blood-knot, but a "realm of gentleness."

This transformation in the text is the inheritance the readers too must now reinvest in their lives. Waller reminds us of the dangers of cynical reason, that realm of "enlightened false consciousness" that trivializes ordinary irrational emotion;[39] he wants to show us how a history of overcoming our learned resistance to nonrepetition will, at least for a moment, revitalize the experience of the intimate, the social, memory, and the nation. It is as though Waller had *Uncle Tom's Cabin* on his lap and answered Stowe's not Marxist enough cry, "But, what can any individual do?" not by deploying the saga form that allows personal stories to be told as soap operas or epics, the forms of communal storytelling. Rather, he answers the question by telling it the way she imagines her own novel's destination: What can the individual do? "Of that," Stowe writes, "every individual can judge. There is one thing that every individual can do—they can see to it that *they feel right*. An atmosphere of sympathetic influence encircles every human being; and the man or woman who *feels* strongly, healthily and justly, on the great interests of humanity, is a constant benefactor to the human race."[40] Individuals are the site of experiment; but to tell the story of sentimental radicalism will be to show how "feeling right" as opposed to feeling "cynical" about change has become embedded in textual and political conventions whose contradictory bargains with pain, domination, terror, and exile remain the unfinished business of the countersentimental, which refuses to confuse survival with freedom, justice, or the good life. But having said this, the thrilling moment of political, public self-transcendence remains limited by the very evanescence of the weapon—consciousness. The revolution that Waller imagines takes the route of the bridge, not the water; as the countless showers and baths in the novel suggest, it is a revolution that refuses to be dirty, or to stay wet. Francesca makes it impossible for her children to inherit her style of intimacy, empathy, survival, and freedom; but Waller contradicts the gesture he writes for her, insisting that this is a story, after all, to pass on, a story about love's power to transform everything important in the world. His is a revolution that preserves the sublimity of the fantasies that already exist, along with what we might cynically call "business as usual."

Speaking of business as usual, I have written the sentimental opening represented by *Bridges* as though it had skirted the embedded history of racial distinction, white compassion, and emotional pseudo-universalism that often shapes the *Uncle Tom* tradition. But the Vaseline-lensed supremacy of white liberalism nonetheless permeates the cinematic senses of the film adaptation—through the soundtrack. Clint Eastwood, the film's star and director, had established his proficiency as a jazz aficionado in *Bird* (1988) and *In the Line of Fire* (1993). The film adaptation of *Bridges* (1995) highlights a vastly popular Eastwood-curated soundtrack (and *two* soundtrack CDs) featuring the work of the African American jazz singers Johnny Hartman and Dinah Washington. Additionally, the film includes an episode not in the novel in which the lovers go on a date to listen to an African American jazz group—it performs the lovers' displacement from the "real" world in which they live and situates the aesthetic, once again, as a space of utopian emotional fulfillment that they can have in memory whether or not they change their material lives. In itself these cushionings of the lovers in the classic jazz tradition aren't "merely" evidence of the paternalist unconscious of sentimental whiteness. But the gesture of associating a white-populated plot with black cultural production typically means to "soulfulize" whiteness and certainly means to do that here.[41] Richard LaGravenese, who wrote the screenplay, also penned the film of *Beloved* (1998).

My aim so far has been to articulate the very different kinds of strength the *Uncle Tom* form has provided the entertainment industry that continues to constellate around it: on the one hand, to negotiate, as the novel negotiates, a radical reimagination of the world, an archive of survival tactics, and to witness critiques of the fraudulent claims to popular consent American political culture has based its legitimacy on, along with its claims to have elicited popular consent to its domination of what counts as political. The politics of rage and pain and powerlessness that motors so much of the sentimental complaint and protest industry has been accompanied, on the other hand, by a desire for amelioration at any cost. In a sense, the sentimental bargain has constantly involved substituting for representations of pain and violence representations of its sublime self-overcoming, which end up, often perversely, producing pleasure both as a distraction from suffering and also as a figure for the better life that sufferers under the regime of nation, patriarchy, capital, and racism ought to be able to imagine themselves having. Sentimentality, after all, is the only vehicle for social change that neither produces more pain nor requires much courage, unlike other revolutionary rhetorics. This ravenous yearning for social change, this hunger for the end of pain, has installed the pleasures of entertainment, of the star system, of the love of children, and of heterosexual romance where a political language about suffering might have been considered appropriate. In these ways the very emphasis on feeling that radicalizes the sentimental critique thus also muffles the solutions it often imagines, or distorts and displaces these solutions from the places toward which they ought to be directed.

Written in 1949, Baldwin's exhortation to refuse to pass on the contradictions of sentimental liberalism might be taken up by Toni Morrison, say: for if *The Bluest Eye* casts Shirley Temple and her ilk to be among the most vicious weapons of whiteness, *Beloved* understands that there is no transcendence anywhere, not through a thrilling or a comforting image. The Morrisonian image connects the subject to history, even when it is fragmented: it does not perform the separation of contradiction, compromise, ambivalence, and uncertainty from the lived or aesthetic life of the subject. Surely *Beloved* quotes "poor Eliza" in its constant return to Sethe's river crossing. But it shows that when you cross the Ohio you do not transcend it; you take it with you. At any moment a woman who has crossed the water, or who is descended from one who has risked the water, might be walking through the grass thinking sentimental thoughts about the love and family and peace she might experience sometime, when she has the time and money and freedom, when suddenly "she [has] to lift her skirts, and the water she void[s is] endless," such that a viewer might "be obliged to see her squatting in front of her own privy making a mudhole too deep to be witnessed without shame."[42] Or perhaps she might be overcome by singing, "where the voices of women searched for the right combination, the key, the code, the sound that broke the back of words. Building voice upon voice until they found it, and when they did it was a wave of sound wide enough to sound deep water . . . and she trembled like the baptized in its wash."[43] Or perhaps, breaking the water of pregnancy while lying flat in a boat she would remember the middle passage, or just think about rain, and other kinds of beloved weather. Whatever the case, the desire to disinherit a community from the stories that bind it to weepy repetitions of sublime death in dry, safe local entertainments motivates the novel *Beloved* to show that rather than seeking transcendence of the self who exemplifies the impossibility of exteriority to history, and rather than merely repeating the tragedies that seemed long ago to constitute whatever horizon of possibility your identity might aspire to, the countersentimental project would have you refuse to take on the history of the other as your realness, or as the solution to the problem of passing (over) water in the present.

Sethe's flood poses a challenge to the tears of sentimental culture because it is stunning, a performance of affect without an emotion, an episode of intensified awareness, like Eliza's escape. But while Eliza is rescued from the space of slippage by the bosom of white sentimentality, Sethe generates the river she steps over as though on the other side of sentimental personhood the ethical stance is not to imitate the normative institutions of privileged intimacy, like marriage, but to occupy a place of corporeal self-knowledge that riddles us, makes experience something that produces new bodies all around on an unstable and muddy ground. Acknowledging the sentimental contact with emotional transparency, Morrison makes her characters and readers sick with surfeit. She counters the desire for performative and transparent community by proposing an inheritance without a mimetic compulsion or fear of emotional opacity, and she rejects the normative presumptions and idealizations of transparency. But this flood is not just a renewed embodiment, like a baptism: it is an emotional experience whose consequences are soon to be embodied in an unfinished sentence—Beloved. That this word tilts toward the desires to be in proximity to love that shape the intimate public of femininity means that *Beloved* too is at least partly ballasted by the affect that wants new forms.

**PAX AMERICANA**   The Case of *Show Boat*

And if the things we dream about

don't happen to be so—

that's just an unimportant technicality.

HAMMERSTEIN AND KERN, "MAKE BELIEVE"

### Adapting—to Racism

This chapter focuses on the centrality of adaptation—aesthetic and subjective—to the ongoing power of sentimental culture in the United States. It uses the supertext of *Show Boat*, spanning Edna Ferber's novel and many dramatic adaptations, to ask why and how specific kinds of pain get turned into modern entertainment, and how to read it when those texts and forms of entertaining suffering are revisited, revived, and revised.[1] It asks what kind of theory or account of history the sublime object of white sentimentality (of which the ur-text here is *Uncle Tom's Cabin*) offers its consuming and witnessing publics; more broadly, it provides a case study for thinking about a project of emotional humanism that wants to turn the enduring sexual and economic politics of racism in the United States into a story about suffering in general, one that offers a liberal lens through which to see all American sufferers as part of the same survival subculture.

In this my argument overlaps with and contests the terms of Eric Lott's *Love and Theft*, which claims that the white male working-class adaptation and appropriation of black minstrelsy in the United States engendered important forms of antibourgeois solidarity while also expressing, against and along with white racism itself, the anxious intimacy of white and black social worlds.[2] From a very different social position—midwestern, middlebrow, and, in the shadows, Jewish—*Show Boat* explicitly laments the evisceration of U.S. racial history by the conventions of optimism in popular entertainment, while offering its own brand of critical liberal universalism. It also redeploys critically the minstrel tradition that Lott and others have engaged as the scene of contact between white working-class, white immigrant, mass consumer practices and African American agrarian and proletarian-related cultural forms, shifting the emphasis from comic absurdity to tragic injustice, while retaining the aesthetic contrasts.[3] While Ferber did not consider *Show Boat* to speak from the intimate public of sentimental femininity as such, the novel uses a love plot to mobilize its conventions of emotional authenticity and its aversion to the political in the name of setting out a general national experience of healing, transcendence, and survival.[4] This is to say that *Show Boat* is a strongly ambivalent text, whose critical historicism addresses racial violence, sexual suffering, and class exploitation as problems over which the right kind of narrative might stage a victory of sorts: like making someone laugh to forget or cry so that you can have the power and pleasure of their consolation.

We live in a modernity that appropriates history in an aversive blur, mythifying and making archaic the authenticity of slave affliction: this is the premise of Edna Ferber's novel *Show Boat* (1926). The story of *Show Boat* follows the dissolution of the geographical U.S. color line into the linked crossover dynamics of the Harlem Renaissance, modernist youth culture, and cosmopolitan entertainments. Magnolia Hawks and her parents live on a show boat, the *Cotton Blossom*, which travels the Mississippi starting in the 1870s; Julie Dozier and Steve Baker, the romantic leading actors, are revealed to have committed miscegenation, with Julie passing as white. They are banished from the boat, with Julie resurfacing during the Columbian Exposition (1893) as the companion to Chicago's leading prostitute. Meanwhile, Magnolia takes Julie's place as an actress; Gaylord Ravenal, the gambler who becomes the lead actor in the melodrama, falls in love with Magnolia, and as real-life lovers they dominate the theatrical scene of the river, their passion burning visibly through the plots their acting sells.[5] They marry, and they go to the exotic and degraded Chicago of the Columbian Exposition, living the oscillating lives of gamblers on the economic periphery of the city. When they hit bottom, they return to the boat, and Magnolia gives birth to a child, Kim, named for the conjuncture Kentucky, Illinois, Missouri. They return to the city, go bankrupt again, and Ravenal, shamed, leaves Magnolia. To survive she joins the new entertainment form called vaudeville, whose profits are surging due to the Columbian Exposition. There she markets not the melodrama she performed on the showboat, but the African American spirituals and popular songs that Jo and Queenie, the ship's servants, had taught her as a child. Magnolia makes these natal slave songs the rage in the North. The book begins and ends in the 1920s, as a narrative about Magnolia's daughter, Kim. She is a celebrity, a full-fledged star on Broadway, the third Hawks generation to capitalize on what she now delicately calls "southern" songs.[6] In the end, Magnolia returns to the showboat and to immersion in the visibly unchanged and psychically unchanging interracial, peasant south of her childhood.

*Show Boat* has been remade into three feature films (along with being featured in the Jerome Kern biopic *Till the Clouds Roll By* [1946]) and six radio plays; it constitutes the first American cast album and the first televised Broadway event; and it has sprouted more than thirty-five major revivals, along with myriad quotations on soundtracks and in television shows (for example, *Uncle Spanky's Show Boat* [1939], an episode of *Our Gang*).[7] As fiction-cum-star biography, the novel is a saga of a celebrity family; and the saga of the celebrity family structures the story of U.S. modernity, as though each generation is itself a modernizing remake of the previous one. In making this mutual introjection of the personal and national into the textual drama, Ferber's *Show Boat* plays out some means by which U.S. subaltern activity, and in particular the public history of African Americans, has been reanimated, expropriated, and adapted for the purpose of creating a modern American culture that might flaunt a rich past while feeling free from accountability to the past's ongoing activity.[8] But the desire *Show Boat* puts out there on behalf of the vague solidarities of liberal conventionality is not a simple one: no historically grounded aesthetic transformation is, even if a work seems ultimately to equate the experience of true democracy with the simultaneity of suffering via sing-along (effected in the musical of *Show Boat* by the soundtrack's constant return to bits and snatches of its big numbers in its closing scenes).[9] The aim of this chapter is to enumerate and coordinate the multiple conventions and technologies of adaptation that contribute to this feel-good and feel-right version of patriotic performance, including figuring in the component of critical anti-normativity that marks the liberal sentimental text's ambition to provide more than entertainment.

In this case, the modern American moment is produced not through the official timeline of national history, nor through a claim that family history is in any sense private, but through a genealogy of entertainments whose place in collective memory makes up a nation that takes on the shimmery, intimate yet detached quality of the commodity form. The effect of commodity historicity is generated, in *Show Boat*, by a national culture industry whose pleasure machines are the showboat on the Mississippi, the Columbian Exposition in Chicago, and the theater on Broadway. This culture industry is dedicated to substituting qualities of nationally coded experience and feeling for class reference and historical memory: as the novel stages the nation's recovery from the legacies of slavery, migration, urbanization, and industrialization, it develops an obsessive relation to futurity. The family form that mediates national history and culture and personal experience in the novel helps to do just that: it holds a wedge open for the future, for reproduction in all its senses—biological, political, economic, aesthetic. In this way the novel tells the story of Americans' increasing dependence on tourism, entertainment forms, and leisure practices for their own self-understanding, sense of belonging, and sense of possibility.[10]

The novel *Show Boat*'s appraisal of modernist mass culture might have predicted the kinds of distortion its plot would undergo in its adaptation to drama: "It was Anodyne. It was Lethe. It was Escape. It was the Theatre."[11] Thus its own mechanism of historical advancement—the mode of entertainment—works against its attempts to narrate critically and sympathetically the costs of the adaptation forced on subaltern populations to, by, and for national modernity. Trafficking heavily in racial, class, regional, and gender stereotypes that point to the bottom of so many hierarchies of value in the

United States, the popular entertainment form can only, it seems, aim to re-populate the image archive of modern American memory by shifting among clichés; *Show Boat* intermixes conventional scenes of elite white life derived from modern cosmopolitan genealogies with the documentary realism of the Depression aesthetic, featuring unglamorous American landscapes and people experiencing their ordinary and extraordinary pleasures, suffering, and exhaustion. The weaving of seeming historical archaism into modernity that the novel effects in the simultaneity of regional difference will turn out to support stereotyping, perversely, as an *ethics* in the novel, though: as I argue below, Ferber uses the literary/printed stereotype to critique the glamorous amnesiac spectacle with which she is also fascinated, and which constitutes the direction in which she sees the United States traveling. Here the point is that while Magnolia ends the novel back in the South, immersed in memory and fidelity to the scene of labor that made her survival possible, the adaptations close by placing her in proximity to a mode of entertainment tending toward modernity, transcendence, and the North.

The plays (first performed in 1927; book and lyrics by Oscar Hammerstein II; music by Jerome Kern) and the films (1929, dir. Harry A. Pollard; 1935, dir. James Whale; 1951, dir. George Sidney) that adapt the novel have made the text a classic vehicle for amnesiac narrative, an authentic piece of kitsch history in which memory converts into memorabilia. Yet even constructing amnesias is not merely an effect of censorship, prohibition, or simple excising. The narrative logic of *Show Boat*'s revisions cuts against the grain of the novel in two primary ways. First, the dramatic versions depict the Ferberesque national culture of sacred stereotypes, but the drama actually gives richer, more elaborate, and nuanced subjectivities to the African American characters it foregrounds than the novel does, while casting into the dustbin of history the white peasantry and urban underclasses to which the novel also attends. Traces of the multiracial and class-fractured U.S. historical past from the novel are replaced in the play by African American—but not always black—faces that sing with feeling about memory, hard experience, and desire. Second, African American history comes to stand for American history itself, at least insofar as history is a record of people and events that pass into pasts. But having elaborated the African American stereotype more fully into theatricalized personhood, the dramas nonetheless increasingly imagine a nation that pushes narratively toward the future, leaving its survivor cultures to a petrified obsolescence, located in the space of the South and in the musical traces of popular song. All occupants of the United States adapt to modernity, and some even counterexploit its emergent vehicles for mobility to gain a better version of their own survival. But in *Show Boat* African Americans are turned into a resource for modernity while the history of structural physical, emotional, and economic exploitation their story embodies remains in the faint echoes of the classic soundtrack.

Thus while the dramas that adapt *Show Boat* differ from the novel in which regional U.S. histories provide the local color and rich past of the modern nation, the adaptations share the novel's contradictory impulses toward historical explanation and national culture making. The modernist desire for a past in aspic can be detected in the place given to passion in *Show Boat*'s historical sweep. All of the versions of *Show Boat* show how one history of subalternity can become reconfigured into the materials for another: specifically, they show how the commodity code "romantic love"/"exotic sex" can mark not only the spectralization of slavery and the "regionalization" of southern history from national popular memory, but also the adaptation of vulnerable and exploited women across race and class divides to the terms of autonomy through glamour offered by cosmopolitan modernity.[12] Both Ferber and Hammerstein recount how women's domestic and sexual service to men, to entertainment culture, and to modern national identity became inextricably linked. At the same time, U.S. "women's history" becomes white women's history, and white women's history becomes narrowed by being linked to a grander scheme of class amnesias: love plots and domestic fantasies come to saturate the narratives of experience and dreams of upward mobility through love with which a class of women are solicited to identify.

The two subaltern codes of *Show Boat* thus diverge in their relation to modernity, with the dramatic adaptations marketing belief in fantasy less ambivalently than does the novel: but neither occupies its internal contradictions in a way that changes the basic plot. The "race" code, central to knowledge but displaced from plot, represents a sign of the archaic origins of collective national consciousness; in contrast, the gender/sexuality code, which takes over the plot, represents both modernity and the transcendence of historical memory. That split is made possible by the technologies of romance and nostalgia in popular culture. In this way, *Show Boat* delivers a meaningfully incoherent account of whether or not white women represent a subaltern class in America. White and light-skinned African American women bear the impact of political history but are rescued from it by fantasies of the kind of romantic fulfillment that turns suffering into something vague one had to go through on the way. Fantasy here operates not as a desire for a thing, but as a desire for a kind of life, a sequencing of events that makes fabulous sense, a biography that, seen from the "outside," would appear to deserve a history.[13] The possibility that anyone's biography might tell of a life lived as fantasy would map it as central to the ways the culture industry makes erotic, normal, and personal the risks and failures, the violence, the deferrals, and impossible promises of democracy under capitalism. It does this first by referring to the life-sustaining longing that people have for particular valued forms of intimacy—for example, the romantic couple, the conjugal family—and then by creating conventions of glamorousness that diffuse whatever might prevent distribution of a vague sense of universality in emotional transparency.

In *Show Boat*, the very same vehicles that imagine the history of the present and the doggerel of the future—the culture industry and its plots of displacement and personalization—are also central apparatuses of violence and exploitation. This is much clearer in the novel, which is about the hard conditions of life that bring work into contact with play, than in the dramas, which focus on the plays of desire. Screen memories, like so many other lacks, appear to us in spectacular forms, forms radiant with the wish they ill-express, fetishes. Fredric Jameson calls these "fantasy bribes": bribes of culture that displace history and condense longing the way a dream does.[14] My interest here is less in the emblem of the bribe than in the scene of its exchange: the ways narratives about intimate life construct fantasy norms that retemporalize ordinary life into a split between the singular detail or "unimportant technicality" of "Only Make Believe" and the conventions of emotional humanism that mark popular modernity as a scene of hazy cosmopolitanism. But *Show Boat* has an aversive relation to the costs of U.S. modernity too. In reading across the supertext that *Show Boat* has brought into being, we see the aesthetic and political techniques that enable the bourgeois project of Ferber and Hammerstein and Kern to be both normative and critical. They name the subjective impacts of economic, sexual, and racial struggle and then deliver plots in which survival appears as something transcendent. This general structure is, as I have suggested in previous chapters, one of the promises and premises of U.S. sentimentality's politico-aesthetic genealogy.

## Uncle Tom's Show Boat

*Show Boat* has been called, by Ferber herself and by critics, a fantastic piece of Americana.[15] Its status as Americana has been said to rival that of *Uncle Tom's Cabin* (Rev. of *Show Boat* 1936). *Uncle Tom's Cabin* follows *Show Boat* around the reviews and the criticism in ways that establish it as a vital and complex pretext for the later work. The fictional show boat itself performs *Uncle Tom's Cabin* as one of its stock melodramas; Harry Pollard's 1927 direction of Universal's *Uncle Tom's Cabin* was explicitly considered training for the first film of *Show Boat*, which he directed in 1929; more recently, Richard Dyer's chapter on Paul Robeson in *Heavenly Bodies* cuts across fiction, stardom, and history in actually extracting a passage from the novel that describes Uncle Tom's body to illustrate Robeson's own atavistic modernist physique.[16] This is to say that *Show Boat* participates in all sorts of direct and indirect senses in the animation of *Uncle Tom's Cabin*'s typological function in U.S. popular culture.

To the degree that *Show Boat* extends *Uncle Tom's Cabin*'s assimilation of the material of slavery into the hardwiring of national identity, it extends the techniques of soft supremacy enumerated in "Poor Eliza" while adding to them as well (chapter 1). Both of the novels perform the cultural work historical fiction of the present typically does: to construct a register of national nostalgia that a) revises what constitutes modernity in the popular public sphere; and b) conflates citizenship and consumer activity. But the styles and consequences of bargaining among nostalgia for lost ordinary forms of humanity, a critical take on the present, and the preservation of a nationalized optimism are quite different in the two novels, and it is worth saying how.

Ending slavery was for Stowe the fundamental pressure behind writing about national life. *Uncle Tom's Cabin* mainly envisions this end by representing slavery's violence in terms of its saturation of the everyday, of ordinary ethical subjectivity, in losses of property and family, mothers and children, as well as in the sacrifice of the body's autonomy and privacy. Slavery is cast as a scandal of displacement: of democracy, inciting corporeal and capital distress; of topography, as Stowe transports the southern slave system from its symbolic place on the geopolitical periphery to a space where, metonymically, the South stands for the nation itself; and, finally, of national aesthetics, for Stowe uses the otherworldliness of the feminized gothic and Christian universes to signify the contingency and fragility of the nation as it stands before the realistic, novelistic, masculine mode that dominates the political public sphere. Stowe's deployment of gothic, melodrama, and comedy as modes of nostalgic history are therefore indices of the nation's present political failure. A truly enlightened nation would produce novels without these temporalizing genres of displacement and excess.

*Uncle Tom's Cabin* intervened directly into a contemporary crisis of knowledge and national power and has therein become the sign of a novel that can work to change the course of history. Its status as a liberal democratic referent has everything to do with the way it cut across distances between privacy and the public sphere. But its status as *Americana* derives from a slightly different domain too, that of the nostalgic self-confirmation its stereotypes have provided as entertainment to postslavery America. As "Poor Eliza" argues, even in *Uncle Tom's Cabin* episodes that enflesh the racial and economic stereotype shuttle between comic and melodramatic representations and use the codes of black music and black death to signify some relation between personal and collective encounters with power. But as time goes on, the black/white, slave/free, South/North formulas put into play by these "period" narratives paradoxically provide an achronic image of national taxonomy itself, onto which other forms of cultural domination become mapped.

I take as an example a contemporary work, *Topsy and Eva* of 1927, which assumes but rings major changes on *Uncle Tom's Cabin* (see fig. 2). *Topsy and Eva* opens in heaven, from which a stork carrying a baby in a diaper emerges. The stork drops Little Eva into a mansion; we see a beautiful angel write into the birth ledger, Miss Eva St. Clare, Valentine's Day 1842; next what the card calls "a stork of darker hue" emerges from the clouds, carrying a dark infant in a diaper. This stork tries to drop its bundle on a single woman's house, but she protests in defense of her reputation; the stork tries to drop the baby on a slave family, but they stone the stork, so that the baby is finally born in a trash can. In heaven the black angels are shooting craps; one of them gets up and writes "Topsy . . . ? 1842, April Fool's Day." This frame relocates the story of *Uncle Tom's Cabin* entirely within the realm of the personal: indeed, at the end of the film, Topsy's love for Eva revives her from her redemptive death, and it closes with the two women cuddling in bed. The erotic prospects of this spectacle aside, this adaptation banalizes contests over race, rank, and sexuality, making the scene of U.S. history into a story of one baby everyone wanted and one baby no one wanted. That is to say, it expresses something imminent in *Uncle Tom's Cabin* and explicit in *Show Boat* after it. Signifying both with regard to specific historical crises and celebrating the technologies of ambivalence—displacement, achronicity, or catachresis—made available by the power this tradition of the novel signifies, *Topsy and Eva* attempts to recast and to change the world.

For Edna Ferber, who was writing in 1926 about a contemporary America whose modernity originated in the Civil War, the construction of Americana from slavery derived from additional pressures to transform or to redistort national consciousness. Like Stowe, Ferber renarrates the nation by mobilizing the slave body, sexuality, American landscape, and fictive truths about subaltern peoples. But in contrast to *Uncle Tom's Cabin*, *Show Boat* aims directly at the field of nostalgic entertainment itself, locating in the banality of "Americana" the ethical and political crisis of modernity, which is whether or not modernity is modern enough, or a wishful periodizing that universalizes certain forms of cosmopolitan liberality to drown out or make quaint the evidence of injustice that perdures. The true but imaginary United States of *Show Boat* is generated by the Mississippi, with its "great untamed" life-force and its "ruthless, relentless, Gargantuan, terrible" capacity to endure violence and enjoy peace.[17] By the end, though, three generations of Hawkses and Ravenals populate three stages of pop culture technology that are characterized by less and less intense aesthetic forms expressing much the same longings and desires for survival and more than that, the aspiration to join a fantasy elite and a wish to participate in democratic culture. The modern nation conflates citizenship with celebrity and its minor chord, consumption, "a picture so kaleidoscopic, so extravagant, so ridiculous" that it virtually makes citizens into infants.[18] What Jameson calls the postmodern "waning of affect" could be said to find a genealogical addition here: history moves into

historicity. But *Show Boat* demonstrates how hard it is to distinguish waning from intensified emotional conventionality in popular culture.[19] Even as the slave intensities fade in *Show Boat*'s version of cosmopolitan white New Yorkers, *Show Boat* is still a melodrama, and "waning" in one part of the diegesis rubs up against a myriad of forms of historicist suffering—conscience making—in others. What do we make of this doubleness? The conventions of emotional immediacy and transparency, as expressed in the supertext of *Show Boat*, make it impossible to distinguish waning and profundity from their appearance in the aesthetic conventions of mass cultural expressivity; the conventionality of public feeling frustrates the adjudication of what constitutes an authentic phenomenological exchange or deep relation to the history that produces the experience of the present. There is no "in itself": the question is how affective pedagogy is taken up in context.

"Americana" is the essentializing trivia of national culture, where the profoundly hardwired meets the banality of kitsch. As I argued in the last chapter, it can turn inequality into adorableness, and criminal evidence into memorabilia. *Show Boat* wants to have it both ways. It was the first social problem musical: it folded realism—read racism and sexual suffering—into the text of Broadway entertainment. "In addition to tackling serious issues like bigotry, spousal desertion, and alcoholism, *Show Boat* was the first large-scale, successful, integrated musical on Broadway," according to John Bush Jones.[20] By making new signs appear as the ephemera of what already counts as "American" life, and turning old signs into classics in a way that preserves and destroys them, *Show Boat* tries to have it both ways, bargaining with the memory of U.S. inequalities and tinkering with the hardwiring of national optimism.

## You're Not the Type

The legacies of inequality Ferber reconfigures in *Show Boat* are haunting but not threatening: her practice of coordinating the histories of race, sexuality, and entertainment in the United States has little to do with enacting aesthetic justice by extracting repressed subaltern histories or cultural practices from the idealizing white supremacist narratives of modern national culture. But the histories embedded in *Show Boat*'s production and revivals are not merely there. Moreover, the recent history of imperialism and global violence that marks *Show Boat*'s revivals interferes with and complicates the process of managing the national memory of intimately consequential injustice. A decade later, Ferber noted that the entertainment strategies of the novel were also responses to the recent trauma World War I had wrought on the nation: *Show Boat* was meant to provide an opportunity for collective affective healing through entertainment about overcoming suffering. So when Ferber produces a critical distance on national culture by means of the stereotyping machinery of a U.S. exotic otherness, her criticism also lays the foundation for a recalibrated narrative of national progress.[21]

In Ferber's writing writ large, though, this stereotypic register is mobilized as a register of lived experience in the context of people's experience of labor. In contrast to many of her peers—Fannie Hurst and Dorothy Parker among them—Ferber was not terribly interested in socialism or analyses of the subjective or material impacts of exploitation, poverty, or suffering as such. Her people tend to be game, survivors. But her focus on domestic and cosmopolitan scenes of service tracks very closely the performance pressures modern conditions place on African Americans, women, and mid-level male white-collar workers, and it makes their interactions more fraught with bargaining and adaptation as tactics for living than merely the molecular bounding of one hardened identity molecule off of another.[22] Deploying modes of identification founded on the linked histories and social functions of living stereotypes and commodities in America, Ferber depicts a *survival subculture* wrought from the physical proximity of people having different but simultaneous experiences of social and political alienation, domination, and waste. How is it possible that the practice of stereotyping could further the narrative project of alliance building?

A digression into a later text by Ferber highlights the kinds of affiliation among the bottom dwellers of U.S. culture she envisions in *Show Boat*. In a story called "You're Not the Type," which begins with the stuttering phrase "All her life—that is, all her professional life," Ferber tells the tale of a fading Broadway actress of light comedy named Vivian Lande.[23] Lande attributes her professional decline to the new conventions of youth and entertainment culture that dominated the United States in the 1930s. She rages at the way that U.S. youth, and especially women, have transformed the trauma of the Depression into a style of acting, as though the ideal career of pain would be to produce new, commodified forms of marketable authenticity. In the following scene, Lande has an attack of "resentment, jealousy [and] fear." She has this attack in front of her maid, Essie: "With the magic intuition of a race born to suffering the brown girl understood. She laughed. It was a superb imitation of mirth. 'Land, everybody says they're going to be an actress. Look at me! I was going to be an actress, nothing would do, I was born to act. But I never did. That's how come I'm maid for Miss Vivian Lande, the famous Broadway star. It was the nearest to acting I could get.'"[24]

The narrator says that the "brown girl" who speaks was of a "race born to suffering." Essie says of herself: "I was born to act." When Ferber details this double birthright, of suffering and of acting, she expresses the liberal presumptions of "women's culture" in a variety of ways. Both women, the employer and her maid, are deemed relegated to theatrical labor in everyday life, performing femininity to maintain the happiness of others and the continued order of things. This style of gender performativity is exacerbated by the acting the woman of color feels forced to do in lieu of acting on the stage, which is specified as an "imitation of mirth" in the white woman's presence, a filter derived from having for a living to manage a white person, a woman, and an employer, which requires skills that link up pride in one's competence and self-abasement in one's intimately executed inauthenticity. Add to this the grandiosity that leads women to think that the emotional labor of the stressful everyday life creates a direct link in expertise between women in their private melodramas and the women who act in the commercial ones. This panoply of responses emanates from the essential association of identity categories—race and femininity—with reactive affect—pain and laughter—and with imitation, which, as the introduction argues, is key both to tracking how people become human and how normativity is reproduced. The emotional exchange that happens between these women is profound in the relation of its simplicity to its overdetermination, and the enormity of the open secret that enables this to be a forgettable, and not revolution-producing, episode.

There is far more to tease out in this relation of the white star to the "brown girl." Ferber here imagines for the brown girl a subjectivity—or, crucially, a "magic intuition"—that is collective and generic. She is barely distinguished by a proper name and a sketchy biography: in America, the semiotic field of the national stereotype *prenarrates* the story of any "brown girl's" particular life. There is no plot for the "brown girl" because a person "born" to a generic identity apparently has neither the autonomy nor the prosaic specificity required for public narratives of personhood: and even in the scandalous event that a subaltern subject does speak the specific pain to which she is born, she deflects it with laughter, and therefore there is either no "story" of her own or else the story she tells is one of her identity's *other* birthrights—imitation, performance, acting. The horizon of identity designated by the couplet "brown girl" and "actress" stands for Ferber as the main available scene of desire and survival for female subaltern subjects in the national capitalist public sphere. But not all U.S. subalterns have the same birthright: Ferber has it that "brown girls" are born both to *racial* suffering and to acting; it remains to be seen what acting does for the white girls who, though born to act, are not, presumably, of a race whose painful confines they have collectively experienced.

"You're Not the Type" attributes both longing and critical consciousness to the subjects who are subject to stereotypical personhood in the public sphere of U.S. modernity. The contradictions of Ferber's liberalism in "You're Not the Type"—as she attributes subjectivity to the stereotype who is nonetheless fated to subindividuality by being born to it—and its pressures on narrative are not as explicit in *Show Boat* the novel as they are everywhere in its dramatic adaptations. Yet even in the novel the resistance of the stereotype to narrative, to incorporation in a history of the present, marks the line between Magnolia's plot and Julie's plot: for example, the moment Julie is revealed as a black woman who passes, she is virtually expelled from the plot, and the narrative energy of romance, which Julie has been shown both to play on the river and to live in her romance with Steve, is transferred to Magnolia in a tableau where they embrace: "And when they finally came together, the woman [Julie] dropped to her knees in the dust of the road and gathered the weeping child [Magnolia] to her and held her close, so that as you saw them sharply outlined against the sunset the black of the woman's dress and the white of the child's frock were as one."[25] The black woman's black dress and the white girl's white dress tell a "truth" about Julie and Magnolia that Ferber reinforces constantly: "In all the hurried harried country that still was intent on repairing the ravages of a Civil War, [the white people on the show boat] alone seemed to be leading an enchanted existence, suspended on another plane."[26]

I have proposed that the plays and the films transform the novel's ambivalence—or perhaps it is merely resignation—toward the attractions of modern life into a performance of fantasies of glamorous transcendence, and that each revival revitalizes the view of *Show Boat* as a history of how slavery generated the wonders of love and the wonders of modernity, with history both a shameful and homey place. The memory of slave pain in the dramatic supertext provides, specifically, two kinds of cultural logic. The dominant and most elaborate one locates in the sexual and economic exploitation of slaves the melodramatic "problem" of U.S. culture, which is "solved" in the narrative by a constellation of factors: the production of metropolitan life in the North, which appropriates and renames the material of what is alternately called "southern," "coon," or "nigger" culture; the transformation of the divisions of race into productive forms of capital, spectacle, and sexuality; and the elevation of romantic love itself into the core bribe of modern entertainment culture.

The second textual logic of slave history and its national effects is much more subtle in the novel and the dramatic or cinematic spectacles. In *Show Boat*, what we have called the "magic intuition" of the postslave population is also located in the characters who had been born into slavery—Jo, Queenie, and Julie Dozier, two servants and an actress. White people are freed from foreknowledge, located between blithe innocence and sheer stupidity. But the soundtrack turns repeatedly to this vehicle for preparing the (white) audience that suffering is ahead, as well as placing African Americans in a different realism than the one that the play actually stages. This off-stage story is present most famously in "Ol' Man River," but also crucially in the hauntingly beautiful song "Mis'ry's Comin' Aroun'." Indeed the whole *point* of Mis'ry's Comin' Aroun'" in the narrative is to foreground—mournfully, beautifully, in minor chords—the affective sensitivity of African Americans to imminent changes in the atmosphere: Queenie can tell an episode of racial injustice is coming on.[27] Sings Queenie, "When I got out a bed dis mornin', ah knowed somethin' was goin' to happen." She sings the phrase "Mis'ry's comin' aroun'" so intensely that Julie stops her: "Stop that rotten song! It's enough to bring misery to us all if you keep singing like that!" Queenie's intelligence hovers, and Julie blames her the way people blame prophets for bad tidings. This kind of shift in responsibility for power is common in popular culture, as when, in *The King and I*, the son is exhorted to "whistle a happy tune" so that good things will happen to him in the chaotic, uncivilized Siam, or the audience is exhorted to clap for Tinkerbell's survival in *Peter Pan*: it is an unserious joke, that thinking makes it so, but it is an anxious one as well, and it incites modes of optimistic belief against the humming, haunting knowledge that also accompanies ordinary action. It is worth noting that "Mis'ry" is mostly not staged in productions of *Show Boat*: cut from the overlong original production, it usually persists in the soundtrack as a ghost. These songs tacitly link the experience of slavery and the organ of intuition; indeed, the songs are introduced lyrically and on the soundtrack to predict the plot right before it turns.

Still, even the African American modes of counterconsciousness that remain explicit in the text become increasingly irrelevant and tacit in the adaptations. Take, for example, the destiny of "Ol' Man River," sung by Paul Robeson in the 1935 film version.[28] This scene comes early, establishing the distance between the naïveté of white people and African American wisdom, derived from slavery, field labor, and life on the river's periphery. Narratively, "Ol' Man River" is not sung simply as another emanation of Jo's capacity to master voice, history, and the trajectories of power in everyday life; it is coupled with Magnolia's duet with her soon-to-be new lover, "Only Make Believe," sung in the previous scene. Magnolia leaves Ravenal and runs to Jo, asking if he has seen the young man:

Noli: "Did you see the young man on the sheriff's buggy?"

Jo: "Yep I seen him. I seen lots like him along the river."

Noli: "Oh, but Jo, he was such a gentleman. Have you seen Miss Julie? I got to tell her. I got to ask her what she thinks."

Jo: "Ask Miss Julie what she thinks. Better ask the old river what he thinks. He knows all about them boys. He knows all about everything.

D'ere's an old man on the Mississippi, that's the old man that I'd like to be. What does he care if the world's got troubles? What does he care if the land ain't free? Ol' Man River . . ."

The context for "Ol' Man River," then, is the simultaneous revelation of Jo's wisdom and Magnolia's rejection of it as plot material. For if Magnolia were to listen to what she hears Jo say, both the love plot and the attendant historical narrative of *Show Boat* would be prevented.

Thus when the song describes what it means for the "river" to "say nothing" and "know somethin'," it refers both to the suppressed and displaced history of U.S. slaves and to the context of white misapprehension of the world, the white will-to-not-know that supports the transcending fantasy norms white romantic fictions express.[29] Meanwhile, the medium of black magic intuition—which is only magic if history is merely a dream, a myth, or a feeling—about pain and suffering becomes essentially Cassandra-like in its profound irrelevance to *anything* that happens in the plot. As it turns the river into material for the more shallow and ephemeral human culture that saturates modern spectacle, "Ol' Man River" is also about the U.S. subaltern

**3**
Paul Robeson as
"Jo," from the
montage sequence
accompanying
"Ol' Man River"
(*Show Boat*,
1936).

experience of being made irrelevant to plot, to the present, and to the national
future by becoming "history."

The manifest content of "Ol' Man River" is not only about the African
American knowledge that does not count; it is also about the intense physical labor that barely distinguishes free black life on the periphery of white
wealth from life under slavery. The African American chorus sings about
the material conditions of its modern life: "Don't look up an' don't look
down, you don't dast make de white boss frown. . . . "[30] As sung by Jo, "Ol'
Man River" refuses to waste the energy of the wisdom Noli has rejected, and
instead it twists the default "public" of *Show Boat* from the white consumers in the text and the actual dramatic audience to the ex-slave peasantry in
the film ("You an' me, we sweat an' strain, body all achin' an' racked wid
pain"), and it violates its own characteristic classic Hollywood style with an
expressionist mise-en-scène loaded with estranging angles and distortions of
perspective. In the film the aesthetic referent is not *Uncle Tom's Cabin*, but
rather the film that had earned the director James Whale his shot at directing
*Show Boat*—1931's *Frankenstein*. Both Robeson and Frankenstein's monster
are shot behind bars, from estranging angles (see figs. 3 and 4). Clearly the
politics of monstrosity is meant to be read politically here, both to signify
the estrangement of black reality from the white narrative spaces of the film,
and also to address critically the forms of distortion and demonization that
simultaneously produce degraded life experiences and images of African
Americans and the iconicity of Robeson, singing his classic song.

**4**
Boris Karloff as the
Frankenstein monster
(*Frankenstein*, 1931).

Little in Ferber's novel would have predicted this intensity of paradox. If Ferber values the African American as part of rural, peasant America, the value of *specific* black people in the novel is to provide material for the Americana of modern national culture, for the "American Theatre."[31] Kim invents with the money she and her mother and her grandparents have earned in the minstrel business over four decades. Although "Queenie and Jo had been as much a part of [Magnolia's] existence as Elly and Schultzy,"[32] Queenie's main legacy seems (appropriately for a story about the theater) to be about a ham:

> It was a fascinating process to behold, and one that took hours. Spices— bay, thyme, onion, clover, mustard, allspice, pepper—chopped and mixed and stirred together. A sharp-pointed knife plunged deep into the juicy ham. . . . Many years later Kim Ravenal, the actress, would serve at the famous little Sunday night suppers that she and her husband Kenneth Cameron were so fond of giving a dish that she called ham *à la* Queenie.[33]

Jo, meanwhile, teaches Magnolia "negro plantation songs, wistful with longing and pain; the folk songs of a wronged race, later to come into a blaze of popularity as spirituals."[34] The songs of "a footsore, ragged, driven race" that "always made her cry a little" are revised in the novel's memory to be material for the Harlem Renaissance.[35] In short, Whale's staging of "Ol' Man River" gives it a special kind of lyric power, the power of a showstopper, which briefly stalls the narrative mode of *Show Boat*, along with measuring the distances between any memory, any knowledge wrought from feeling, that a U.S. slave genealogy might offer people who wanted to learn from it. Ferber's take on the culture of black song reproduces its subaltern status as episode and soundtrack, not narrative history: her affect toward modernity's remaindering of blackness to the off-screen, the exotic, and the nostalgic slides around from disapproving (when bad people do it) to adoring, as in the fawning tones cited above.

By the 1951 adaptation of *Show Boat*, "Ol' Man River" denotes no monstrous difference—of race, class, body, or national fantasy: the song's status as "classic" overtakes its plot and political function. It is no longer even putatively part of the story—until late in the film, when it is briefly sung as a bit of existential wondering by William Warfield, "Ol' Man River" is merely hummed by the disembodied chorus on the soundtrack to remind the audience that there is "something" implicit the "river" knows that entertainment culture no longer needs to say. Here, as elsewhere in the score, the muffled music comes to signify a vaguely pervasive generic African resistant subjectivity, which provides nebulous pedagogy for the white actors in the narrative. As for the audience, its pleasure in the dramatic spectacle of U.S. history is now located in its mastery of *Show Boat* as a classic text: thus African American "magic intuition" and rememoration become themselves superseded or "unsung" in the dramatic adaptations.

You can see from this description that *Show Boat* follows a process of extracting "black style" from African American life and enfolding its traces into the pulsating contemporary culture of this book.[36] Because it is written as Kim's celebrity biography, and because Kim's talent is performing stylistic innovations on what the novel variously calls "nigger," "negro," "plantation," "coon," "American coon," "real coon," and "simple" songs, imitation and renaming can be said to be the central aesthetic and ideological mechanism of the dominant and marginal U.S. histories *Show Boat* tells.[37] (Magnolia sings "in unconscious imitation of the soft husky Negro voice of her teacher [Jo].")[38] To be a name, of course, is to be a celebrity; to have a name is to have a place in a cultural domain; to be restlessly, repeatedly renamed is simultaneously to be a register for someone's epistemic and ethical unease with both the word and the thing the word connotes, to be a structure that comes to mean serial obsolescence itself, and to designate as if from a source the collective amnesia that follows the trail of the "new" the narrative teleology suggests.

The history of the word "nigger" in the adaptations of *Show Boat* reconfirms this instability of the text's scene of history—it is the soundtrack's first word: as Miles Kreuger tells it, "First it was '*Niggers* all work on the Mississippi,' in the 1935 film it was '*Darkies* . . . ,' in the 1946 revival it was '*Colored folks* . . . ,' in *Till the Clouds Roll By* it was 'Here *we all* work on de Mississippi,' and by the 1966 revival it was—*Nobody* works on de Mississippi, because the Negro chorus was omitted altogether from the opening number."[39] Robeson, long identified with the role of Jo and the song "Ol' Man River," spent his life restlessly rewriting the lyrics to make them less abject, less complicit with the subordination of black history to the forms of U.S. elite culture. For example, he frequently changed the lyric from "I'm tired of living/An' skeered of dying" to "But I keeps laughing/Instead of crying/I must keep fighting/Until I'm dying": in so doing he asserts a performer's countermemory of the modes of racial and economic evisceration the dramatic texts of *Show Boat* disguise as Americana.[40] Yet even Robeson used the power of celebrity, of personal commodification, to provide a spectacular model of what U.S. citizenship might be.

The function of magic intuition in *Show Boat* is thus manifold, but clearly it serves the plot by providing wise discipline from the margins. It becomes, to be vulgar, the servant of the plot, glossing the emerging modern text of white melodrama—sex, love, and family trauma here merged with melodramas of celebrity and capital. In addition, the historical sweep of the play, and the construction of its black population as a chorus, sutures this instance of Americana with the form, though not the content, of national epic. It does not do so uncritically, however: the peripheral consciousness of African Americans provides critical commentary on the spectacles of transcendence, imitation, consumption, and fetishism that dominate U.S. mass culture. But even if the novel specifically seeks to ally its America with U.S. racial, economic, and regional peoples, the dramatic supertext of *Show Boat* builds its alliance not with the wisdom or the *ressentiment* of chastised populations, but with technologies of fantasy.

What Love Has to Do with It

*Show Boat* eroticizes the history of the development of an apparatus of adaptation, displacement, and transcendence; its modes of entertainment succeed each other, as dominant spaces do, along with the evolving lexicons of power that change slaves into "peasants,"[41] peasants into consumers, consumers into career actors, or at least actors in the theater of everyday life, who play with the fantasy of being consumed, like a celebrity. The aesthetic code that supports its progress is the love story the novel tells, which integrates ex-slaves and gamblers into entertainment culture, which enables racial crossover, the repression of signs of labor, the development of new forms of capital, and the production of metropolitan nationalism as a force of nature, fate, libido, and "consent."

In the dramatic supertext, the vehicle for this crossover is the song "Can't Help Lovin' Dat Man." "Can't Help Lovin' Dat Man" directly follows the scene of "Ol' Man River" in the 1935 version, and it repeats many of the themes Robeson intones as well, both musically and lyrically.[42] This repetition continues the pressure to displace slave history for love's sake. But the costs of the displacement are explicit in the film's and the play's staging of this knowledge transfer, which has no analog in the novel at all. Sung in the feminine space of the kitchen, this song is a female complaint about the way love fates a woman to love one inadequate man and to suffer from that love.[43] The syllogism "Fish got to swim and / Birds got to fly / I got to love one man till I die" posits love as a force of nature, much like the river. The death drive of love is similar to the "river Jordan" that Jo would like to cross in "Ol' Man River," which will relieve him of his suffering in a beyond-life land of freedom (from pain and labor). But such repetition is also comic, substituting the situation or screwball comedy of heterosexual love for the tragedy of slavery, racism, and exploitation. Finally, the "magic intuition" of Jo emerges here as the commonsense philosophy of Julie, who has also learned from experience: "Love is such a funny thing, there's no sense to it."

In the original libretto and the film of 1935, Julie teaches "Can't Help Lovin' Dat Man" to Magnolia in an act of loving sexual pedagogy. Yet when Queenie hears Julie sing it, she comments not on the epistemology of compulsory heterosexuality it sets forth, but instead on the racial history embedded in the song: " . . . ah didn't ever hear anybody but colored folks sing dat song. Sounds funny for Miss Julie to know it" (see fig. 5). Prior to Queenie's intervention, the song Julie sings appears to expose her intimacy with the ordinary tragic disappointments of love; but, recast as an artifact of racial

**5**
Queenie haunts
Julie during "Can't
Help Lovin' Dat
Man" (*Show Boat*,
1936).

history, it comes to reveal her criminalized racial and sexual identity to the audience, and it initiates the juridical scandal that divides the plot into black diaspora and white romance. To intensify the paradox of Queenie's magic intuition Magnolia, who will soon be seen doing the excruciating blackface number "Gallivantin' Around," celebrates the up-tempo ending of this song by imitating (some would say grotesquely) the "shuffle," a dance step associated with slaves and minstrelsy in the United States (see figs. 6 and 7). Given what follows, it is as though musically the frenzy of pleasure needs to be stopped by the slow, sonorous death of tragedy.

As might be expected, in the 1951 version of *Show Boat* "Can't Help Lovin' Dat Man" is extracted entirely from its racial context and is, likewise, transported from the basement kitchen to the public deck of the boat. Rather than affirming a long relationship between the older woman and the younger one, Julie now teaches Magnolia the song as she sings it to her—on screen, for the very first time: and so this version simply signifies Julie's man troubles. The women dance in this as in the other version; but as the dance they do here is simple and simply improvised around the song Magnolia newly hears, it is fair to say that this revision empties their bodies and the music of any relation to history—at least to the history of America, to the history of "Ol' Man River," and to race, for both Jo and Queenie are elsewhere—Jo is exiled to a lower level on the side of the boat (see figs. 8 and 9). Their knowledge of the archive is irrelevant to what becomes an impromptu scene of female bonding over love's complexities. The history of *Show Boat*'s soundtrack thus

**6**
Magnolia dancing
the "Shuffle" (*Show
Boat*, 1936).

powerfully reinforces the text's analysis of national amnesia: by displacing
the "race" crisis onto a love story at every moment it can, and by refusing to
specify whatever it is that Ol' Man River knows. Magnolia's and Gay's love
plot, intricately bound up *as realism* with the melodramatic love they perform
as actors, thus coordinates a number of transformations: it retroprojects slavery as a nostalgic origin of the narrative of modern life; it establishes acting
as a means of flight and of deliverance for women, who have no public access to power outside of careers on the stage that dominates the modern U.S.
public sphere; it establishes imitating what gets acted as a realistic means of
securing women's cultural and affective value; it also installs the love plot,
here an amalgam of fantasy plus realism, as an index of female subalternity
in America. In this regard the revivals of *Show Boat* mark this text as a classic source of love's overcoming of nature and history, even as the show also
provides a vehicle for female complaint.

## The Consolations of Landscape

I have suggested that the supertext of *Show Boat* thrusts slavery and the
South into the margins of the national diegesis. It does this, in part, by turning African American and southern history into a property of the landscape
we pass by, like tourists and space travelers, on our way to the national
future. In contrast, fish that swim and birds that fly have a transitory relation to landscape: they move through time and space, and in this case, from

**7**
Magnolia "Gallivantin' Around" (*Show Boat*, 1936).

the South to the North, from the archaic to the emergent, from slavery and race codes to gender and entertainment, from coerced subordination to the simulacrum of free consent. One example of this is in Magnolia's mixing up of "her" south with commodity aesthetics, which separates the region decisively from any aura of modernity. The dramatic supertext confirms this spatial cleavage with the song "It's Getting Hotter in the North." Kim performs this song on Broadway, in southern drag and peasant blackface, while flecked with the metropolitan cool of the Harlem Renaissance. "Hotness" is the vehicle that both links and sunders the music from its lived context; the song tells the story of mass culture's foundation in African American culture, and it stands not merely as the virtuoso song of Kim's celebrity repertoire, but also as the sum of her inheritance from her mother and America itself. The lyrics of "Ol' Man River" again provide another kind of instructive gloss; as Miles Krueger has pointed out, the twelve-line refrain has only one true rhyme: "He don't plant 'taters,/He don't plant cotton,/An' dem dat plant 'em/Is soon forgotten,/But ol' man River,/He jes keeps rollin' alon'." "Cotton" and "forgotten" here clearly quote the historic instance of that rhyme, in Dan Emmet's confederate anthem "Dixie's Land": "I wish I was in de land ob cotton, Old times there are not forgotten. Look away! Look away! Look away! Dixie land."[44] *Show Boat*'s gloss on the Confederate/pseudo-black vernacular/minstrel text evokes a breathtakingly complex set of revisions and elisions. It locates in turns of phrase the

**8**

Julie and Magnolia dance to "Can't Help Lovin' Dat Man" (*Show Boat*, 1951).

power to stimulate the transformation of slavery, and later of the Civil War, into the negative space of modernity in turn-of-the-century America. Look away—from what? Ferber has commented that the success of *Show Boat* was probably linked to Americans' desire to escape consciousness of the "blood and hate and horror" of violent wars that marked the globe during the 1920s.[45] The production of Americana in this light is indeed juxtapolitical, with the displacement of power into the healing spaces of the aesthetic and the affective.

The transformation of pain and labor into Americana is thus effected by the separation of racial or "historical" memory from love's forgettable, and therefore infinitely repeatable, performances. This dissipating function of the aesthetic commodity is telegraphed in other instances as well by the staccato breaking apart of the consumption experience into memorial units that evoke what Ferber calls "a glorious world of unreality," in which the lines of power, desire, and identification are so morally and melodramatically clear they are overdrawn.[46] The value of aesthetic experience here is also that it provides a forum for the exercise of agency: audiences of workers actually seek out the pleasure of unlearning or forgetting.

But if the novel of *Show Boat* reveals the relation between love plots, race, and the erasure of history to be the cultural dominant of U.S. modernity, it also promotes its own mode of cartography that resists the seeming inevitability of these deflections. Magnolia's consciousness is the locus of much of

**9**
Jo accompanies from the lower deck (*Show Boat*, 1951).

what we know about life on the Mississippi and its place in generating U.S. culture. Lists of faces, of spaces that flow by the show boat and through her eyes generate a kind of countermuseum that holds the ephemera of U.S. underclass life and experience, while also pioneering a mode of memory entirely adaptive to the capitalist public sphere. In particular, the specificity of local detail that overwhelms Magnolia's consciousness bridges the sensual experience of history and the commodity logic of serial consumption: "As for geography, if Magnolia did not learn it, she lived it. She came to know her country by traveling up and down its waterways. She learned its people by meeting them, all sorts and conditions. She learned folkways; river lore; Negro songs; bird calls; pilot rules; profanity; the art of stage make-up; all the parts in the Cotton Blossom troupe's repertoire. . . ."[47]

In this context, aesthetics are inseparable from everyday life: but their blending has many different implications for understanding the nationalist project of *Show Boat*. Magnolia's commodification of the songs she learned from her ex-slave servants links the exalted ambitions of the ordinary citizen to what Ferber calls the "weird spectacle of the commonplace" that underlies the aesthetics of the modern U.S. culture industry.[48] Magnolia creates patterns, mnemonics of social identity, through these short, object-dominated sentences. To live geography turns out not to mean experiencing the land, but rather to take the peripheral traveling consciousness itself to be the source of a new modernity: "They were known to the townspeople as

Show Folks, and the term carried with it the sting of opprobrium. . . . [But] [t]hey looked, Magnolia decided, as if they had just come from some interesting place and were going to another even more interesting."[49]

## Stereotypes, Survival, and Narrative Ends

Having experienced both an actor's and a laborer's relation to body, landscape, and narrative, Magnolia imagines another way of inhabiting and transforming America. Repudiating history's disembodiment in the North and in mass culture at the end of the novel, she performs a *different* imaginary reconciliation of commodity logics, labor, desire, and national history. *Show Boat* investigates the cultural work of entertainment in part by representing entertainment *as* work, as an industry in which people labor. In one sense, this consciousness of the commodity's location in a system of production works against the text's representation of consumption, for popular and mass culture are cast as utopian spaces for audiences, places where labor, the thing that happens on land, away from the river and the metropole, is forgotten, and where aesthetic consumption is seen as the *negation* of work, the only such activity—control over time, space, and the body—that the U.S. peasantry has. Ferber's quarrel with the collusion of technological modernization and modernist art is that modernity requires an aesthetic that moves from place to place, name to name, according to the ideology of the new. In mass national culture, as it stands, there is no accumulation, no activity of public memory; instead there is a shedding of prior knowledge on behalf of new promises and consolations.

Thus the paradox of national memory in the culture industry: underclass populations consume melodrama and comedy to displace the absurdity, drama, and afflictions of their own lives; but these pleasures are momentary, in contrast to the privileges metropolitan pleasure addicts enjoy, and are to be consumed as a means of generating and propping self-identity. But Magnolia does not promote radical rememoration or resistance to capital—nor indeed does she reimagine the U.S. theater as a documentary form, a witnessing of the hard genealogical facts of the national history of racial and economic subjugation. Instead, negotiating the contradictions of a critical bourgeois consciousness, she posits the value of fictive truths and strategic displacements to champion the cause of survival itself.

But best of all [Magnolia] liked to watch the audience assembling. Unconsciously the child's mind beheld the moving living drama of a nation's peasantry. It was such an audience as could be got together in no other theatre in all the world. Farmers, labourers, Negroes; housewives, children, yokels, lovers; roustabouts, dock wallopers, backwoodsmen, rivermen, gamblers. . . . Seamed faces. Furrowed faces. Drab. Bitter. Sodden. Childlike. Weary. . . . They forgot the cotton fields, the wheatfields, the cornfields. They forgot the coal mines, the potato patch, the stable, the barn, the shed. They forgot the labour under the pitiless blaze of the noonday sun; the bitter marrow-numbing chill of winter; the blistered skin; the frozen road; wind, snow, rain, flood. The women forgot for an hour their washtubs, their kitchen stoves, childbirth pains, drudgery, worry, disappointment.[50]

The function of these lists of faces and lives in *Show Boat* is to provide the material for what Ferber, a sentimental nationalist, images as a U.S. "survival subculture." This subculture is constructed not through simultaneous collective struggle, but in a mentality: in a collective translocal consciousness of collective pain, a solidarity magnetized almost telepathically through diasporic, aesthetically mediated identification with other survivors. In the face of the dissolution of U.S. history by the mass culture that represents its modernity, survival seems to her like an important victory over nature and nationality, a vital form of historicity, and material for a critical Americana. Thus, in *Show Boat*, the "magic intuition" of "races born to pain" casts "acting" as a mechanism of survival, not mere celebrity, and it suggests that the audience's shared consumption of a memory of someone else's pain—the material of melodrama, sentimentality, and comedy—takes over the space political and politicized discourses typically inhabit to organize identity and identification in national life. And while this commodified mode of historicity is a form of accommodation to capitalist culture, simply to denigrate the utopian aspirations of affirmative culture would be, in her view, to impugn survival itself. For Ferber, the process of desubjectification becomes the price the reflective citizen pays for the protections of the stereotype or the performative role. In other words, the sentence "black faces dotted the boards of the Southern wharves as thickly as grace notes sprinkle a bar of lively music" amounts, here, to a lexeme of survival politics.[51] *Show Boat* would argue that the shell of the stereotype secures the capacity to survive in America and counters the same powerfully dislocating forces of modernity the dramatic texts virtually celebrate. In this sense, like all of the works discussed in *The Female Complaint*, *Show Boat* demonstrates enormous faith in the vitality of conventionality to provide a world for the disenfranchised, to encode and protect their optimism for living, and to produce aesthetically a sense of comfort akin to that which cannot be provided by the material world of inequality and the political world that destroys life.

*Show Boat* demonstrates how what Gramsci calls "passive revolution" works: the phrase designates the means by which dominant parties try to persuade subordinated ones to perform acts of deference, perhaps through some notion of consensual democracy, thus affirming an incomplete hegemony as indeed a comprehensive one.[52] *Show Boat* figures the transition from race to love plots both as an unethical and a "natural" transition of U.S. culture into middlebrow modernity, with the love plot itself coming therefore to bear the burden of articulating and hiding the contradictions among a whole lot of factors: it signifies expectations for women's disappointment in desire, their economic contingency, their abandonment to emotional isolation, their fantasies to be "somebody" one way or another (in someone's or a public's eyes and arms). It always signifies the ratcheting up of narrative intensities toward displacement (of someone's life, or narrative attention to structural injustice, for example) and at the same time represents a utopianism toward establishing new and better foundations. In the intimate sphere of femininity, it also provides an archive of the tactics that women can use to survive privacy and that a survival subculture might use to endure the modern conditions of identity formation, in which the stereotype, the commodity, and the history of collective pain establish a juxtapolitical image of "democratic" mass culture. The novel resolves these contradictory readings of racial, sexual, and economic subalternity in a democratic space by separating out from "living" modern landscapes and narratives the archaic stereotypes whose resistance to representation according to the biographical norms of modern personhood actually, in Ferber's view, *preserves them* from annihilation by the amnesiac technologies and styles of the culture industry. All of these impulses are proximate to each other, enhancing the pleasure of experiencing multiple episodes of specific intensity.

This form of aesthetic bargaining is conventional in U.S. popular culture, using the textual proximity of dominant and nondominant types to provide a way of forging unthreatening representations of equality within the scene of soft supremacy, and positing conventions and clichés as placeholders for the universal. As a prime example of Americana *Show Boat* exemplifies this style of light-risk liberalism—its popularity seeming to confirm the progressive intentions of its crossover spectacles, distillation of African American history into a vogue of black style, celebration of women's erotic desire for publicity, and belief that one day transcending fantasies will cash out in new forms of justice and realism. But *Show Boat* only hints at a United States in which the pain of dominated classes would neither be entertaining nor entertainment.

## *Show Boat*'s Unfinished Business: Once upon a Time, a Little Jewish Slave Girl . . .

The tradition of the white appropriation of the history and experience of black suffering in the United States—sometimes to chart national legal and social progress and sometimes to chart the incompleteness of the process in which legal freedom becomes social equality—continues prolifically to generate award-winning Hollywood cinema (*Monster's Ball*, *Crash*, *Million Dollar Baby*) and mainstream fiction (*The Human Stain*, *The Rainmaker*). The culture industries use these events to publicize progress in the dismantling of antiblack racism: still, white-emanating popular culture seems to have an infinite appetite for the story of racism's episodic transcendence by compassionate individuals. I have suggested that in laminating the structure of romantic fantasy and its conventions of overcoming obstacles onto the history and posthistory of slavery, *Show Boat* transferred to the Broadway musical the historical novel's traditional way for structural social change to seem imaginable at the human level. The fact that a narrative of a subaltern's survival can be read as a romance that heralds justice for the collective seems to provide evidence that the system isn't all that rigid and that we are all human, facing the same obstacles with the same desires. The white race film and its aligned genres are recommitment ceremonies to a view of the universality of the emotional experience of struggle and survival that does not ask if anyone in the congregation objects. When the objection does exist—and there are always narrated racist resisters who have not yet been brought around to experience the compassion their racism tries to suppress—the films' main narrative aim is to show how not to break the sentimental contract with recognition of common suffering as the basis of human solidarity. Popular culture relies on keeping sacrosanct this aspect of sentimentality—that "underneath" we are all alike.

This tradition of coerced solidarity has nonetheless produced static in ways that haunt the shape of *Show Boat* beyond the evidence, cited above, that producers feel compelled to tweak the ways the play refers to the African American laborers whose culture provides the material for the narrative's claim to historical and ethical veracity. Contemporary reviews frequently comment on the ways its fantastic spectacles are tarnished by its reliance on African American stereotypes, for instance—gestures of liberal guilt in the face of the play's musical pleasures.[53] More specifically, the 1993 Broadway-bound revival of *Show Boat* in Toronto animated a collection of protests about all sorts of things: the need for Canadian support for indigenous multicultural art; U.S. cultural imperialism; and U.S. racism. M. Nourbese Philip's incendiary broadside *Showing Grit: Showboating North of the 44th Parallel* was perhaps the most public polemical response to the event in Toronto, protesting the staging of both *Show Boat* and its contemporary *Miss Saigon*. Providing fierce analyses of the racism of the novel, play, and films while exposing and critiquing the national, economic, and cultural structures promoting their revival, *Showing Grit* phrases all of its objections in terms of an ethnic/racial struggle that both did and did not translate transnationally: relations of cultural imperialism between the United States and Canada; African Canadian versus Canadian white; African Canadian versus Canadian Jewish; liberal multiculturalists versus all of their others. Furious that "cosmopolitan" Toronto denied its complicity in the racist pleasures of *Show Boat* (its liberal institutions responded to protests by pointing out their well-funded antiracist education programs), Philip also addressed his revolt at the "tradition" of black-Jewish solidarity that misrecognizes racist nostalgia as white/Jewish racial sympathy with enslaved and degraded blackness.[54]

The haunting presence of Jewishness in *Show Boat* was manifest from its conception. *Show Boat* was born out of the commercial and artistic failure of the play *Minick*, cowritten by Ferber and George S. Kaufman. Adapted from Ferber's short story, "Old Man Minick," *Minick* is about an old Jewish socialist from Chicago who has been made to feel irrelevant by the commodity-driven youth culture of his children, and it tells the story of his decision to leave their home for an old age "home" full of Jewish men who discourse endlessly on world politics and do not find consolation in commodities and light drama. Ferber saw this story sentimentally, as a universal tome about human feelings of inclusion and exclusion. But the dramatic version was panned by critics for being too ordinary, too predictably realistic—banal: its figures of the immigrant generation surpassed by its assimilated, cosmopolitan, consumer-oriented, and upwardly mobile children were already types, in the United States, by the mid-1920s.[55]

Depressed by this rejection of her small drama of ethnic archaism, Ferber's producer, Winthrop Ames, offered up a plan for them to flee to an alternative world unmediated by critics, where the laboring classes would come and be grateful for any entertainment at all—on a Mississippi showboat. Ferber's autobiography describes her response to this image of places where audiences are sentimental and not cynical:

> Now I sat up and up and up like a cobra uncoiling. . . . Here, I thought, was one of the most melodramatic and gorgeous bits of Americana that had ever come my way. . . . At the very thought of the Mississippi there welled up in me from some hidden treasure-trove in my memory or imagination a torrent of visualized pictures, people, incidents. I don't to this day know where that river knowledge came from. Perhaps, centuries and centuries ago, I was a little Jewish slave girl on the Nile.[56]

Ferber's appellation of this as a *melodramatic* scene tells a lot about the mise-en-scène of *Show Boat*: the image, the incident, the gorgeous spectacle are the primary units of "American" memory. Add to the mix her immersion in the Jewish tradition: she writes as though *Show Boat* had a generic kinship with the Passover Haggadah, which, among other things, contains prayers by the historically enslaved Jews for all other dominated peoples. This tradition of projective alliance was especially powerfully animated in the U.S. culture industries during the 1920s, as Michael Rogin, Andrea Most, and Stephen Whitfield have attested: Most argues that the influx of immigrant Jews to Hollywood produced many allegorical translations of the Jew into a figure for Americanization as such in the period after World War I, an allegory,

Rogin points out, that often involved the mediation of blackface both to connect Jews to and separate them from African Americans, while Whitfield traces Broadway music's powerful crossover impact to the contemporary presumption that Jews have a genetic relation to Africans.[57] I have already suggested the powerful contradictions at work in the *Show Boat* supertext's play with blackface, black music, and black history: the genealogy of Jewishness Ferber manifests here intensifies how convoluted it was from the start, in its anxious gesturing toward a revision of the terms of liberal universalism.

Soon, though, Ferber came to worry about the veiling of the Jew behind a vaguely capacious U.S. nationalism. This worry intensified dramatically in the decades following *Show Boat*'s emergence as an event of middlebrow popular culture. In 1938 Ferber wrote her autobiography, *A Peculiar Treasure*, from which the anecdote about the novel's origin comes. Not at all near the end of her life, Ferber wrote her story, she said, for one main reason: the mounting evidence of anti-Semitism in Europe.

> Deep down, I knew why I wanted to write this book. Actually it had been seething in me since first the poison of Nazism had begun to ravage Germany. The Jews of Germany, the Jews of the world, were to be destroyed. This was part of Hitler's stated program and he had begun briskly and efficiently to carry it out. By 1938 little or nothing had been done by the civilized world to arrest this savage plan. I was a Jew, born in the United States of an American-born mother and a Hungarian-born father. I knew that I wanted, more than anything else, to write honestly and informatively about a family of middle-class Jews in the United States of America. . . . This, then, isn't a story of my life, written because I am fatuous enough to think that anyone is interested. It is the story of an American Jewish family in the past half-century. . . . [58]

How does this reflection change the implications of the "little Jewish slave girl" passage? In one sense, not at all: experiencing her vision as a gift of magical memory, Ferber seems entirely self-satisfied. At the same time, though, the motive for telling the story at all provides another context for her admission that Jewishness was a source of inspiration for a play that was already deemed to be a classic piece of Americana. It establishes the logic of archaic memory in the construction of the present; the multiple locations of

American racialism; and the importance of racial memory and the stereotype as preservers of a history never fully integrated into the dissipating activity of survival that makes *Show Boat* a performance of cosmopolitan shallowness that archaizes the ongoing life of white, working-class, ethnic activity in the contemporary United States. The story of *Minick*'s failure is written into the dissipation of blackness in *Show Boat*. The story of Ferber's Jewishness is written into the idea that stereotypical memory has a monumental status that must be honored by popular culture. Her later observations that anti-Semitism in the United States produced her instinct for hypervigilance and identification with professional actors is embedded in Essie in "You're Not the Type," since both associate the glamour of acting with the labor of contested survival.[59]

At the same time Ferber felt that more than the Jews were vulnerable to American and European anti-Semitism—the future of the practice of freedom required interfering with *her own practice* of the writing of assimilative optimism. In 1939, Ferber performed the role of Parthy in Orson Welles's Campbell Playhouse radio production of *Show Boat*.[60] After the performance, Welles gave the microphone to Ferber, and she read the following speech:

> Today, in 1939, I never could have written *Show Boat*. I am too distressed, too agonized at what I see and hear in the world about me. *Show Boat* carries no stern message. It is just a romantic novel about a rather glamorous phase of American life. Since it was written in 1926 and this is 1939 there must be in it a quality that strikes a sympathetic chord. It never could have been written in a war-torn world. Those of you who prefer to go on with your life as it is—conducting your business, arranging your life as seems best to you—would doubtless know a feeling of panic if you now, instantly, had to shoulder arms and take up the life of a soldier. You'd doubtless make good soldiers for a cause you think right and just. But you'd rather—oh, so much rather—live your normal daily existence—your peaceful, prolific, orderly daily existence. But slowly, poisonously, the miasma of hate and fear and intolerance is seeping into our lives here in the United States. And because it must be fought with the written and spoken word we writers are turning from the lovely paths of creative and imaginative writing to the stony road of propaganda. The uniform for

this journey is rough and unaccustomed; the shoes are stiff to our feet, the collar rubs, the gun bruises the shoulder, but wear it we must or know no peace or self-respect within ourselves. I don't in the least mean that fine and moving and even great books and plays have not been written that are based on propaganda. But the writer should feel free to write as he pleases—and in these times he is deprived of that feeling.

Those millions of you in America who have chuckled over Huckleberry Finn and Tom Sawyer; those of you who have thrilled to that majestic piece of prose, the Gettysburg address; who have read and heeded the wise sayings of Benjamin Franklin, whose pulses have thickened to the beat and march of Walt Whitman's poems—if you love these things and believe in their beauty and worth, then stir out of your lethargy and save them. [Then a long blacked-out section.] Walt Whitman tells you. Listen to what he says:

> Long, too long, America,
> Travelling roads all even and peaceful
> You learn'd from joys and
> prosperity only,
> But now, ah now, to learn from crises
> Of anguish advancing, grappling
> With direst fate and recoiling [not]
> And now to conceive and show to the
> World what your children en-masse
> really are . . ."[61]

Ferber argues here that, under political duress, there is no "ordinary existence"—it is a scene shorn of a default sense of confidence about the simple pleasures. In times like these, art has no autonomy, and the ethics of authorship are such that only a harsh directness will do—the aims are clarification and persuasion, not the pleasures of absorption in the circumlocutions of irony, allegory, satire, or melodrama. This does not mean that her art was always *radically* ahistorical or apolitical: in 1939 she archaized *Show Boat* by locating its aesthetic as a response to the pressures of the posttraumatic United States, which was reeling from World War I. Thus the historicist aesthetic of attractions and distractions I have described in *Show Boat* in terms of sentimentality's attachment to the dialectic of suffering and the romance of overcoming overwhelming odds has a nationalist motive as well, to work through a national war trauma whose reverberations found their most brilliant explicit musical expression in the "Forgotten Man" number of *42ⁿᵈ Street* (1933).

In 1926 this trauma became allegorized in the American "recovery" from slavery in the registers of modernist entertainment, northern migration, and the heartbreaking optimism of love. In 1939 it would be unethical to pretend that this shifting of register was melodramatic realism of the sort that claimed respect for the populations it allegorizes away. Instead, the U.S. literary canon stands in here as a simple pleasure whose very simplicity is the ground of the political freedom *not* to think about the Jewish and African American slave legacies. Ferber's postplay propaganda reframes the admission of Jews to the white melodrama of slavery and indeed the entire project of emotional humanism as a *pleasure* of melodrama, a fading of political consciousness in episodes of emotional intensity that feel like living, a form of living at once extremely embodied and abstracted too, in a way that equates conventionality with unconflictedness and simplicity.

*Show Boat* typifies the messy conjuncture of adaptation, commodification, and emotion that extends the nineteenth-century genealogy of sentimental expression introduced in "Poor Eliza": to encounter its cluster of embedded contexts required a series of historical arguments about how the semiotic substance of sentimentality has been used in complicated ways to produce a simplified popular account of modern American subaltern identity. It is "complicated," first off, because in sentimental culture suffering is used to suggest someone's depth of being: there, what is simple does not appear shallow, but the opposite, a pool of profound grief, whether in defeat or in the terms of toughness survival requires. But entertainment is the condition under which this scene of critique finds its social expression; the guise of "feeling" as a thing distinct from and superior to public sphere norms of politics and instrumental rationality requires the modern sentimental text's central moments of instruction and identification to appear only as sublime ephemera, in punctuated events like the musical number, the knowing glance, and the telling gesture, or episodes in which a damaged character fails and flees into narrative exile. These moments shape the fragile temporal material of feeling and memory that make an entertainment text also a "serious" one that requires the exercise of compassion and empathy. But its relation to convention and repetition also provides alibis for the privileged, who, seeing the impacts of inequality and injustice, are trained into demonstrating *and identifying with* a sense of overwhelming helplessness about how to interfere with the machinery of social destruction, apart from having appropriately haunting feelings. This is why people often say they feel "manipulated" by sentimental texts: they feel forced to repeat conventionally virtuous feelings and do feel them while also not feeling integrated with their own performance. To feel manipulated toward compassion is to experience an exile from the vague space of belonging made available in the culture of true feeling as though it were the simple feeling of democracy.

## NATIONAL BRANDS, NATIONAL BODY *Imitation of Life*

> Advertising ministers to the spiritual side
> of trade. It is a great power that has been
> entrusted to your keeping which charges you
> with the high responsibility of inspiring and
> ennobling the commercial world. It is all
> part of the greater work of the regeneration
> and redemption of mankind.
>
> CALVIN COOLIDGE, 1929

### On Prosthetic Embodiment

In Nella Larsen's *Passing* (1929), two light-skinned American women of African descent bring each other to mutual crisis. The gaze of one woman virtually embodies the other, calling her back from her absence-to-her-body, an absence politically inscribed by the legal necessity to be nonblack while drinking iced tea at the Drayton Hotel in Chicago in 1927. Lost in thought about domestic matters, abstracted from her juridico-racial identity, Irene Redfield senses the gaze of the alluring blond "ivory"-skinned woman who watches her: "Feeling her colour heighten under the continued inspection, she slid her eyes down. What, she wondered, could be the reason for such persistent attention? Had she . . . put her hat on backwards? . . . Perhaps there was a streak of powder somewhere on her face. She made a quick pass over it with her handkerchief. Something wrong with her dress?"[1]

Something must be wrong with her; she suddenly has a body. She associates this sensation with the colonizing gaze whites wield when trying to detect whether a light-skinned person is white (a white icon) or black (a white hieroglyph): "White people . . . usually asserted that they were able to tell; and by the most ridiculous means, finger-nails, palms of hands, shapes of ears, teeth. . . ."[2] Yet Irene has already similarly cataloged and policed the body of her nemesis, disapproving her explicitly sexual display, her "peculiar caressing smile," "those dark, almost black eyes and that wide mouth like a scarlet flower against the ivory of her skin . . . a shade too provocative."[3] It turns out that the women, Irene Redfield and Clare Kendry, were childhood friends. But they share more than this in that they mutually usurp the privilege white Americans have to assume free passage within any public space they can afford to lease or own—such as a taxicab, a table in a restaurant, rooms in a hotel, a private home.

The whiteness of blackness here requires the light-skinned African American woman to produce some way to ameliorate the violation, the pain, and the ongoing crisis of living fully within two juridically defined, racially polarized bodies—and perhaps, if Hortense Spillers is right that American genders are always racially inflected, two genders as well.[4] Passing for nonblack allows these women to wear their gender according to a particular class style. Irene affects the bourgeois norm of good taste, which means submitting her body to a regime of discipline and concealment; Clare wears the exotic sexuality of the privileged woman as her style of publicity. One style of femininity tends toward the normatively invisible or the "abstract," which involves a wish to cast off the notable body, and the other tends toward the erotic, the sensational, which hyper-emphasizes the visual frame.[5] Nonetheless, each of these styles of femininity aims to deflect the racializing scrutiny of white culture, as it abstracts the woman's public identity from the complex juridical, historical, and memorial "facts" of her racialized body. Thus each woman returns the other to her legally other body by seeing her, and seeing through her—not to another real body, but to other times and spaces where the othered identity might be inhabited safely. To Clare, who passes racially in her marital, familial, and everyday life relations, it is a relief to leave the specular erotics of the white female body under the gaze of a similarly racialized friend. But for Irene the embodiment resulting from their encounter thwarts her desire—which is not to pass as a white person, but to move unconsciously and unobstructed through the public sphere (which is, in this case, a marketplace where people participate through consumption).

Deborah McDowell has argued that these two women desire each other sexually. *Passing*, in her view, is a classically closeted narrative, half-concealing the erotics between Clare and Irene.[6] But there may be a difference between wanting someone sexually and wanting someone's body: and I wonder if Irene's xenophilia isn't indeed a desire to occupy, to experience the privileges of Clare's body, not to love or make love to her, but rather to wear her way of wearing her body, like a prosthesis or a fetish.[7] What Irene wants is relief from the body she has: her intense class identification with the discipline of the bourgeois body is only one tactic for producing the corporeal "fog" in which she walks. "It was, she cried silently, enough to suffer as a woman, an individual, on one's own account, without having to suffer for the race as well."[8] This ideal model of bodily abstraction is understood, by Irene, to be nationally endorsed: despite suffering as a twice biologized and delegitimated public subject—a "woman," a "Negro"—she displaces her surplus body onto the metaphorical logics of American citizenship, which become the "truth" of her body, her "person." Even though Irene desperately wants to save her rocky marriage, she refuses to emigrate to Brazil with her husband because national alienation would replace the racial kind: "She belonged in this land of rising towers. She was an American. She grew from this soil, and she would not be uprooted."[9] Irene is married to this constellation of pain, her body the register for brands of race and of gender that specifically refer to the American context from which she has, apparently, parentless sprung. Irene's embrace of the nation seems a pathetic misrecognition. But what kind of body does American national identity give her, and how does the idea of this body solve or salve the pain that the colonized body experiences? And if a desire to be fundamentally American marks one field of fantasy for Irene, how does this intersect her other desire, to be incorporated in another woman's body?

In Irene's case, as often happens in bourgeois-identified "women's literature," this moment of political consciousness takes place in desperation,[10] and rather than think systemically about the state she is in, she reverts to the tendency to faint and fade out that has served her so well, and so analgesically, in the course of her life. But political theory has investigated more extensively the complex relation between local erotics and national identity, between homosociality and political abstraction.[11] So far almost all of this work, for clear historical reasons, has circulated around the construction of the male citizen in the political public sphere. Feminist political theorists, for instance, are reconsidering Enlightenment constitutionality and specifically how white male privilege has been veiled by the rhetoric of the bodiless citizen, the generic "person" whose political identity is a priori precisely because it is, in theory, noncorporeal. Before moving to *Imitation of Life*, where a narrative of profound female identification is interarticulated with the national public sphere, it is worth spelling out specifically how such a model of political affiliation has figured the American male body, setting up a peculiar dialectic between embodiment and the sense of abstraction in the post-Enlightenment body politic.

The Constitution's framers constructed the "person" as the unit of political membership in the American nation; in so doing, they did not simply set up the public standard of abstract legitimation on behalf of an implicit standard of white male embodiment—technically, in the beginning, property ownership was as much a factor in citizenship as any corporeal schema. Nonetheless, we can see a real attraction of abstract citizenship in the way the citizen conventionally acquires a new body by participation in the political public sphere. The American subject is privileged to suppress the fact of his historical situation in the abstract "person": but then, in return, the nation provides a kind of prophylaxis for the person, as it promises to protect his privileges and his local body in return for loyalty to the state. As Pateman, Landes, MacKinnon, and others have argued, the implicit whiteness and maleness of the original American citizen is thus itself protected by national identity.[12] This is a paradox, because if in practice the liberal political public sphere protects and privileges the "person's" racial and gendered embodiment, one effect of these privileges is to appear to be without notable qualities while retaining cultural authority. It is under these conditions that what might be an erotics of political fellowship passes for a meritocracy or an order defined by objective mutual interests.[13] The white male body is the relay to legitimation, but even more than that, the power to suppress that body, to cover the event of its tracks and its traces, is the sign of real authority according to constitutional fashion.

American women and African Americans have never had the privilege to suppress the event of body: and thus the "subject who wants to pass" is the fiercest of juridical self-parodies as yet authored by the American system. While this system prides itself liberally on the universal justice it distributes to its disembodied or "artificial" citizen, the mulatta figure is the most abstract and artificial of *embodied* citizens. She gives the lie to the dominant code of juridical representation by repressing the "evidence" the law would seek—a parent, usually a mother—to determine whether the light-skinned body claimed a fraudulent relation to the privileges of whiteness. By occupying the gap between official codes of racial naming and scopic norms of bodily framing conventional to the law and to general cultural practices, the American mulatta's textual and juridical representation after 1865 always designates her as a national subject, the paradigm problem citizen—but not only because she is indeterminate and therefore an asterisk in the ledger of racial and gendered binarism that seems to organize American culture, as some critics have argued.[14] Irene Redfield's case suggests another way of looking at the national reference of the juridically problematic body: her will-to-not-know, to misrecognize, and to flee her body by embracing the Liberty Tree suggests that she experiences herself as precisely not abstract, but as imprisoned in the surplus embodiment of a culture that values abstraction; and that her affinity for the bourgeois, the individual, the subjective, and the unconscious symptomatize her desire to shed her two racially marked gendered bodies in fantasies of disembodiment, self-abstraction, and invisibility. The very vulnerability she feels in her body would be solved by the state's prophylaxis: identification with state disembodiment might suppress or deflect what Spillers calls the "pornotroping" of racist patriarchy.[15] I do not mean to say that embodied subjects in the culture of abstraction always seek invisibility; following Scarry and Spillers we see that abstraction from the body's dignity and the subject's autonomy has been a crucial strategy of political oppression.[16] Moreover, we see in "camp," in youth, in sexual, and in ethnic subcultures strategies of corporeal parody that recast and resist the public denigration of the nonhegemonic othered body. But sometimes a person doesn't want to seek the dignity of an always already violated body and wants to cast hers off, either for nothingness, or in a trade for some other, better model.

In *Passing*, when women drink iced tea, shop, and have parties, and in *Imitation of Life*, when women make pancakes, picnics, and movies, the colonized female body is not abstract, but hyper-embodied, an obstacle and not a vehicle to public pleasure and power. At the same time, the erotic sensation released in the conjunction of women with each other affirms and reasserts the body in a way more in line with the oft-used feminist and colonial studies interest in the transition from invisibility to presence, and margin to center. It is the logic of this dialectic between abstraction in the national public sphere and the surplus corporeality of racialized and gendered subjects—its discursive expressions, its erotic effects, its implications for a nationalist politics of the body—that I want to engage in this chapter. What would it take to produce the political dignity of corporeal difference in American culture, where public embodiment is in itself a sign of inadequacy to proper citizenship?

*Imitation of Life*—which exists in three versions, the Fannie Hurst novel and the films of John Stahl and Douglas Sirk—addresses these questions by linking the struggles of an Anglo-American woman and an African American woman, both single with a daughter, to a tale of economic success: in this complex text the women fight for dignity and pleasure by mutually exploiting the structures of commodity capitalism and American mass culture. As we trace the various embodiments of *Imitation of Life*, we will see its "stars" transformed into trademarks and corporate logos, prosthetic bodies that ideally replace the body of pain with the projected image of safety and satisfaction commodities represent. In this sense *Imitation of Life* recasts the fantasies of commodity transcendence we have just been tracking in *Show Boat*. From some angles these commercial hieroglyphs look like vehicles of corporeal enfranchisement; but we will also see the failure of the erotic utopia of the feminized commodity, as the success montage of one American generation can not reframe the bodies of the next.

Specifically, in every version of the text the white woman struggles to achieve economic success and national fame while living in a quasi-companionate couple with the black woman, who does the domestic labor; the black woman, who is also instrumental in the white woman's mastery of commodity culture, remains a loyal domestic employee, even in the wealthy days.

But once the women have leisure and security, their bodies reemerge as obstacles, sites of pain and signs of hierarchy: the white daughter falls in love with her mother's love object; sexual motives also propel the light-skinned African American daughter to want to pass for white and so she disowns her dark-skinned mother, whose death from heartbreak effectively and melodramatically signals the end of this experiment in a female refunctioning of the national public sphere.[17]

For purposes of economy, my discussion of these narratives will be organized around the form of commodity aesthetics through which they trace the American female body: the trademark. Hurst's novel of 1933 represents the business and life history of a white person named Bea Pullman, who assumes professionally her husband's name and gender after his death and, "passing" for male, opens a hugely successful pancake franchise named "B. Pullman." The visual logo that accompanies her masculine signature, however, does not represent the pseudo-body of its white, male producer (whose race and gender are deceptively presumed by the concealment of "his" given name), but rather is displaced onto yet another corporeal other, her African American housemate, Delilah Johnson. As a visual icon, Johnson is known, not surprisingly, as "Aunt Delilah." In contrast to Hurst's novel, Stahl's film of 1934 associates the pancake business only with the trademark and brand name "Aunt Delilah." Miming the passing from novel to film, he honors her with both a logo and a huge, hieroglyphic neon sign; finally, Sirk's film of 1959 isolates the white woman in the neon sign and the public body. Sirk renames the trademark characters and some of their professions: Bea Pullman, "the pancake queen," turns into Lora Meredith, an actress with her name up in lights on Broadway. Delilah turns into Annie Johnson and remains a domestic laborer, but with no cachet in popular culture. Thus more than names change in these interpretations of *Imitation of Life*: I will not attempt to do full readings of these texts; rather, I attempt to see how they collectively imagine the American body politic from the points of view of the overembodied women who serve it.[18]

## "B. Pullman" and "H. Prynne": The Feminine Uses of Camouflage

Fannie Hurst's *Imitation of Life* occurs in the midst of carnival. It opens in summertime, in Atlantic City, in 1911. But the crisis of the body we witness there has, at first, nothing to do with leisure culture, or the service industry that lives on the cycles of its pleasure. Instead, in the novel's first scene we witness a paradigm moment of sentimental fiction, a daughter's private response to her mother's death. But the content of this moment is remarkable in its grotesque embodiment of the feminine: "It struck Bea, and for the moment diverted her from grief, that quite the most physical thing she had ever connected with her mother was the fact of her having died. She found herself, crying there beside the bier, thinking of her mother's legs . . . her arms and legs and breasts and her loins there, under the bengaline dress . . . stiff and dead."[19]

"There had been so little evidence, during her lifetime," she thinks, "of any aspect of her [mother's] physical life": and yet "the physical fact of [Bea's own] coming of menstrual age" (1) revealed to her the repulsive and upsetting fact that her mother had "committed the act of sex" with "that crumpled figure over there in the corner of the darkened parlor, his back retching as he cried" (4). This primal scene, of sex after death, is unbearable to Bea: her response is mentally to dismember her mother, to protect her after the fact from the embodiment that had made her whole and therefore penetrable. This style of mourning, and of preserving the memory of the maternal form by breaking it apart in a kind of catalog, is not only Bea's awakening to her mother's body.[20] It is also her initiation to sexual self-consciousness: mourning "had felt like wine" to Bea, "fizzing down into, and exciting and hurting her" (5).

The erotics of feminine identification, then, are here tied up with a sublime amalgam of pleasure, pain, and physical defamiliarization that comes from Bea's mother's death. Bea's attraction to this mix of sensations is reinforced by her father's subsequent domination of her life: not only is she, at seventeen, forced to replace her mother functionally in the household, but she is pressured into marriage to Mr. Pullman, a man her father chooses. This idea in itself does not upset Bea, who is rightly accused of "marrying marriage" rather than a man (42). Marriage, with its usual transformations of a woman's name and sexual practice, is the conventional mode of female self-abstraction, and in marriage, Bea experiences abstraction doubly. While sex with Benjamin Pullman is simply a "clinical sort of something, apparently, that a girl had to give a man," "it was amazing what feeling secure did to the front one put up in the world" (55, 57). Being fitted with the false front and the mental prophylaxis of marriage also admits Bea into the world of "girl-talk," as she and the neighborhood women now speak frankly about deviously managing men and faking orgasms (58). This is to say that her entry into marriage provides Bea with a prosthetic identity, estranges her from her body in both an alienating and a pleasing way, and consolidates her relations to other women. Bea wishes that marriage weren't physically self-alienating, but this, she learns, is a fact about marriage. Her intuition is further confirmed by her father's tyranny: debilitated by a stroke soon after her marriage, his physical brutality to Bea throughout her entire life makes him an ever present "symbol of littleness from which she needed emancipation" (177).

But there is something good about her association with men, and this is in their connection to the national public sphere: specifically the activity of national politics and of capitalist enterprise. Men sit around the bourgeois home speaking their political opinions, which Bea registers but has no interest in; but Hurst's narrator provides a counterconsciousness to Bea's mental limits. She repeatedly analogizes the personal choices Bea makes to the political agency of the American citizen: for example, "Thus in the year when men were debating whether a college professor was of sufficient stamina for Presidency of the United States, Bea lifted her face, which intimated yes, for the betrothal kiss of Mr. Pullman" (33). They marry two days before the election, in the midst of a raucous political parade; the house in which she marries is bedecked with the double symbology of a wedding bell and the American flag. Since these events take place before women had the national franchise, Bea's private acts are the only "votes" she has; and insofar as her later successes mark her *for other women* as a protofeminist, this self-abstracting private event becomes, in retrospect, the first of a set of steps she takes into national existence.[21] It should be said that the historical and ideological pressure of feminism on American women's public self-presence explicitly follows Bea everywhere throughout this book; but, like Irene Redfield, Bea needs to see herself as acting without agency under the pressure of necessity and has no affective relation to collective life, to politics, or history. Indeed, women's history is always in advance of Bea, who only belatedly understands her position in a symptomatic way. Hurst stages this isolate sentimentality as a problem Bea has, a mental blockage symptomatic of her sex class.

Along with gaining closer proximity to the political life of the nation, Bea's affiliation with Pullman brings her closer to the capitalist public sphere.[22] Hurst's representations of the capitalist presence in American everyday life are quite institutionally specific, as if she had contracted to advertise via product placement commodities in her narrative the way Hollywood films do now.[23] But the status of brand names and well-known corporations in *Imitation of Life* isn't simply referential or commercial: by the turn of the century, product consciousness had become so crucial a part of national history and popular self-identity that the public's relation to business took on a patriotic value. As political parties became less powerful, and as capitalism became less local and more national, the imagined co-presence of a consuming public in the emerging and transforming mass culture became a central figure of America and was crucial for its intelligibility;[24] indeed, Robert Westbrook writes that around this time political parties began using the strategies of advertising to vitalize American citizenship in the political public sphere by characterizing it as consumption behavior.[25]

Like Bea's father, Mr. Pullman works for the great "Pickle and Relish Company." Daily he stands on "Amusement Pier" lecturing on "the life history of the tomato from the vine to the ketchup bottle," while handing out pickle stickpins and samples (13). His authorized biography of the tomato, which exists in an ironic linkage to a plagiarized biography of Abraham Lincoln's life he also delivers (14–15), discloses a corporate strategy to posit the commodity form and the brand name as the last stage of natural and national growth. By 1911, this form of suturing nation and nature was also associated with the sexual and commodity desire traversing Atlantic City, an interpenetration that makes Bea feel uncomfortably sexualized: pictures of Heinz Pier, to which Hurst clearly refers here, reveal scantily clad advertising beauties in the space of national/commodity history and distribution, linking up food and women in a public erotics of consumption, leisure, and knowledge.[26]

This conjunction of leisure culture and its servants subverts the discriminations of the bourgeois domestic economy. The capitalist public sphere absorbs the erotic investments of bodies in proximity, of contact through public exchange, and even of information culture, which emerges here as the new history of the nation, seen through its commodities. Meanwhile, the conventional topographical distinction between the home and the work spaces of the bourgeoisie does not hold: when the family travels, it travels to company functions; when the family moves, it is passively "transferred"; and a side business Mr. Pullman runs, selling maple syrup to local hotels, takes place within the home's instrumental space. In addition, Bea attends to the little "economies" of domestic labor with the zeal of an entrepreneur: but she is a formalist and needs to see the home she runs as a sentimental nexus of consolation and escape. Bea does not live a split between domestic ideology and practical social relations, but she sees it as her job to maintain and intensify "the private's" reality at the level of theory. Then tragedy strikes. Soon after her marriage, Mr. Pullman dies in a train wreck. Bea is pregnant, then, and gives premature birth to a girl, Jessie; she is also thrown into poverty, burdened by a child and an invalid father.

Simultaneously Bea is imbricated more deeply into separate spheres: the domestic/maternal and the public/capitalist. For her this is an impossible position, mapped out according to two mutually reified gender logics. Hurst stages Bea's mutation serially: first, her ether-inspired corporeal dissolution in the pain of childbirth evokes the sublimity of mortality the specter of her mother raised— "and when they started to try and amputate her legs by pulling them out from the sockets, she screamed, and there was the upper half of her separating from the something going from her . . ." (72). She emerges from this event reconstructed and regendered in a new, maternal body. In the next chapter, Bea is startled out of sleep, as if the sleep of childbirth, and is inspired to look at her husband's business cards. They reveal graphically that she can assume Pullman's business and gender identity because they share a first initial, B (73). This initial solves a problem she has been having on the job market, where her bourgeois female body has been exposed to the indignity of being all wrong for all the positions she seeks. But the maple syrup business (run, suggestively, by H. Prynne of Vermont) is mail order, and so her female body would be suppressed, nonknowledge: Bea thinks of her paper transvestitism as simply a wedge into the capitalist public sphere, but it is an identity she never fully relinquishes.[27] Bea emerges, then, from the first stage of female abstraction, marriage, to the second stage, where identity is marked by labor and self-alienation. Maternal and masculine work works the same way on Bea's body, however—she is exhausted, anesthetized. Both labor in the family and labor for money absorb her libidinal energy, or, as

Hurst puts it, "Countless little budding impulses seemed to have been nipped in the frozen garden of her expectations" (88). She nonetheless retains her theoretical commitment to producing an unalienated domestic scene: but her need to earn wages disrupts the separate spheres on which her theory was based, and she displaces her need onto the capitalist public sphere, where she goes from serving her husband's leisure to serving as her husband in the leisure industry. The contradictions of Bea's position threaten to disembody her permanently, an outcome she both wants and doesn't want.

For the next fifteen years, Bea "buckles herself" into the worker's body like a suit of "armor" (186). At first, she lives, "on a minus sign" (93), selling maple syrup in the back alleys of Atlantic City. At the height of Bea's exhaustion, she walks up to an "enormously buxom figure of a woman with a round black moon face that shone above an Alps of bosom, privately hoping that the scrubbed, starchy-looking negress would offer herself" as a sleep-in maid (91): this woman, Delilah Johnson, tenders the offer and comes not only to run the house, but to provide Bea with the candy and pancake recipes she soon turns into commodities in search of a franchise and a fortune. Later, selling "Delilah Delights" pancakes and candies in hotels, and then in her own restaurants, Bea becomes more like a classic capitalist, increasingly distant from production and the public scene of consumption. As the brains and the name behind the business, Bea remains almost entirely behind the veil of the male moniker. In addition, Bea uses "Aunt Delilah's" body to stand in for her own. When Bea imagines Delilah as a mammy-like trademark, Delilah protests and says she wants to dress beautifully, to create a stylish image inheritance for her daughter to remember her by (105). But Bea forces Delilah to play the mammy, and in this coerced guise she becomes the prosthetic public body of "B. Pullman," the store, and Bea Pullman, the woman.

Bea relies on Delilah to do much more than to protect Bea's body: the "social hieroglyphic" or trademark representing Delilah serves to create consumer desire for the products of the "B. Pullman" restaurants. As Stahl's film displays, when Delilah stands framed in the store's plate glass window making her authentic pancakes, the mise-en-scène of capitalist aesthetics merges with actual production. Bea relies on Delilah's double embodiment as icon and laborer to engender public "need" for her commodity. Delilah can do this because she is a professor in the true religious sense who trains "imitations" or "replicas" of herself in the "University of Delilah" (184): there, she teaches "Jemimesis," or, how to commodify the "mammy's" domestic aura, which each waffle, pancake, and candy she makes is supposed to instill in the consumer, like a communion wafer. In Delilah the religious aura of the commodity and the everyday imitation of God merge, in an uncanny repetition of Marx's analysis of how commodities become invested with soul and pseudo-agency: to Bea, this is imitation in the good, the best sense.[28] But Bea displaces onto Delilah more than her need to manage the public sphere. Delilah is also Bea's private maternal supplement, raising Jessie and caring for her father. And finally, she is Bea's wife and mother, the only person who touches her body during the 1920s, massaging her back and feet after the long day at the office. In short, Delilah solves for Bea "the corporeal problem of being two places simultaneously," both in everyday life and in the capitalist public sphere (140). Because Delilah can "be" both places, Bea has to "be" in neither. In Delilah, Bea achieves the condition of prophylaxis she has sought since her mother's death.

Never for a moment does Bea question her structural relation to Delilah: to Bea, their cohabitation is as a priori and untheorized as are their different places in the racial and class hierarchies of the dominant culture. Because Bea herself is so desperately liminal, masquerading as the difference between the white man's name and the black woman's body, she has no consciousness of her privilege. Rather, like Delilah's light-skinned daughter, Peola, Bea has the perverse opportunity to capitalize on racist patriarchal culture by creating a compensatory "body" to distract from the one already marked by the colonial digit. Peola "passing" creates a juridically fraudulent white body, while Bea incorporates public "persons"—companies and copyrighted trademarks—whose passing breaks no law or norm because a sense of autonomy is the promise of control over capital.

Then one day Bea awakens to the distance she has traveled from the sensational body in which she might live. This is, in part, because fame and money eroticize her in the public eye, which is curious about how she pleasures her body under the stress of success. Second, she discovers the body as a site of potential pleasure because it is "sex o'clock in America," and the New Woman of the 1920s reveals to Bea another way to negotiate the public female body: in an armor not of bodiless abstraction, but of cosmetic masquerade. And finally, because capitalist practice carries its own erotic charge, its processes of abstraction are homoeroticized by Bea: she is openly attracted to other women who engage in what she calls "the racy ingredient of competition" (244) within the national public sphere. These feelings are congealed when Bea meets Virginia Eden, a beauty magnate whose own name is a hieroglyph (a means of passing) that condenses the erotics of "sex solidarity," the American/Jeffersonian *locus amoenus*, and distracts from a Jewish background (she was born Sadie Kress). Eden opens the erotic floodgates in Bea: she dates her, makes her a business "proposition," and seduces her into a contractual collaboration. "You and me ought to work together, Pullman. You make women fat and comfortable. My job is to undo all that and make them beautiful. You're grist to my mill. I want to be grist to yours" (193).

Awakened in the garden of Eden, Bea then becomes an erotic object for her female employees (she opens a gym so that they might also turn their bodies into erotic armor, and they fall so in love with Bea that her male secretary starts intercepting their "obnoxious" gifts and love letters [189]). But when their business deal, which involves gentrifying tenements, falls through, Bea experiences the erotic pain of female alliance once again: for "Virginia Eden's teeth were as pointed and polished and incisive as a terrier's, and with them, when she sank, she drew blood" (201). Then, the feeling of being embodied and excited by Eden scares Bea. She begins immediately to hyper-heterosexualize herself and falls in love with an unattainable man, Frank Flake.[29] After this embodied interlude, she returns to the life of abstraction. For Bea has not finally attained her national position by identifying with women, or with anything sensual. She has achieved success, within the auto-containment of the commodity form, by reinforcing the very apparatus whose practices she flees: in hiding behind the colonial simulacrum of a "male" employer who owns the copyrighted image and labor of an African American woman.

A trademark is supposed to be a consensual mechanism. It triangulates with the customer and the commodity, providing what W. F. Haug calls a "second skin" that enables the commodity to appear to address, to recognize, and thereby to "love" the consumer.[30] Bea repeatedly turns to this abstract erotics for love and protection. This is what Delilah is and represents. And in this sense, Delilah's fractured public identity—as herself, as an autonomous iconic image, as a servant of "B. Pullman"—foregrounds the irregular operations of national capitalism on the bodies of racially and sexually gendered subjects. In other words, at the same time as Delilah brings dispersed fields of exchange into proximity and intimacy, she also shows their non-analogousness. While Bea is protected by hiding behind Delilah's tremendous public body, Delilah's status as a living trademark takes over her own meaning and history: she married a bigamist and gave birth to a daughter cursed with Ham's opposite—light skin in a racist culture; she escaped the South to protect her daughter from the most brutal forms of racism. But when Delilah dies, the press reports that "her people" love her because the popularity of her facsimile legitimated blackness in public white culture. She is also, the press says, a constant reminder to white "national consciousness" of the dignity of her race; during World War I she becomes a domestic icon of the doughboys, who dream of a safe domestic political space after the most horrible of wars. It matters not to the public that she dies a most humiliating, lonely, and grotesque death, "in her huddle on the floor, a heterogeneous twist of pain, her back in an arch, her torso writhing" (319–20): for "Delilah" has become the trademark who lives on, interminably. Through her forced archaic, nostalgic abstraction, and not her biographical person, Delilah reconfigures the capitalist and the national public spheres to include, even to foreground, the American class of overembodied, colonized subjects. In this she provides an alternative image to the logics of liberal culture. At least this is someone's liberal fantasy projection of what such a trademark might do.

## Aunt Jemima and Uncle Sam

It is, for sure, the fantasy condensed in the face and history of Aunt Jemima, whose aura in American pop culture Hurst borrows for "Aunt Delilah" in *Imitation of Life*. Aunt Jemima was introduced to America at the Columbian Exposition in 1893. This links her up with the origin of American progressive modernism, the alliance between industry and the state to produce new "frontiers" of production and invention, and the induction of advertising itself as an arm of American sovereignty: it was to promote this event, after all, that the Pledge of Allegiance was written.[31] A huge success, Aunt Jemima became associated with a line of new products that included the "skyscraper, the long-distance telephone, the X-ray, the motion picture, the wireless telegraph, the automobile, the airplane, and radium."[32] She herself was an example of state-of-the-art technologies: the invention of the "half-tone" printing process at the turn of the century that enabled advertisers to install a new realism in the human trademark; the emergence of a new "logocentric" style, which encouraged consumers to link products with personalities;[33] and the invention of ready-mix convenience foods, of which her pancake mix is the first to "emancipate" the housewife.[34] She did not, however, contain the promise of further racial emancipation. As Hazel Carby's discussion of the fair's contempt for African Americans shows, the exoticization of Aunt Jemima would surely mark the limit of what the consuming public could bear in the linkage of African and American.[35]

The "promise" of Aunt Jemima thus went much farther than household convenience: her condensation of racial nostalgia, white national memory, and progressive history was a symptomatic, if not important, vehicle for post–Civil War national consolidation. At the fair she was embodied by a woman, Nancy Green, who lived in an enormous flour barrel. Periodically she would come out to sing and tell tales: "Some of her script was drawn from the words of the old vaudeville Aunt Jemima song, some from [pseudo-] memories of her own plantation days in the Deep South," and some from her own invention.[36] The association of exotic, primitive women with pancakes and domestic consolation was reinforced by popular fantasy, as the renown of *Little Black Sambo* suggests. One other context is relevant to Aunt Jemima's phantom presence in *Imitation of Life*: the analogy embedded in the trademark's address to the notion of the bourgeois housewife's domestic "slavery." In one advertisement of 1919, for example, the copy is explicit: Jemima's pancakes were the last hope this side of Abraham Lincoln to maintain the union of the North and the South; housewives who bought Aunt Jemima would not only be emancipated from labor, but would keep the family together by keeping politics out.[37] In this way the trademark itself bridges the nuclear household and national history along with helping to produce the kinds of historical amnesia necessary for confidence in the American future.

Something like this amnesiac activity is narrated in Hurst's *Imitation of Life*. The accumulated "pancake wealth" of the nation does not transform the injurious conditions of the national/capitalist public sphere. But since the commodity is the modern embodiment of the legitimate "artificial person,"

Americans in the text equate personal emancipation through it with shedding the collectively shared body of pain to gain a solitary protected self. This is Bea's strategy, which works so well that she ends up alone, enfranchised but not empowered. But John Stahl's *Imitation of Life* of 1934 reads the text's utopian potential. Without looking away from the culture of abuse that saturates even American leisure, Stahl imagines *Imitation of Life* within an affirmative female economy. This utopia is not the abstract "paradise" of heterosexual, natural bliss Steven Archer (Warren William) offers Bea (Claudette Colbert), on an island "elsewhere," outside of the frame; nor is it in sentimental womanhood, where differences dissolve through maternal identification—as in the cry of Delilah (Louise Beavers) to Peola (Fredi Washington), "I'm your Mammy, child! I ain't no white mother!" Instead, Stahl derives from Hurst's text the positivity of difference: of female households and work-places that protect the hyper-embodied frame; of an unalienated capitalist public sphere; and of an identity in labor that eases the psychic burdens of gender and race. These "spaces," however, are really temporalities, moments in time when certain possibilities coalesce. This means that the film's "solution" is also framed as failure: in Delilah's commercial and in Peola's racial hieroglyphic, and in the impossibility of their suture in the United States.

Delilah enters Stahl's *Imitation of Life* by accident, misreading the address of an advertisement and ending up at Bea Pullman's door. To convince Bea that Bea has indeed asked for her, Delilah reads her the ad's text, which describes her own subject position in the marketplace: she's a "girl," "a house-maid, colored, not afraid of hard work." She says that she has been looking for jobs, answering ads like this, but no one will take her because she has a child, and the ads don't call for a child. Then she advertises her child: she's been "brung up right, not drug up, like most of 'em is." Peola comes in and performs for Bea: she says "Good Morning" in patrician diction, an act she has clearly practiced. While at first Bea protests that she cannot afford financially to succumb to Delilah's hard sell, seeing Peola induces her to fold this female family into her own equally impoverished unit: no longer a "girl," Delilah becomes to Bea "200 pounds of mother fighting to keep her baby."

This scene is extraordinary in the way it shows Delilah textualizing, characterizing herself in little sound bites: it is apparently the lot of the marginal subject to self-commodify verbally, to objectify and promote her own

qualities in a culture that, corporealizing, presumes her insufficiency. Advertising rhetoric, then, starts to look like a mode of colonized discourse. Delilah's insertion of Bea into the generic slot of the white housewife who consumes "colored" domestic labor is misguided, however. To rent the abandoned Boardwalk poolhall that turns into "Aunt Delilah's," Bea is forced to sell herself in roughly the same way: without capital, as she later says, "All I had was talk."

These two contradictory structures mark the relations of Bea and Delilah in Stahl's film: in one mode, the traditional nomenclature and spatialization of the domestic worker in the private home still obtains, especially as the women achieve leisure. Delilah is always "Delilah," while the other is "Miss Bea"; when they can afford a spacious house, the "domestic" lives beneath, and the employer, above (see fig. 10). In addition, as they gain leisure, their bodies diverge, becoming more socially proper to the public iconography of race, class, and gender in early twentieth-century America. The African American woman grows larger and darker, and her clothes get slightly better; the Anglo-American woman becomes a vital "new woman," wearing corsets and bobbed hair and slinky things.[38] But during the first ten years of struggle to gain financial stability and public dignity, the women live in the closest of quarters. In physical style they are equivalent, dressing in uniforms appropriate to their work (see fig. 11). In addition, they inhabit their bodies in much the same way—they are exhausted; and they are shot at the same respectful distance by Stahl. But the film moves away from its accent on their

shared class and maternal difficulties. The recurrent success montage that traces Delilah's transformation into a trademark begins by emitting the same odor of racist expropriation that permeates Hurst's novel.

For Bea takes Delilah's pancake recipe, her maternal inheritance, and turns it into a business; she takes Delilah's face and turns it into a cartoon trademark. Stahl stages Delilah in this scene as a buffoon, a position that provides her an opportunity for ironic commentary. On hearing Bea manipulate the rhetoric of credit to bilk businessmen into advancing their wares, so that she might transform a boardwalk poolroom into a women's domestic business space ("Aunt Delilah's Pancakes"), Delilah acts as a comic soundtrack, singing in a worried tone, "I puts my trust in Jesus," as she washes the windows. When Bea asks Delilah to smile for the trademark sign, Delilah smiles a small and hesitant smile. But Bea forces her to assume and to freeze in a "blackface" pose, which she dutifully maintains long after Bea needs her, to Bea's great delight. Stahl shoots the huge face of smiling Delilah in extreme close-up and uses shot-reverse-shot cutting back to her frozen, smiling, saucer-eyed face as if to underscore how mentally insufficient Delilah is to her situation in the white patriarchal capitalist public sphere. But the grotesque hyper-embodiment of Delilah in this sequence violates her own and the film's aesthetic codes: I feel certain that her graphic decontextualization is specially designed to allude to and to ironize both Bea and Aunt Jemima in her role as a site of American collective identification (see figs. 12a–e). The film's interference with the Aunt Jemima in Delilah is reinforced elsewhere. After Delilah's visual

Delilah turns into her trademark (*Imitation of Life*, 1934).

degradation, we see her making pancakes in the store, dressed as her trade-mark likeness; then, the film depicts a mass of imitation Delilahs, originating in her human face and fulfilled in her neon sign. But these women, who are shown packaging and mass producing Aunt Delilah's Original Pancake Mix, are explicitly industrialized, associated frame by frame with the disembodied human labor that generates their "product"; bodies without heads, they are filmed in an expressionist and not a cartoonish mode. They are surrounded by history: they are produced in history.[39] And when Delilah's product finally makes it into boxes, which are shown repetitiously moving along the produc-tion line, the soundtrack refers to the humanity abstracted by and condensed into the commodity, playing a sharply escalating series of the musical phrase

"Nobody Knows the Trouble I've Seen," which is also featured in the very opening moments of the film, over the credits.

In Delilah, Stahl gives Aunt Jemima a body dignified by labor and inscribed by struggle; but, distorted by racist magnification, she is "very deceivin' as to proportion." Indeed, in this seemingly stereotypical guise, Delilah utters the film's most political sentences. In that sense too she is decommodified, an anti–Aunt Jemima. She ironizes the tradition of grotesque African American representations in American consumer culture, which includes the distortions of the Hurst novel itself; and, most important, Delilah talks back to the nation from within her fictive frame, in the mammy's costume. We hear no tales of the sunny south from her, or sweet memories of the plantation: when she steps out of her flour barrel she speaks of the political brutality of the national public sphere. When Peola explodes in rage at being called "black" by Jessie, Delilah, on screen in uniform, tells Peola to "submit" to the cross her light-skinned father bore. And in an intense close-up that reflexively undermines the comic quality of the earlier caricature of her "trademarked" face, she faces the question of who is to blame for the pain of racist embodiment (see fig. 13): "It ain't her fault, Miss Bea. It ain't yourn, and it ain't mine. I don't know rightly where the blame lies. It can't be our Lord's. Got me puzzled."

At the moment Delilah settles on her perplexity, she looks away from the people on the screen and turns her face toward the camera. Thus the unspoken word in this speech is national, as she looks directly out at the audience: here, in her white, fluted chef's cap, she addresses her audience specifically as

Americans. Delilah is generally read as an apologist for the discriminations of racist culture because she argues that Peola must reconcile herself to the pain of her embodiment. Despite the manifest power of religious belief that ameliorates her own experience of racial violation, Delilah also engages in political analysis; in fact, this entire scene reveals, in brief asides, the rage at the other side of her resignation. Two comments in particular frame both Delilah's reading of her own history and her desire to protect Peola from repeating it by way of spiritual and financial support. Just prior to Peola's first public outburst against identification with her mother's blackness, Bea and Delilah work in the store and fantasize about what they want for their lives and the lives of their daughters. Bea comments that Peola is smarter than Jessie; Delilah replies, "Yesm. We all starts that way. We don't gets dumb till later on." What is "dumbness" here, if not Delilah's name for the mental blockages to rage and pain—what I earlier called "the-will-to-not-know"—that distinguish the colonized subject? Delilah's personal wish is just to get off her feet; but before then she will make certain that Peola is prepared, financially and educationally, to become a teacher, never to do housework for anyone. Teachers are "smart": they are not dumb, not full of sublimated rage, not sentenced to the life of the body as Delilah is, although she says she accepts the burden of her frame as part of the Lord's work.

The irony, of course, is that Delilah can pass through American culture because she has given her body over to its representation of what her subject position is: her very darkness, which overembodies her in the national public sphere, also domesticates her because she is entirely intelligible to the juridical satisfaction of the white mind. The film's pictographic move from her surplus body to her gigantic neon luminosity emphasizes her objectification: it always seems to be night in the sky behind her luminous body. In contrast, Peola's resistance to the official and popular rule of racial classification makes her body a different kind of obstacle: Peola would have to choose to be "black," to submit to a colonial corporeal regime, according to her own agency. But to choose to be visible in a culture of abstraction, to be a racial hieroglyph in everyday life, would be to choose a form of slavery. She simply can't inherit her mother's strategies of passing because she doesn't have her mother's body—as juridically defined and culturally staged. She looks and dresses much more like Bea (see fig. 14).

**14**
Delilah and Peola look in
the mirror (*Imitation of
Life*, 1934).

Thus one way of reading the racialized sign in this film is to see the contradictions, within its regime of visual representation, between the commercial and the personal racial hieroglyph: the cultural capital of the mother's public hyper-embodiment versus the juridically constructed enigma of the daughter's, which can and cannot be registered in the mirror and the film. Each racialized corporeality requires a special kind of self-licensing: thus Delilah looks forward to leaving her body completely, as it is so saturated by unrequited cultural fantasy; while Peola wants to be "white," which means she wants to relinquish one of her bodies, to become less meaningful and more American. Since Bea and Jessie share the same frame, the same color, the same class style, they will not have this problem and can affirm themselves while choosing each other.

But the contradictory and fracturing logics of race here produce another form of homosocial fantasy, which requires relinquishing the individual body as the primary unit of social meaning. When Delilah asks Peola to be a good girl and go to a high-toned college, we might think, as many critics do, that the film endorses the racial assimilation of African Americans. But she is also asking Peola to understand and to live her class interests as a member of a contested collectivity. Delilah herself did not have the privilege to do this in the 1920s; like many of her race class, she was dependent on the national market for "colored" domestic work. But for a film that takes place on the New Jersey boardwalk and then in New York City, *Imitation of Life* records almost nothing of American leisure culture or the political public sphere; for a film that takes place during the Depression, we hear only fleeting references to unemployment. In contrast to the novel, which is manifestly national and institutional in its scope, Stahl's film doesn't seem to believe in the value of an abstract, coherent, national or capitalist space. He finds America directly on the body, on its surfaces; but the surfaces of the body are marked almost solely with collective signs, which map out the subject's vulnerabilities, the routes her pain travels. This kind of pain is not the individuating, isolating kind; it is the source of a political confederation, the public world women might make. But female alliance across race is not the film's solution to the fragmenting effects of American hierarchy. Rather, the film offers it as a first step in effecting a shift away from the centrality of national identity as such. Delilah's funeral reveals on screen a concealed but vital and ongoing public sphere within the black community. In contrast to the novel, where all of America melts into the public space of mourning for Delilah, this funeral is run by the black churches and lodges that specialize, among other things, in ritualizing the passing of an individual person from a world where pain is a collective burden. The emergence of this suppressed locus of costume and ceremony isn't merely a species of colonialist "artefacting" on Stahl's part:[40] it deconstructs the simulacrum of "one" American public sphere and reveals that the notion of one dominant culture is one of the culture's most powerful myths. What if *Imitation of Life* were told from Delilah's point of view? The film approaches this by excluding the elements of cultural life to which she has no access. And by having her speak from within the trademark, it creates a space for political agency that exists elsewhere, and here, in her death as well. As Bea's final embrace of Jessie under the neon gaze of Delilah confirms, one must recognize that the body wrought by pain, memory, history, and ritual is collective. It is not aberrant or objectively in excess. In so shifting the public meaning of the "over-embodied" body, the Stahl text imagines a crucial victory over the abstract and individualizing lure of paradise, whether in America or elsewhere. This anti-nationalist message is, paradoxically, brought to us by a national trademark. Perhaps this was the only voice to which the audience would listen.

## White Neon, Black Gold: The Sirkean System

In the 1930s versions of *Imitation of Life*, national nostalgia for a safe domestic space was played out in commodity culture through the production and

transcendence of a black trademark. The idea was that public investment in a commodity form, with its humanoid skin and soul, would consolidate a nation shaken by a monstrous war and debilitating depression: and so Aunt Jemima, who had served so well after the Civil War, was "modernized" in "Aunt Delilah," displacing Uncle Sam. In the novel, this trademark is appropriated callously from the body of a black domestic worker as part of a white woman's emancipatory strategy. In Stahl's film this trademark is given public speech and speaks from the political place of surplus embodiment and the personal rage of collective suffering. Twenty-five years later, Douglas Sirk pulls back the black trademark's curtain and reveals the white woman hovering there: in one of the great *tu quoque* sequels of our time, his *Imitation of Life* exposes the form of the white woman to the commodification she has for so long displaced onto the black woman's body.[41]

As in Stahl's film, Sirk's narrative of female commodification hinges on a woman's relation to publicity. Advertisements do much of the critical work of this film: the opening shot of Lora Meredith's face, which is repeated later for emphasis, shows her bending over a sign that announces the "1947 Coney Island Mardi-Gras." This frame reasserts the film's symbolic link to Carnival, on the "Fat Tuesday" of public culture that portends Lent's impending melodrama (see fig. 15). But this film occupies the very public spaces excluded in Stahl's rendition—as if in a shot-reverse-shot relation, Sirk shoots the boardwalk from the beach that Stahl never represents. Sirk puts "the masses" back in mass culture and condenses the national identity of their taste and their desire in the surplus corporeality of Lora Meredith (Lana

Turner). While in the 1930s texts of *Imitation of Life* an ethic of bourgeois propriety motivated light-skinned women to escape the hyper-determination of the public body, in the 1950s the culture so embraces spectacular things that to be American means to want more body, more presence. But since presence, in mass culture, is signified by the image, Lora Meredith's stardom merges her embodiment and abstraction in a way peculiar to women but symptomatic of the gaudy culture at large. And so Lora Meredith becomes her own prosthesis, projecting herself into simulacral public spaces where the commodity, representation, and the body meet. That her fraudulence is America's has been widely discussed, by Sirk himself and by every critic who writes on this film: my interest here is to show specifically how Sirk determines the female trademark, transforming its public iconicity, its stereotypicality, into a national problem.

The transformation of Lora Meredith into "Lora Meredith" involves a self-instrumentalizing contract with her director, David Edwards. The montage sequence in which he proposes to make her sexually and professionally generic involves photographically removing her body from his apartment, moving the shot across the public space he calls her "empire," and scattering her across the nation. In the ten years that this sequence covers, Lora's body becomes progressively reified: her name replaces Edwards's name in the lights and increases in prominence; her face floats, separated from her body, amid overlapping marquees; her image is delaminated from her face and splayed on national magazine covers; and, toward the end, women in the audience mime her look so that projection of her visual image is no longer necessary to transmit to us her dominion in the national/capitalist space of fantasy consumption (see figs. 16a–f).

Although the montage transmits a ridiculous brightness, and although all the evidence is that Lora is a shallow actress—since Broadway and Hollywood apparently seek only a "girl with a certain *Je ne sais quoi* . . . that something [she] managed to get with the dog"—the humiliation to which Lora is exposed is mainly not professional but domestic. The film establishes its disciplinary home economy in its very first scene, when Lora loses her daughter—now named Susie (Sandra Dee)—on the beach. This loss introduces Lora both to Steve Archer (John Gavin), her soon-to-be-suffering lover, and Annie (rather than Delilah) Johnson (Juanita Moore), her soon-to-be-suffering "maid": they themselves are linked by their spatial proximity

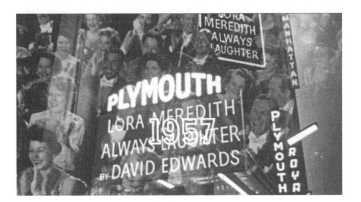

to a policeman, whose job is also to find the mother who has lost her young blond child. Everyone in her household polices Lora, including the children; each pronounces a monologue that catalogs explicitly Lora's inadequacy as a lover, mother, and employer in part because she really does lie and self-deceive to further her career, but mainly because public life is "imitation" and private life is "real" where women are concerned.

Yet there is something odd and ambivalent and even masochistic about the family's compulsion to repeat the argument for domesticity. More than anyone, Steve Archer brings this message to Lora. When they meet, he aspires to hang his pictures in the Museum of Modern Art—for example, the picture he takes of Lora on the Mardi Gras sign titled "Mother in Distress." But falling in love with Lora compels him to give up his dream and to ask her to give up hers. He tells her: "What you're after isn't real." What's "real" to him is "the nicest looking green folding money," and sex, besides. When she says, "What about me? What about the way I feel?" in defense of her lifelong dream to act, he replies, "Stop acting." (In a later scene, when she offers to give up Steve for her daughter's sake, as Claudette Colbert's character does in Stahl's production, Susie repeats this: "Stop acting, Mother.") Yet Steve returns repeatedly to the scenes of her acting: twice we see him in loving audience, both on the stage and off. He is addicted to consuming her product: he says, "You know, I still have you in my blood. . . ."

This dynamic of attraction, rejection, discipline, and performance has its uncanny "blood" repetition in the maternal relation of Annie to her daughter, now named Sarah Jane. Sarah Jane is light-skinned, an inheritance from her father, who "was practically white" (Susan Kohner, the actress, is in fact white). Throughout her youth Sarah Jane blames her mother (rather

than, say, the state or the law) for her condition and chooses a style of racial passing that negates her mother's "servile" mentality and manner, featuring instead libidinous, assertive physicality. Sarah Jane's racial passing is simultaneously sexual and theatrical: but in this she is typical of women. For in this film a woman who lives with difference—either gendered or racial—enjoys no prophylactic private sphere, no space safe from performance or imitation. This internal estrangement is as real for Annie as it is for her daughter: Annie comments that Lora's home has got to be better than the racist brutality of the South, but this is the closest she comes to saying that she feels at home where she lives. In any case, Sarah Jane mimes Lora in understanding that physical allure is the capital a woman must use to gain a public body. But this capital turns out to be as counterfeit for Sarah Jane as it is for Lora.

The writing on the wall in the scene where Frankie (Troy Donahue) beats up Sarah Jane for camouflaging the "trouble" with her mother (she tells Frankie that she is the daughter of rich, conservative parents; but the trouble she has is maternal shame) stages Sirk's negative homage to Stahl's *Imitation of Life*. The empty store in front of which the young lovers meet sports a prominent FOR RENT sign, but this empty store will not provide a secure space for a female affective and economic unit. Rather, it reflects the brutality that takes place outside that unit—in the public space. Moreover the plate glass window that had contained the authentic embodiment of Delilah's icon now reflects the public truth of American culture: the word "liberty," reflected backwards off a marquee from across the street meets up with the word BAR. In conjunction—or in "disjunction"—they condense the story and the conclusion of both of the narratives Sarah Jane lives, in her Anglo- and her African American frames (see figs. 17 and 18).

**19**
Sarah Jane
on the sexual
conveyor belt
(*Imitation of
Life*, 1959).

After Frankie rejects Sarah Jane she takes to the life of the white showgirl. She is not good enough to achieve the self-iconicity of mass culture: she earns no success montage. Instead, Sarah Jane's mode of self-instrumentality is to hyper-emphasize her body in the present tense of performance, in the mode of the naked gold figurine that is the trademark of the Moulin Rouge, where she works. By making herself a thing, she takes over her own cultural objectification as a racialized subject, relying on male narcissism to separate her sexual "value" from her genealogical body. Both of her performance scenes are extremely carnal, although opposite in their mode of allure. In the first, she dresses and sings raunchily about her need to embody herself sexually so that she might avoid the fate of passive, feminine women who have "empty, empty arms."[42] In the second, at the Moulin Rouge, she is one of a chain of indistinguishable mute showgirls on a conveyor belt (see fig. 19). They mime en masse a scene of seduction, drinking, and intercourse. You might even say they mime a success montage, in its mix of seriality and repetition; however, the success referred to in this sequence belongs not to the persons who embody it, but to the audience, whose mastery is one with the privilege of consuming. In contrast, the audience of Sirk's film is not exactly positioned like the public consumer of the female sexual fetish. When the film shows these scenes, it routes them through Annie's maternal eyes. Twice Annie and the audience see Sarah Jane in a sexual and racial performance: we watch Annie have an inverted primal scene, transfixed and sickened as her daughter does a "number" (see fig. 20). As with Steve and Lora, Sarah Jane is in Annie's "blood": it is as if the light-skinned female body in performance is irresistible to its consumers, even when it produces

pain and not the arousal of the theater's Aristotelian emotions or the girlie show's carnal sensations.

If Lora and Sarah Jane produce the "unreal" simulations, what does Sirk hold out for authenticity? I have already suggested that Annie and Steve, who police imitation with an unwavering moral passion, become implicated in female fraudulence by their addiction to it. Steve and Annie assume pain the way Lora and Sarah Jane want pleasure: and if the star-crossed women overinvest in the ecstasy and value of being public objects, the star-crossed blood lovers turn their pain into its own kind of spectacle. In short, if the film spends its most explicit time on the "problem" of the prosthetic public female body, it also shows how the problem of the female body itself becomes a commodity.

The paradoxes involved in this double commodification come together at Annie's opulent funeral. As the final scene in the film, the funeral might look like a privileged site of authentic public display, as I have argued that it does in the Stahl version. For like Delilah, Annie has a secret nondiegetic life in the black community. This life has not made it on screen because, Annie says plainly, "Miss Lora, you never asked." The funeral scene at the church brims with pomp and costume, but the ornate procession seems to reclaim the potential for public spectacle to produce dignity within American life. And the song Mahalia Jackson sings, "Trouble of the World," describes the weary one's relief at leaving for the Lord's house, where presumably there is no back room or basement. Finally, the ornate procession itself seems to perform its own distinction. Compared to the rest of the film it is unfrenetic, measured, subdued. It is also the only time we see men in costume, as if

perhaps signaling a patriarchal reclaiming of public spectacle. But as the procession rolls down the street, the camera pulls back: one window reads "costume rentals," another suggests "fakery" (see figs. 21 and 22).

This ironizing text is authentic, like graffiti. On the walls of consumer America, as in this film of *Imitation of Life*, public advertising seems to be the only "agent" of truth. Sirk himself has said that he intended to undercut the funeral by making it bizarre and embarrassing; he also shot Mahalia Jackson deliberately to look grotesque (see fig. 23). He could not understand why Jackson moved the audience in her luminous cry for relief from her body; and, suspicious of public culture and popular expression, he could not imagine that a representation of public female dignity might seem emancipating after all the corporeal humiliation his characters endure.[43] Sirk preserves in his *Imitation of Life* the American loathing of the enfleshed public body; he plays out, even in his own irony, how the ethic of universal and abstract dignity also embodies the citizens it deems illegitimate.

I have argued that, by designating certain forms of legitimacy in abstract personhood and not the flesh, in American culture legitimacy derives from the privilege to suppress and protect the body; the fetishization of the abstract or artificial "person" is constitutional law and is also the means by which whiteness and maleness were established simultaneously as "nothing" and "everything."[44] In *Passing* and in *Imitation of Life* Anglo-American and African American women live the effects of their national identity directly on the body, which registers the subject's legitimacy according to the degree to which she can suppress the "evidence." One of the main ways a woman mimes the prophylaxis of citizenship is to do what we might call "code-

crossing." This involves borrowing the corporeal logic of an other, or a fantasy of that logic, and adopting it as a prosthesis. The way women have usually tried this is heterosexual: but marriage turns out to embody and violate the woman more than it is worth. Thus other forms of bodily suppression have been devised. This is how racial passing, religion, bourgeois style, capitalism, and sexual camp have served the woman; indeed, in *Imitation of Life* this ameliorative strategy has become the "trademark" of female existence across race and class and sexual preference (see figs. 24 and 25).

What does this tell us about the potential national identity holds for the subjects it has historically burdened with bodies? We have seen that in the modern United States, the artificial legitimacy of the citizen has merged with the commodity form: its autonomy, its phantasmatic freedom from its own history, seem to invest it with the power to transmit its aura, its "body," to consumers. We have seen, in *Imitation of Life*, light-skinned women embracing the commodity's promise, although this embrace itself results in many different forms of embodiment. Sometimes the commodity becomes a prosthetic body, an apotropaic shield against penetration and further delegitimation; sometimes the body itself becomes the object of public consumption, protected by the distance between the image, performance, and actual form.

But the films and the novel give the lie to the American promise that participation in the national/capitalist public sphere has emancipatory potential for the historically overembodied. First, the strategy of abstraction that distinguishes white bourgeois style "solves" the problem by disciplining and shedding the public body, which forces the woman to live with the torture of its perennial return. Second, the body of the dark-skinned African American

**23**
Mahalia Jackson sings "Trouble of the World" (*Imitation of Life*, 1959).

woman is apparently unabstractable on her own behalf. Even Aunt Delilah's nostalgic public form represents a history of violence that is simultaneously personal and national in scope. This is why the amelioration of religion is so crucial to the black mothers of these texts, for there is no imaginable space in America, not even in the most benign white woman's house, where she will see relief from the body's burden. In Stahl's version, Bea and Delilah do escape into the sisterhood of the laboring body, but once leisure is achieved they revert to the default forms of their culture. For light-skinned African American women, then, the choice of public identity comes to be between two bodies of pain, not two possible modes of relief from indeterminacy.

There is a moment in Hurst's *Imitation of Life* that crystallizes the distances between the nation's promise of prophylaxis to the "person" and the variety of female genders it creates. At the moment before Bea has her first experience of intercourse with her husband, she goes upstairs to put on the nighttime garb of the virginal bride on her way to the hymeneal altar. She has never before entered their "master bedroom": the "darkies" put it together during the wedding day. Bea, frightened, thinking of her mother, catalogues the objects on Mr. Pullman's mantel.

> Framed photographs of an exceedingly narrow-faced pair of parents, deceased. One of quite an aged aunt, deceased. A framed program of the Pleiades Club, the one on which Mr. Pullman was announced to read his paper on Abraham Lincoln. And of all things! Dear knows from where, the black girl had unearthed a picture which must, in some way, have got mixed up with his other belongings. A horrid cabinet-sized thing of a

woman, which Bea turned face down, in stockings and no clothes, trying on a man's high hat before a mirror. With what seemed like actual malice, that picture had been propped up against one of the china pugs. Those darkies. . . . (50)

At the moment when Bea is to leave her ignorant girlish body behind for the sexual knowledge of womanhood, she finds her husband's pornography. The "thing" of a woman represented there violates everything she knows about her proper New England husband; and Bea understands that this woman has preceded her in his fantasy life. Bea turns the picture face down because she does not want to face it. She wants instead to blame it on the "black girl" who set up the room; she wants to displace her disgust at the masculine embodiment of women onto the black women who serve her. I have suggested that Hurst's version of Bea habitually relies on black women to be embodied: but along with revealing Bea's own racial and class instrumentality, the picture suggests a politically "malicious" correspondence between Anglo- and African American women.

The "thing" of a woman the picture depicts is having a wonderful time. She is fantasizing in a mirror, which itself frames the genitaled trunk of her body for the husband's pornographic gaze. However, the text does not

consider what the man wanted from the picture. Let us imagine, then, for a moment, what this woman might be thinking. Surely, her costumed appendages signify a fantasy of agency: she might assume a male body or masquerade as another kind of woman. But the hat this "thing" of a woman wears is not just any hat: it is Lincoln's hat. The text clues us in to this by referring to Mr. Pullman's speech about Lincoln: the one he plagiarized from the *Encyclopaedia Britannica*. This article from 1911 about Lincoln reminds us that he was for white women's suffrage, as well as reluctantly for the emergence of black slaves from property to personhood; the article also characterizes Lincoln as the most feminine of presidents because of his sensitive heart.[45] In conjunction with the prop of the hat, the woman wears most likely a pair of dark stockings. Perhaps she is enjoying imagining how an amalgam of races and genders might look if legitimately embodied as citizens, or even as president, within the national frame. Bea is certainly not thinking this: she is too busy blaming the "darkies." Or maybe the "thing" of a woman parodies Lincoln's promise, revealing the bodies of light and dark women to be "things" his proclamation did not liberate. Thus Lincoln's hat reminds us that the nation holds out to the woman a promise of emancipation and a pornographic culture both. And that, as Delilah says of Peola's picture, "never done her justice."[46]

**UNCLE SAM NEEDS A WIFE**   Citizenship and Denegation

> He has seen but half the universe who never
> has been shown the House of Pain.
> R. W. EMERSON, "THE TRAGIC"

### Sentimentality's "Unfinished Business"

Sentimentalists strive to save the political from politics. To do this
they constitute the citizen not as someone with potentially jeopar-
dizing qualities or with a status in a hierarchy—for example, as a
*subject of politics*—but as someone with attachments and intentions
and pain capacities—for example, as a *subject of feeling*—who longs
for what everyone is said to long for, a world that allows access to
vague belonging, a sense of unanxious general social membership
that ought to be protected by the institutions that bind power to ordinary life. Whereas other workers in the field of political feeling
might ask you to mobilize self- and world-transformative emotions
with which you had never identified—such as utopian anxiety or
nihilist desires to risk the potential destruction of the world as you
know it on behalf of a better good life—the sentimentalist tells you
that you are already there emotionally to bring the world into line
with your felt need, and that when the world is brought into line
with you, you will feel transformed into a richer version of what

you already are. To risk change in the conditions of ordinary identification and the structural management of it, the political sentimentalist therefore denigrates politics on behalf of saving the political as a site of aspiration for change; the institutions of extimacy that flourish in inconstant democracies have to be pushed aside from the focus of consciousness in order for sociality to seem something other than a threat to happiness and fulfillment.

Thus, in chapter 1, "Poor Eliza," politicians who work in politics in the conventional sense were always revealed as degraded, compromised figures of shallow principle. But the sentimental texts suggested that rather than merely serving the interests of established power, the politicians had simply not sufficiently thought through their principles. Yet in a sentimental context the way truly to think through something is to *interrupt* cognition, to test a view against feeling's higher truth. This also involves exhortations to overcome feeling's lower untruth, the debased appetites so often associated with political avarice. Stowe and her legatees redirect a Christian legacy from politics into the political by arguing that a sense of genuine affirmative collective sociality best can be achieved by embracing the identity among souls through transactions of pain and recognition, suffering and compassion. Only then can the domain of politics turn from a gross place of covetousness and violence into virtually sacred tableaux of a better good life that features calmed nerves, de-fractured loves, and an aesthetics of absorption that embraces strangers who warrant inclusion into the best version of the social world that one already inhabits.

The fantasy of changing the political by transcending politics through gestures of emotional humanism is especially associated with nations and women—in the United States and globally, with Stowe and the tradition associated with her—but it is, I have been arguing, a quality of intimate publics generally. In sentimentally mediated worlds, optimism is not organized around unimaginable transformations but around structural adaptations whose justice the sentimentalists can already affectively pre-experience internally as a flourishing intensity (this would be true in terms of the emotional registers of nineteenth-century psychology and the disciplined yet unconscious ones of the twentieth).[1] Yet in lived liberalism American style, sentimental-political optimism *for change without trauma* is haunted by anxieties about the potential disfigurations of ordinary subjectivity, fantasy, and pleasure implied in large-scale imaginaries of social transformation. Chapter 1 tracked the utopian aspirations of the sentimental. This chapter tracks what is on the other side of the sentimental-utopian: the fear of too much change, and the adjustments and adaptations endemic to that fear that seek to minimize in advance potentially destabilizing eruptions. Predictably, the sentimental foreclosures move between the circulating registers of national sentimentality and national sexuality.

I open my archive with women's suffrage, a moment of tremendous optimism for the potential within national culture to repair its own juridical errors. Particular states allowed women to vote in all but federal elections starting around the end of the nineteenth century and the beginning of the twentieth. Not until 1920, though, were most women deemed full U.S. citizens (whites and African Americans were, but not immigrant Asians until mid-century) and permitted to vote federally.[2] In the moment of suffrage's achievement by women, however, a specter of feminized nineteenth-century sentimentality seemed most to threaten the modernist cosmopolitan project to make women "of the world" rather than of the local and the intimate. Ida Clyde Clarke's *Uncle Sam Needs a Wife* (1925) is a citizenship manual published shortly after women received the vote (see fig. 26).[3] It is a work wildly at odds with itself, in ways both predictable and unusual. As we will see, most citizenship training manuals directed toward the legally uninitiated are dry as dust, oriented toward inculcating citizenship as a set of noncontroversial knowledges and habits. But saturation in pragmatics does not imply a lack of interest in orchestrating patriotic emotion. As one manual avers, "Votes for women is a movement concerned far less with numbers than with inner meanings. It means informing the whole field of public life with the woman spirit, if it means anything at all."[4]

The closer these manuals get to women, the more impassioned becomes their rhetoric about rational political participation. *Uncle Sam Needs a Wife* is variously comic, tragic, goading, critical, and apprehensive as it pursues its anxious sense that women are squandering the potential power of their citizenship. (Many of its arguments about what constitute women's "political interests" in everything from the social importance of mothering to education to war are shockingly resonant with debates in contemporary U.S. popular culture.[5]) Like so much commentary about suffrage, *Uncle Sam*

26
Frank Goodwin, frontispiece for Ida Clyde Clarke, *Uncle Sam Needs a Wife* (1925).

UNCLE SAM NEEDS A WIFE

makes inconsistent arguments about the ways that the entry of women into the body politic might still transform both the nation and women. Women already have all the expertise necessary to run the political sphere but have been trivialized and seek only narcissistic knowledge; women are less sentimental and more emotionally skilled than men but are also exhausted, fickle, emotionally volatile, and banal; women have better instinctual politics, being, for example, natural pacifists, but work too closely to the instincts and the personal. That Clarke's polemic proceeds amid a jumble of accusations and observations does not invalidate it as a historical exemplum or a site of ideas: political and social worlds are inevitably built across fault lines of contradiction and bad conceptualization that not only do *not* threaten the general project but make its endurance possible.[6]

In the United States, the vote was the prize agreed to by a coalition of radicals, reformers, and social conservatives, even as they imagined a quite divergent range of social transformations to be the consequence. Clarke enacts pretty much all of these. But her polemic's fundamental anxiety rests in its ambivalent loosening and restitching of the sutures that bind women to sentimental politics. Like most texts in the political sphere, it manifestly abjures sentimentality, seeing it as a harm to women, a mode of hyperbole that masks its diminishing effects. Seeing women stuck in nineteenth-century feminine paradigms of idealized privacy, *Uncle Sam* provides a cosmopolitan update of the ideology of women's separate sphere by repurposing the skills engendered there to a new "field" of potential political action at home, locally, nationally, and globally (239; Clarke's phrase is "transmuted motherhood" [195]). Women remain entirely identified with feeling and emotions in ways that do not interfere that much with the conventions of femininity whose endurance amid structural economic and cultural changes enables the intimate public sphere of women to seem an ongoing place of general recognition for any woman. This process of bargaining with and within femininity is evident in Clarke's strongly argued final chapter, called "Unfinished Business" (245–79). Articulating broader feminist and civic calls to step up to effective citizenship, Clarke locates the unfinished business of femininity in women's habit of cultivating strategically weak political "convictions" (245). The sheer weakness of political will suggested by this description should not be mistaken for Clarke's judgment against political longing; rather, it reflects a desire to name how its pervasive conventionality works as a defense against serious political struggle. *Uncle Sam* names sentimentality a primary culprit in the maintenance of structural inequalities in the United States and the world while wielding its lures to appeal to women's pride in the virtue of their affective knowledge.

Insofar as *Uncle Sam Needs a Wife* tells a story about political emotion in which political dissatisfaction runs up against affective commitments not to risk much change while witnessing the need for it, it predicts the later twentieth-century politics of pain where political failure foments not revolution but the reproduction of a wistful fantasy that things might be otherwise. The second part of this chapter shifts to the contemporary U.S. political sphere, tracking Clarke's anxiety about femininity, suffrage, and politics and tweaking the terms of collective intimacy in relation to ongoing sentimentally normative practices of collective ambivalence toward the relation of politics to the political. Contemporary concerns about the political event of the vote and the citizenship form it expresses also suggest something other than a sense of national optimism about continuities between political being and the politics of belonging.[7] More than ever, as the vote itself is seen as a corrupted vehicle for the misrepresentation of political will in the United States, citizenship is measured in the broader sense of social membership and is more likely to be enacted optimistically in responses to events in mass culture, especially those signifying evidence of democratic "accident" or ongoing violence—for example, the police beating of Rodney King, the Thomas-Hill controversy, O. J. Simpson's murder trial, and the attacks of September 11, 2001. My claim here is that a juxtapolitical citizenship form thrives in the contemporary United States not simply as a sign of sentimental liberalism or as a container for its utopianism about the power of affect and performed emotion to reroute the world toward a vaguely imagined horizon of justice. Its third function is to perform what I have established as the tradition of aversion to democracy's political instantiation within national-political sentimentality. When political desire is failed by politics, participants in the sentimental tradition have come to choose traumatic cultural mediations as a way of expressing passionate detachment from politics as such. Does this mean that the body politic now "votes" for national continuity by investing in events of mass violence and death that are deemed diminished when they are "politicized"? What destinies for politics and the political can we track in the voracious consumption of disaster? Juxtapolitical citizenship might represent a foundation for translocal political identifications, in the mode of "grievable life" or movement politics, but not usually.[8] The history of its flourishing reveals individuals en masse hoarding a sense of belonging *against* what politics as usual seems to offer—a space of aversive intensities, increased risk, shame, vulnerability, exploitation, and, paradoxically, irrelevance.

## "Drop Complaints Here": Making (Up) Women Citizens

*Suffrage* has nothing to do with suffering—etymologically, if not historically. Between 1865 and 1920, the U.S. political public sphere was cracked open like a fresh egg whose purpose was to leak some limited, uneven sovereignty onto the then formally excluded female occupants of the United States: then, the model of political and social membership that dominated the formalist public imaginary was enfranchisement.[9] To be enfranchised was to be free to vote, to self-alienate a political opinion; it was to be deemed a sovereign citizen who could self-represent autonomously and therefore be represented. The capacity to hold, to alienate, and to delegate these private properties was what electoral democracy seemed to secure. This is to say that the franchise was the form of alienable expression that confirmed a subject's political existence, like breath on a mirror. It established the citizen as evolved beyond the flesh—not dead, politically speaking. Yet, as we will see, where the politically depressed personhood of the enfranchised but historically subjugated citizen is concerned, one never strays too far from the specter of suffering and death.

The history of civil rights in the United States shows that gaining the franchise is both an event and a process that always crackles with contingency. Thus it is that the African American men who were enfranchised as abstract individuals by the Fourteenth Amendment struggled for another century until the "qualifications" to vote were no longer read right off of the body[10]; thus it remains, at this writing, that despite having the formal franchise, gays and lesbians remain excluded from many of the protections allowed to American heterosexuals. Reproductive and labor safety laws formally speak to generic rights of citizens while actually designating women not of childbearing age and whites and people of color who work for wages as relatively disposable. Still, the franchise is the precise difference between zero and one for members of a historically excluded population: it changes the conditions of survival in relation to the domain of justice and enables the experience of one's life to be expressed in terms of the self-interest of "a constituency." Additionally, the vote not only signals something like full formal belonging to the body politic but also registers a grounding that enables subjects to move across time and space regardless of their particular or individual genealogies and verifies for local, national, and international law the individual's distinguishing marks. After all, the vote means that someone lives somewhere both local and national. Like the signature, the fingerprint, and the photographed right ear, the voter's registration confirms that someone was in fact at a jurisdictional place at a proper official time (at birth and at naturalization, for example).

Since the 1840s, thousands of citizenship training manuals have been generated in the United States for making both native-born and immigrant occupants literate in national culture and its various locales: states, townships, counties, school districts, villages, and so on.[11] Produced by federal, state, and local governments for immigrants, students, and the military, and by private organizations for immigrants and new citizens such as women and children, these manuals provide for us an image of the nation as it is imagined to be, insofar as it needs to be navigated, negotiated, and managed—lived in. Before looking more closely at *Uncle Sam Needs a Wife*, it would be useful to get some sense of the generic conventions. What kinds of citizen subject do these texts generate, and what do their fantasies of participation in politics imply for images of a common culture?

A manual is a pragmatic pedagogic genre, an opportunity for retraining a reader into something different and yet more herself—in this case, into a socially intelligible form of person whose politico-ethical sensorium is in the right order. Although one encounters citizenship workbooks throughout the twentieth century that test the imminent citizen the way children are tested in some version of the basic dates and facts of U.S. history, the citizenship manual usually raises the stakes of adequate citizenship beyond the minor empiricisms. The law of this genre is to impart the normative knowledge and practice habitus of the citizen and to orient the citizen toward acting appropriately. "Citizen" becomes a synonym for the undramatic practice of social as well as political membership. The manual makes citizenship ordinary.

Rhetorically, these civics texts evoke a combination of baby talk and the image of an English speaker who, on encountering a foreigner, tries to communicate by yelling loudly and slowly in English. These are not merely metaphoric associations: just as immigration law placed pressure on the status of native-born enfranchisement at the turn of the century, so too was newly compulsory public education of previously excluded minorities and women cause and effect of constitutional change. Frequently, when the handbooks presuppose their utility as textbooks, they presume such multiple audiences, whose differences become nullified through the metacultural form of the nation and the juridical form of the vote. But the dehumanizing species associations among women, the poor, and the black continue to emit a powerful vibe as well, as their ignorance and "inclination to measure everything in terms of the personal" suggests subcivilization, the negative reign of instinct over thought (207).[12]

*Uncle Sam* archly notes that men have never taken classes in citizenship, that citizenship training schools are being run for women, and that women are wasting their time studying what men have taken for granted (91).[13] It is astounding to read, repeatedly, the manuals' elaborate definitions of the city, the state, the village, the school board, the ballot, the ballot box, the political party, and so on. They make new citizens responsible for the most minor details of bureaucratic process and public sphere codes of behavior, such as how to write a letter to a congressman. They talk about being polite.[14] *Uncle Sam* actually engenders an image of the uneducated woman citizen as a political "moron": but it also claims that both genders share in large quantities of political idiocy (224). Men do not understand or respect women, writes Clarke; patriarchal politics is a terrible, spoiled, corrupt, economically inefficient, and degenerate "household" that needs a wife. Moreover, men are too sentimental, emotional, and narcissistic really to run a government well (27, 30, 58).

In this bolus of hyperbole resonates a longer struggle within the women's suffrage movement over the formal education of citizens. During the struggles of the late nineteenth century, the phrase "Educated Suffrage" marked a compromise developed by white middle-class suffrage activists. The purveyors of this model of suffrage meant to sacrifice working-class women of all races in order to gain patriarchal approval. It tapped into the hegemonic embrace of particularized universalism by admitting the presumption of "qualifications" to notions of the abstract individual with rights.[15] Despite this resonance, however, African American activists who refused such a compromise nonetheless lectured widely on the need to educate black women to the demands of citizenship. For some, education did not mean separation from the totality of black people but uplift for all, while for others suffrage activism involved elevating black women over black men deemed incompetent to citizenship during the nightmare of Reconstruction. In any case, all understood the importance of the deliberate dissemination of the tools that would promote African American social and political legitimacy.[16]

At the same time as *Uncle Sam* hectors women not to commit the "crime" of being uneducated as to economic and imperial policy, it elevates what they already know innately and as managers of households. Like many of the middlebrow manuals, *Uncle Sam* claims neither a feminist nor a sentimentalist viewpoint, but rather the standpoint of clear-eyed realism (58). Of course it was conventional even in the nineteenth century for sentimental texts to call themselves realist in contrast to the ultra-emotional, personal, feminine "sob" stories associated with a parodic version of the women's magazines. But what makes this particular claim for realism distinct historically and significant theoretically is its characterization of women's failure to take up an aggressive position within politics as a *psychological* symptom of becoming a subject under patriarchy in its traditional and modern forms (75, 163, 179, 193, 214, 222). Clarke sees the bodily consequences of "subjugation" in a variety of biomental experiences of political depression and spends multiple chapters imagining their undoing.

Clarke says that women create at least part of their nontransformative political impact. Women have "super-knowledge"; a greater capacity for improvisation in hard circumstances; empathy with struggling others; a peaceful, not warmongering nature; a tendency toward virtue and away from vice; more experience managing budgets; more courageous realism; more inventive longing; "superior" psychology; and a lot of wasted talent (18, 57, 69, 136). They are mainly maternal and oriented toward helping intimate others flourish, but a minority of women has surplus labor from which politics could benefit: Carrie Chapman Catt is Clarke's prime example. But women are also trivial and trivializing: amid the noise of their complaints, they manifest an "inferiority complex" involving psychological obstacles to attaining full citizenship (66–67, 106, 118–36).

Indeed, what makes this manual at once singular and exemplary is the manner in which it articulates the state of women's citizenship in terms of the new science of psychoanalysis, claiming that whatever ails women requires not hypnosis or the talking cure but sublimation through politics (133). In deploying this register of analysis, *Uncle Sam* articulates citizenship training with therapy culture, which was also emerging in women's culture at this moment. The Adlerian anti-Freudian language of the inferiority complex establishes that political oppression produces "submerged" personality; it refers to contemporary European experiments in releasing the body's biosocial energy to advocate for derepressing women politically (133).[17] In this it was like the many suffrage plays and novels that associated the politically uninformed or disenfranchised woman with states of lethargy and depression, the turning inward of atrophied social energy that produced the lamest, most paralytic versions of the female complaint.[18] "The social diseases and the economic diseases from which women are suffering are as distinctly women's diseases as are those of the physical body" (185).

But *Uncle Sam Needs a Wife* sees politics as the cure for depression. It spends many chapters showing how women dissipate their political energy in "conferences" that distract and exhaust them in their urge to reform everything: "See [women] plunging idly through superficial studies of superficial subjects under hypnotic headings while wars and strikes go on!" (136). As a result, Clarke avers, women become masochistic and bitter toward each other, refuse the challenges of difficult knowledge, and attach themselves to trivial pursuits and other dissipation.

This political development in the terms of therapy culture is itself a product of many forces. First, there were significant transformations in modes and norms of privacy and publicity in these early days of the modernist intimate public sphere, with its foregrounding of women's cosmopolitanism. Among these was the invention of national consumer markets in the United States after World War I; these markets addressed their particular incitement to expertise—usually implicitly—to middle-class women and mothers. Deploying a distinction typical of the period but unusually explicitly defensive, one manual notes that

> in this connection it is an interesting fact that the women most interested in voting appear to belong to the respectable middle class. Thus, in a fall election in 1912 the election commissioner of Denver found that in three small, prosperous or rich districts, 2,774, 2,496, and 909 women voted, respectively, while in the crowded "Red Light" district of those days only 143 women voted and many of these were respectable wives of working men whom necessity forced to live in that section.[19]

Respectability was the key to establishing competence in civil society.[20] Respectable women would produce a respectable world: this requires libidinal or appetitive self-mastery. But above all the therapeutic ghost in the citizenship machine emerges in the manuals' normative neutralization of what the structural transformation of women's political legitimacy might mean. "*It is up to every woman to get her ballot's worth*," one manual writes. "And how do you get your ballot's worth? By application of the very principle you employ in the purchases you make . . . you are an experienced shopper; you are a recognized expert on values; you know quality and how to get quality; you can bargain skillfully; you know how to avoid being cheated. And I'll wager you did not learn to cook without a good cookbook at your elbow."[21] This author calls her text the *Fanny Farmer* of citizenship, a place where practical feminine knowledge is simply put to new use. It becomes a commonplace that women's practical agency gives them both an interest and an expertise in engaging the political public sphere as mothers of the race, as home economists, and as managers of money, crisis, desire, and moral leadership. As new citizens of the world they will be too busy adapting to the urgencies of consumer desire to have surplus or unwieldy desires that register beyond the normative machinery.

The very existence of *Uncle Sam*, indeed, which was published in a panic that women had not sufficiently developed into full citizens even after the franchise was achieved, signals that other stories of sociocultural bargaining might be divined from the minor event of these pamphlets. One of these links the question of women's practical and visceral citizenship education to the pressure placed on U.S. cultural reproduction from the postwar influx of European immigrants, whose women were deemed to be in a better juridical situation than native-born women who had married male U.S. citizens. Furthermore, the return of underemployed military veterans, already decimated by the war's unprecedented brutality, conflicted with the transformation in the greater experience and expectations of the metropolitan women who had taken on greater public responsibility during the war, both in industrial and white-collar contexts. This latter element, usually associated with the project of national remasculinization after World War II, actually played crucially in the formal political advancement of women, just as John D'Emilio has argued that it did for gay men and lesbians in less politically formal ways.[22]

Additionally, at this moment women's suffrage became a part of a general expansion of the conditions of thinkable democratic form in the U.S. political public sphere. An intense education in a variety of potential U.S. socioeconomic destinies was made available. The Mary Sumner Boyd volume *The Woman Citizen* (1918) spends 50 of its 250 pages describing the platforms of the Socialist, Anti-Saloon, Prohibition, and National parties, along with the Democrats and the Republicans. Each of them is described with dignity, performing non-normative political thought as integral to patriotism itself. In addition, throughout this and many other manuals of the moment, arguments for cross-segment alliances especially around issues of class are central to the reparative work women's suffrage was claiming it would do for industrialized worker populations, both in the United States and elsewhere. "We are the realists of the sexes," *A Political Handbook for Women* typically observes, explaining women's deeper understanding of more varieties of work.[23] The right of workers to tolerable work environments and adequate pay merged with the older sentimental rhetoric about women's essential and practical linkage to children and to the everyday. As often is the case, sentimentality returns here as a mode of realism that asserts women as best placed to ameliorate the harsh conditions of survival for the economically and politically subordinated. The rise of the international labor movement was crucial to the vitality of women's suffrage in this domain, as the depleted bodies of children and the poor were recognized as kindred symptoms of capitalist democracy's failure.

At the same time, the federal or state governments of western democracies took up competitively championing the cause of women's suffrage, if not feminism.[24] A progressive stance on women's suffrage would demonstrate a nation's moral and economic superiority to the nations and peoples they sought to dominate: "Woman suffrage is preeminently a war measure," *Uncle Sam* avers. It notes that "Great Britain and Canada have extended suffrage to women . . . [that] France and Italy have virtually promised to do so" and that even Woodrow Wilson recognized it as crucial to any representation of democracy as the most humane and morally evolved political system.[25] As many historians have shown and as Gayatri Spivak would have predicted, the tableau of white men saving brown women from brown men in the colonial context was a site for the enunciation of this strategy of U.S. imperial publicity.[26] In any case, by 1920 there was a general consensus that the emancipation of the oppressed woman into formal participation in U.S. democracy was crucial to the conversion of what *Uncle Sam* calls women's unused "Social Capital," their knowledge and expertise, for the global advancement of national life.

These tropes are patriotic, but again, the patriotism is an argument for women to attach to *politics* and not just patriotism or vague political belonging—for example, to transform the sentimental into the agential. The citizenship manuals authored by and directed toward the white middle classes are critical of national and capitalist violence toward workers, children, and weaker countries. But they express little ambivalence toward the promise of the national, and this at a moment wherein the trauma of world war made internationalism a real option for the more socialist and anarchist sites within feminism. To some degree, the ironies of strategic universalism were not lost on the white middle-class suffragettes. The narrator of *Uncle Sam Needs a Wife*, for example, self-mockingly appropriates a flirtatious mode of patriotic critique:

> We love you Uncle Sam! Of course we do! Haven't we brought you into the world, and nursed you, and petted you, and spoiled you, and flattered you, and adored you? Haven't we taught you all you know? Haven't we lectured you and tried to reform you when you haven't turned out to be all that we expected you to be? . . . What better fate can befall a likely, promising, but unstable and spoiled young man than marriage to some wise, comprehending, intelligent, devoted woman! (19)

Acerbic jokes and lightness of speech are central rhetorical forms of the female complaint, providing one version of the acid wash of critique, of which the other side is melodrama. *Uncle Sam* is unusual in the ambiguously chipper tone of its ridicule of men. But whether ironic or sincere, the citizenship manual directed to women inevitably mediates its critique with consoling references to the ongoing proprieties of married life. Emotional heteronormativity remains the fundamentally stable point in the internally and externally directed pedagogy of the women's citizenship manuals. In the United States, heteronormativity should be understood to describe both white middle-class and "respectable" working-class aspirations to national universality. I do not mean by this that white and African American suffrage workers had no critique of the patriarchal family and capitalist inequalities: quite the contrary. But as a site of consent that secures the intelligibility of a particular image of a general national culture, the franchise is to citizenship what heteronormativity is to social membership—whether the sign for such normativity is the family or the couple. Both are particular means to an end that register as the taken for granted. Whereas the sovereignty of the individual is a central magnetizing figure for the generalized citizenship manuals, women's training in U.S. citizenship links their education to the production of more and better intimate normalcy in general as well as to a better "United States."

Historians of suffrage love to point out that other historians of suffrage overvalue the importance of the vote in telling the story of women's complex entry into the national and capitalist public sphere. They emphasize what I have emphasized, that a wide range of reform movements—antipoverty, antiracist, anti–child labor, antiliquor, antiexploitation, antipatriarchal—were linked by the time women's suffrage turned into modern feminism. Still, in all accounts scholars argue that misogyny and antifeminism were so strong in the United States that it was deemed necessary to articulate coalitions across vectors of difference around the form of the vote. The vote became the least common denominator in a variety of political struggles for greater racial, sexual, and economic equality. And in exchange for these compromises, women's vote came to be seen as a confirmation of U.S. sexual and political superiority.

## From Sarcasm to the Sacred

To the degree that they were ironic or *knowing*, the rhetorical purveyors of political bargaining during the women's enfranchisement struggles cannot be read as motivated entirely by expediency. The consoling image of an intimate sphere with strong but strongly differentiated men and women that enabled the victory of women's suffrage while minimizing what might be scary about it deployed a standard means of hegemonic persuasion. It is common to hold still a beloved social norm so that other changes can seem less threatening. Sexuality frequently plays this role, the role of the potentially anarchic force that must be bound conservatively so that adaptations might be made within the hegemonic field. One might say that sentimentality manages sexuality— that was true in the nineteenth century in the United States, surely, and this is its conventional function. But *both* are equally powerful features of the emotionalization of the modern subject—the person who knows herself insofar as she knows what she feels. The seeming moral hierarchy of cultivated empathic feeling over appetitive acting out masks the similarity of the threat of lack of control each poses to an amalgam of desires for there to be a general social world whose continuity can be predicted. *Uncle Sam Needs a Wife* presents one version of the sexual/sentimental double threat to the flourishing of the general world; two juxtapolitical deaths of the 1990s—those of Princess Diana and John F. Kennedy Jr.—mark a return of sorts to the mass social pseudo-competition between sexual threat/politics and sentimental management/the political.[27] Like many events associated with great inconsequential displays of emotion they seem almost silly now: and yet the very waning of their impact reveals something important about the circulation of juxtapolitical intensities in the modern intimate publics.

At the place where she was killed in Paris in 1997, there is a statue now associated with Princess Diana—an arm, perhaps the Statue of Liberty's arm, jutting out from a stone foundation.[28] Tourists come to this statue from all over the world, leaving offerings and writing graffiti on it that testify to Diana's ongoing significance, marking her death as a vibrant event that continues to teach something about something to someone. When John F. Kennedy Jr.'s plane crashed in 1999, the statue of Diana became a means for his secular deification: throughout the weeks following tourists left notes and signs and other traces of homage to Kennedy on Diana's monumental body. The iconic proximity of these two figures creates a linked destiny for them. World citizens by accident of family, their lives ended tragically "before their time." They are joined somewhat like the famous picture of Elvis and Nixon shaking hands that made its way into Thomas Pynchon's *Vineland* or, more soberly, the photo of Malcolm X and Martin Luther King that Spike Lee features in *Do the Right Thing*. These startling images of public figures in figural intimacy circulate not only as evidence of lost personal futures but also as histories unfulfilled. But whose history? Capturing unlived potential, the imaged pressing of posthumous celebrity flesh comes to signal for a certain segment of its public a broken engagement with a better destiny. It is embodied, yet it resonates impersonally; it is unreal and yet it is experienced emotionally.

These images and events are not official propaganda for a political good life circulated to enhance anyone's power. Partly, they are produced to generate reliance on media so that people come to define collective experience as a dense web of mediatized events. They can also be seen as evidence that in the United States celebrity attachments are preferable to a reality in which ordinary human relations seem less worth investing in, as intimate domestic and work situations become less likely to stretch over lifetimes. One could return, additionally, to Fredric Jameson's argument that celebrity or nonhuman icons such as the shark in *Jaws* mark at least a collective sense of lack and longing for an underdefined *something*.[29] I want to focus here on the proximity of the mourned-for personage to the political world. Is the dead-too-soon celebrity citizen, like the shark, an event that calls out what would otherwise be political optimism, the form of the attachment that, at one time, would have circulated through the promise of universalist politics? How is it that ordinary people see themselves, their destinies, any qualities at all apart from mortality, in these scenes? What does it mean that an optimistic visceral politics seems to resonate most unambivalently in this afterlife-laden affect world of postpolitical signs?

Kristin Ross argues that the period after World War II in France (and, I think, generally, in the West) was distinguished by a retreat from identification with national history, an emptying out of public memory as a suturing device.[30] What replaced it was a national universalism organized by the privatized concerns of the everyday: homes, family, tactile experience, and an interest in augmenting hygiene everywhere. This shift in the domain of national identification, she argues, shaped the postwar critical interest in everyday life as well, serving the interests of nations and capital by distracting citizens and intellectuals from feeling accountable for the nation's ongoing imperial and capitalist relations. The year 1968 was a direct challenge to this shift and yet also extended its new focus on the subject and experience as the site of history. If this is so, critical theory rooted in the subject and in modes of psychoanalysis and interpretation uncoupled with materialist politics must continue to carry the traces of the privatization of experience, the inculcated view that subjective cultures are the apolitical real that must be protected from the political surreal. In the United States, the continued emphasis on moral feeling as the center of political value continues the postwar pattern while also tapping into the longer tradition that elevates proper feeling as the ethico-political norm.

The possible future president and the quasi-princess were said to have touched "ordinary" people even though they were already in a space beyond that when they were living. Like the centaurs that intermix gods and humans, they seem, mainly after their deaths, to mediate alterity and intimacy, ordinariness and greatness, without fully embodying either. This is why they can represent mass futures along with tragic and farcical repetitions of power's chaos. But the collective investment in the strangely animated icons now hovering both beyond and within the political is not just an effect of postwar mass culture. As Claude Lefort, Michael Taussig, Louis Marin, Marina Warner, Giorgio Agamben, and Slavoj Žižek have argued,[31] dense and radiant images of the politically saturated and especially the governing body have long been employed as vehicles for shaping a collective sense of social belonging. It is as though an aesthetic of fascination or absorption by the image *is* the fulfillment of the promise of belonging and of disavowal or deferral that an icon holds out. Taussig tracks the posthumous cultural destiny of the state icon he calls "The Liberator":

> But as we look at the fate of this body of the father stronger in death than when he was alive, we discern another body forming, not only of joy as well as of sorrow but of an underground grotesque as the body comes to be divided between the state and the people, interlocking entities hovering indeterminately between being and becoming in the glow of each other's otherness, irradiated by increasingly sacred remains.[32]

In other words, attachment to a collectively held thing marks, among other things, a fantastic transpersonal intimacy, rendering a seam at the place where the political exists as an intimate sphere to one side of politics. Marina Warner links this to ancient and Catholic assumptions that a god's human embodiment is not mimetic but representation plus, a scene of encounter with numena, not of masochism, anesthesia, or overreading. Agamben extends this story, arguing that it is wrong of Ernst Kantorowicz to compress the king into the two bodies human and political, a bifurcation dedicated to explaining how it can be that the sovereign is the law and yet does not take the law with "him" when he dies.[33] The political body becomes the sovereign's, Kantorowicz argues, when he comes to embody the articulation of the human to the transhistorical right of law. When the sovereign dies, however, the right of law does not die with him but transfers to whomever replaces him at that conjuncture.

Agamben argues that this model does not account for the element of the sacred that imbues the sovereign with something inhuman and impersonal that becomes his quality and not that of the formal office. For example, he points out that the murder of the sovereign is never deemed a homicide because the sovereign is not an *homme*. His murder is not a sacrifice either, although the language of sacrifice might be deployed to distract from the fact that the law cannot be sacrificed to the law. Even when the modern representative politician transgresses, he cannot be laid bare to the law as such while he is in office, merely exposed to the pseudo-law of, say, the impeachment trial, which can remove him from office. But even then he would only be human in a juridical sense, continuing to carry in his person the sacred illumination that derives from his embodiment of law as such. This is perhaps why the courts yielded to President Clinton's oft-asserted refusal to testify in real time: they were trying to preserve something of his inhumanity, his sacred superhumanity.

What difference does it make to think of the sacred aspect of contemporary mass iconicity, especially where it intersects with the political? Agamben's and my own main interest is in understanding the relation of democracy and state violence. He wants to shatter the paradigm that claims the law's rational sovereignty to itself according to the engines of interest that drive the Rousseauian general will. He uses the inhuman body of the sovereign who can be killed but not sacrificed to establish the performative consecration of law's absoluteness as in fact the "operative presupposition" of nations, democratic and otherwise.[34] This does not mean that there is no difference between sacred and secular states, or sovereign kings and representative presidents, but that the sovereignty of law in modern political worlds retains the traces of the logic of hallowed embodiment.

Agamben and Lefort associate the seduction of spectacular political embodiment with fascism and fascistic tendencies within capitalist democracies: whether or not one accedes to this bodily analogy, however, the analysis fortifies the mass cultural context of explanation for the phenomenon of overvaluation of the dead-too-soon icon whose popular appeal I have been tracking. It links these icons to the sublime and ridiculous ghostly representations of dead presidents, such as the now queerly supervalent nineteenth-century image of the heavenly George Washington taking Abraham Lincoln in his arms, and the ghostly homosocial utopia of the 1969 Dion song "Abraham, Martin, and John."[35] Both of these scenes now can be read to show that the president has never been human, but instead circulates in a realm of principle, desire, and sacred autonomy that turns the democratic ideal of representation and representative democracy somewhat on its head. The sovereign, as embodied law, sublates the fallen flesh, taking it to something beyond ordinariness or the human. Diana and John F. Kennedy Jr., in turn, represent this hallowed aspect of publicness that citizens and subjects are trained to desire, but they go the politician one better as celebrities in the political sphere who possessed only symbolic power and so whose deaths are not accompanied by the ambivalence of the memory of their power over life and death. To love the law in this displaced yet sacred way is to ratify its irrationality, its auratic linkage to the beyond of history and humanity. This is one reason why the language of love is never out of place enough in the discussion of law; its fulfillment is also ultimately confirmed in a beyond of life in which it cannot be experienced.

These figures, then, at once human and superhuman, circulate as an achieved intimacy, a performative condensation of a collective desire to be possessed by a future that the ordinary person has no access to living, and the opportunity for which has now passed on. These figures displace attention to questions of the efficacy of social movements, politics engendered not around repetitions of spectacular failure and optimism but around political claims. In particular, the doubled ghost seems to speak of an attachment to public figures that move in undivided and undivisive realms near but not in politics. These are juxtapolitical intimate publics in nuce, auto-poetic in that they are formed in a flash around an event that they also create—for example, the event of the death turns into the event of mourning. But they do not last as publics long after the intensity of mourning fades, except as a memory. It is as though these dead-too-soon personae represent a hole in the historical fabric through which the hierarchies of violence and alterity that we associate with the lawlessness of the law might, finally, *not* be reproduced. In their estrangement from sovereign normativity they might represent something like a lost revolutionary wrinkle in time, as the articulation of the sacred *against* the political, here seen not as sovereign but as fallen law. In this way a juxtapolitical celebrity culture of mourning expresses a critical political position indeed. But it can only find negative articulation as personal loss and narcissistic wound, and political *relation* not to the nation-state but to other spectators of the failures enfigured by these dead-too-soon ciphers. What else does one make of the repetition of Diana-like mourning in the mass precipitation of flowers onto the New York City sidewalk right where Kennedy lived? Offerings like these constitute the mode of social participation du jour, for sure. But the gesture is a way of marking that one has been touched by the optimism of an attachment to the pre- and postpolitical, now made into the intimacy of belonging to an impersonal collectivity organized by loss that can serve as a topic for intimate conversation among strangers. This is a time of strange intensities if vigils and flowers dedicated to celebrity deaths and big suffering count as gestures toward salvaging civic optimism.

Stjepan Meštrović argues that the United States is a postemotional society.[36] This counterintuitive observation makes a kind of uncanny sense in that one so often sees performances of empathic attachment that can, one feels, barely resonate beyond the moment in which a confirming recognition happens. Meštrović dryly refers to President Clinton's capacity to "feel your pain": but who is to say that emotional artifice is empty if insincere, or when it is? In this context it makes no sense to trivialize as a kind of mass bad taste the collective urge to mourn the political in these cases of recent mass witnessing. The situation is much more complicated than that. First, the kitsch version of political trauma lays bare the importance of technologies of feeling for organizing a mass national experience of structural violence into a form that gets sensed as ordinariness. Second, historically viewed, national sentimentality has legitimated imperial and internal violence by linking opinion to right consciousness or feeling. It is not that empathic feeling is itself a bad thing, as the desire to feel inside of an intimate impersonal collectivity can have many different effects. It might ground resistance to political powerlessness; it might be a counterhegemonic drive that survives on small objects until the right one comes along; it might confirm what we already know, that publicity marks danger while private but collective spectatorship protects participants in it. One can spin a dozen optimistic and pessimistic stories about the traffic in violence with which citizens of mass society are trained to identify: from schadenfreude, pleasure at the suffering of others, to self-confirming pain, to an experience of the unlivable event that induces a will in someone or a public to take risks for change. But the repetition of empathic events does not in itself create change.

Third, the activity of this technology of generalization into an intimate political public does not homogenize all violent events into an equivalent logic of importance. Different forms and scales of articulation are taken on by formal events of public mourning. For the superhuman icon, special issues of paper and broadcast magazines and journals generate a buzz and a memory of the excited feeling the celebrity used to elicit, along with the frenzy of mournful attention that marks a continued attachment to normative democracy, even though the figure of democracy is of a generalized lost or wasted potentiality. For those whose violent destinies also distinguish them from the iconic liberal human whose life flows out from his sovereign acts, other sites and practices of mourning register ordinary traumatic impacts. These events are barely memorialized in the mass-mediated public and circulate thereafter very differently in semi-privatized worlds of collective memory.

The difference between these two scenes of privatization in the face of the failure of politics measures the ongoing and painful life of what Elspeth Probyn would call *outside belonging*.[37] Jacques Rancière points out that the *proletarii* are etymologically "those who do nothing but reproduce their own multiplicity and who, for this very reason, do not deserve to be counted."[38] The bodies are *too much*; the people are *not enough*. This is why I have adapted the philosopher Sue Golding's language of denegation to mark the limit of the democratic discourse of rights and legitimacy. Liberality is a necessary procedure, and yet as ideology it is a "pacifying procedure"[39] that works as a hegemonic lure only at the moment that democracy looks like a level playing ground or a mode of general admission. In a universalist culture whose units of inclusion and exclusion are formally legal the incommensurateness between legal standing and social membership (between formal inclusion in the law and informal domination) militates against the general citizenship of the enfleshed or sarco-subject.[40] She may become politically denegated but this has never yet erased the genealogy of inhumanity her body represents for its privileged others in so many symbolic, institutional, and economic contexts of production.

Mass longing for figures harmed and made sacred by proximity to politics reenacts the dynamic of optimism that has solidified the seeming inevitability of unequal bodily destinies in the United States. Intimate publics periodically are taken over by such longing, the longing that returns consciousness to mourning or rebelling against the lived historical field of democracy's failings. But when these emotional reinvestments in the political over politics take up idioms of belonging rather than revolt, the question remains: Must the critical act bind people more passionately to the attenuating promise or can it fray that binding at the same time, embodying a transformative sarco-politics that forces the logic of democracy to change in the face of the limits of the capaciousness of formal "recognition"?

Even as I consider the question, though, spectacles of sexuality, suffering, and impeded suffrage always take me to *The Island of Lost Souls*.[41] In this film animals are transformed into men in a room they call "the house of pain"—the one to which Emerson also refers at the outset of this chapter. In this room animal beings become capaciously human. "Take me to the house of pain," they plead, where through unanaesthetized suffering and cutting they become "men." To be more human is to understand pain as the pedagogy that engenders respect for the law: it is an ethics of cruel optimism. Abstraction is held out as an ideal to which the men can aspire, and surviving pain on behalf of the political produces the ghost that guarantees the right to abstraction. At the same time, though, bodily pain is a burden the animal-men seek proudly to bear, as if submitting their bodies to the law, becoming cuts of meat for the body politic, were almost as good as enjoying the conceptual freedom of the law. Maybe it is. Nevertheless, the scientist cannot make more than one woman, and she cannot be a man before the law. The female animal is even more embodied than the animal-men by becoming a person; yet she is even less human than they are because she attracts the law, bringing it down to the shameful sensation of its own bodily particularity. Of course this is the standard critique of the embodied: they reduce the world to their level. Flesh begets flesh. This is a story about sexuality as a figure for political embodiment in a system that claims to abjure it. But contradictions like this cannot be dissolved, only sublimated, and barely that, within the liberal regime of law's promise to relieve subjects from their bodies and locate freedom in their feelings.

## REMEMBERING LOVE, FORGETTING
## EVERYTHING ELSE  *Now, Voyager*

> I wish I understood you. . . . There's something
> about you, yourself, that I can't get hold of. . . .
> Why, I simply don't know you!
> CASEY ROBINSON, *NOW, VOYAGER*

> Falling in love is not a good way of getting to
> know someone.
> ADAM PHILLIPS, "ON LOVE"

### The Ideology of Normal Love

Love is the enemy of memory. But this is a paradox. For love is a much memorialized, mourned, and fetishized feeling that invests institutions of intimacy such as the couple and the family with the power to organize life and the memory of life across generations and millennia, nations and worlds. But in order to twist its public and world-ordering function into a matter of personal and private agency, love's conventional practice is antimemorial. In the modern ideology of normal love, lovers learn to aspire to forget the stories they already know about the self-amputation, vulnerability, and social coercion so frequently and so intimately linked with what love's institutions identify as mature happiness.[1] I am not suggesting here that all couples and families survive on a diet of toxic optimism in the face of inevitable amorous failure, or that the noise of romantic love is the activity of false consciousness. Rather, there are multiple motives for the desire to forget—to drown out, to diminish, to reshape, to repress, to remotivate, to sublimate—the standard traumas of intimacy, whenever love enters in.[2] This is a chapter about femininity, optimism, and some therapeutic genres of bargaining to stay near love that shape so much of what magnetizes consumers to the situations circulating in women's intimate public.

When I write here of love, and of the nostalgia for amnesia it brings, I am working from the archives of modern heterosexuality in the United States, a public domain of personal life whose conventions saturate the documents of women's culture.[3] In previous chapters I have described women's culture as a capitalist, culture industry phenomenon dating from the nineteenth century in the United States that promotes a core form of gendered personhood for women; its diverse texts are linked by the claim that women identify with each other *as women* despite the myriad economic, social, and political forces that create differences and antagonisms among them. What links women across these fractures is the identification of women with the pleasures and burdens of reproducing everyday life in the family, which in the United States, since the end of the nineteenth century and the beginning of the twentieth, has meant, among other things, being charged with managing dynamics of affective and emotional intimacy. The identification of women with affect and emotion is a complex thing, not just a projection of the view that women feel more powerfully than they think, a cliché that can make women seem both trivial and magnificent. In the intimate sphere of public femininity the passionate irrational attachments of affect and the normative transactions of emotionality shape women's psychic and social lives and their responsibility to other people's lives.[4] Women's emotional expertise and the improvisations around it animate investigations, debate, and advice about managing shared and unshared feeling, and femininity emerges as a scene of affective and emotional experience, expertise, and ethics. Women are not only expected to be compassionate and understanding, but to act both as teachers of compassion and surrogates for others' refusals or incapacities to feel appropriately and intelligently. This intimate public circulates capacious debate about the fairness and consequences of this circuit of emotional responsibility. Its discussions of the affective and emotional work of intimacy tend to take the shape of debates about the costs of and desires for heteronormative convention. The main conventional frame for such debate is the plot about the causalities and the casualties of love—a conventional plot about conventionality where comic, tragic, and melodramatic modes all circulate through discussions of the emotional extremities, stresses, and moments of relief women face within ordinary life.

The modern love plot requires that, if you are a woman, you must at least *entertain* believing in love's capacity both to rescue you from your life and to give you a new one, a fantasy that romantic love's narratives constantly invest with beauty and utopian power.[5] To be needed (by a lover, children, a family, or all of them, in a nimbus of intimate connections) demonstrates your feminine worth: it is in this sense that the institutions of heterosexual love provide normative locations for imagining the feminine good life. During the Victorian period, experts located in the *family* form love's main capacity to build worlds; in the period after World War I it became love's purpose to place the *couple* at the heart of social being, to designate its two-as-one as at the core of normative personhood. Even in an era of rhizomatic connections across networks of intimates a romantically unsutured person is exposed to public commentary about not "really living" and being abjectly "alone." This chapter's historical archive is located mainly between the world wars. But insofar as women's intimate public preserves the logics of previous promises for institutionalizing or making dependable the feminine good life, I would claim that popular culture constantly reinvents the love plot as a figure for optimism, while maintaining women's culture's strong ambivalence about believing in and relinquishing this promise.

Meanwhile it has been the purpose of love's commodities to make its institutions of intimacy seem like social relations that flow naturally from urges and desires for attachment. It is said that being in a loving couple or family should make you feel safe from the world, in the world, and for the world; and even if, at the threshold, intimacy feels risky, the institutions of intimacy are supposed to protect you from remembering and therefore from feeling that risk acutely, so that you might build up a sense of love's reliability, its promise of stimulating yet balancing security. At the same time, the ideology of normal love secures security against the specter of utter exposure that is said to be experienced by those who live their lives in public, outside of an institution of privacy. The failure to achieve privacy is still a charge that defines gays and lesbians, as well as single people, adulterers, and the stereotypical family on state welfare. People who are unhinged or unhitched, who live outside of the normative loops of property and reproduction, are frequently seen both as symptoms of personal failure and threats to the general happiness, which seems to require, among other things, the positioning of any person's core life story in a plot of love's unfolding, especially if that person is a woman.

During the first four decades of the twentieth century, the heyday of film melodrama leading up to the Hollywood "women's film,"[6] Olive Higgins Prouty wrote a series of five novels about the erotic and economic upheavals in an aristocratic Boston family named Vale: *White Fawn, Lisa Vale, Now, Voyager, Home Part*, and *Fabia*, the main archival resource of this chapter. The geographical, class, and racial specificity of this family and the multinovel saga organized around it provide a great test case for comprehending the techniques of generalization through plots about love that remediate the details that bind people to women's intimate public.

In the way that an effectively executed genre can produce "the license one feels with another victim of a common malady," these novels are saturated by popular theatrical and cinematic markers that have penetrated the ways literary figures encounter themselves, each other, and the world.[7] Gestures are called melodramatic and memories are called flashbacks; intense gazes are called close-ups and long shots; and frivolity is likened to what happens in vaudeville and circuses. Prouty even theatricalizes the "troupe" of emotions and represents characters processing experience as though they are watching themselves performing cinematic interior monologues. "Charlotte's information, as far as knocks were concerned and what goes on afterwards behind closed doors, was confined to the stage, the screen and the written page" (Prouty 97, 282–84). Triangulated through genres marking intensified emotion, these literary techniques aim to produce, while seeming merely to confirm, a sense of intimately shared affective continuity among producers, viewers, and readers: but it is important to emphasize that continuity is not the same as alikeness. Often in Prouty's work people do not know who they are or what they feel: indeed, the more uncertain the figure is, the more likely her status as heroine. Here the bar for inclusion in the intimate public requires little more than a general sense of recognition of someone's *situation*. The "situation" is a central genre of the intimate public. Prouty expects the consumer to affirm that *x* situation would likely produce suffering, desire, vulnerability, and/or confusion and to be interested in the managerial response the story details in the face of such results, even if accompanied by alterity or critique: *I can understand why someone would feel that way; I don't know if I would have handled it that way.* But in the intimate public maintaining the circuit of continuities requires that the participant sense realism in the staging of life lived at the emotional extremes.

In the Vale saga no lover of any gender escapes conscious bitter knowledge of the vexed relation between love or the love plot's promise of rescue and the real life of intimacy, where maintaining devotion to forms of optimistic attachment requires convoluted bargains with practices of social obligation, insincerity, and sexual self-alienation. But love's promise to rescue the subject from her default life by installing her in proximity to intimate conventionality is not merely posed as a struggle between fake freedom and real imprisonment, delusional optimism and inevitable disappointment. The interest of the love plot in women's intimate public is as a scene of bargaining, calibration, adaptation, technique. Prouty's corpus opens up love as a traumatic environment *and* a compelling scene of desire, both the worst *and* the best resource for fulfilling someone.

Prouty is unusual in women's popular culture for the clarity with which she foregrounds ambivalence as an inevitable component of desire. The novels presume familiarity with the experience of extimacy: the strangeness and unpredictability of one's erotic attachments, the estrangement at the heart of the intimate, the constant swerve between the desire to be known and not, to be enigmatic and not, to know and not know who the lover is and what one wants to receive and to give.[8] Prouty is deft at portraying people who are easily overwhelmed by the normative demands of intimacy and the strange, wavering intensities of erotic attachment. Her figures live life optimistically only so long as they can negotiate intimate attachment from a near distance while maintaining proximity to it.[9] For her literary figures, the best, livable love thrives by being *around* love, not being taken in possession by it.

The tragicomic saga of the Vales' familial intimacy is, nonetheless, a forum for hetero-female complaint about the inadequacy of most intimates to step up to the bar of affective reciprocity. But it is more than that too. The novels are populated by asexual, autotelic, gay, lesbian, and self-described "queer" characters as well as fretful heterosexuals. (In Prouty's work the word "queer" has the most contemporary of meanings—it is assigned to people whose sexuality makes them anomalous to the whole field of normalizing taxonomy.)[10] While the protagonists are women, both genders suffer terribly from unhappy transactions with the intimate world; what makes women special and singularly women is the burden they bear of producing emotional clarity for others and protecting everyone's optimism for intimacy's potentially lifting effects, while often feeling queasy about it themselves—until love returns to remind them of its centrality to optimism and living itself.

The first novel of the series, *White Fawn*, opens on the day that its heroine, Fabia Vale, has a coming-out party, by which I mean the kind that officially announces her heterosexual availability to the marriageable male members of her class. Androgynous and ambivalent in her ordinary body, Fabia has never fit into the gendered expectations of her social context, as she has associated more with tomboy grit than feminine glamour: and on the day of her coming-out party she is especially uncomfortable. But on the way to the room where she is meant to make the requisite sumptuary transformation into adult heterofemininity by putting on a slinky dress, Fabia sees her mother necking illicitly with a male lover, a treasured old friend of the family. This primal scene sunders Fabia from the normal love plot for about a decade's worth of novels: she threatens to become cold, a career girl. The novel named *Fabia*, though, forces her back to love's conventional narrativity only in the very last sentence on the very last page, as her lover leaves to risk his life for his country in World War II. The fourth novel of the series, *Home Port*, is also set during the war. It chronicles two related sexual crises: that of Fabia's brother, Murray Vale, whom everyone (including himself) thinks is gay, as he is a so-called pansy; and Nora Brock, whom everyone (including herself) suspects is gay as well because of her extreme masculinity. The two come to make the perfect modernist couple. They embody the sexologist's view of what distinguishes modern personhood: bigendered heterosexuals.[11]

All of the novels in this saga perform a fantasy reconciliation of everyone's sexual ambivalence: the messy trajectories of attraction, identification, aversion, desire, aggression, coercion, loss, and sheer self-incoherence all bound up in love make a kind of narrative peace with the heterosexual couple and the family form. But it is only a kind of peace. In Prouty's work the family is not a space for the successful performance of love but rather a scene in which the trauma of love's failures can be experienced, endured, and mourned as a kind of loyalty oath to an ideal image of fulfilling intimacy. Heterosexuality, as Étienne Balibar has said, provides that image of metacultural unity.[12] Prouty queers the Vale family by making it remember heterosexuality. Her love plots are wedges, providing openings for exploring women's psychological and social compulsion to imitate conventional intimacy modes; but she makes love into a crisis in the terms of the subject's coherence rather than an expressive performance of someone's subjective authenticity. I have suggested that in her oeuvre people in love do not know what they are doing: they chase after and run away from their attachments, and when they get exhausted, they become depressed. Their depression leads to drama, then adaptation, but not to revolution.[13] The novels, in short, address and remake the impact of erotic ambivalence by exploiting the love plot's negativity, the way it tends to raise and erase its own complexity as it accumulates story in the service of its apparently inevitable resolution. To be in proximity to the *sense* of resolution without the trauma of revolution stands in for something like mental health for lovers, as we will see.

This family saga significantly departs from the one Prouty wrote in her earlier novel, *Stella Dallas*, where modern love's promise of transcendence and deracination from the determinations of history are available as grounds for and explanations of dependable life only to people with money. For the rest, romantic heterosexuality provides a motor for class mobility. In contrast, the class privilege of the Vale family opens up the space for queerness to be legitimated in the folds of the love plot: or, the normative love plot flourishes within the folds of the improvisations dramatized around it. How does Prouty manage to sustain both? That is the question of this chapter.

For the Vales generally, the class aristocracy of New England breaks down as an effect of contact with the fuzzily popular yet avant-garde process of cosmopolitan *embourgeoisement*. In the novels the culture industry condenses experience into a continuous present of desiring, while the family and re-production produce obligations to the dead and to history. Queer being in the family is made possible by the victory of the culture industry version of love over the traditionalist normative love of familial life. It is not as though mass culture models of personality aren't conventional, however. But, as Eli Zaretsky has argued, the complex articulation of mass social conventions of normative personality and an increasingly intensified subjective experience in modernity seems to promise unprecedented sensual self-development. It becomes impossible to pry apart self-cultivated subjective experience from mass cultural mediation: the main trick of capitalist modernism is to make one's self-performance feel like a choice and not a submission to tradition or banality.[14] In this case the remediation of personality and personhood relies on a shift of class markers within whiteness (see fig. 27). As the aristocratic Vale family turns middle class, its ancient and lifeless hereditary bodies become live ones wearing fashionable clothes and talking in jive vernaculars. In *Now, Voyager*, the once fireless living room where hot tea was once sipped by cold people is now the place where family members of all generations come to eat "wieners" and chips and swing to the "primitive rhythm of a rumba" and the atavistic strains of jazz (338–39). When white aristocrats imagine emancipation, they curse like sailors, make casual racial slurs, and say aloud that they want to be made love to.

Yet the seeming exhaustion of the aristocratic habitus among the Vales does not comprise a radical shift. Prouty focuses on what is therapeutic about the recalibration of imperial banality and traditional aristocratic white racialism. She prefers the off-color white universalism of mass society, with its "benign" notions of racial mixing as something that happens in the culture, not among bodies. If the culture is more jazzed than the subject, the subject does not have to claim ownership of pleasure. Tourist and pop-culture imperial racism can also make entrenched hierarchy seem thoughtless, like littering, so that it is possible to continue feeling racially and socially superior while the body experiences expressively the intensities of slumming rhythms and deshamed pleasures. Thus when one character says, "What seems to be my type may be just my technique," he refers to the therapeutic and liberating effects of seeing personality as a skill that releases the subject from his singular negativity and historical legacies (Prouty 78). Seeing personality

## 27

In a descending trail of dirt and darkness, the *Now, Voyager* poster associates sexuality with a fall from class and sexual superiority.

as an aspirational technique that interrupts your habit or history of being rather than makes you into what you imitate enables Prouty to write love as wonderfully and dangerously queering. Love becomes a relay to a domain of fantasy-mediated ongoing presentness where a general emotional atmosphere of entitled belonging makes possible anyone's potentially unlimited enjoyment of "everything and everybody" (Prouty 185).

Narrating change without shattering trauma, then, Prouty's love plots operate according to a logic of benign variation and soft-seeming supremacy: racial and economic superiority in the new cosmopolitan modernity are always overshadowed by love's lifting, abstracting, and shimmering luminosity. Love makes possible flourishing and living on amid all sorts of converging contradictions. In the end, all novels in the Vale chronicle perform a bargain between what they know about the social and subjective operations of the institutions of intimacy and the dream of love's superpower they cannot relinquish for fear of having no hope about anything. This bargain is the subject of this chapter: what does it cost to remember love while forgetting everything else?

## The Business of Love

As many scholars have argued, since the early twentieth century in the United States this dream of modern love has marshaled vast cultural resources to produce people who identify with it. Social historians of the couple, the family, and sexuality see the selling of heterosexual and heterofamilial love as central to understanding a cluster of transformations of U.S. society during the period after World War I. The first of these is economic, involving developments in the circuits of capital and the production of new subjectivities. A "new order was evolving that was characterized by giant corporations oriented to national markets": and "getting individuals to identify a range of their physical, psychological and social needs with [national] commodities [was] integral" to their project.[15] At the same time sexuality itself was becoming a more public form, accompanied by expanded premarital modes of sexual experience such as dating, as well as by a commodity culture of its own.[16] The public campaign to normalize national culture after the war advocated a marriage between sexual and commodity desire, but this social energy had to be regulated by a model and modal middle-class family.[17]

Feminist historians have shown how complex, how liberatory, and how constraining *the sexualization of all desire* was for women.[18] On the one hand, the increasingly public scene of erotic plenitude allowed women finally to own their sexual desire legitimately, independent of identification with any particular partner; on the other hand, sex radicals, sexologists, and social conservatives worried that the feminist and capitalist promotion of erotic intensity would encourage women to become lawless serial monogamists, or lesbians, or both. Conjugal heterosexual intercourse was then reinvented as both *a* normal need and *the* normal need a woman must fulfill in order to be healthy.[19]

The women's culture industry was one site for the production of such a feminized subject. The woman who was adequate to its version of normal femininity was as powerful as a feminist would aspire to be, but she was *mainly* invested in the family and cognate emotional networks. She was socially important because she could mediate the worldly temptations of capitalist culture and the processes of family intimacy. Then, as payback for her absorption in the service economy of family life and social reproduction *and* for her own mental and physical health, she was encouraged to fulfill her sexuality, but only through monogamous heteromarital practice.[20]

Given this mix of emancipations and constraints, it is not surprising that myriad forms of therapeutic publicity accompanied the utopian suturing of desire to ordinary life promised by mass cultural conventions of modern love. In particular a burgeoning industry of expert and quasi-expert advice columns and self-help articles in women's and "family" magazines became dedicated to helping women identify their lot with the constant disappointment that comes from life's failure to fulfill love's promise.[21] This is to say that the therapeutic ideology of women's culture was both half-critical and wholly affirmative: validating the fantasy of love that assigns it the power to make a safe and lasting intimate world; and providing therapeutic explanation and tactics for surviving once the project of rescue fails. In other words, it reproduces the mistake or the lie of the ideology of normal love, which markets love's utopian project as a practical one whose failures do not inhere in its conceptual or institutional shape or social contexts, but in the lover herself or her faulty intimates. The individual bears the burden of adjusting to bad theory. The ideology of normal love can only survive when the relation between the utopian and the practical contexts for loving is a relation of amnesia or displacement. In what follows cliché will stand as the main genre of displacement central to securing a place for normative love in U.S popular culture.

This is why love's attack on memory is not usually considered a bad thing. Love is supposed to transcend or at least to neutralize the contradictions of history. When people enter into love's contract with the promise of recognition and reciprocity, they hope memory will be reshaped by it, minimizing out the evidence of failure, violence, ambivalence, and social hierarchy that would otherwise make love a most anxious desire for an end to anxiety. A fantasy norm unevenly bolstered by the institutions that are said to be its main supports, then, modern love requires the lover to produce an epistemology that works against the defenses of knowledge. In this convention, when love fails, the trauma of memory becomes a scar the failed lover carries around for life, declaring it as deserving of care, nostalgia, and mourning.

But what is the failed lover ultimately mourning, if not the amnesia love's optimism creates?

## The Intimate Journal of Miss Charlotte Vale, Spinster

Prouty felt ambivalent about the embrace of her texts by the gendering machine of women's culture. Referring to radio, stage, and cinematic remakes of *Stella Dallas*, she angrily disparaged the heroic claims about suffering in women's melodrama and soap opera, where love's career as a traumatic ordeal so often ends up as a test of simplified moral clarities.[22] The novel of *Now, Voyager* tries to inoculate itself from ahistorical and apsychological sentimental appropriation, but in many ways Irving Rapper's 1942 filmic adaptation is a cliché version of the novel, largely sanitized of the novel's ambivalence toward the demands of love on femininity. In fact, both Prouty and Bette Davis expressed dismay at the normativity of Casey Robinson's screenplay, and together they all reworked the script.[23] I will return to this difference later but will also move across the novel, screenplay, and final film cut where they converge. For these versions of *Now, Voyager* display important similarities, specifically in the optimism they show about what therapy can do for women who suffer from disorders of love, women paralyzed by memories of family trauma and failed desire, barely surviving the history of their amorous disappointment, their saturation by failure in the present, and their inability to think any future without love's promise of coherence. This is what motivates the novel's totemic citation, Walt Whitman's poem "The Untold Want." This poem is given to Charlotte as a gift from her therapist as she departs from a sanitarium: "The untold want, by life and land ne'er granted,/Now, Voyager, sail thou forth, to seek and find" (Prouty 66). Providing the book's title, the poem also stands on the title page of the novel as a gift to the reader and the condensation of Prouty's therapeutic ambitions.

In *Now, Voyager*, one version of the "untold want" is the anomalous life and scandalous knowledge normal culture suppresses, and its method is tourism. Charlotte's only strong erotic attachments take place on cruises where she practices a sort of erotic tourism—"be interested in everything and everybody," admonishes her doctor. She even chronicles the first love affair in a fetish object of love's photographic memorabilia that she calls *The Intimate Journal of Miss Charlotte Vale*—in the film, she adds the word

*Spinster* bitingly to the title (Robinson 70). This addition derives from a story the novel tells elsewhere about the threat that one might become a spinster, a so-called queer one, an unlovable one. Charlotte's mother threatens her with this possibility and mentions one case, clearly derived from the Salem witch trials, whose story circulates in the Vale caste to strike terror into the hearts of other women with abnormal or untold wants. The spinster's name is Stephanie Stebbins; she is a local woman whose "queerness broke out . . . when she was only fourteen."[24] As an adult she is said to be "one of those pathological cases of a spinster masquerading as an irresistible young girl, usually found in insane asylums, but sometimes seen wandering around at large. . . . in absurdly youthful costumes" (Prouty 184–85).

*Now, Voyager* is the homeopathic other to Charlotte's book and to the spinster's story. Set against these images of the queer, unlovable, insane, unpleasantly sexual, and unpleasantly nonsexual spinster exposed to scrutiny and public commentary is Prouty's optimism about the value therapy can have for those suffering the effects of erotic and familial love trauma. This optimism is derived, in major part, from Prouty's own life. *Pencil Shavings*, her largely cheerful autobiography of 1961, tells of a life full of her crushes on women, her and her husband's marital and maternal abjection, and their numerous nervous breakdowns (for which the designated therapy was *writing*). Her therapist, Austen Fox Riggs, was a proponent of mental hygiene ideology and advocated tricks and techniques of rational self-interruption as a neutralizing force against nervous disorder.[25] The novel of *Now, Voyager* directly utilizes Prouty's shattering experiences of gendering and sexualization and fictionalizes her treatment. But for all its critique of the rhetoric of feminine passionlessness and feminine duty, Prouty's writing offers its own version of the genericizing dialectic of women's culture narrative as a whole. It sees the mental and emotional *interestingness* of women as directly related to the arsenal of intricate maneuvers they must develop in order not to be suppressed entirely by the world of banality they are supposed to desire. It also presumes that at some level all women want at least approximate membership in the world of heteronormative femininity, however ambivalently. In Prouty's work the intersection of life and love at the core of feminine gendering keeps being rejected and resurrected: from this perspective the "untold want" may express the simple desire that the promise of romance to enable a general flourishing be fulfilled, after all, but not in a dominating way. But how is it possible that good can come from formulas and clichés that claim to express every woman's desire for a love plot, despite what she already knows of the costs of the normative institutions of intimacy? *Now, Voyager* takes up this question—of love as a traumatic disorder; of clichés and their relation to mental health; of memory as a danger to the project of living optimistically—as its explicit narrative situation. More than many texts of women's culture, it attempts to imagine a better bargain between the woman's historicized erotic self-understanding and that seemingly more positive thing—the memory of optimism for love's transcendence.

Here is the novel's story. Charlotte Vale was born when her mother was in her late forties, shortly before her beloved father's death. Mrs. Vale takes consolation in the "unpleasant fact" of Charlotte by making her live only as a daughter, only in terms of the mother's drives and desires. Under pressure from her mother's resentful, possessive, and authoritarian style of loving Charlotte constructs a secret, sensual life: this doubleness eventuates in a serious nervous breakdown. Charlotte goes to a sanitarium named Cascade, which is headed by a Dr. Jaquith. There, in the course of her recovery, she transforms from a "fat lady with heavy brows" into a svelte sexual woman with closely cropped hair; and she comes to assume a public autonomy from the love plot and the family narrative (Prouty 82).

As the novel opens Charlotte has just left Cascade and is taking the sea voyage the title speaks of.[26] At first, she remains crippled by two powerful memories of love, one involving her mother's discipline and the other the romance that Charlotte had had a decade before on another pleasure cruise, that time to Africa. That affair was interrupted by her mother, whose antipathy to heterosexual lust was matched only by her antipathy to the leveling effects of consumer culture and the working-class origins of Charlotte's chosen lover. Charlotte's newly beautiful body radically interrupts the personality and the history that had been organized around it by her mother (Prouty 14–15, 20–21). She feels that she does not know how to act in this new body, and so she reproduces what she has "absorbed" from other women—her sister-in-law, Lisa Vale, and her friend Renée Beauchamp, women casual in their comfort with the performance of feminine elegance and lubricative social ease (Prouty 14). Notably, Beauchamp is well-known for her "imitations"; her capacity for improvisation is her most valued feminine skill, and everyone who meets Charlotte when she is passing as Beauchamp expects performances of it from her.

As for Charlotte, "Somewhere she had read, 'act an emotion, and you'll be more likely to feel it'" (Prouty 255). And, yet, "One cannot escape from one's personality by dressing up in costume" (Prouty 53). So the *therapeutic* point is that embodied imitation of what she has absorbed of femininity is not emancipatory performativity, as Charlotte does not aspire to be who she is acting as. As I argued with regard to *Imitation of Life*, however, sometimes imitation is a route not to becoming another kind of being, but to shedding the being one is dragging around unhappily. Here, imitation as self-negation provides a route to health. As the book opens, Charlotte accepts an offer of a cigarette: "[It was the] first time in her life she had smoked a cigarette except opposite her own reflection behind closed doors. . . . But she hadn't smoked the cigarette to assert her own personality. On the contrary she'd smoked it to conceal her own personality" (Prouty 3).

If prior to the breakdown Charlotte concealed her erotic openness, her new method of open concealment is a mode of embodied but inexpressive inauthenticity directed first toward becoming not herself and eventually toward *licensing her to imitate her own bodily practices emotionally*. Her body becomes a horizon to which her subjectivity has to catch up.

Doubly unbound to history and personality, Charlotte opens to unprecedented and reckless experiments in seduction, sensation, and public heterosexuality. On the ship she has an emotional and lightly sexual affair with a married man, J. D. Durrance. When she comes home she becomes engaged to Elliot Livingston, a conventional man who can offer her the three magic things she has learned that every woman "marries for": "a home of her own, a child of her own, and a man of her own" (Prouty 232–33). (In the film, Charlotte invents this phrase to describe her desire; in the novel, her sister-in-law, Lisa Vale, says it, and Charlotte imitates it as per usual, taking it on as a mantra that she utters to absorb it into her self-understanding [Prouty 264].) When Eliot kisses her erotically she worries that, though she feels nothing now, she will eventually become sexually attracted to him because she is made of "common" or "carnal clay" (Prouty 239). But, "instinctively attracted" only to her lover and not her fiancé, Charlotte cannot pull off the artifice of normalcy long enough to feel it (Prouty 255). Her ensuing refusal of a life story made from within intimacy's institutions so infuriates her mother that she dies while arguing with Charlotte about it. This cluster of catastrophes spins Charlotte into a second nervous breakdown, and not just from a sense of her own sexual and criminal guilt. Without the institutions of the couple and the family to structure her existence, she has nothing else permanent through which to imagine her life.

So she reinvents the institutions of intimacy. During Charlotte's second institutionalization at Cascade she meets up with someone who evokes her youthful self: a tiny preteenager named Tina, a girl who closets herself in a room and paints, who calls herself "queer," and who has become anxious, anorexic, and neurotic in response to *her* mother's aversive love (Prouty 241). Charlotte saves the abject girl from her family, taking her into the Vale family home as a kind of surrogate daughter. Charlotte also turns to rescuing other victims of love, using her wealth to build a wing of Cascade specifically for children traumatized by the family, here figured in toxic mothers and patriarchal, absent fathers. However, the child Charlotte rescues is Durrance's daughter. Under the guise of their shared concern for Tina, the lovers can meet pseudo-legitimately.

However, this act of rescue requires that Charlotte sacrifice any prospects for sexual contact with J. D. The sublimity of this sacrifice at the film's close has helped to make it a classic American melodrama. As he had done so many times in the early days of their affair, Paul Henreid (J. D.) lights two cigarettes in his mouth and gives one to Bette Davis (Charlotte). As their smoke intermingles, he asks Charlotte if the unwed life she must lead to ensure her access to Tina and to him will bring her true happiness. She says, "Oh Jerry. Don't let's ask for the moon! We have the stars!" (Robinson 223).

What does Charlotte mean by this phrase? Don't ask for a totalized object in love when we have so many bright and scattered opportunities? Or don't desire what you can't possess, and, ergo, desire what you can? Or, embrace your queerness, Jerry, don't be distracted by the big satellite when you can preserve the multiple practices and possibilities your desire has already created? Something about the difference between shining and twinkling? In the movie, the music swells when she makes this bargain, and the camera moves up to the starry sky, leaving the two lovers to their privacy. The aesthetic of endingness emphasizes the significance of this event in the gestures and sounds of melodramatic resolution, implying their new future ordinariness, their protection of that "little strip of territory" they call their own, a space of lived fantasy where they share what they call "our child" (Prouty 339, 336). In the novel, there is no soundtrack, of course: the book simply ends. But this ending *is* resonant, haunted by an earlier phrase: "The last words written in a book have only an artistic value" (Prouty 284). What is the artistic value of this phrase, the phrase that seals off the story? What does it mean for value to be "artistic" and is the implied "merely" itself part of the tragedy of what it takes to make love flourish? To answer these questions, we must go into therapy.

The person who predicts the mere formalism of the starry-eyed ending is the book's animating spirit, Dr. Jaquith. Dr. Jaquith's appearance in the Vale household initiates the narrative of the film of *Now, Voyager*, and his therapeutic strategies are at the core of the novel, competing in flashback with the mother's voice and replacing her as a source of advice about how to negotiate the intimacies that define living. As I describe love therapy in *Now, Voyager*, I will move between the novel and the film, as they mainly, with an exception I will detail below, reinforce each other.

Insofar as *Now, Voyager* legitimates a plot in which a woman chooses neither to reproduce nor to marry in the eyes of the public that knows her, it is virtually unique in the history of cinematic engagements with women's mental illness. Since the 1930s the Hollywood breakdown plot has almost entirely involved stories that track a woman's failure at heterofamilial love, a failure for which the cure is achieved through a therapist's success at bringing her to a happy adaptation to it.[27] But Jaquith not only lacks a family of his own; he does not believe that its achievement through love equals mental health for anyone (Prouty 286).

Corresponding to Jaquith's alienation from a conjugal life plot is his alienation from Freudian psychoanalytic practice. Jaquith believes that depression occurs when people's world-building drives become so damaged by a permeating memory of failure at love that they can no longer sustain any optimism about the world or about their prospects in it. In addition, he believes that for the depressed patient, the family is not a private haven from the alien public or the stressful world. It is the patient's main alien public.

Thus, in Jaquith's view, a cure can only be had within an alternative space of intimacy. He builds Cascade into a total institution that enables patients to reinvent themselves via changes in their cognitive and practical relation to their bodies, talents, and habits (Prouty 311).

Jaquith supplements this new landscape with a kind of talking cure, but his method does not involve the use of transference to dissolve symptoms by reconstructing the patient's memorial fragments into a narrative that makes a new context for them, as in Freudian psychotherapy. Patients come to Cascade when they feel disordered; they eventually leave when they feel ordered. But the world they rejoin has defined them as failures to achieve normal mood and behavior. So the second therapeutic tactic Jaquith offers employs what we might call the homeopathy of the optimistic countercliché. The analyst provides the patient with catchphrases whose utterance is like a passport into an alternate memory and personality. His formulaic images and mottos seek to displace the stifling stereotypes and normalizing customs of conventional life. Jaquith says, "Cascade is just a place in the country. People come [to it] when they're tired. . . . It's very simple really, what I try to do. People walk along a road. They come to a fork in the road. They are confused, they don't know which way to take. I just put up a signpost. Not that way, this way" (Robinson 63).

Coming from Prouty, this conceptualization of mental health in the genre of the catchphrase is not surprising. Austen Riggs, Jaquith's prototype, was more a mental hygienist than a Freudian, and his book *Just Nerves* advocates a program of rational self-interruption over Freudian models of disease that require rehardwiring the affective circuits of the person suffering from nervous disorder.[28] The novel comments constantly on the ways popular Freudianism produces new anxious self-evaluations among the lettered classes (Prouty 105, 110). I will return to Riggs's work later. *Now, Voyager* itself swerves between many different schools of popular psychoanalysis: it *is* popular psychoanalysis in aesthetic garb, as the opening poem's hybrid status as title, gift, and therapeutic self-help mantra would suggest.

The signposting strategy Jaquith uses to direct his voyager-patients "may sound preachy, but it's good talk" (Prouty 287). It involves the analyst's gift of abstract formulaic images and phrases to displace the stifling stereotypes and normalizing customs of conventional life: the stock phrase holds open a space of possibility and aspiration that the patient might use to substitute for the feeling hardwired in her: *a phrase to replace her personality*. In both the novel and the film this technique of fixing up the self appears frequently in flashback, as Charlotte repeatedly calls up pithy maxims Jaquith has given her: the aim of "her new technique" is to drown out the brutalizing idiom of maternal and familial love (Prouty 69).[29] Here is a selection from Jaquith's wisdom archive: "Independence is freedom from subjection, and reliance upon one's own will and judgment" (Prouty 202). "Ignore sensations. Discount emotions. Think, act, feel, in this order. Then thumb your nose at what you feel" (Prouty 66, 69). "Pull your own weight. . . . We've taught you the proper technique. Now go ahead and practice it on this cruise. Respond! Take Part! Contribute! Be interested in everything and everybody. Forget you're a hidebound New Englander and unbend. Loosen Up. Be nice to every human being who crosses your path" (Prouty 5). In sum, "To rid oneself of false fears by the intelligent application of one's own knowledge was one of the fundamental principles of Doctor Jaquith's philosophy" (Prouty 64). These phrases provide the evidence for why, both in the novel and the film, Jaquith is considered "professionally . . . a psychiatrist, and unprofessionally a philosopher and very wise man" (Prouty 203) who hands out "common sense" instead of "sympathy" (Robinson 187). "His speech . . . was always filled with homely similes" (Prouty 281): the book describes him as possessing Asian-style wisdom and the film likens him to God (Prouty 280–84; Robinson 205).

Jaquith's method highlights the centrality of rhetorics of stereotype, aphorism, euphemism, and rote phrases about necessity and reality to the image of women's mental and emotional health in U.S. popular culture. But why would the displacement of one set of conventionalities by another provide a relay to sanity? *Now, Voyager*'s use of case study logics to narrate Charlotte's story suggests some answers to this. First, the film and the novel present the family as a place of coercion around the subject of its collective identity: a general family view of what "we" do, who "we" are justifies the constant public measurement of every person's virtue, value, and adequacy. In Charlotte's family this judgment takes place through the exchange of valorizing or contemptuous catchphrases. For example, in the opening scene of the film and throughout the novel Charlotte's mother spouts only brutally characterizing phrases about her: the twenty-nine-year old spinster is scathingly called "the child of my old age," "my little girl," "my ugly duckling," "a moulting canary," and an "excited servant girl" (Prouty 16–17; Robinson 57, 60, 73).

Charlotte responds to this brutal deployment of anerotic orthodoxy and animalizing insult not by contesting it explicitly with her own arsenal, but by developing expertise in the field of feminine cliché, which becomes for her an elaborately developed site of coveted shameful autoeroticism. As though trying to protect a sense of Charlotte's authenticity, though, the novel and the film are unclear about how *strategic* her expertise is. On the one hand, she insists that in her thirties her relation to feminine performance is "more the result of absorption than conscious imitation" (Prouty 14); and the film never suggests that she looks to other women for ways of being that she might imitate. On the other hand, since her youth she has read intensively in works where people learn to be sexual. She does not read romance novels—but she reads everything as though it were a blueprint for a future sexualized femininity. "Charlotte had always been an omnivorous reader of fiction," Prouty writes.

> She never let a novel by Hemingway, D. H. Lawrence, Proust, Maugham, or Aldous Huxley slip by her unread. A lending library supplied her demand for modern literatures. The lending library books were all covered with uniform paper jackets, and it was not difficult to conceal from her mother all those of which she would disapprove. The books she could not obtain from a lending library she purchased, and, after reading, hid in the dark tunnels behind her sets of approved literature. The prim white bindings of Jane Austen concealed Boccaccio's *Decameron* and Flaubert's *Madame Bovary*; Thoreau, in dark green cloth and gold, screened *Ulysses*, and *Sons and Lovers*; and behind the hand-tooled leather backs of Ralph Waldo Emerson crouched Bertrand Russell and Havelock Ellis. (Prouty 97–98)

Here, transcendentalist individualism meets an autodidactic education in the radical pro-sex adult books of turn-of-the-century heterosexual high culture. To Charlotte's mother Emerson's, Thoreau's, and Austen's "hand-tooled backs" cover "good, solid" books that emphasize conscience, distinction, a disdain for ordinariness, and an upright personal style (Robinson 76).

She allows Charlotte to read them because they are antimodernist, not because they legitimate a modern, radical, self-reflexive, perfectionist individualism.

But the encounter of nineteenth- and twentieth-century elite letters here means something altogether different to Charlotte. It does not mean that she is any kind of radical, sexual or otherwise. Nor does it mean that she is bisexual, as Prouty was, or involved in a fantasmatic acting out of lesbian romance, as Patty White, Stanley Cavell, and others argue. Those readings base their conclusions about Charlotte's sexuality on the broken circuit of identification with and desire for her mother and for mothering generally; they read the film as ultimately a performance of a legitimated feminine personhood and a homosexuality enfigured in the trade Charlotte makes between heterosexual practice and caring for Tina.[30] Choosing Tina in a way that helps her queerness flourish heals the wound of Charlotte's having been so aversively chosen by her own mother. In this reading Charlotte is involved in a lesbian economy because she is choosing herself by choosing Tina.

I do not dispute that Charlotte is intensely motivated sexually, or that in choosing Tina she skirts the necessity of marrying or having sex with men. But Charlotte's sexual subjectivity is not organized by a gendered object choice; she desires something far more abstract. Conventionality is her object choice. This is how she can seem queer and normative simultaneously. She desires saturation by multiple conventionalities—stars, instead of moon. But there is nothing simple about wanting to be proximate to conventionalities.

This view of erotic object choice and sexual attachment as something other than organized by gender can best be explained by tracking what Charlotte *does* with her reading during her one and only previous love plot, which previously I have described as having taken place on an African cruise with a young working-class officer named Leslie Trotter. Prouty details what happens to Charlotte when love theory becomes passionate practice:

> She and Leslie had sat there in the dark for over an hour. He had kissed her finally. Her response had been quite different from what he had expected. Charlotte hadn't been sure what he expected. In the novels she'd read men didn't like prudes. She wasn't a young girl any more. Then Leslie had kissed her again. And still again. The third time Charlotte had felt the response which the first time she had only pretended. By the end of the fourth day she was deeply in love with Leslie Trotter. (Prouty 43)

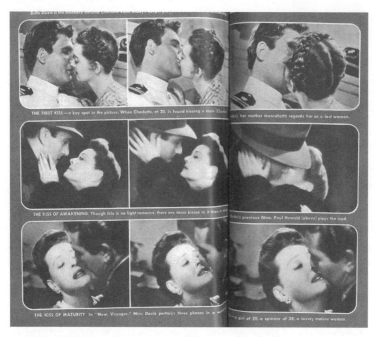

THE FIRST KISS—a key spot in the picture. When Charlotte, at 20, is found kissing a man (Char... ...el, her mother thenceforth regards her as a lost woman.

THE KISS OF AWAKENING. Though this is no light romance, there are more kisses in it than in any ...tte's previous films. Paul Henreid (above) plays the lead.

THE KISS OF MATURITY. In "Now, Voyager," Miss Davis portrays three phases in a w... ...e girl of 20, a spinster of 28, a lovely mature woman.

**28** *Now, Voyager*'s publicity uses the kiss to measure Charlotte's sexual development.

First comes reading, then experiment, then heterosexual desire, not the other way around: the aesthetic mediation of erotic practice leads Charlotte straight to normal love's narrativity (see fig. 28). As the book's ending would predict, however, the "aesthetic" is no stand-in for the sublimity of signification beyond cognition or intention. There is nothing creative or innovative about Charlotte's feeling of freedom in love. As it is, she barely understands what is happening to her: when Leslie honors her "warm, generous, gorgeous, love-making," Charlotte thinks: "No man had ever told her such a thing before. She didn't know what he meant by 'gorgeous,' exactly, but she wanted terribly to deserve his adjective" (Prouty 55).

These seven words express with devastating clarity the ways the institutions of intimacy can make a subject understand herself newly, in revolutionized ways—and yet these ways are *less* complicated than the ways she had always known. Love's gift is the subject's simplification. Charlotte wants to be adequate to the obscurity of its simplicity. To deserve an adjective she doesn't understand will give her life true meaning, somehow, so long as she can perform the experience of what she has learned to recognize as true feeling. It is as though the phrase holds open a space for escape from pain into something monumental, spectacular, and public: she feels placed on a throne by Leslie (Prouty 56; Robinson 75). The aesthetic of a conventionally romantic "as if" sexuality is a placeholder opening up a vein of vaguely imagined possibility.[31]

A decade later, the exciting memory of this prospect haunts and paralyzes Charlotte. Details and photos of the love plot she briefly lived convert into bedroom fetishes that substitute for living: "We are what our memories are," Charlotte thinks (Prouty 54). She becomes fat and aversively ugly, broadcasting on her body her *inadequacy* to the adjective, and yet for all the resignation and depression it signifies it is also the most aggressive fat that ever lived, a virtual billboard of angry femininity. How does this happen? Earlier I described how Charlotte's mother intervenes and abridges the shipboard romance. Mrs. Vale then remainders Charlotte to the isolation of filial duty. "I am my mother's companion. I am her servant," she says (Robinson 76).[32] At first, in response to this contraction of her life into phrases about its wholly and depressingly imaginable prospects, Charlotte becomes a double person: a traditional daughter in public and a cosmopolitan woman in private. In public, by which I mean in the family that *is* her public, she gives her body over to her duty to her mother and her relatives, and with their distrust of diets she becomes fat. Charlotte becomes so much the public image of familial duty that when her body is photographed she resembles the stereotype she is supposed to be: looking at her family portrait, J. D. asks Charlotte, "And who's the fat lady with the heavy brows and all the hair?" She replies "That's a poor, pathetic spinster aunt. . . . The name of the spinster aunt is 'Charlotte'" (Prouty 82). Caught within the discourse of the stereotype through which she has come to know herself as public, she is unable even to say the word "I" in connection with the alienated image of her familial self.

Meanwhile, during the decade of her depression, Charlotte's bedroom becomes a locked and private shrine to her memory of normal love and the clichés of a femininity forbidden to her. The first shots of Charlotte in the film display this acutely. There is a knock on her door. A servant says, "Miss Charlotte?" The camera answers this question by cutting to Charlotte but not to her face. It focuses instead on Charlotte's hands. Her hand, which is carving small ornamental, typically feminine incisions into an ivory box, gashes the box when her name is called; then her hand puts out a cigarette and throws the ashes into the garbage. The camera rests on the garbage can. "Miss Charlotte" is waste, wasted, a trace of a person: she is cigarette ashes tossed into the can, lipstick smeared onto a tissue and discarded with the ashes. Five full minutes of the film pass before the camera shows Charlotte's face and the mouth that has been so sensually active; it is close to eight minutes before we hear her first words: "Introverted, Doctor?" (Robinson 64).

Later we learn that Charlotte's secret feminine masquerades are indeed an introverted way of life that she has developed to protect from familial disdain the vestiges of her ambition for normal sexual self-pleasure and a life narrative of her own. We also learn that she has developed the kind of psychoanalytic expertise you get from immersion in the therapeutic genres of mass culture. Even then, however, having the skill to name pain does nothing to give it a new shape that would free Charlotte from the way she lives her traumatized femininity. Rather, the word "introverted" hangs somewhat like an epitaph, a monument to the vestiges of her ambition for self-pleasure and a life narrative of her own.

The novel does not narrate much of the material that opens the film, although it folds some of it into Charlotte's flashbacks. It does not narrate the exchange about "introversion," for example, but attributes that psychological condition and its overcoming to the Vale manse itself, which converts from "a silent, gloomy introvert, preferring its own company" to an "amiable, people-loving" space issuing forth "new sounds—jazz, giggling, laughing, barking of dogs, the rattling of a cocktail shaker" (Prouty 323). But the spirit of that cinematic exchange does appear in the novel—in a debate between the patient and her doctor about the desirability of "sublimation" (Prouty 285–86), a term not uttered in the film but manifested in Charlotte's life practice at the end. In the novel, though, Jaquith hectors Charlotte out of depression by encouraging her to use her imagination to achieve nonfamilial happiness through ascendance to sublimation's "high ethical plane" (Prouty 287). Rather than atrophying into self-pity and depression, one is *obligated*, he argues, to develop skills for converting libidinal energies into practices that, if effective, can relieve the lot of damaged or non-normative others who also need help in finding avenues toward better world-building. He argues that Charlotte should sublimate even if she does not feel like it: for "motives, like muscles, have to be exercised to become strong and driving" (Prouty 287). As in Charlotte's experience of feminine masquerade and love, the motive as Jaquith imagines it is produced retroactively. One acts rationally and then projects its good effects back as animating intention that is emotionally expressive of a true self, not the other way around: in this sense normative formalism binds the damaged subject to practices of acting *as if* he or she were a whole uncompromised person (Prouty 286).

From this we can begin to see how *Now, Voyager* positions the cliché's centrality to its portrait of women's mental health. Most of the women in Charlotte's family are entirely conventionally feminine, acting according to the norms of their race, caste, and generation. Following the family system, Charlotte's strategy is not generational, however, because what she wants is everything; she wants to master all conventionality, to feel powerful in her administration of the secrets such multiplicity requires. She thus splits into good and bad objects, first becoming in public an abject stereotype—the spinster, or eternal daughter—and then in secret, a modern stereotype, a sexual woman of mass society. Jaquith intervenes in this circuit of masquerades by substituting new conventional signs for the old ones. But while he frees his patient from her family this way, he continues to affirm her desire to occupy the genre of conventionality that has always made her intelligible to herself and to others. Throughout, as in the "aesthetic" last line of the film and the novel, Jaquith promotes an image of the optimistic life that involves *the courage to live better clichés*.

## The Real Miss Beauchamp

We have been tracking the freedom in the cliché that binds the aristocratic to the popular, the therapeutic to the sentimental, and the normative to the passionately, irrationally erotic in *Now, Voyager*, and the culture of feminine therapeutics in which its plot found intelligibility. But the conversion of *Now, Voyager* to film suppressed two important elements of the novel's psychosexual situation. First, any U.S. consumer of popular psychoanalysis or middlebrow aesthetics from the early twentieth century would have recognized Charlotte's simulation of an absent "Miss Beauchamp" as a clever citation of Morton Prince's famous case study of Clara Fowler / "Sally Beauchamp" in *The Dissociation of a Personality*.[33] Prince identified most of "Beauchamp's" personalities by roman numerals or first names, but "Sally Beauchamp" was Prince's name for the hypersexual, androgynous-modernist personality who seemed most to threaten the patient's well-being; "The Real Miss Beauchamp" was his name for the "normal" personality his treatment would produce. Ruth Leys notes that the wildly popular narrative went quickly through two editions and generated over five hundred plays and remakes, and therefore must have been a source for Prouty.[34]

But to what end? The referentiality seems obvious, Leys writes, presumably because both narratives are about depressed, sexually disrupted women. The case study patient and the case study literary figure generate singular, completely separate selves distinguishable according to feminine style, and they are also anxiously attached to and absorbed in all of the scenes of personality they project. Leys might call them lesbian or bisexual not because they are attached to their mothers or to other women but because they are attached to themselves in the guise of the partial personae they project as full, real, or authentic ones. But it would be more accurate to say that Beauchamp and Charlotte have no sexual subject position in the classic psychoanalytic sense of the term, as I have been suggesting all along. How is it possible to have no position if what is expressed are multiple positions?

It could be uncomplicated, after all, for Prouty to represent through Beauchamp the split between Charlotte's depressive bodily hexis and her coming out as a new person:[35] like Prince's patient, Charlotte feels deeply ambivalent about her mother and sexually guilty in a class sense ("common" or "carnal clay"); and a therapist puts both women on the right path to normatively sexual and mental health. (Prince used hypnosis, not the cognitive practice of freeing the will that mental hygiene advocated and Jaquith uses, however [Prouty 64; Robinson 205]). Prouty might also be tweaking Prince's presumption that the frank and sexual woman "in" Beauchamp imprisons the normal one, rather than the other way around. Many other echoes between the sick and the sexy versions of Beauchamp and Charlotte abound. But any straightforward amalgamation of the two personae or the two plots begs questions otherwise important to the *Now, Voyager* supertext. How should one understand and *work* the relation between clinical and popular therapeutic vernaculars? What is the difference between being dissociated and disordered, clinically and habitually split, and sexual but sans position (for example, "queer")?

For Prince, a clinician determines the presence of a *disintegrated* personality versus a *dissociated* one based on whether or not the patient is functional. Dissociated people split in order to live well and to flourish; they do not become disorganized beings, like hysterics.[36] Each of Beauchamp's personalities is true to herself and her vision of honesty and when faced with the unbearable truth of her incompleteness generates another "alternating personality" who can bear a different facet of the burden of what is overwhelming.[37] This very dysfunctionality is therefore functional and enables the subject to endure—until it doesn't, when the machinery of symptomatic displacement breaks down. Indeed, the very fact that Beauchamp "could be disintegrated without wholly losing those distinctive qualities that characterized her" meant that her symptoms were a sort of perverse armor around what was healthy and integrated in her, her "real" personality.[38] Leys claims that Prince can maintain this view only by not acknowledging his theoretical incoherence, his swerve between mimetic and antimimetic understandings of the multiple: "Beauchamp" is deemed both to be absorbed uncannily in re-enacting her trauma and distant from it, theatricalizing it as an actor of symptoms.[39] This suggests two important, if unsurprising, conclusions, held unawares by Prince and explicitly by Leys. First, "identity" as such and "sexual identity" are the same object in both classic pre- and post-Freudian psychoanalysis, with sexual lability seen as turning identity into a *problem*. Second, seen through the dissociated or multiple personality, the person is fundamentally contradictory: autonomous and capable of sexual self-integration *and* fundamentally disrupted or homo/bisexual.[40] This is why Hacking calls the whole mess a "docudrama."[41] The psychoanalytic case study produces a propositional version of the healthy subject, a consensual fiction about what psychoanalytic expertise can do to determine what health is: for example, a "normal, healthy-minded" person appears when "the real Miss Beauchamp" loses the "bad temper and willful self-determination . . . and emotional idealism" she had advanced.[42] The drama to which Hacking refers is itself doubled. The psychological profession acts out its theoretical contradictions, and those contradictions could themselves refract the subject's own inevitable internal battle between one view of herself as fundamentally shattered, disorganized, or incoherent and another view of herself as solid and complete but vulnerable, desperately needing the ego armor that the personality is *supposed* to provide.[43]

But for our purposes this history of obsessive tinkering with varieties of multiplicity provides a way of understanding the incoherence of the improvisations of subjectivity, sexual subjectivity, styles of gendering, fantasy, and questions of liveable doubleness in *Now, Voyager*. In the narrative of *Now, Voyager* Charlotte's faux occupation of "Miss Beauchamp" on the cruise produces a tragicomedy of errors. The situation emerges from the haste and secrecy with which she made her last-minute move from Cascade to the voyage through which she enters the now of the novel, the film, mental health, and public, androgynous, modernist femininity. Because Charlotte took Renée Beauchamp's place at the last minute she is known publicly on the ship as "Miss Beauchamp." Because Charlotte is still ill and still attached to the bargains with being misrecognized that have shaped her life, she is too fragile to interfere with the alienated public persona that points to her. Luckily the nervous breakdown has made her capable of wearing a thin elite white woman's elegant clothes as though she was born to them, which she both has and has not been. In contrast to the referential "Real Miss Beauchamp," to be healthy Charlotte has to *practice* being a multiple, to cultivate her *personalities*. What does it mean to be multiple without being *a* multiple?

Misrecognition is the a priori of sociability for Charlotte. Of course, misrecognition is inevitable in any transaction of desire and attachment. But negotiating and living with misrecognition by loved ones is what women talk about as one of femininity's special burdens when they are just "being girls together" in the intimate public of women, *and* it is Charlotte's especially burdensome singular condition (Robinson 115). Earlier I noted that Renée Beauchamp was a member of the feminine elite who was well-known for her hilarious impressions and monologues at parties. She also has great taste in clothes, some of which land in Charlotte's ship closet—notably the beautiful cape with "fritillaries" embroidered on it that eventuates in Charlotte's exposure and confession to J. D. that she is an imposter Beauchamp. This is to say that the woman Charlotte poses as already has a reputation for manipulating feminine masquerade, a slightly dangerous form of deployed doubleness that produces local celebrity out of its pleasure in exaggerating other people's personalities imitatively. Another way of putting this is that Miss Beauchamp does at parties what Charlotte's family does to Charlotte, namely rephrasing personality in distorting mirrors of estrangement, for fun, a kind of impersonal teasing. (J. D. notes that Beauchamp/Charlotte is much more "comfortable" to be with than he had expected.) From this perspective Prouty is just playing the symptomatic-sick doubleness of "the Real Miss Beauchamp" against the light manipulativeness of her literary namesake's normativity and playing both against Charlotte's own style of doubleness. Charlotte adapts the space of ellipsis or suspended personhood made possible by passing to expand the meaning of occupying the now doubled name of Beauchamp: as embodied by her it is a defense (against the other passengers), a prison (of misrecognition), a pleasure (providing both a sense of social normalcy and anonymity), and a weapon (against her mother). None of this is a plan, exactly. Charlotte passes as Beauchamp because it is easier than not passing: the occasion of passing merely changes the situation of misrecognition. "Beauchamp" becomes gloriously incoherent, a vague cloud of impossibility and possibility. Charlotte passes "this way" *and* "that way" because she can.

What turns this situation from a tragic heap of humiliatingly exposed, failed, and inauthentic impersonations to something more positive is J. D.'s centrality to Charlotte's conduct of her situation. When Charlotte enlightens J. D. that she is not the real Miss Beauchamp, this binds them emotionally and opens up the narrative to the new love plot. J. D. enables this hedonic duplicity by converting Charlotte's public splitting to a secret one: from the start, the two lovers and the narrator comment on how precious it is to share secrets and to hoard their hidden world of belonging.[44] He alleviates Charlotte's early melodramatic anxiety by making it into social slapstick. To prevent her from feeling more discomfort at being expected to act imitative and satirical like Renée he tells people that Charlotte is not the real Miss Beauchamp but another one named "Camille." She worries that "Camille" is another joke on her, another denigrating intertextual gloss, but he says he has no idea if *Camille* is an opera or a book and is using the name merely to refer to the surface, the color of her dress, which is like the flower. We believe that J. D. is shallow culturally: he likes being "typical," simple, and conventional in a way that relieves Charlotte immensely of her obligations to reproduce the orientation toward most of the signs of social distinction she has inherited.

However, the experience of shared freedom in belonging that J. D. affords her does not spur Charlotte into a lifelong commitment to transparency and openness in intimacy. Furthermore, she passes on to Tina this association of love with secrecy and hoarding (Prouty 31, 302). Their very first interaction is structured around secrecy, with Charlotte keeping secrets *with* Tina from the nurse and *from* Tina, about her identity, ultimately in collaboration with J. D. Later, lightly, Charlotte asks Tina to call her "Camille" when they realize they have no familiar moniker to bind them (Prouty 33, 35–36, 319), but Charlotte does not tell the child that J. D. had already given Charlotte that name. Parrying a name without knowing its resonance, Tina enacts a relation of which she is unaware, but the film and the novel seem to argue that the child is empowered by being kept in the dark. (Jaquith argues, "I can't be kept in the dark when there's a child in the picture," but he never says that the child should be enlightened.) The distorting Beauchamp intertext and the habits it reanimates thus confirm and expand the field of Charlotte's habit of and need for splitting and displacement. Splitting and secrecy protect all of her attachments while bolstering the mirage of singular sovereignty that she wants to perform in the social world, even when she is not up to it emotionally. They also maintain the priority of adults over children established in the Vale legacy—although this time, too, it is a softer supremacy.

It seems, then, that Prouty is playing around with "the Real Miss Beauchamp's" split personalities: while they are a patient's symptoms of illness they are a literary figure's ticket to remastering feminine experiment. Not merely a scene of compromise with femininity, Beauchamp opens up splitting as a sexually and intimately aggressive tool: Charlotte gets everything she wants. But to this understanding of what it means to use nominalist lag or the opportunity of renaming we must add another elided aspect of the novel: J. D.'s biography of depression, dissociation, and normativity. The relation of these two plots provides another revealing context for the meaning of "aesthetic" in the novel's closing gesture, in its sublimely greedy, pseudo-renunciative bargaining. This will also gloss in different terms the novel's commitment to cliché and the conventional formalism of the personality in the intimate public sphere.

The decision to cast Paul Henreid as J. D.—in the film a foreigner from an unnamed somewhere who has nonetheless not traveled—contributes to the film's simplification of his story. It also helps to undermotivate Charlotte's passionate attachment to J. D.: in the film their love happens very quickly, and for her it seems based on the relief his personality provides her from her own. She feels "gratitude" for his hedonic exuberance, unpretentiousness, ordinary kindness, extraordinary empathy, and risk-taking love and, although this is less explicit, perhaps some identification with and favoritism of Tina. Even in those terms Jerry is not all Charlotte had hoped for. She files a female complaint in their very last scene, calling his sensibility "conventional, pretentious," and "pious" and reeducating him all over again about what makes their love worth preserving (Prouty 334; Robinson 219). Nonetheless in the end J. D. is good enough to remain bound to if he follows her directions in that "don't let's ask" way. But in the novel Jerry's personality is not the key to their bond. The key is in his personal experience of nervous breakdown and gender dysphoria, matters cut entirely from the film.

J. D. is Charlotte's twin in masculine form. More than a gallant man who understands feminine vulnerability and feels his obligation to managing it, he is a case study subject like Charlotte. Prouty details carefully the story of his psychological makeup: he responds to Charlotte's confession about Cascade with one of his own.[45] When she declares she is ill and has just finished a three-month stay at Cascade, he touches her and says, "'I couldn't afford to go to Cascade when I was ill. . . . I know all about it. I understand now'" (Prouty 69–70). Charlotte calls herself a fool; he replies, "'Thank God for that! So was I! Why, it's like discovering we've got a common ancestor, and are cousins of something'" (Prouty 70). He closes off this scene by giving her fingers "a therapeutic squeeze of encouragement." Later, they pursue their likeness. She asks him what "the underlying cause" of his illness was, and he says "a long-drawn-out period of a sense of failure" (Prouty 86). She repeats this phrase precisely when he inquires as to her etiology. But their likeness splits when it hits sexual difference. Particularizing his sense of failure, he points to "'what makes most men feel it—not making good at the chief object for his existence—as a provider . . . . Strikes pretty deep sometimes.'" She points, in turn, to the female complaint so conventional it barely needs enumeration (for more on this convention of the complaint's expression in contracted forms, see the next chapter's discussion of Dorothy Parker): "'A woman has a chief object for existence too, you know. And if she fails to make good at it, why, it, too, can strike pretty deep' " (Prouty 86). They soon depart together feeling an "ecstatic sense of companionship," having progressed from cousin on the journey to lover (Prouty 88) (see fig. 29). The novel elaborates this sense in echoes between his letters home and Charlotte's dreams on the first night after their meeting. Finally, after their first night of bonding, as she rereads "The Untold Want," he reads this passage in *The Autobiography of Henry Adams*, the story of yet another man who could only there call himself "he": " 'Then he found himself launched on waters he had never meant to sail' " (Prouty 53).

The novel details in case study fashion J. D.'s history of split or disso-ciated gender performance. At school, he was well known as a cut-up, an impersonator, called to parties to imitate the famous imitator Harry Lauder and the vaudeville types "Mack and Mike." He was, as it were, the male "Renée Beauchamp," an imitator whose authenticity was affirmed and not threatened by his mimetic play. But on being married his story begins to look like Charlotte's, a public life of anhedonic duty diluted by folds of pleasure gathered up in a secreted scene.

> He had always been "Duveaux" to Isobel. The difference between Isobel's "Duveaux" and the old college crowd's "J. D." was as great as between two contrasting characters in a monologist's repertoire. To the old col-lege crowd J. D. had always been the most straightforward, single-minded fellow in the world—one character under all conditions. But Isobel had developed in him a dual personality. Whenever in her company he was perpetually trying to be, or to appear to be the kind of man she wished he was. But whenever she was absent, he resumed his instinctive one-tracked personality. (Prouty 50)

J. D.'s very language reveals the pleasures of being multiple advanced by *Now, Voyager*. This is how their first meeting after months of silence runs, amid the hubbub of a party where they run into each other:

> "Yes, I've been to Boston several times this winter. (You're looking sim-ply glorious!) George Weston and I have business dealings. (I've wanted horribly to call you up!) Well, yes, I know Boston fairly well. Chiefly from the Cambridge side. No, not Harvard. Sorry, M.I.T. One year only. (I've walked by your house on Marlborough Street.) No, Miss Vale, I'm

## TEASER INTRODUCTION FOR PAUL HENREID

Paul Henreid's performance in this film has been hailed one of the finest on the screen in many years. Cash in on his expected popularity among your patrons with one or all of this quartette of teaser suggestions. For throwaway, use scene mat 201, page 3. Still used is NV 604—10c—from Campaign Editor, 321 W. 44 St., N.Y.C.

**29** Although the film of *Now, Voyager* deletes the plot about J. D.'s nervous breakdown, the film's advertising points to what the novel meant to say.

not an architect. I'm a jobber. (Once I almost rang the bell.) . . . (Oh, Camille, Camille! It's so good to see you! I'm still horribly in love!)." (Prouty 241)

This doubled discussion turns to Tina, as it always does: J. D. here reveals to Charlotte that Tina is in Jaquith's care. This news enables her subsequent manipulation of Jaquith into letting her take care of the child; it also produces the child's rescue from her family, her implantation in a new one, and her ascension to a world in which her fantasies of being held and happy in a home where her father comes are secured by secrets and lies. Charlotte and J. D. thus finally prepare Tina for an experience of femininity as something other than a space of negative commentary, unwantedness, and humiliating exposure. This rescue requires a new shared open secret (with each other and the intimate public of the audience); it involves an agreement on the importance of disavowal in sustaining love, for without disavowal there would be no way to secure optimism for the promise of affective reliability in conventionality. And without optimism there is no mental health.

There is, then, a significant divergence from Prince's model of personality dissociation in the multiplicities and duplicities of *Now, Voyager*. The supertext offers managerial splitting of the personality as a *cure* for those who cannot adapt to the rationalizing pressures of normal culture or who refuse to be implanted in its rhythms from the start. Prince argues that a multiple personality or victim of dissociation is in a debilitating internal war of reified types, each type a kind of personality that threatens the other's sense of solidity. In contrast, for J. D. and Charlotte splitting is not a *type* but a *technique* crucial to love; it drowns out the memory of love's impossibility in the normal world and replaces it by multiple scenes of secrecy. From this perspective *Now, Voyager* is not just a maternal or women's melodrama but a queer melodrama, a melodrama of the anomalous subject wrestling not to be free from conventionality but to find collective spaces for emotional thriving in proximity to it.

### The Enabling Cliché

I have described the centrality of formulaic personhood to the production of mental health for men and women in the novel and women in the film of *Now, Voyager*. The natal family demands that the family member perform affectively in a way that is intelligible to the family's established practices: its demand is formalist, apsychological, directed toward practical agency. As mothers, wives, and daughters, women bear a special burden for reproducing and sustaining family identity, protecting what seem to be its core forms so that it appears invulnerable to change, but there is also a conceptual surplus to this function. In the ideology and institutions promoted by women's culture, women are the emblems of intimacy: and when a woman negotiates its conventions and institutions it is read as a plebiscite on love's very forms, which are deemed implicitly to ballast the ethical center of society *tout court*. Any queer impulse someone might have to cultivate an anomalous sensorium or alternative identification reappears as a kind of immature stubbornness and serious threat that must be worked through not only on the family's behalf but on behalf of love itself (see fig. 30).

**30** A promotional summary of *Now, Voyager* as a fantasy of being normal, using clips from the film.

For the women who aspire to normal life, the conventional love plot is a cliché dressed up as a maxim, a piece of practical wisdom as well as the mark of a utopian aspiration. Jaquith's aphoristic method does not unsettle this structure of subjectivity. Instead, it protects it by sublimating or aestheticizing it, marketing forms and phrases that serve as placeholders for the good life that the women have not yet secured. All the women need to do is to pronounce the phrases and make that journey toward the something else not quite visible, yet. Yet in these texts, for the most part, the women do not see the placeholder function of the phrases they learn to say. They are incited to mistake sublimation as a fulfilling variation that will interfere with the doomed destinies that they have already feared are intractable. Sublimation may well be an opening up to another logic of having a life, an undoing of a habit without a fully formed project of alternativity. But the texts of women's culture never pass beyond a certain point: the signs always say "Go home."

Even after Charlotte is cured, after all, she takes the cliché about man, home, and child as her prospect in life. In public, of course, she is still a spinster, now made glamorous by wealth and the aura of modernity she radiates. But in her secret life before and after her breakdowns, she performs a hyperconventional femininity. The difference in the second is that J. D. now shares it with her: they end the book, after all, playing imaginary house. But all Charlotte wants, and all she has ever wanted, is the right to live her own clichés. She wants the exuberance of such conventionality to be Tina's inheritance, too—it is more important than money and social standing. So does Tina's father: in the film, when J. D. says "I love you" to Tina, he is looking over her shoulder at Charlotte.

You might say that is what freedom is in liberal culture: this is Stanley Cavell's argument about the film, that the woman's consent to conventionality dramatizes the ur-form of American liberty.[46] But my argument has been that the therapy form of women's culture misrepresents the value of the therapeutic banality and therefore of popular culture. Pop psychotherapy authorizes the desire for unhappy women's self-interruption through therapeutic banalities about the management and sublimation of emotion. The genre of the enabling cliché adds an aura of expertise to the self-talking cure, and this in return reauthorizes the redemptive pedagogy of women's culture. At the same time, the critical consciousness of public sphere femininity does express longing for a radically revised life prospect for women and less burdensome affective transactions in the meanwhile. It also alleviates and thematizes the alleviation of women's loneliness by respecting women's desire to embody and make possible other people's rest in conventionality, that stand-in for the experience of belonging to a world that welcomes them. But the narratives that flow from these conventions almost inevitably obscure the contradictions of "sentimental realism," which perform rhetorically the enmeshing of the most contracted and contradictory conditions of intimacy as the freedom love provides to look forward, again.

Unfinished Business

A decade or so after *Now, Voyager*'s composition and translation into film, and while surviving nervous breakdowns cured by writing and catalyzed by feelings of sexual anomaly and maladjustment to family life, Olive Higgins

Prouty engaged in a project of rescue very much like Charlotte's own. You might have read about her in *The Bell Jar*: she was Sylvia Plath's scholarship sponsor at Smith and paid for her psychiatric care as well. The letters between them and between Prouty and Plath's mother, Aurelia, reveal another intricate network of love's institutionalization, where signs of mental health and signs of heteromarital love are debated, confused, and suppressed.[47] Meanwhile, Prouty oversees Plath's budding career as a writer for women, consults with her doctors, and supports her electroshock and her occupational therapy, by which I mean weaving on a loom as well as writing.

Jacqueline Rose writes that everyone who comes into contact with Plath, even long after her suicide, becomes obsessed with the rescue/therapy plot—in other words, they fall in love with Plath, wanting to supplant retroactively the bad mother and the bad husband who are blamed for her failure to endure. She argues that Plath herself was violently split between wanting to be a good heterosexual girl who writes high cultural poetry and a bad girl who wants to get down into the passionate and radically phallic bisexuality that is, paradoxically, associated with the ruthlessness of desire set loose by the erotics of popular women's fiction.[48] I would argue that these readings of Plath's sexuality reduce her and it to a symptom of a greedily confused sexual subject position. In any case, neither Prouty nor any kind of writing saved Plath from feeling or being impossible. The story of her sacrifice to heteronormativity, like Charlotte's and so many women's, has been memorialized in the archive of love's posttraumatic institutions, popular therapy and women's culture. There, women are taught "to seek and find" a form of therapy that affirms love as the source of and cure for a psychic disorder and social contradictions whose effects are made to seem inevitable *and* a small price to pay for optimism or its fading memory.

(6)

# "IT'S NOT THE TRAGEDIES THAT KILL US, IT'S THE MESSES" Femininity, Formalism, and Dorothy Parker

> Listen. I can't even get my dog to stay down.
> Do I look to you like someone who could
> overthrow the government?
> DOROTHY PARKER

## On Wanting (To Be) "Somebody"

Dorothy Parker's, Alan Campbell's, and Robert Carson's *A Star Is Born* (1937) ends with the actress Vicki Lester intoning the phrase "This is Mrs. Norman Maine," a tragically defiant assertion of something about what her marriage has meant (see fig. 31).[1] But what, really, does she mean by this, what kind of closure does it provide, and why does it carry no personal pronoun while being so radically personal? Is *A Star Is Born* simply *Now, Voyager* redux, a text whose shift of idiom at the moment of closure reveals a nest of unsaids?

On the face of it, Lester (Janet Gaynor) merely echoes the phrase "Goodbye, Mrs. Norman Maine" that the head of her studio, Oliver Niles (Adolphe Menjou), has said to her two scenes before in response to her desire to sacrifice her life and quit show business to protect the fragile ego of her husband, the star Norman

"This is Mrs. Norman Maine" (*A Star Is Born*, 1937).

Maine (Fredric March). On overhearing the plan for his wife's professional suicide, Maine kills himself. Thus in this final scene Lester needs to be reintroduced to her public because both she and her star aura have undergone trauma. The phrase "This is Mrs. Norman Maine" acknowledges to her public her mourning for him. But the fuller story of the phrase begins in the film's opening scene.

Lester enters the film in her pre–stage name phase as Esther Blodgett, a star-struck farm girl from the Great Plains. Aglow with pleasure, she sweeps into her family's house fresh from seeing a Norman Maine romance with lots of "mush" in it, and she is teased mercilessly by her family about her compulsive celebrity imitations and her fantasy of becoming a star. Esther runs upstairs and weeps until her grandmother quells her tears by financing a trip to Hollywood, but "granny" does this only after admonishing Esther that to "become a somebody" like Maine you have to "break your heart," a phrase the film repeats throughout as the cost of the devil's bargain with fame.

On reaching Hollywood, Esther appears in the usual chirpy montage sequence featuring classic tourist entertainment sites, which culminates in a visit to the galaxy of stars memorialized in concrete on the sidewalks outside of Grauman's Chinese Theatre. Immediately she steps into Norman Maine's shoe prints: not only do they radiate his physical aura, they immortalize his stardom and make it seem magically available for channeling through spatial cohabitation. Esther Blodgett's feet, though, cannot fill Norman Maine's shoes, a fact that makes the young girl laugh exuberantly.

The final scene of *A Star Is Born* returns to Grauman's Chinese Theatre. Having been "discovered" by Maine, married to him, his superior at the box office, and widowed by his suicide, Esther Blodgett, now Vicki Lester, is making her first public appearance since his funeral; it is the premiere of a new film for her as well. She did not want to attend the opening: Maine's alcoholism and suicide had indeed made her want to cast off her star facade and to return to being Blodgett. But the grandmother, who subsidized this whole plot, has flown to Hollywood to exhort Vicki not to waste a talent whose star value is so great that her husband sacrificed himself to save it. Granny attends the opening with Vicki. But Vicki exits the car alone.

As she steps out of the limousine that delivers her to the premiere, we can see that Lester is putting on a brave face, imitating unbrokenness in the face of tragedy, as public figures will do. But on her resolute way to the microphone, her gaze alights on her late husband's star and his empty shoe impressions, and for a moment she swoons, almost faints, mimes dying. When Lester rights herself she steps up to the host's request that she say a few words to her fans "here" and on the radio, and she speaks to them while looking unsteadily toward a point on the off-screen horizon. Saying "Hello everybody: This is Mrs. Norman Maine" confirms her decision to survive in and for her public. But it also gestures toward the terrible privacy to which she has been remanded, as though her married name is a jury sentence that shrinks her to the size of a phrase.

Alternatively, one could say of the ending that in uttering "This is Mrs. Norman Maine," Lester is performing a remarriage of sorts. Earlier we have seen that when Vicki Lester married Maine, she did not marry him but his prior incarnation, for their marriage is pronounced to be between Esther Blodgett and Alfred Hinkle. Yet in this final moment when she comes out as a widow, she is not the widow of Hinkle but of the name Hinkle married himself to when he signed his studio contract. In other words, the widow proclaims herself married to her late husband's stage name because this tragically is the life left to her now, a public life, a sacrificial space of private brokenness in which the authenticity of being just a wife, a nobody, must be drowned out by the spectacle of being a widow, a shadow, a somebody-for-others, a condition intensified by the celebrity status of the beloved, of whom she is now and forever an echo.

Lester's gesture is also a grand refusal. It repudiates an industry and a public that have spurned a living man from making a living within the holding chamber of his stage name, a performance of solidarity with someone who had been made obsolete before he was dead. It is an embrace of the value of that man in the only terms a mass public schooled in the ways of Hollywood can be sure to understand, the terms that marry a fantasy of true love's absolute authenticity to the power embedded in cliché and conventionality, which support the very fantasy of recognition and transcendence that Maine used to enact in the days when he was a heartthrob for people such as Esther Blodgett. So, for anyone who wanted to hear it, "This is Mrs. Norman Maine" would be an acid wash of truth telling against the view that becoming somebody involves fulfillment in transcendence rather than sublimation, the destruction of one element for the production of another.

At the same time, though, Lester's phrase makes it possible *not* to hear the truth about the costs of the desire "to become somebody" while retaining conventionality. Her final act positions their story within the genre of perfect, ghostly love preserved by death that classic Hollywood fans consume greedily.[2] In this mode life flourishes in intense emotional situations or episodes of apotheosis, not in realist plots of anxiety, disillusion, dissolution, and/or triumph. In veering back and forth this way, in being genuinely emotionally incoherent, *A Star Is Born* also brandishes Lester's membership in the survival sisterhood whose offer of recognition of femininity's special burdens is said to magnetize women to other women's stories in the emotion-focused genres of women's culture in the first place.[3] The rhythms of this final scene and the ways they rhyme with earlier moments stand as an emblem of a peculiarly modern conjuncture of femininity, formalism, the lure of normality, and the fear *and* threat of not being in "the" story, which, being a conventional plot about conventionality, is not a story about uniqueness but about the politics, ethics, aesthetics, and erotics of desiring to be somebody while being unoriginal to the point of heartbreaking absurdity.

I have been arguing that, for the people who identify with it, femininity is a B movie, a genre of the unsurprising that is deeply fulfilling because it is unsurprising. What follows extends our investigation into the satisfactions of the normal, the predictable, the usual, and the formal in U.S. women's popular culture by focusing on genre and using the *oeuvre* of Dorothy Parker as its case. But this is a strange case, a case of estrangement of sorts. Parker is a middlebrow writer and a writer who locates her claim for the universality of her version of common sense in its difference from other modes of middlebrow feminine publicity: she is "Dorothy Parker" and not "Edna Ferber" because of her cosmopolitan, cognitive superiority to the leaky, fraying, diminishing sentimentality Parker associates with the fantasy-saturated practices of normative femininity. These knots of identification and aversion produce what Rhonda Pettit catalogs as the wide range of incompatible assessments of Parker's relation to sentimental femininity: too close and too aversive to the emotions, too leaky and too edgy, too popular and too genteel.[4] This chapter argues that these charged evaluations can arise because of Parker's characterization of form and genres as *needs*. In Parker's work, aesthetic conventionality itself is always proximate to gendered and sexual normativity. Formalism denotes normalism. But its failure induces crisis. This is one thing that Parker means by the phrase that titles this chapter, "It's not the tragedies that kill us, it's the messes."

This chapter pursues Parker's aversion and attachment to messes of sociality that span the intimate, the aesthetic, and the political.[5] Widely considered the best and most memorable U.S. female complainer, Parker was also a left-wing activist. The paradoxical relation of her sexual-aesthetic normativity to her political risk taking will seem less so when read as an expression of her take on what it means to be committed to something, a lover or an idea. Tracking the couple in the couplet, the melodramatic gesture, and the comic episode, I will suggest that Parker's work focuses on the centrality of genre to the elusive experience of being held by the promise of the normal as ideal. Genre is her scene of *whateverness*, Giorgio Agamben's term for the condition of an ethical belonging to the social as a matter of its being such, regardless of program or content. Parker's fidelity to the social is expressed in her commitment to genre.[6] So is her fidelity to need. Articulating the consequences of this double commitment will require some thought about what a genre is, how modes of personhood and aesthetic events are mutually mediated by the affective expectations congealed around generic mappings, and how Parker plays with the open secrets of generic expectation, coding a kind of strong ambivalence in the rise and fall of aesthetic and affective intensities.

I will argue that, in this body of work, women's disappointing experiences of the normal forms of personhood and intimacy do not induce rejection of them, but improvisations on the *fear of the loss of the melancholic position* that arises from stark consciousness of normalcy's apparitional solidity. As Parker plays heavily in the affective registers of women's intimate public, with their constant recalibrations of what counts as reciprocity, she adapts the lability of its affect-saturated genres to stage normalcy not as a place of rest, but as an anxious nonplace characterized by the overwhelming self-evidence of the failure of language and love to be adequate to the world-building mission that is their constitutive legitimacy in femininity's intimate public. Thus there is the importance of the lived repetition into form and aesthetic genre itself. There would be no imaginable intimate or political life were form not achieved, and it matters not whether one lines up behind it affectively. Without genre, attachment could be transmitted but not received, engaged, or endured.

Improvisation, as we know, is a formalism that hides itself in the richness of variation. What distinguishes Parker's version of attachment to normative sexual form from classic melancholia is the status of the object: in classic psychoanalysis, melancholia keeps your ego attached to the lost object so that emotionally it is not lost, or you are lost with it, whether or not the object or scene of desire is actually present. But the reflexive melancholic accepts the impossibility of possessing the object of desire and can ironize, play with it, and joke about it while dramatizing possession and loss all the same. Reflexive practices such as these enable her to stay in the scene as though unmastered by it and in this continuing tipping over and righting of herself to show that her object of desire is not the apparent object at all, but an opportunity for courage, or optimism. It is as though life is but a film loop of an approach to a position that cannot be occupied, but that can be vitalizing so long as she is moving toward it and being moving to herself or you, her audience. Whether the object of desire is a person, a feeling of transcendence, a risk, or a place of rest and confidence is merely a detail whose consequences can be pursued narratively: what Parker brings to the table is her unerring focus on the mess of disappointment that *might* have taken another turn and itself demands a form.

For Parker, disappointments in men, women, and love do not induce rejection of the desire for romance to be realism, intimacy to feel like recognition, or reciprocity to feel like reciprocity. Her disappointments in democracy do not induce her disidentification with its potentiality. They induce, instead, reanimations of the demand that generated the intensities of attachment in the first place. They manage ambivalence formally as a way of staying in the room with desire. For the position of the reflexive melancholic can amount to the same thing as *commitment*, Adorno's term for art that signals that " 'it should be otherwise.' "[7] How can one tell the difference, though, between the rhythms of bargaining in maintenance mode and the rhythms of refusing a defeat?

This chapter concentrates on the spectacle of the unsteady woman that Vicki Lester embodies briefly at the end of *A Star is Born*, a revelatory tableau of shaky vocality, unfocused gazing, and emotional wobbliness that is central to women's culture's revelation of the processes and rhythms and threats to survival of staying proximate to normative idealities. But, being middlebrow with higher aspirations than that, Parker asserts constantly a distance from the dreaminess that substitutes for feminine agency in sentimental realism. Protected from the imago of simple mimesis of the literalizing script of the good life they think they know better than to want, the women she writes often feel simultaneously superior, singular, and conventional. *They are emboldened by the courage not to have learned from their experiences.*

Yet, the situation of moving toward desire's impossible horizon is not only pathetic or tragic. Being emotionally flooded by wanting the impossible is never quite the end of the story, which still contains evidence that a woman has had a life because she has been in proximity to love, and that having had it she may again have it. Failures, after all, reproduce the opportunity for optimism, fantasy, and the enrichment of genres of alternativity;[8] they induce a kind of hypervigilance that seems potentially a resource for changing the pattern of repetitions and the rhythms of attachment. At the same time, hypervigilance is not the opposite of disavowal and self-deception; it is also, and often, their guardian.

This tenderness around protecting the scene of longing is a very complex phenomenon, on which each chapter of this book has shown a different angle. Fantasy always expresses a desire for continuity with a better world than yet exists: in this it is always utopian and critical, a measure of a lack that, at the same time, is often expressed in an attachment to objects that do already exist and that therefore misrepresent inevitably the desires that bring people to them. Key here is the concept of the placeholder. A sense of normalcy is mainly a free-floating affect, a generalized sense of comfort and continuity with a loosely experienced world, and the desire to be normal involves cultivating a studied vagueness about the relation of any object of optimism to the nexus of things that proximity to that object might bring. (In *Imitation of Life*, for example, Bea is accused of "marrying marriage" but her nonresponse to the charge amounts to something like "Maybe! I'm not going to think about it too much!"⁹) The stubborn aggression and tenderness of the subject who fantasizes protects fantasy from being too pierced by realistic plots, as opposed to realistic transmissions of affect. In "women's culture," to want "a life" is to want those virtually closeted experiences of affect to have amounted to something beyond merely surviving. The compensation promised by membership in the imaginary world of commonality provided by women's culture is the elevation of these gestures to the scale of having achieved, through suffering, sacrifice, and aggressive fantasy, a collectively acknowledged density of a style of being. Even the kinds of dissenting expressions so conventional to the female complaint can be expressions of tenderness toward and continued attachment to the impossible situation. For to dismantle completely the normative circuits would be to disrupt the porous terms of personal and mass intimacy that have provided reliability for close to two centuries.

Parker's corpus can be characterized as a literature of failed disavowal of this material, even as it attributes these tensions to mass culture's central contradiction regarding the normal—that it harms individual sovereignty but is a relief from singularity, which is deemed a burden. The texts of women's culture tend to express this contradiction and their ambivalence toward it in anxiously formalist dramas of bargaining, as though surviving intimacy and femininity in capitalist modernity were just a question of choosing a balance among the right forms and living that stabilizing process in as close a proximity to the fantasy norms as possible. But the texts of women's intimate public vacillate significantly in calibrating how much women can and ought to bear to face what Joan Copjec calls the groundlessness of the world for feminine fantasies of reciprocity, acknowledgment, and security.¹⁰

For Parker, this reduction of life to a relation between bargaining and fantasy produces conventional women as a community of stuck subjects who live only to return to the intensified situation. At the same time, and despite being so highly mediated and conventionalized, the experience of intensity, of bargaining *as* fantasy, is *so* threatening to the shape of the subject that the question of whether or not she *can* return to form often takes over the discussion, leaving her women treading water and collecting memories of optimism in the scene of their disappointment. In this way her women sustain proximity to "whatever optimism," the optimism whose intensities must be maintained even when there are no imaginable forms adequate to the desires that seek them.[11]

This balancing act and the flurry of activity it generates as evidence that living is taking place are central to the magnetizing story of femininity in women's intimate public sphere. Parker participates in the sentimental world of feminine pleasures and sufferance by deploying genre reflexively—staging feminine normativity as a formalist fantasy about the pleasures and burdens of adaptation. But her investment in female complaining goes beyond noticing that people do it, return to its scene, and revel in its big tragedies and petty survivals. She wonders aloud and makes art about whether or not the circuits of affective normativity reinforced by aesthetic conventionality can be interrupted by will and knowledge, the assurance of better arguments. In this she straddles the sentimental attachment to pain as the truth of the subject and to rationality as that which elevates people over their appetites and impulses. Additionally, her attachment to thinking as a protection against femininity inflects her political critique of U.S. class and racial inequality.

But contemporary readers of Parker rarely think about her as sentimental: her ambivalence is read in the vernacular sense, as a smart person's *refusal* of its stupefying seductions.[12] She is known, after all, not for her tenderness but for her hard-edgedness, her pleasure in making the pithy, skewering quip with a frankness beyond what is conventionally acceptable. This view of her grew, in part, from her own public self-representation: she dismissed her own poetry as "whines" and always sought to surpass the caricature of her that located her wit at that ground of love's disappointments.[13] Likewise, many critics locate her very claim to importance in her superiority to a specifically feminine sentimentality. Jessica Burstein argues that Parker's contribution is to supplement the female complaint with a new affect of reflexive modernity, the blasé, Georg Simmel's designation for a mode of cosmopolitan boredom in which the subject dissolves in anonymity yet rises to a new height of muted consciousness in the face of new spectacles of suffering.[14] In *Making Love Modern*, Nina Miller attributes Parker's hard edge to a new form of sophisticated citizenship, in which love is no longer a scene of women's privacy but a vehicle for a kind of publicness unique to modernity, providing a new ground for a sophisticated sovereignty unhindered and indeed enhanced by sexuality.[15]

But as Simmel himself argued, I am suggesting that for Parker these performances of cognitive superiority are not triumphs over these emotions but defenses, failed defenses, ways of managing affect through the mediating pacing of form (tropes internal to the text) and genre (the codes that generate readerly expectations about the shape of the narrative event). Parker acknowledged this explicitly. Reporting from the Spanish Civil War she writes about seeking the right tone and form in which to represent the pleasures and stresses of ordinary life under conditions of crisis: "I heard someone say, and so I said it too, that ridicule is the most effective weapon. I don't suppose I ever really believed it, but it was easy and comforting, so I said it. Well, now I know . . . I know that ridicule may be a shield."[16] What does it mean to think about a genre as defense, once genre is seen as the formalization of aesthetic or emotional conventionalities? This question is central to comprehending the promise of form and genre's holding warmth that women's popular culture—even Parker's version of it—provides for the subjects of femininity.

## On the Pleasures of Being Generic

An interview with Dorothy Parker in the *Paris Review* in 1956 alights on the high points of her career as a figure with special observational gifts about love and politics. It is an extremely pleasant interview, full of musings about her own professional unoriginality: she reveals herself to have been a keen imitator of Millay, Sitwell, and classic writers of the sonnet, and she even asserts that, on reading Gertrude Stein's claim that her cohort was a "lost generation," she imitated being lost. But in response to a question about the original of her story "Big Blonde," Parker closes up and acts flinty.

> Interviewer [Marion Capron]: What about "Big Blonde"? Where did the idea for that come from?

Parker: I knew a lady-friend of mine who went through holy hell. Just say I knew a woman once. The purpose of the writer is to say what he feels and sees. To those who write fantasies—the Misses Baldwin, Ferber, Norris—I am not at home.[17]

"I knew a woman once" is a conventional phrase, a placeholder for a story about women that can almost go without saying. A variation of it is repeated in the subtitle to a film whose story was written by Parker, *Smash Up: The Story of a Woman*. And it is also repeated, with slight adjustments of the seam, throughout her poetry, drama, and prose, in phrases such as "Yet this the need of woman, this her curse: to range her little gifts, and give and give, / Because the throb of giving's sweet to bear."[18]

"I knew a woman" is a most efficiently told story of love as the gift that keeps taking. It is a story repeated so often that it has become a phrase, a code, a byword, like that joke in the joke about jokes in prison (the prisoners have only so many jokes and recycle them so much that they just yell out numbers; when one of them yells out a number and receives no laugh, he moans, "I never could tell a joke"). In this feminine economy too, it seems, there are also only so many stories and they are so bad and so pervasive that they are like curses the world has made on women rather than stories that emerge from their lives.

In this interview and elsewhere, Parker demonstrates exemplary knowledge about the exemplarity of this story about a woman, an expertise she demonstrates by *not* telling her friend's whole story in all of the gory details. She refers to it and indeed demonstrates a real pleasure in its withheld or contracted unfolding. She adds value to this pleasure by implying that her demurral derives from a sisterly ethics, the ethics of friendship: by not revealing the map from real life to fiction, while saying that a map could easily be drawn, she solicits curiosity about it while blocking traffic in the epistemological pleasures of misogynist and sentimental schadenfreude, with their studiously pornotropic cataloging of the details that would make this woman's singular "holy hell" recognizable generally. Instead "Big Blonde" does this work of erasing singularity from individuality to create the generic woman. It makes her into a case, an example, the instance of a structure. It does this by shifting constantly across women's internal and external compliance to feminine norms and contrasting this compliance to the aesthetic performance that houses it.

In general, Parker can be sure that we do, indeed, already know the story of the story about a woman I'll just say I once knew—it is about the bargain "a woman" makes with femininity, which is to measure out a life in the capital of intimacy, opening herself to a risky series of sexual and emotional transactions that intensify her vulnerability on behalf of securing value, a world and "a life" that are financially, spatially, and environmentally stable and predictable enough. A woman does not have to have experienced physically or unironically the sublimity of the great love to take up emotionally normative femininity: nor does she have to have been drastically burned by it. The normative position includes a whole range of variations of closeness and distance as long as the intimate referent thrives. She can seem guarded and distant from it—but no one is fooled that she hasn't already recited it with her own name filling the blanks.

In other words, Parker's wielding of the "story of a woman" merges living a life, the work of surviving, with having a life, a fantasy that women's ordinariness exists on another plane, where the details of the everyday transform into meaningfulness; what being in love secures is evidence that you have had an impact on the world by being a condition of possibility for someone else. It relies on a fantasy of reciprocity that is also a fantasy of power; it relies on a fantasy of having been recognized. Parker contributes intensity to this already complex scene of tectonic shifts by emitting empathy, bitterness, and sadism toward her friend, the story about her friend, the scene of solicited storytelling, and her own mixed feelings, in a few single phrases: the economy of detail expresses in inverse the flood of emotional exposure the person who engages in feminine transactions will inevitably undergo.

What is stunning about Parker's *oeuvre* is how general its stories are when they are about women. Across decades of writing there is little change in the outline: women are sensually and cognitively alive but wasted as resources for making life because feminine culture is stupefying and trivializing; their story of hope and love and pain is repetitive, like a compulsion, or an addiction, like verse itself, and the genre film. Her late melodrama *The Ladies of the Corridor* was even published with a preface detailing sociological studies about the wasting away of women widowed in their forties, women who live out their repetitive lives imprisoned in hotels for the erotically unwanted.[19] This is why the social death of women articulates with the desire to be conventional in Parker's work at an astonishing distance from the material of biography: women's lives move on in general, as their fate is generality. The intensified generic aesthetics of this material are, therefore, metalevel performances of the encounter of the subject with her desire and/or the normative demand to want to be conventional.

Unsurprisingly, Parker writes many poems about the problem and process of living like this, in which the repetitions of normative desire and the predictability of verse merge. They are poems about the emotional experience and social consequences of conventionality, as in "Ballade at Thirty-Five":

> This, no song of an ingénue,
>> This, no ballad of innocence;
> This, the rhyme of a lady who
>> Followed ever her natural bents.
>> This, a solo of sapience,
> This, a chantey of sophistry,
>> This, the sum of experiments—
> I loved them until they loved me. (PDP 105)

The repetition of the *this* with no verb points to the intractability and objectivity of the object: this reality, this poem, this form, this scene of balance without emotional reciprocity:

> Always knew I the consequence;
> Always saw what the end would be.
>> We're as Nature has made us—hence
> I loved them until they loved me.

The poem is an argument about love, which is standard for a certain kind of poem. But the woman mimes the love plot without wanting to live it, which is not standard for the love poem or the woman. So this is a story that *has* to be told. But at the same time, with the same timing, the poem can only exist under the shadow of the standard story whose form it otherwise performs prettily and poetically, with an overload of internal rhyming and repetition. Thus the overload releases as a sense experience the impossibility of emotional reciprocity in real time: at the same time, successfully accomplished genre is a utopian performance, a scene of mastery in contrast to disappointing life, with its rhythm of failed experiments. Love is the seeking out of form, here defined as a "natural bent." Genre and aesthetic form release the potentiality in the seeking in love but mainly overproduce memorials for witnessing the ways lovers miss each other, as though it is just a question of timing, "coincidence," aesthetic skill. The story that does not need to be, but *has to be* told even fails to numb the senses in its prolific formalism.

Such an aesthetic performance of numbing as a relief from the work of managing attachment is shaped, in the end, by Parker's splitting off the tone from the rhyme at the end of line phrases, verses, and poems and by making unpredictably unsuccessful rhymes, and in so doing miming the sour turns of love.[20] Strictly executed conventionality in desire and poetics are allowed an appearance: indeed Parker builds this cramped space of desire only to shame her reader for wanting to be held by tone and genre as though poetic form itself provided the experience of reciprocity in love. As she got famous, her readers would no doubt read her in order to be spanked a little by the failed couplets and couples whose wrecks were expected to make an appearance there. But the work of genre demands that reading the actually complex semi-failed poem about the non-blasé world of desire force a kind of suspension of cognitive identification with the armor of emotional intelligence. It is in this way that genre and gender as spaces of emotional transaction merge with each other in Parker's work and seduce readers to ferry back and forth across the field of their ambivalence about using their knowledge in the field of desire: we are incited to be lulled into the stream of details that make conventionality seem alive in the process of its re-enactment. The work demonstrates both control and the absurdity of fantasies of competence; it provides a form of secure or regressive reliability and then codes the affective pleasure in form and genre as both necessary for thriving and very, very wrong.

To take another example: like many of her poems, "Sonnet for the End of a Sequence" does not even bother to tell the story that propels us to the predictable end.

So take my vows and scatter them to sea;
Who swears the sweetest is no more than human.

And say no kinder words than these of me:
"Ever she longed for peace, but was a woman!
And thus they are, whose silly female dust
Needs little enough to clutter it and bind it,
Who meet a slanted gaze, and ever must
Go build themselves a soul to dwell behind it."

For now I am my own again, my friend!
This scar but points the whiteness of my breast;
This frenzy, like its betters, spins an end,
And now I am my own. And that is best.
Therefore, I am immeasurably grateful
To you, for proving shallow, false, and hateful. (PDP 304)

If the details did matter to the story of a woman, one might talk about the poet's irony, detailing her measured assertion of immeasurable gratitude at being so beautifully and confirmingly disappointed and abandoned, and showing how intricately the sounds of the double lettered words—silly, little, cluttered, betters—resonate with the other couplings expressed in the end rhymes, distressed in the enjambments, and inverted in the end, where the poet belies her earlier demonstration of virtuosic femininity in love and in the genres of love that she can write, with emotion, and shape, into beauty, and imitate, as from an elevated tradition of witnessing, what is finally identical to her own soul's desires. It is as though Parker wants to show that she has mastered (poetic) convention rather than being mastered by it (emotionally). But the process of the poetry is to master the compliant reader until that compliance hits the female complaint. It is a political complaint too, the kind that arises when the dream hits some hard truths: that people are ambivalent about what they want and incoherent too. It seems frank to say so in a short sentence. What Parker works here is the revelation of the process of holding on to the form and staying thereby in proximity to the norm.

Parker's poetry always engages the rhythm of the feminine compulsion to repeat, vigilant even when it betrays little pleasure apart from the rhythms of knowing. This specific image of the patterned subject who adapts to the echoes of its own movement resonates with Freud's formulation of subjectivity in "The Economic Problem of Masochism." *Pace* many critics' conflation of the pleasures of poetic form with masochism itself, Freud first refers *not* to the masochist but to the general subject in asking why people submit to regimes of unpleasure when the purpose of the ego and of the libidinal system is to minimize the discomfort of the highs and the lows. Admitting that, in the end, he does not know, he wonders if people after all amount to what they encounter in echoes of a "rhythm, the temporal sequence of changes, rises, and falls in the quantity of stimulus."[21] Tracking oneself in the echoes or lag time of the changes one is always making is not masochism but subjectivity: the masochist's relation to the pleasure of self-extension in form thematizes the constraints of form as punishment, but that is one of many tones and not intrinsic to the structure of being held in a rhythm of varying intensities.

In the shadow of this thought it is unsurprising that, against better knowledge, Parker's "woman" returns to the rhythm of love and the fantasy enacted by the couplet that two people too might rhyme and in rhyming drown out the fresh hell of loneliness. Her subject-in-general associates being a human with a rhythm; her feminine subject associates it with the affects and emotions of normative femininity. Parker, meanwhile, distinguishes herself by mastering aesthetic conventionality so that even when she loses she wins. But it is a displacement, not a detachment.

Without the girdle of the couplet, it all points to affective attrition, pathos, and psychosis. The everyday of uncoupled femininity in these pieces, and performatively in Parker's prose, is a space of spreading out, of no response to the call, of dissolution toward a death in life or suicide. The solo subject listening to her own echoes in Parker's work cannot be like a lovely verse because without a lover to rhyme with she is limerant, disorganized by the overwhelming immediacies of crisis and the contingencies of bargaining. Parker's much anthologized story, "A Telephone Call," begins, "Please, God, let him telephone me now. Dear God, let him call me now. I won't ask anything else of You, truly I won't. It isn't very much to ask. It would be so little to You, God, such a little, little thing. Only let him telephone now. Please, God. Please, please, please" (PDP 119). Other pieces, such as "Sentiment," also take the form of the *récit*, a psychological genre whose mode accumulates the detail of autobiography while performing, paradoxically, the subject's disintegration into mere repetition.[22] Derrida's "The Law of Genre" uses the *récit* to theorize the conventionality of genre itself, focusing on the centrality of sexual difference to it: for Blanchot in *The Madness of the Day*, even the performance of madness takes place according to rules. In the *récit*, therefore, the subject's textual dissolution marks paradoxically that even the subject who is becoming destroyed dissolves according to the logic of the law's demand for reliability. All we need to make up a form are repetitions: we do not even need the capacity for intention. Only an elitist, someone who cannot bear her own generality, would force the reading of the subject toward a place of uniqueness.

"Big Blonde," which has incited this reverie, manifests this skeleton of a plot in the register of bodily experience, sensually mediated knowledge, and miasmatic consciousness. The story tracks Hazel Morse over the decade in which she turns from a woman who was "prettily colored and erect and high-breasted," a "good sport," and a fun "form of diversion" into someone whose "days were a blurred and flickering sequence, an imperfect film, dealing with the actions of strangers" until even the strangers leave, the credits roll, and it is just Mrs. Morse and her maid, Nettie, in her apartment drinking to cheer up and toasting, "Here's mud in your eye" (PDP 186, 211), an anti-epistemological wish if ever there were one. In the story Mrs. Morse is enervated by the memory of the details of her slippage into slurring vagueness and spreading enfleshment (even her freckles are blurring). The details matter to Parker, who distinguishes herself, in her courage for knowledge, from Mrs. Morse, who is trying not to remember or feel remorse for stuffing her once beautiful feet into the "stubby champagne slippers" of Cinderellaesque femininity (PDP 209). Here being drunk is the heightened feeling of femininity peeled off from the barely enumerated plot of optimistic self-remaking that I have called bargaining, a brightening activity that tries to but never fully blocks out the imminence of abjection, that eviction from socially habitable subjectivity where the confirming pleasures of *jouissance* split off from any actually fun experience of pleasure. But this elliptical subjectivity is no avant-garde transgression of metaphysical personhood: this version of slurring into a repetition takes no courage or cognition, or even intention. It is not an act, but a succumbing to the rhythm of repetition that is the zero sum of personhood.

What does it mean, then, to Parker, that subjectivity involves a choice between the bad rhymes of the realist couple and the subject reduced to mere repetition, a purposeless rhythm of rising and falling, all failures in love, here the figure of normative social form? Adorno would argue that conventional rhythm is narcotization and that the constant shifting between daydreaming, anxiety, and panic constitutes "pseudo-activity," that which "overdoes and aggravates itself for the sake of its own publicity, without admitting to itself to what extent it serves as a substitute satisfaction . . . the attempt to rescue enclaves of immediacy in the midst of a thoroughly mediated and rigidified society."[23] For Adorno pseudo-activity is a habit of fake self-symbolization in dramatic agency to which capitalist culture relegates the subject's need to experience mattering. Parker is even more skeptical than Adorno, insofar as she sees no way out of being bound up in episodes and gestures of bargaining to become "someone" and surviving extreme and ordinary disappointment. At the same time, she takes consolation by playing around with the forms that bind: ironic formalism is the normativity of the middlebrow author, who can have her sex and hate it too.

Take, for example, the wedding proposal scene of *A Star Is Born*, repeated intact across the Gaynor and Garland versions while much else changes between them. In this adaptation, Vicki Lester (Janet Gaynor) and Norman Maine (Fredric March) are at a boxing match when he proposes (see fig. 32). Imagine each of these couplets crosscut by a shot of two boxers battling it out.

N: Do you like me?
V: Sure I do.

N: That reminds me, will you marry me?
V: No, thank you.

N: Why won't you marry me?
V: 'Cause you're not dependable; you throw away your money; and you drink so much.

N: Well suppose I quit drinking.
V: (Yes)
N: Suppose I save my money.
V: (Yes)

**32**
Pugilism meets screwball comedy: the lovers banter (*A Star Is Born*, 1937).

N: Suppose I become absolutely dependable on all occasions? W . . . (fight escalates into a knockout).

V: Norman, would you do all that for me if I said I'd married you?
N: No, certainly not. I was just supposing. (Cut to Maine telling an off-screen Oliver Niles: "We are going to be married.")

Note that this scene is exactly like a Parkerian lyric: each blow rhymes with a phrase and each phrase is a phase in the narrative whose journey is not predictable but whose end is as inevitable as that knockout in the ring. Yet it is a pseudo-conversation: he asks, she says yes. In between, some questions are raised and put to rest. So does it matter that Lester shows what she knows? Never before in ordinary life has Lester/Gaynor acted hard-boiled; only when she imitates other stars or stock accents or plays "wife" during their honeymoon do we ever see her even imitate the inelegant.

What are we supposed to think about protest and resistance in the context of the ongoing rolling of the machinery of the fight, the film, and the marriage? The betrothal scene requires the film to marry two styles—women's culture realism and Hollywood fantasy. It does this by wielding an almost *vérité* camera to match its style of screwball verbal pugilism: but the content, as we would predict, tells another story, this one about the fear of losing the opportunity to enact conventionality. Because this film distinguishes itself the way Parker's work always does, as not merely sentimental, its hallmark wit involves being explicit about that which it is inconvenient to be explicit about in love, which is that one's object is always more or less a bad object.

Varieties of this humiliating observation are central to all versions of *A Star Is Born*. "Drunk or not drunk, Norman Maine is nice," Judy Garland's Lester says, on the way to falling in love with "The Man Who Got Away," proving once again that ardently felt incoherent emotions are the most authentic of all. At the same time, there is a feminist inflection to Parker's analysis of the splitting off of emotional performance from emotional knowledge: I have described this split as a hallmark defense in Parker's style. In *A Star Is Born*, as in every film this book engages, and others—*Alice Adams* comes to mind—femininity is seen as a training ground for the profession of acting. Acting, like many forms of engagement with convention, requires the subject to sublimate her being into another's shape while nonpsychotically having a personality to snap back to when the intersubjective moment is over: method acting, of course, called for more temporal leakage between the performance and the being manifesting it. For ordinary women represented in women's culture, life is all about method acting, and it is the revelation of the labor of representing hypocrisy as emotional transparency that elevates ordinary femininity into situation tragicomedy. These plots about ordinary people just being one makeover away from being legendary actresses just amplify the convoluted and incoherent world of promise and revelation held together in women's intimate public, where the work of being somebody for others' emotional well-being produces massive apprehensions of desire and disappointment along with the woman's sheer pleasure in being a mistress of conventionality as such. Even though, as actresses, Gaynor and Garland are said to transcend imitation, as women they are compelled, by and for love, to be most artificial, or formal. The irony for Parker is that this open secret does not interfere much with the reproduction of the desire to remain within the scene of intimate bargaining, without whose intensities there is no evidence of life, only failure to thrive.

This was the point of continuously returning to "the woman" in the "story of a woman I know," to see the wiggle room within normativity as the basis for feminine optimism, which engenders conventionality as a protective layer that manifests itself sometimes as rhetorical hardness and sometimes as its opposite, in behaviors and genres of leaky, porous, blurry, grotesque, or lovely softness. Parker details this form by splitting the registers of "woman" into the aversively soft and optimistic and the aversively knowing and stuck.

But while the former is left to her virtuous disappointment, the latter has poetry and drinking and new seductions to drown out the impossibility of living the life fantasmatic. The vernacular gestures of cosmopolitan feminine survival only appear as liberation from the merely sacrificial, sentimental, privatized ones of the conventional or archaic women. In Parker's *oeuvre*, these freedoms are also ways of maintaining the desire and the demand to be walking toward love.

Meanwhile, gathering up the shards generated by the rubbing together of persons with desires for attachment to the normative worlds they try to fit into, and seeing no whole into which we can glue them back together so expertly that we can hide the sutures, we are left with the measure of the complaint. A mode of address available to many genres, complaint is the means through which Parker and so many women bound to femininity find a way of archiving experience and turning experience into evidence and evidence into argument and argument into convention and convention into cliché, clichés so powerful they can hold a person for her entire life.

Responding to restlessness with normativity by so much activity of resolution is a central process of mass culture, as Richard Dyer and Fredric Jameson have argued, concluding that the utopian is encoded in totalities that otherwise seem saturated or weighted by the conventional, thus delivering a doubled sense of affective satisfaction to those otherwise saturated by the world to which they are also bound in the continuous present.[24] Dyer in particular shows how the fulfillment of generic expectation itself is a form of *jouissance* that Hollywood engenders regardless of the images of totality or details of dissolution particular plots might enumerate. I have argued that this dialectic of fulfillment through genre takes on a particular minor cast in the way it organizes Parker's couplets too, in that she produces explicitly what does not socially exist—the couplet as couple. This is also a form of high-middlebrow resistance to homogenizing mass culture.[25] But Parker ups the ante in her deployments of form against the messes of social and self-betrayal from which she everywhere dissents sentimentally. Her poems are located outside of mass culture by virtue of their manifest self-reflexive seriousness, inside of mass culture by virtue of the venues where the middle-brow find their art, and in the thick of low things to the degree that they are doggerel that loves and cultivates failure: the love sonnet as wisecrack. This is why her poetry is not exactly light verse, and why its vernacularity lists precipitously between the feather and the anvil. It wants its value to be secured by the distance made by reflexive intelligence: but it also doesn't want that; it wants contact with the world.

Thus in Parker we are encountering the convolutions of the middlebrow text, as it does not rest with producing the self-confirming pleasures of generic contracts that actually work, but is restive with those pleasures and condescending toward them. It ought to matter, she suggests, that *she* is able to infuse form with intelligence, and yet this very intelligence foregrounds the failures of the rational subject to make a world that makes a sense that approaches justice. She can only approach the absurdity of the rationalization of injustice, though, and this means that in her corpus the transformation or sublimation of structural subordination—the "social problem"—that marks middlebrow conscientiousness about entertainment requiring instruction reaches its limit when it is the *subject* who dissolves and not the world of the subject.

In other words, the female complaint is that the little ladies are forced to know, to be conscious of, and to protect their intimates from knowing what they know about the world to which they are attached. They know a lot that they are displaying to each other in the open secret structure of the intimate public. One of their secrets, which Parker can almost not bear to learn, is that self-cultivation toward more refined sensibilities does not neutralize the stupidities and irrationalities of attachment; and that knowledge does not break repetitions but can be a prison of its own that creates loneliness and self-consciousness without diluting the subject's saturation by, well, everything.

The non-optimism of this account of knowledge shows that the complaint and the love plot are both sites of sexual knowledge *and* sexual practices. In the texts of women's intimate public, sexuality is a scene of adjustment in which the oppressiveness of a social situation of vulnerability converts into an attachment to a need to be near to the story of how the subject lost her form and lived to tell the tale.

## Unfinished Business

While she was gaining fame as a witness to women's amorous contortions, Parker was known for developing an active political sense, from her arrest in 1927 for "loitering and sauntering" in protest at the imminent executions of Sacco and Vanzetti to her radicalization during the Spanish Civil War. Biographers say conflicting things about how deeply committed she was to the Communist Party, but all agree that she risked her career through leftist political activism public enough that she was named repeatedly in testimony before the House Un-American Activities Committee and appears as well in documents produced by that committee listing reds and their fellow travelers.[26] Characterized in these documents as " 'an undercover Communist,' 'an open Communist,' and a Communist appeaser," she was also suspected of soliciting many a "fellow traveler" and taking her aesthetic orders directly from Russia, rather than from the communist-saturated unions that were actively organizing rank and file actors in the 1920s and 1930s.[27] This part of her career, although forgotten now, made her vulnerable to anticommunist cultural activity such as public picketing at performances of her work and, more obliquely, blacklisting. She dedicated much of her later aesthetic work to this commitment, although not her poetry: in her radicalizing revisions to *It's a Wonderful Life*, in the political rantings of the freaks and the blind man in Hitchcock's *Saboteur*, and in gorgeously didactic stories such as "Little Curtis," "Clothe the Naked," and "Song of the Shirt," all of which represent fantasy as fundamentally shaped and cramped by class and racial inequality and detail their devastating consequences to life materially, which includes to fantasy. Parker's tone is always tremulous when she details the imaginative damage wrought by mass injustice—she skewers the lame vagueness of feminized empathy toward the "unfortunate" and veers rhetorically between extremes of satirical antibourgeois outrage and melodramas of the suffering.

So it is strange, but characteristic of Parker's style of political stylization, that in the *Paris Review* interview that frames our discussion she diverts a question about the blacklist to a discussion of grammar.

Interviewer: How about your political views? Have they made any difference to you professionally?

Parker: Oh, certainly. Though I don't think this "blacklist" business extends to the theater or certain of the magazines, in Hollywood it exists because several gentlemen felt it best to drop names like marbles which bounced back like rubber balls about people they'd seen in the company of what they charmingly called "commies." You can't go back thirty years to Sacco and Vanzetti. I won't do it. Well, well, well, that's the way it is. If all this means something to the good of the movies, I don't know what it is. Sam Goldwyn said, "How'm I gonna do decent pictures when all my good writers are in jail?" Then, he added, the infallible Goldwyn, "Don't misunderstand me, they all ought to be hung." Mr. Goldwyn didn't know about hanged. That's all there is to say. It's not the tragedies that kill us, it's the messes. (18–19)

What hangs on this critique of vulgar vernacularity? On the face of it, Goldwyn's bad grammar manifests the failures of aesthetic self-cultivation that also produce his dangerous politics, about which she waxes ironic. The blacklist isn't deemed anti-democratic here: it's vulgar. The analysis hinges on an argument about proper form. Over and over, in Parker's work, and in the class axis of the complaint culture in which she reigns, to know something and to cherish and distinguish yourself through what you know is to get the social grammar right. To know when to withhold and when to tell a story is to be an insider and to belong. To have mastered the performance of conventionality approximates an appearance of an idealized self. Having expressed it all in the cool rhythms of trained cognition, expressing a cultivated and acculturated consciousness, gives one the right to judge politics and also to be satirical, superior to the conventional popular cultural belief in one's ethical obligation to go into any new scene with sunny good intentions.

And so it is here, in form, that the political Parker meets the sentimental one. Parker locates herself in a cultural elite by cultivating an edge that separates her from the vulgar political world and the sentimental sisterhood. This edge merges class, classiness, and a highly refined vulgarity: she always selects the clean lines of style over the misshapen abreactions of the ordinary. Even when her metaphors and emotions are all kinds of mixed and her desires pretty simple, she will always have wanted to seem set apart in a glow of sharp-witted clarity. A tragedy is magnificent and organized by logic; a mess is depressing and disorganized by failure. A melodramatic gesture telegraphs a clear feeling; a female complaint, another messy situation.

What is fascinating to Parker, and all of the female complainers, are the stories of learning to adapt, an education in disappointment management that is critical without trafficking in the big political refusals. The end of the poem, the couplet that marks, like a tear, the impossibility of the idealized couple; and the end of the film, the episode and the caption, which mark the insufficiency of glamour and love plots to secure the conditions of self-love, of being somebody; these are weapons to make you sick with despair but also consoled about how hard it is, especially for women, to detach from the drama of adjustment and obligation. The generalized affective recognition offered by women's intimate publicity actually saves the day. For it looked like being *somebody* was the only way to not be *nobody*. How do we reinhabit fantasy concretely, in a social body, given the politically, socially, and imaginatively cramped world that creates an abyssal nonmediation between the fantasy of being somebody and ordinary life? Parker's semi-solution was to identify in public as "a woman who," an *anybody*. Averse to conventionality, but relieved of singularity through it too, sometimes it is all a girl can do to show you a once beautiful shape, a failed conventional form, or an instance of tinny courage that can gesture toward the broken utopian while making you feel the optimism of having an infinite number of second chances at it.

# THE COMPULSION TO REPEAT FEMININITY

*Landscape for a Good Woman* and *The Life and Loves of a She-Devil*

From the different perspectives developed in the preceding cases, I have been arguing that, in the literature of women's intimate public, the restlessness that desire creates is not the same thing as an imminent politics or a drive to detach from the disappointing object world. The insider conversation that circulates there, about the details of women's *situation* and the strategies of survival and affect management emerging from it, becomes also a way of musing about what identifying with fantasies of conventionality can do for and to women amid the project of surviving a world that can wear you out.

As the feminist activists of *Uncle Sam Needs a Wife* (see chapter 4) would have suggested, it would have been possible in this book to posit feminism as a resource for a variety of historically available solutions to the crisis situation of a normative femininity that turns the intensities of bargaining activity into evidence that one is living life richly. Sometimes feminism is not sentimental and does not bank on the association of femininity with the authenticity of true feeling. Sometimes it is a vehicle for an imaginative refusal of what in intimate and political life has not worked for women; and sometimes it gives permission to women to make a more extreme break—and strategies for doing so—with a conventional object world no longer worthy of the promises historically projected onto it. But, from the perspective of what has bound women historically to their sense of belonging to a general femininity, feminism has been a much better resource for critique than for providing accounts of how to live amid affective uncertainty, ambivalence, and incoherence. That has been a primary historic contribution of women's intimate public in the United States.

This ambivalence has not only exposed the couple form to a variety of critical gazes, but has also focused on what has been made possible and impossible in the project of earning autonomy and sovereignty promised by capitalist meritocracy. All of the novels and films we have looked at see economic autonomy as crucial to a woman's sense of limited sovereignty in the world; all of them see exploitation as an unavoidable problem with predictable consequences; and all of them want the world of lived love to provide ballast for the stress of all that striving and surviving. When love fails, therefore, it diminishes the meaningfulness of whatever economic and public success the protagonists have scraped together through hard labor and luck (this describes the affective economic shape of *A Star Is Born*, *Imitation of Life*, and *Show Boat*, for example). Fractures in intimacy almost always expose the drive toward economic attainment in these plots as a mode of entrepreneurial pragmatism that builds confidence and wards off loneliness, without, alas, snuffing it out.[1] The historical articulation of feminism with economic radicalism and the tone-deafness of feminism about many women's ambivalent relation to autonomy and aloneness therefore usually does not seem helpful in middlebrow texts that work in the idiom of survival. But in the long history of sentimental publics, economic and intimate precarity have inevitably produced reflections on what would happen if radicalism were a general way of life and women's labor were seen as a potential resource for a flourishing intimacy outside of intimate and economic normativity.

This chapter looks at some cases where feminist fantasy transacts with the fantasy conventions we have derived from the legacies of feminine sentimentality, with its aggressive organization of life around desires for emotional transparency and affective confirmation, and with its positioning of fantasy as a blueprint for the real. Its aim is not to speak about feminism in general, but to point toward zones of affectivity where feminism and feminine sentimental conventions have a hard time meeting. It pursues what can happen in a moment of loss, when the forces that have overorganized fantasy into conventional forms, scenes of improvisation, and negotiated contradiction seem to be discarded as rules for living in a way that threatens the proximity and endurance of fantasy as the context of practice itself. What happens when the forms that have stood for virtue, value, social intelligibility, and optimism generally are seen to have exhausted their unifying function, their role in allegorizing the activity of the everyday as adding up to something? What does it mean to lose the way you have lived without knowing what else to do?

Sometimes radical political imaginaries characterize traditional forms of social intelligibility and discipline as supernumerary limbs, or accretions that weigh down the potentially empowered subject of history. Established patterns of conventionality are seen as forms of stupidity, unimaginativeness, and automaticness. This is not my view, but even if that were the case—even if conventional desires made people live unthinkingly, and even if contemporary economic and intimate practices have surpassed some historic forms and no longer organize or describe the world of power, knowledge, and desire in which people are managing life—what about the ongoing life of the archaic? Is moving past a form's historical dominance the same thing as witnessing its breakdown? If not by substitution, how do new metacultural figures of the emergent subject of history—the hybrid, the queer, the feminist, the migrant—transact with previously ascendant patterns of normative identification?[2] The aim of this chapter is to establish some methods for adjudicating the anachronism of the sexual present, using two contemporaneous hybridized encounters between femininity and feminism: Carolyn Steedman's autobiographical *Landscape for a Good Woman* (1986) and Fay Weldon's novel, *The Life and Loves of a She-Devil* (1983).

In both texts, the metacultural or universalizing forms to which the texts point—the nation form and sexual difference—come into contact with practices and spaces that are noted for their unwieldy and shifting improprieties—sexuality and the city. For both, the city is the place where economic and cultural membership are lived complexly, while the nation is the space where law establishes rules and norms and persons gain simpler, formal value as citizens; likewise, sexuality is the practice that shakes things up, while sexual difference organizes identity and all sorts of other taxonomies into their normative locations. But both works problematize this distribution of instability too. *She-Devil* is written partly in the frank yet florid style of a Barbara Cartland romance, but it tells a feminist story. *Landscape* is a postsentimental autobiography, looking for a genre to give shape to the relations among its diverse explanatory structures (fairy tale, social history, psychoanalysis, working-class and women's autobiography). Both texts reopen the question of feminism's difference from femininity, which has to do with the latter's overvaluation of individual struggle at the expense of social critique and revolt against exploitation. As these are texts from the early 1980s, the lag between the idiom of their critical concerns (socialism versus capitalism, sexual liberation versus male privilege) and the ones that animate contemporary questions of capitalism, transnationality, and erotics can become an opportunity to interfere further with the fantasy that a better form (of analysis, as of being) will solve the problem of living.

Carolyn Steedman's *Landscape for a Good Woman* provides a history of the failure of radicalism and feminism to speak to the affective disappointments of her working-class mother in England after World War II. When Steedman renders her mother's desire for the good life, she tells a story about feminine desire as a scene of class-related subjectivity that gets enacted through migration, marriage, the management of knowledge, the manipulation of money, and the marginality of children. In this cluster of movements and positionings, desire is something that makes you restless, defensive, and ambitious; it propels you toward an elsewhere that, you imagine, will offer you a fresh start, a new horizon of possibility and fewer economic impediments. In this view, desire merges the intimate ambitions of your life narrative with the economic ones, while pushing back the demons of a burdensome past. In other words, the ideology of desire Steedman chronicles casts history as a weight on the capacity to live now as if in an ongoing future shaped by fantasy, not by forces or relations of production.

The coproduction of intimacy and economy in the idiom of desire opens up for Steedman other modes of meaning that have less to do with the linearity of moving stories than with the circularity of static signs. Here the subject's life is made not from movement, but from relations to *things*.[3] Addressing the ways commodity cultures work to organize fantasy, Steedman suggests that the cultivated appetite for things both tempers and temporizes desire by attaching it to concrete and potentially attainable objects, fixing people in thing-oriented circuits of repetition that promise a life of something like sublimity, but without its risk or pain.

Many women of the postwar era, for example, identified the pleasures of their ideal world with beautiful fabrics, beautiful hands, beautiful clothes, and good food.[4] In advance of class security, Steedman says that her mother turns in on herself for practice, performing the feeling of belonging as solidity and superiority; she lives these dreams in the cultivation of her body and the bodies around her, from managing familial programs of culinary discipline to working as a manicurist for an elite class of fashion model. In this way the alienation of production and the self-elaboration in consumption become fused beautifully, muting without entirely drowning out the hard lived distances of unfairness and inequality. The body, Steedman writes bitterly, is what the powerless work on when they have nothing else:[5] a certain skirt and certain foods can populate what counts as imaginable satisfaction in the face of other frustrated social relations. This constellation of need conventions has enabled a quasi-literal reading of the social to gain popular legitimacy, such that the things and practices of self-discipline identified with women's desires came themselves to seem evidence of the good life's good value and possessive potential.

Steedman means to expose here much more than a tendency toward feminine fetishism. She suggests that these conventions of the beautiful object convey a less-enunciated desire for a world that can sustain families, love, and dignity and that can overcome the economic strain and shame that working people experience in their effort to reach that plateau of satisfaction, the unanxious space and time of attainment that is the "good woman's" fantasy.[6] Much of the work and the moving, monitoring, and accumulative fussing that go into survival as well as into the reconditioning of the social body are condensed in objects. The move toward a specific goal is about whatever value or use it explicitly conveys, but such a move is also a vehicle for tactical moves to produce yet a third kind of space. There, one would feel protected by an aura of plenitude and invulnerability like that which radiates from one's ego ideal or the experience of "social standing." The mother's fantasy is, more simply, for her life to become a space of perfect time *where that change has already happened* and where, therefore, the activity of living was maintenance, not striving. The objects she desires, like any cathected object, are therefore both expressions of a cluster of wants and also defenses against experiencing how rawmaking and destabilizing it is to be driven to make a world amid a scene whose standards of reciprocity are underwhelming and worse. Nonetheless, the mother cannot not feel the ambivalence that drives her toward her satisfaction via the object.

Steedman uses the artifice of the landscape to describe the interpretive devices people invent to make sense of their disjointed realities: the landscape tableau provides a clue to understanding how the contradictions of capitalist culture become livable, desirable, explicable—or at least endured. This process is literalized for Steedman in the Lowry landscape of a mill town in northern England that her mother hangs over the mantel. Steedman puzzles that her mother would display a world from which she had fled and hidden, as though she wished after all to acknowledge what she had abandoned for the project of uplift. No doubt the mother's motive is derived in part from nostalgia's ghosts and from a desire not to be *of* somewhere but *from* somewhere. But given Lowry's celebrity as the *auteur* of a fading Britishness in the popular art world of postwar England this landscape turns the detritus of her past into cultural capital, augmenting her claim to be, after all, the *thing* of her own fantasy.[7]

The substitutions Steedman's mother makes confuse Steedman by not being confusing enough. Somehow the mother's drive to inhabit a metropolitan space where financial and cultural networks make ingots of opportunity available for the ambitious is embodied in the national iconicity of the landscape form where a former place of production can be displayed as quaint and provide pleasure and leisure at the point of consumption. Somehow the mother translates the hot complexity of a sexuality and a marriage marked by secrets and shaming into the register of proper femininity and "decent" class aspiration. She turns the stress and compromise of life in metropolitan zones into an imaginary space of absolute value that is never, or not yet, lived, by insisting that fantasy is the scene of life that must be protected from the fraying of the everyday.

Fantasy is where the mother really lives—she is a sentimentalist in the traditional sense, and she believes in the intelligence that brings her to longing's objects. In the meantime, she and those around her do what they need to get by, taking nourishment from the hoards of happiness that they keep in little pockets of sense experience and sense memory. But this hoarding needs to be disavowable, too. In *Landscape*, children, women, and the working classes always accept their obligation to maintain a surface that shows no wrinkles, tears, or bruises. As though there could be plastic surgery on the real, the experience of betrayal, disappointment, and flawed intimacy that shapes all of their stories must be contained in the open secret whose keeping preserves the composure, if not the dignity, of everyone bound to it by fantasy and solidarity. To explain the consequences of this and the difficulty of moving beyond the convention that maintains it to something emancipated, the next section glosses how the book closes, asking its readers not to celebrate what they have just learned about (working-class, feminine, children's) suffering but instead to "say 'so What?'; and consign it to the dark."[8]

### The "So What?" Question

How do we comprehend an imaginary that occupies terribly unsettled spaces but locates fantasy as what really gives life its meaning? We might begin by thinking about substitution as something other than a form of repetition. Christopher Bollas describes the optimism a new object of attachment organizes as a "transformational environment."[9] Extending Winnicott's notion of the transformational environment, Bollas argues that when someone recognizes a new attachment she seeks to desire herself in the desire she elicits from another. This version of herself is not someone who already exists but one that the transformational environment provided by the new object will help to bring into being.

To the extent that the loving subject is asking for the object to provide her with a sense of herself that does not yet exist, Bollas's model is akin to the Lacanian view offered in the introduction to this book. But Bollas's version of attachment love splits from the Lacanian account in significant ways. In both views, the subject of love finds her new optimism for herself in the potentiality released by the love object's recognition of her. This desired change, embodied in the other's desire, will fabricate the desiring subject's fantasy of what she will be as the story of who she already is. But in Lacanian parlance this structuration of the subject of love in a collapsing of the will-have-been with the already-is enables the subject to disavow and project out her sense of incompleteness and lack. In Bollas's contrasting view, this transaction additionally confirms the self-ambivalence of which the lover's desire to change is evidence. The beloved's confirmation of the sense of oneself as loveable coexists with the other sense of oneself as insufficient, unworthy, a mixed bag. But in Bollas's work the negative part of ambivalence does not defeat love. It is what makes love possible. The transformational environment absorbs contradictions, convolutions, and paradoxes of attachment. They can flourish all at once, protected in the environment's capacity to hold together someone's being despite and amid what is transitional, ambivalent, illogical, and incomplete about her. In this model, love creates a space for proliferating logics of attachment and self-endurance, a proliferation that would only threaten the subject's continuity if she had to reduce it all to one structure, one way of being, one focus, and one fate, as we will see.

Steedman's mother learns to seek transformational environments and to accumulate evidence for her goodness within regimes of normative ideology that link intimate desires to political realms of social membership and self-development to the assimilation of bourgeois norms. To remain endowed with the virtually legislative power of normativity, the fantasy or theory of a particular identity must be literalized in practice. To sustain optimism for the project of the feminine good life in the practical world, she requires spaces where the labor of producing a better self can take place. In *Landscape* the city is central to the production of the "soft subversions" subjects generate to negotiate capitalist hierarchies of value.[10] Félix Guattari argues that subjects of capitalism are reduced to a "microfascism" of the body, a masochism or pleasure disorder that subjugates consciousness in self-directed fixations that distort the subject's perception of her generic place in regimes of structural subordination. The subject is reduced to telling history as a story about herself and begins to embroider her conventionality with consoling and conventional signs of uniqueness. Agency feels diluted into incremental acts in the capitalist cityscape; time is absorbed into a space that only slowly registers effects.

These distinct but proximate temporalities render ordinary living relatively oblique to the flow of communication and capital that moves along rapidly in the metropole's networks.[11] In the unmapped spaces and intervals of anonymity, one can cloak those aspects of class history whose exposure might obstruct the fantasies one might live by the accumulation of capital, whether cultural or economic.[12] Steedman charts her mother's appropriation of a prosthetic life through the story of her migration from one city to the next. In London she uses her noncosmopolitanism, her anonymity and genericness, to provide the camouflage that will enable her fantasy self to emerge unmarked by its unpleasant past. To her, the city is an economic space where life can be contingently carved out, but it also grants a space of opportunistic loss and instrumental proliferation where the will can be exerted against the strain of history's determinations, just as women's sartorial and bodily habits can seem to eclipse history's distinguishing marks.

This particular desire for a dehistoricizing abstraction, which coded class ascension through feminine style, emerged at a conjuncture with a shift in national policy regarding English class hierarchy. The post–World War II generation extracted a promise from the state that rebuilding England would mean more fully including all classes of citizen in the nation's resources. The so-called welfare state expanded, but the political impact on working-class subjects of its redistributive program was not necessarily progressive.[13] Over time Steedman's mother became righteously conservative, identifying not with the lot of the laboring classes but with an aspiration to *feel* free from structural impediments the way she imagined the elite must feel. She desired to embody the best of "culture." Following Enoch Powell and others nostalgic for the eminence of imperial Britishness, she adopted patriotic nationalism, with its codes of xenophobia and racism, to give shape to what lay in the way of this freedom. Along with feminine bodily discipline providing public consent to the values of the visibly superior proper world, these normative forms and practices of citizenship were crucial to sustaining the mirage that her "I" was both particular and (potentially) universal: unique, superior, typical, law-abiding, and unfettered where need be.[14] While Steedman's mother exploited the cityscape to cultivate her aspiring brand of uniqueness and conventionality, her attachment to proper form impeded the development of a critical relation to the very conditions of national economic, sexual, and gendered subordination that produced her anxieties and induced her to work for a gratifying future in the first place. The body and the nimbus of intimacy it generates became the archive or the hoard that she could spend in order to make a world that would confirm the power of the feminine thing, her fantasy. Meanwhile, the body magnetized the activity of consciousness so that its destiny seemed also to be the destiny of the nation. In this context, the centrality of the city to fantasy's enactment is lost in the roar of the universal.

To the degree that Steedman uses her mother's life to exemplify the fantasies that characterize women of the postwar working classes, it would be unwise to read this approach as a story about the ways they used commodities to express what would otherwise be critical theory. Instead, commodities are cast as an aesthetic solution to the complexities of aspirational social relations, an understanding of the aesthetic that Steedman places at the center of her class analysis of regimes of subjectivity. Clothing styles and norms of bodily performance are managed by individuals, who negotiate social membership through them. Meanwhile, she argues, one's sense of place and expectations for agency are profoundly influenced by the narrative genres in which subjectivity is conventionally represented: for the middle class, the psychoanalytic case study; for the working class, social history; for children, fairy tales; for citizens, political speeches.

This list of subject-producing genres is surprisingly incomplete. Although *Landscape* is mainly about women—it is Steedman's own story told as the unhappy extension of her mother's unfulfilled one, as well as a story about the uneven devolvement of gender's costs and privileges on men and women of different classes—its argument that class locates gender and sexuality in history does not articulate its analysis with an appraisal of the irrationality or unclarity of sexual attachments. In her view everything her mother and father did were tactics for survival that made sense given their backgrounds, their styles of affect management, and their individual and mutual agreements to keep constitutive secrets. Acts are manipulative, they serve a function and a purpose, and they evidence clearheadedness, never a muddle.

But even when there is clarity about what it is that someone wants to escape, and even when commodities represent the possibility of attaining a legitimate, uncontested, and even glorious foundation in the world, it is likely that the ordinary situation of the people she describes was as reactive as it might have been active; unselfconscious as it might have been deliberate; numb or impulsive along with being intense. It must have been—indeed, she shows it was, while reading it as all of a piece—ambivalent, managerial, and inconsistent. The building of life was the scene of its attrition and in between there was getting by and acting from the gut. So while I am not saying that her mother did not identify having things with having achieved a solidity in the world at terms of reciprocity she could idealize, I am saying that alongside an analytics of interest must go an understanding of the *improvisations* of affect.[15]

This association of the feminine with the capitalist nation is rooted in the political moment in which Steedman wrote *Landscape for a Good Woman*. In contrast to the postwar prosperity that helped to shape Steedman's mother, the context for much of Steedman's own critique is the politics of the Left after 1968 generally, especially socialist feminism. Some central claims and tactics of the movement are expressed in the way *Landscape* tracks the double narrative of the mother and the daughter across national, sexual, and class divisions and employs a rhetorical analytic that mixes theory, history, literary reading, and autobiography: briefly, that challenging the institutional and subjective effects of patriarchy requires dismantling traditional divisions and hierarchies of knowledge as well as those of the state, capitalism, the family, and the law; and that a simultaneous revolution in sexual practices, institutions, and ideology will further liberate feminine desire from its identification with emotional and domestic service economies. A socialist, sexual, and conceptual liberation would be required to disorganize the normative world, freeing persons from their destinies within the "real" of subordination and exploitation.[16]

*Landscape* tacitly endorses these views; at the same time, however, Steedman suggests that by presuming the universality of feminine subjectivity and desire, feminist psychoanalytic thought of the same period participated in the normative work of maintaining femininity's generic status, in large part by simplifying men and diminishing the importance of class and national politics to the histories and futures of women. Yet Steedman cannot fully reject psychoanalytic configurations of gendered subjectivity—in part because the strategy of her text is to respect the different genres of subjectivity that represent the Real for different categories of person; and in part because the compulsion to repeat abjection to norms of sexual difference is the fundamental condition Steedman narrates, as it historically arbitrates the way class, racial, and national relations are lived. Against her will, she inherits a feminine location, along with the Oedipal mommy-daddy-me story that so frustratingly refuses to go away. The "So what?" that hangs as the epitaph to her mother's and her own life at the end of *Landscape* is meant to be a rhetorical question about the value of all these details, these species of feminine and feminist negation and desire.[17] The book's most melodramatic moment points to a wish to be beyond these stories. But the very desire the ending expresses *not* to participate in the very intimate public of femininity that makes this book intelligible and a gesture toward communication among strangers says something about the impossibility of and ambivalence toward retrivializing the survivalism that marks its own gesture.

This chapter reconsiders the hanging question about the compulsion to repeat femininity. "So what?" asks about the centrality of the logic of cliché to the popular understanding of the feminine; it queries the "pseudo-activity" of feminine genres, which produce narratives that seem to risk transgressing the structure of cliché while all along posing threats as conventional as any happy ending, any blue sky or love song.[18] This does not mean that the threats to fulfillment are mere mirages, but that frequently the drama of their overcoming requires disguising their conventionality. In *The Life and Loves of a She-Devil*, the conventions of romance are so intensified that they generate an aura of stop-time in the continuously anxious present of feminine identity: yet the constancy of resistance to it has a timelessness to it as well, such that the sense of treading water or drowning in the present can also mark the pleasure and even the comfort one might derive from the most painful repetition.

At this level of generality it must be asked if femininity is mainly the ur-example of the routinization of all identity in national-capitalist culture; if the articulation of commodity logic with psychoanalytic notions of attachment, ambivalence, and repetition specifies women historically in modernity; or if there is something irreducible, though not trivial, about the feminine, period. Yet these phrases seem off, too absorbed in a project of a reading that seeks identity's true shape. My task is to turn the compulsion to repeat femininity into the problem the essay addresses, rather than—once again, on behalf of feminist optimism—reconfirming that the always incomplete process of feminization can open up spaces for subversive kinds of improvisation, negotiation, and change. "So what?" can be read as a response to such a claim, as well as a demand to account for the clichés of desire and complaint that constellate around feminine and feminist fantasies, a demand to come to some conclusion other than the one in which the pains women take to remain attached to the pleasures of the feminine undertaking seem inevitably like femininity itself.

As in many historical romances, *The Life and Loves of a She-Devil* uses a love triangle to universalize its image of personhood. But the novel is also *knowing* about the libidinal tricks such formalism plays. Informed, like *Landscape*, by English feminism of the 1980s, *She-Devil* speaks critically of women's relation to love, locating it within the political economy of feminine suffering shaped by global and patriarchalized regimes of intimacy and labor. Neither text much deals with the postimperial *racial* struggles that marked the Britain of the same moment: crises in the political economy of sexual difference operate solely on a white national and familial class axis. That the default image of proper femininity is white and upwardly mobile in these works matters—not just because normativity should always be called out but because the fantasy of finding, making, and reproducing *likeness* that shapes the stories these texts tell becomes merged here uncannily with a racialized rhetoric of solidarity.

At first it will seem that the novel locates the merger of women with femininity and femininity with love plots in a satire of their normalizing institutions, discourses, and desires. Yet by the end of the book, as so often happens, political knowledge drops out of the narrator's consciousness and, once again, it is only the personal sphere that is susceptible to radical change. "Since I cannot change the world, I will change myself," the She-Devil resolves.[19] Yet prior to this the first-person narrative of *She-Devil* has pursued the question of what it would take to destroy the conditions of feminine sub/abjection. The She-Devil's first tactic is unsurprising: to destroy the compulsion to identify with the fantasy of normal love. The second aim conjoins a critique of feminine and feminist projects: *She-Devil* queries the belief that will, consciousness, or reason can save women from desiring the conventional world that normal love maps out. It is an argument for the centrality of the unconscious to any critical practice, whether juxtapolitical, as in feminine culture, or political, as in feminist. Accordingly, alternate chapters are composed in two strikingly different registers—the satirically slanted but acutely rendered language of the romance novel and the rage of feminist realism. That is, two forms of realism, the feminine and the feminist, appear to signify different but cognate representational approaches to the analysis of the world. These modes struggle internally throughout the narrative, addressing as if from different ends the undervaluation of women and the overvaluation of consciousness that characterize the situation of the female and the feminist complaint—the movement of desire and critique that women have felt compelled to repeat.

### "I Sing a Hymn to the Death of Love"

Here is the novel's story. It is written in the voice of a woman named Ruth, who is hampered by many things: very tall, very fat, and abjectly ugly, she has a hairy mole on her face that makes her not only very hard to look at, but repulsive to imagine. Ruth is a product of a working-class environment in which normative, pleasing femininity is especially overvalued as a vehicle for class aspiration. Rejected by her family for her bodily anomaly and the ungainly personality formed around it, Ruth moves through her youth isolated, graceless, and inarticulate. As she ages, her physical strength becomes her only valued attribute: she is a good worker, not a good woman, and work makes a place for her in the world. The first job we hear that she has is at a switchboard: her competence depends on her body's suppression.

Ruth's depression about her bodily destiny is so complete that one cannot even call what she achieves "survival": it is simpler than that, a sentient stubbornness. When the book opens she is a suburban mother of two hateful children whose adulterous husband, "Bobbo," an accountant, calls Ruth "his best friend," which means in practice that she gets to hear detailed accounts of the affairs he is having. Bobbo marries Ruth to spite his mother (and because Ruth's huge body, in the dark, provides a sort of maternal comfort to him): but he soon realizes that such a deviant-looking creature will hold him back in his quest for success. Ruth tries everything to make a Victorian-style suburban world for Bobbo, but who she is visibly stains all of her gestures of taste and attempts at beauty.

Under these circumstances, it is not surprising that Ruth is also, in her spare moments, an addicted reader of romance novels. She especially fancies those written by Mary Fisher, a novelist whose graced personal life is said to enact the fantasies and theories her novels weave, demonstrating by example that romance is both utopia and a reality that can be lived if a woman gives herself over to making beauty, and not just on her body: her language must be luscious, and she must create an exquisite home and landscape: "Mary Fisher lives in the High Tower," writes Ruth to open nearly half of the chapters: she lives on a rugged cliff near the "surging" sea, "where the new morning sun glances over hills and valleys and trees. . . . She is a woman: she made the landscape better" (231). To Fisher and to Ruth (and implicitly, to all participating readers of the romance) the contrapuntal and material relation between reading and living suggests the value of the romance form to women: it is a tacit map of how to use fantasy to shape living, from the space of dreams to the landscape of the everyday. But because of what she looks like and what she cannot do, Ruth must separate fantasy and the real. Consuming Mary Fisher's novels with the insensate avidity of a bulimic, Ruth's compulsive pleasure is also a kind of knowledge—not of the real, but of her distance from fulfilling the values of the feminine world: "I need to know the geographical detail of misfortune" (4).

Ruth's love of the generic is a mirror of her failure at achieving every aspect of it. Since her body has always provided no consoling and distracting mirage for the anxiety that is femininity, that might be the end of the story of Ruth: she even suggests that an aerial photo of Eden Grove, her suburb, would show her as an irregular blob lumbering through a harmonious landscape. But then Bobbo becomes Mary Fisher's accountant as well as her lover. Ruth's first response to this crisis is traditional. To keep alive the fantasy of love's beautiful form, Ruth moves through the usual stages of feminine reseduction—straining to cook beautiful meals, to dress elegantly, to speak pleasingly, and to disappear when she fears she is on the verge of "ugly and discordant" excesses and improprieties that may produce discomfort (7). Unfortunately, the intense pressures of Ruth's performative normativity make her spill the food, tear the dress, trip, pout, speak, and cry at all the wrong places and times. Eventually, Bobbo decides to leave her. He encourages Ruth to get a job. Repeatedly, she says, "but there are no jobs" (39, 48). He considers her pathetic, clumsy, ugly, and dull-witted: "You speak in clichés and talk in clichés" (19).

But during the couple's final fight, there is a sea-change in Ruth's consciousness. Humiliated in front of Bobbo's parents, Ruth locks herself in the bathroom. Angrily, he declares, "You are a third-rate person. You are a bad mother, a worse wife, and a dreadful cook. In fact I don't think you are a woman at all. I think what you are is a she-devil!" (41). Then, quietly, there is "a change in the texture of the silence" that emanates from her (41). Ruth embraces the hysterical gravity of her new appellation: it releases her from the world of pleasant feminine cliché.

Soon after Bobbo leaves, Ruth gives the children money to go to McDonald's, burns down the suburban house, and deposits the kids at the romantic "High Tower" where Mary Fisher and Bobbo live; she disappears from her old life and identity and takes on the project of living as a she-devil, a being of Nietzschean master proportions who uses her wisdom, bodily strength, and will to build a world that suits her. To be a she-devil means not only to live beyond the rules of normativity, but to go beyond sexual difference: "A she-devil is supremely happy: she is inoculated against the pain of memory. At the moment of her transfiguration, from woman to nonwoman, she performs the act herself. She thrusts the long, sharp needle of recollection through the living flesh into the heart, burning it out. The pain is wild and fierce for a time, but presently there's none" (163).

For Ruth, this is a theoretical, practical, and sexual transformation into the negative. The homeopathy of self-inflicted pain derived from the incineration of her memory (the memory of desires) numbs the general pain of failure at competence to femininity: but what is there for desire or identity when what was there for it is expelled?

No longer contracted to femininity, Ruth sees nothing at all utopian about the stabilizing fantasy of gender—it is one of the lies of romance.[20] This does not mean that she becomes postsexual or denies the fascination and desire that sexuality (especially heterosexuality) shapes—quite the contrary. Ruth's response to her marital betrayal is to embark on a life of sexual adventure: every intimate contact she makes is triggered by her ability to become the sexual object her lover needs in order to feel confirmed in the world, which places her paradoxically in the feminine position of absolute power over the lover's grandiosity. Her failure to be feminine releases its power to her—but only in the event that love and desire not be part of the story, which is instead a story about power, about other routes to the feeling of plenitude and unconflictedness that love in a heterosexual family had never delivered to her.

Giving her lovers the gift of her fearlessness and her repudiation of sentimentality, Ruth receives from them access to modes of being she cannot produce from her will—money, safe space, influence, and bodily transformation. An expert reader of the diseases of subjectivity sexual normativity creates, she acts instrumentally on behalf of anger and hate, the purifying pain that defeminizes: "I want to give hate its head," she says (43). Each personal conquest she makes also advances her aim to destroy the institutions that keep women addicted to love and to the intimate scenes of their subordination: this means blighting the adulterous couple along with the "world of judges and priests and doctors, the ones who tell women what to do and how to think" (120).

To do this she moves from Eden Grove to the city. As for jobs, she makes a discovery: "There is always a living to be earned doing the work that others prefer not to do. Employment can generally be found looking after other people's children, caring for the insane, or guarding imprisoned criminals, cleaning public rest rooms, laying out the dead, or making beds in cheap hotels. . . . There is always, as governments are fond of saying, work for those who want it" (110).

She migrates from job to job, working in pseudo-domestic and semiprivate arenas as a nanny for poor women, a nurse for the insane and the aged, and a maid for the privileged. In each job, she takes on a new name, a new vita, a new history: Vesta Rose, Polly Patch, Molly Wishant, Marlene Hunter. In the city, it is presumed, women are hidden and in hiding even when they are on the street or at work. Their zone of privacy is portable, labile: they make an intimate scene wherever they go. Yet in the metropole femininity is also put at risk constantly in its proximity to bargaining and exploitation: this is to say that the putative universality of the feminine (as a space of activity) is marked by the difference between "negotiating" alterity to only just survive and negotiating it with the kind of symbolic capital that makes femininity feel like an aspiration rather than a name for negativity. In *She-Devil*, as in *Landscape*, the city is a place of constant instrumental activity, but not a space of revolution.

The She-Devil works the ambiguous relation between threats to and the fulfillment of the fantasy in this next stage of her life. While working in a prison under the name Vesta Rose, for example, the She-Devil takes on as a lover Nurse Hopkins,[21] another misshapen and inassimilable woman whose sexual gratitude produces a political consciousness ("Women like us . . . must learn to stick together" [119]) and sexual pleasure that bind her to "Vesta" for life. After a bit of time passes, Ruth convinces the nurse to leave the prison with her—" 'Out there in the world,' said Ruth, 'everything is possible and exciting' " (120). This seduction convinces the nurse to bankroll "Vesta Rose," an agency for women "shut away in homes performing sometimes menial tasks, sometimes graceful women trapped by love and duty into lives they never meant, and driven by necessity into jobs they loathe and which slowly kill them" (120).

Once in the metropolitan world, saving women's lives through nondomestic labor becomes the lovers' manifest aim. "The agency specialized in finding secretarial work for women coming back into the labor market—either from choice or through necessity—women who had good skills but lacked worldly confidence after years of domesticity. Those who signed on with the Vesta Rose Agency would receive retraining in secretarial skills and what Ruth called 'assertiveness training' " (121–22). The agency merges employment with self-help, as well as with a quasi-socialist understanding of the degrading aspects of the household economy. Merging this comprehension with the logic of the company town, Vesta Rose offers to the women it employs many extra life-sustaining services—and for a substantial fee: day care, laundry, shopping, and cooking, for example. Thus while minimizing the contradictions of the double shift, the agency actually bolsters the domestic service economy in which femininity operates as an ideology extending the aura of the labor of love. These happy and competent workers become proudly known as Vesta Roses. They are intensely loyal to their leader.

In migrating to the city, then, Ruth creates jobs and supportive economic and emotional public spaces for women. Vesta Rose is so successful that within six months Ruth's women are posted all over the city, in every low level white-collar working environment that counts—courts, jails, hospitals, schools, and financial institutions. The geography of her misery turns into a fantasy space, a city produced by women's collaborative work and emancipated will. The intimate public is joyous, neither a space of critique nor compromise: the female complaint seems ridiculous and outmoded as the force making women's collective binding.

But Ruth has an ulterior purpose. She takes a spare key she had kept from the marriage to go to Bobbo's office at night and shifts funds from his clients' accounts to the joint checking account they still maintain. Some months later Bobbo's office calls—he needs a typist. Vesta Rose sends Elsie Flower to him—a Mary Fisher clone, "little and sweet in looks, who bowed her neck as she bowed her mind, as if forever expecting some not altogether unpleasant blow to fall" (124). Bobbo, a sexual profligate, "seduces" Elsie, and Ruth, on hearing this, encourages the girl to fall in love with him and to tell him so. When Bobbo predictably dumps her, Ruth uses Elsie's rage to exact further revenge. She exposes him to Mary Fisher in a detailed letter with photographs; and, knowing the books of the business as well as she was trained to do, she (plus another Vesta Rose employee who works in Bobbo's bank) helps to transfer money from his account to a Swiss bank account, making it seem as if Bobbo has embezzled the funds for his own purposes. The She-Devil notes the sum—$2,563,072.45—as she notes many figures: her revenge on Bobbo requires mastery of his craft, plus even more precise accounting of who suffers love and how much it costs. Bobbo soon gets arrested. To exacerbate his pain, Ruth ingratiates herself with the judge who hears Bobbo's case: she becomes his maid, his advisor, and his S/M slave, with the result that Bobbo is given a cruelly harsh sentence.

Ruth also revenges herself on Mary Fisher by getting her mother expelled from her nursing home and returned to Fisher's house. Obliged to care for the sarcastic and vocal aged woman and the jailed Bobbo's anarchic children, Fisher is dragged down into the muck of practical femininity she had previously dedicated herself to avoiding, which means disillusionment in the everyday and alienation from the project of making a life as beautiful as a romance novel. As a result, she can no longer write romances. Her sublime estate decays. Her fingernails become jagged. Her friends desert her. Her publishers complain that her texts now alternate jarringly between romance rhetoric and housewife realism, like Weldon's novel itself. Her only pleasure is in her sexual thrall to Bobbo, with which she loses contact on his imprisonment. Creatively disabled with an imprisoned lover and no longer believing in feminine will, Mary converts to Catholicism and tries to have faith sustain her. At this point Ruth completes an affair she is having with a priest and convinces him to go to save Mary Fisher's soul: they too have a sordid and sadistic affair until, at last, Mary Fisher contracts terminal cancer, which she and the priest both think she has brought on herself by her sins.

Ruth's revenge on those who were once her objects of unambivalent desire is only part of her she-devil aim, however. Once Bobbo and Mary Fisher are taken care of, Ruth prepares to come to America. Here unfolds an aspect of the plot of which we have only previously seen glimmers. As she begins to embezzle money in London, she also embarks on a project of dental surgery, which involves a very painful filing away of every other tooth in her mouth; she then goes to a plastic surgeon and asks him to shorten her jaw and to give her new teeth, on behalf of what she calls "the first step to the New Me" (162). Her doctor even tells her excitedly that she "will be making facial history!" (175), which costs $1,761 to do. Then Ruth goes to a plastic surgeon who "believes in the power of intimacy" (177): and when he asks her what she wants, she says she "want[s] to look up to men."

This daunting task involves neither electroshock, drugs, nor psychoanalysis, but the reconstitution of her body through amputation and prosthesis: she reshapes her nose, her lips, her eyes, her hairline, and then chops six inches off of each of her legs. The model for these changes is a picture of Mary Fisher that Ruth rips from the back of one of her novels: and in this Ruth is merely taking to an extreme what ordinary women are taught to do when consuming other women visually, that is, segmenting the female body into ideal erotic parts and presuming that their sum would produce an erotically pleasing totality, a version of femininity that is both utopian and ordinary. (Thus it becomes relevant to consider the other intertexts to Ruth's remodeling as well: explicitly in the novel, "The Little Mermaid" and *Frankenstein*; around the novel's edges, *The Life and Loves of Casanova*, and *Don Juan*.)

The doctors, overwhelmed, confused, and in love with Ruth for having such big desire and such faith in them, turn Ruth into a simulacrum of Mary Fisher. The novel goes into excruciating detail about the procedures performed on her body: the skimming of fat from beneath the skin, the use of lasers to burn away scars, the hacking off of thick leg bone, and other acts of sculpting that involve gentle verbs like "tucking," "pinning," "trimming," "bracing," and the experimental one, "heat-sealing" (207–8). This litany of detail is not expressed in the registers of pornography or fetishism. It is written in the dead, scientistic language of accounting: $110,000 for the face, $300,000 for the body, $1,000,000 for the legs. Ruth takes no pleasure in the physical pain, nor does she see herself as heroic for enduring it. Rather, she views it as a way of focusing and mastering the pain she has otherwise confronted in her life. She says that it cleanses her by diverting the mental pain she so long suffered for her failure to be beautiful. Now, mentally a she-devil and no longer a woman, Ruth is postoperatively physically a woman, in all the usual feminine senses. In transsexual terms, she is a monster-to-woman post-op.

After Ruth has healed and sealed the new reality that extends from her new body, she returns to England for Mary Fisher's funeral. Ruth buys and refurbishes the romantic high tower, but she distorts the beautiful landscape in which Mary Fisher had crafted it; she rehires Garcia, Mary Fisher's servant and lover, but now she treats him as a slave, in terms both of labor and of sex. Finally, Ruth reclaims from prison a now broken and overmedicated Bobbo and takes him back to the high tower, where he abjects himself to her for the rest of his days. She takes many lovers in front of him and makes just as big a show of rejecting as accepting them: she tortures Bobbo with her lack of overwhelming need for him or for anyone, even her children, who have reentered the working class (the son is said to be ordinary; the daughter both fat and lesbian). The right of refusal, Ruth emphasizes, is what defines the She-Devil: "I want to be loved and not love in return . . . the future lay in refusing men rather than submitting to them" (43, 232). In contrast, the normatively feminine woman thinks that her world depends on the success of her improvisations around the realities men make for themselves: Mary Fisher the romance writer softened these scenes by insisting that romance is woman's realism, and that the harsh realities of capitalism, property, exploitation, sexual alienation, and domestic inequality can be transcended through pastoral fantasy and a commitment to maintaining and living the beauty that fantasy can fold into the everyday of intimacy.

It is on this point, the articulation of fantasy with the material relations of the everyday under global capitalism, that we began our exploration of what it might mean to interfere with the conventions of desire's formalism and the compulsion to repeat, to defetishize our attachments to *kinds* of things—a particular body, body politic, or body of knowledge. *The Life and Loves of a She-Devil* narrates a process of formal interruption in the flows of capital, the clarity of gender, and the utopia of (hetero)sexuality by the She-Devil herself: but the logic of desire that solicits content to these normative forms—whether suburban, national, or heterosexual—is never terribly unsettled. When Ruth transmigrates into the Mary Fisher prosthesis she switches her bodily destiny, but she changes nothing about the ways any identity congeals a bodily destiny when it's imagined as a type.

In this regard *She-Devil* demonstrates how easy it is to forget the conventionality of those forms of identity that organize collective and personal fantasy and self-understanding. Central to that forgetting is the overvaluation of bodies and subjectivity to the stories we have learned to tell about history and power. In *She-Devil* "genre" stands as the aesthetic trace of the wish for the simplification of universality, reminding us that rhetorical convention strongly organizes the shape of the subject's desire for social belonging and social value. Style and species, which merge whenever we talk about "genre" texts here, give the gift of appropriateness to the subjects who desire to consume their "law": like a good citizen, the reader is "free" within the law of genre to pre-experience the flow of unconflictedness unachievable elsewhere than in the genre's horizon of expectations.

It would not, however, suspend the compulsion to repeat the pseudo-adequate relation between desires and their forms simply to eject "the subject" from our analysis because her desires are so powerfully on the side of the law of (world-ordering) form; nor would a turn to retelling history from the standpoint of transpersonal systems—capitalism, nationality, heterosexuality—disable the reality effect of the conventions and monuments that allow the subject to feel organized within them. The current solutions to this critical desire, the conjunctural models of "reiteration," "negotiation," or "practice," do bring to bear a productive consciousness of the lack of fit between conventions of structural determination and subjectivity, but they weigh in too heavily on the side of the subject's temporality and sense of agency and overvalue the way power or law *appear* to the subject, as though there operated no misdirection in the system to produce absorbing mirages, maps of social orderliness, or tricky conventional images of the good life—somewhat like the dream of standard sizes for women promised by the department store.[22]

I have tried to demonstrate the urgency of this conundrum by reading the books at hand as a doubled case. I began with psychoanalysis to say something about a limit: the formalism of desire is a hardwired fact of life, but what it really trains us to do is track the proliferation of forms in situations that are overwhelming and managed by fantasy. The nation form and the fetishes of racial and gendered identity whose interarticulation is shielded by their formal separation can be projected back from an imagined future as archaic formations, as they already currently are by theorists of the postnational and hybridity. But sometimes archaic formations provide foundations. Meanwhile the normative process of disciplining people into their generic taxonomies remains, and we know the rest: after great pain, a formal feeling comes. The questions are how does the formal feeling work when it stabilizes someone, in the good, the bad, or the mixed sense? What conditions its conventional zone of reference and consolation, and under what conditions and in what kinds of space would it be possible to delaminate the radiant form from the desire that organizes it, makes it a *thing* not of realism, but of fantasy?

*The Life and Loves of a She-Devil* takes on the formalism of desire—its alternately consoling and aversive condensation in the fetishistic object—and its relation to normativity. Central to the translation of the form to the norm is the *scene* that enables the subject to experience her subordination to proper type as also a feeling of a freeing uniqueness. In *She-Devil*, as well as in the political contexts from which it speaks, the spaces of metropolitan capital and geopolitical fantasy provide the architectonic of modernity that both staples one to the identity form one is burdened by and frees one to occupy the nooks and crannies of anonymity, generality, *and* universality. These relations describe more than the paradox of the general will: under capitalist regimes of law in which property is the condition of symbolic mobility, individuals are free only to the degree that they appear to generate value within the rules of the proper or the normal. It matters that the proper and the normal are absorbative of many kinds of form. But their metafunction as indices of simplicity and authenticity can distract from what is fundamentally unstable about them.

In *She-Devil*, the flow of capital and people through houses and across cities and oceans does show us other routes of meaning lived in ordinary life by people who manage survival in non-normative ways. But as these ways are forged under the pressures of precarious lives, they do not constitute redemptive *models*. Meanwhile, for women (and other migrants) the violence of intimacy with the law (of desire) is liveable because of the temporalizing promises of love, femininity, and heterosexuality—those most ruthlessly *locating* of institutions that are at the same time vehicles for identifying with a version of personal history that transcends the materiality of the present.

The She-Devil's own story suggests, nonetheless, that consciousness, or paying attention to the proliferation of anomalies, does not reorganize life: recognition or redescription of a thing does not constitute its destruction or transformation. If there is such a thing as a "sad fact," it is that gender and nationality mark the space of an ever attenuating optimism that the law (institutions, apparatuses, and norms) might be reworked, reseduced, or reformed so that what is given but toxic does not remain so but becomes untraumatically or incrementally obsolete over the long haul. (I take this to be the dream of liberalism.) I must close dissatisfyingly, then, by reconsidering the postnormative fortunes of desire in *She-Devil* across the three urforms we have been tracking—the nation, the gendered body, and literary genre—without concluding anything about their future from the "lesson" of their backstory.

### The Nation Form

In the beginning, before she raised hell and earth, Ruth understood as a fact of life the suffering of women across many terrains both national and cosmopolitan ("Women in Korea and Buenos Aires and Stockholm and Detroit and Dubai and Tashkent, but seldom in China, where it is a punishable offense" [46]); the superexploitation of women globally and at home and in the unliveable jobs at the bottom of the heap; and the need for women to pool their knowledge and resources in order to refuse to be banalized into the silenced spaces of reproduction. But, significantly, however, the internationalist feminist and socialist-tinged structural view of the novel's first half drops out when Ruth leaves for the United States. In England the reduction of women to body and feeling became sickening to her, and so she embarked on a pilgrimage that involved refuting the complaint form and encouraging women to enter the exciting present-tense world of public value (through labor, travel, and agentive sex). Only then do we see her instrumentalizing those women for her own private ends.

When Ruth migrates she leaves her gender utopianism behind. She comes to "America" to lose her body, her history, and her political consciousness: she arrives to assume the freedom of the sovereign individual who thinks that her mind, her will, and her control of capital by rights should make a new world on the model of her new body, which, as an unnatural thing, is the closest a body ever comes to being an abstraction. What happens instead, after all of her plotting, is that she loses her optimism for anything but the repetition of the negativity she knows.[23]

This novel is a melancholic form that signals its pleasure in these kinds of loss, for its procedure is to abandon most of what it shows through the proliferation of detail, scene, and movement: failures of possibility are what make the novel dramatic. In She-Devil the loss is signified by the pilgrimage to "America," a place dedicated to the ascendency of generic or normative individuality over any other national story, whether about capitalist processes or other paradoxically related matrices of contingency, determination, and identity in collective life.

"America" enables the cancellation of Ruth's socialist knowledge and here, as so often, its loss folds the violent forces of money and property back into stories of the body and the intimate sphere. How much of this effect of narrative self-erasure is a performance of the compulsion to repeat, in which the love plot, nationality, and capitalist triumphalism represent the conventionalized forms of fantasy? Is this narrative overvaluation of the subject's emergence from a complex field of detail inevitable, because reading produces subjects, not acts, and because the classic pedagogy of the novel represents changes of mentality on the same scale that it represents social redemption?

Ruth's tactic suggests that if a subordinated subject aims for survival in the mode of liberal individuality her desires can indeed find ways to negotiate or refunction ongoing systems of normativity—she can figure out a way to pass as well-adapted when necessary. But the minoritized subject who wants to live throughout the entire range of her personality (without closeting its bigness in the shell of a body) pays a huge cost if she also seeks a *representation* of it, in the nation or through surgery: the fictive totality of universalism and particularity requires the subject not to believe but to act *as if* her autonomous individuality and her generic identity are the same thing, the simultaneous fulfillment of her omnipotent fantasy (mastery of the world) and her desire for belonging (mastery by it). The formalism of identity in the liberal nation produces hierarchies of abstraction called identities: meanwhile, they deliver the bribe of a free and complex mentality to the citizen, who can develop any consciousness she wants so long as she declines to interfere with the pleasure and order her readable body creates for everyone else.

## The Body

In the beginning of *She-Devil*, Ruth is a mute abject shell who has no positive impact on the world. At the end she has a shell of dead cells (a beautiful body) that protects her from showing feeling. At the same time, by taking on as a bodily project the urge for "self-creation," Ruth endows her conscious self with a form of superpersonhood that subordinates everyone who encounters her. She-devils, she says, absolutely refuse to assume the redemptive-pedagogical position of generic femininity. There is no trace of cyborg-style optimism here. Indeed, she calls herself a failure for being unable to change any body of land, water, or language apart from her own (231).

Could the postoperative Ruth teach, if she wanted to, a story that is not about failure? Does it turn out that the horizon of possibility the fantasy world femininity provides is the *only* material she has? In the space between her new bodily ego and the scarred traces of her historical one, she riffs on the feminine in yet a third way, derived from her knowledge of what it has cost for her to survive her fantasies. Would saying what she knows from the new body that refuses historical knowledge leave her nothing, no potential for pleasure, no possible life narrative, no resources of self-development? Ultimately, neither the nation, the city, the body, or sexuality are redemptive sites for her, as they have been for others: in *She-Devil*, as in *Landscape*, where women are concerned there is no privacy, only exposure; and survival comes only to those who can find prosthetic protection in the generalizing haze of normativity.

At this juncture, then, the compulsion to repeat femininity is the only condition of Ruth's life narrative: it involves a return home that should be impossible but is not because the compulsion to repeat—the impossibility of breaking attachments and of experiencing self-sovereignty as such—*is* femininity. Yet to say this is not to finish with the question of history past and future, for different women enter the impasse of their gendering differently; and the form that expresses the animating attachment is not an inevitable resting or organizing place for that attachment. It is a placeholder.

This is where politics and ideology critique reenter. The body is the main screen on which Ruth exists to the world, because she is female—it is the determining economy. All of her gestures of refusal can come only after the consent to her femininity and the fantasy it sustains *for others*. Despite the explicitness of her masquerade, it reminds her and everyone who sees her of romance, the vanquished ghost: as a mnemonic of the compulsion to repeat a never experienced sublime, it demonstrates once again that one's libidinal position is not one's own, but a content that the world has given one to suffer and to fantasize through by calling it "individuality." It is also the portable limit one carries around, the very sign of the conventionality of one's desire.

## Genre

In this chapter, genre stands as something like a conventionalized symbolic, an institution whose modern translation through the commodity form affixes it with both genericness and a uniqueness derived from the particularity of its distinguishing details. Genre also figures the nameable aspiration for discursive order through which particular life narratives and modes of being become normalized as the real, the taken for granted. (In *She-Devil*, genre is strictly formal—for the affective version of what genre intends, see the final chapter in this book.) Romance, with its negotiation of desire and institution (marriage, reproduction, property, dynasty, nation) is in the not-strange-enough position of being identified intensively both with the fantastic unreal and the real that constitutes what "a life" should be, especially for women. Thus along with the rules of social membership that seek to saturate the political with the nation form, genre establishes the place of reading in the production of normative law. But what does it mean to think about subjectivity as literalized in the law of genre?

As histories of the novel have long attested, the genre concept generally presumes a reader's competence in textual conventions, a competence not necessarily linked to a plot or setting as such, but to modes of causality, desire, enigma, and affective response associated with that setting. To be competent in a genre is therefore to be cultivated as a certain *kind* of subject, a type. The association of different kinds of subject with different categories of represented desire in turn leads to a popular culture organized around types who are characterized by interior and exterior habits and narratives that are said to flow out of them in invariably recognizable ways. Read from within the law of genre, these kinds of fictional subjects literalize their desire in acts and identities. It is as though both the narrative and the persons within it take on the form of cliché, a proposition repeated until it takes on truth value, a truth that is repeated until its resonance dies, a phrase that converts into a ghost of meaning, a tough transparency. This aura of the taken for granted around genre's institutionality (its common law, established by precedent) suggests the power fictional genres have to mediate identity normatively, to cast proper identity as the seed out of which an imaginable affective future inevitably springs.[24]

Even the most blazingly generic texts are a mix of aesthetic elements (the western's coupling with romance, or the historical novel's articulation of melodrama, epic tropes, and documentary verity, for example): yet it is also the case that generic conventions work according to an implicit contract that guides reading toward appropriateness. The instabilities of genre are thematized in the threat any text poses *not* to fulfill its contract to produce satisfaction: and if readerly *enjoyment* is played out in the narrative obstacles to or deferral of an anticipated resolution, the possession of and by that end is also a stabilizing attachment for the consumer.[25] The death of pleasure foreshadowed in *jouissance* remains central to the capacity to endure it. This dialectic is crucial to the compulsion to repeat.[26] The conventionality of this dialectic in love plots has been crucial to the reproduction of femininity and heteronormativity.

### Unfinished Business, or The Return of the Repressed: Pleasure

This raises questions typical of the era after 1968 about the value narrative pleasure might come again to have in the formation of critical cultures and consciousness. In the 1970s the translated notion of pleasure that also went by *jouissance* (as first incited in the United States by Barthes and Sontag) articulated a liberatory aim, much as the feminist movement reconceived sexuality as a site that demanded and would provide a new, revolutionary sensorium. Currently, that mode of critical pleasure through reading has been replaced by a professional incitement to make readings engaged with material practices through ethnography and history, in part to repudiate the implied universality of interpretation set forth in the early manifestos. Still, I remain enchanted by the critical potential of pleasure and knowledge.

Sheila Rowbotham argues that feminism has had two phases: the emanci- patory one of suffrage that produced juridical and cultural enfranchisements and the liberationist one of the generation of 1968, which tended to see his- tory as a Bastille from which subjects need liberation.[27] For Barthes as later for Foucault, pleasure was the least public and least rationalized of practices. On this repetition, perhaps, the hierarchy of mentality—rationality, will, consciousness, affect, fantasy—over material determinations can be shaken up, not on behalf of the body's or practice's superior freedom but on behalf of thinking the thought of pleasure as a thought about cathexis and its appar- ent opposite, ambivalence.

The common-sense understanding of ambivalence emphasizes its negativ- ity: uncertainty, obscurity, or relentlessly assertive doubt. But like pleasure, which can be rephrased as the compulsion to repeat an attachment that one likes, doesn't like, or feels neutral about, ambivalence is, in its strongest ver- sions, a pulling apart or antithetical attraction, an impossibility that cannot be overcome by synthesis, will, or better reason. As I suggested in the introduc- tion, the usual solution to the conundrum of ambivalence is to temporalize the intensified fraying the concept suggests: to understand it as a crisis that can first be fixed by attachment to a new form from which one can then be liberated until the next crisis, and so on. In contrast, the pleasure concept involves understanding that the feeling of freedom is not freedom, pleasure not pleasure, disavowal not disavowal, but ways we have learned to identify knowledge and sensation. They are maps to causality but not the truth about it. In contrast, the forms that codetermine crises of self and the pleasures of social intelligibility can be seen as transformational: in liberal culture love and the nation are the ur-types of the forms that have become saturated by their content, which makes it harder to see the fantasy motives for which they once seemed a solution and for which, like many a neurotic symptom, they may no longer work. The risk one takes with pleasure is not to presume, as the She-Devil does, that a better form will release one from the pressure of fantasy and the optimism of discontent.

The concept of the transformational environment describes why people enter new attachments, given what they know about the attenuation of the old ones: Bollas suggests that the new attachment expresses a subject's desire to change, but not traumatically (which would render the subject impossible).[28] But the transformational environment is a way that the attachment to form speaks against itself, as the subject's (or a mass's) desire to move beyond whatever is dead or deadening rubs up against the comfort that the form's stability brings. It may wish to accrue history like a dust ball, a mystic writing pad, or a self-reproducing story, but it also signifies an aggressivity toward the scene of history.

This chapter is not written in the self-help genre or with an eye to providing a conceptual solution to the lure of absorbing conventions and norms. Like *Pilgrim's Progress* before it, *She-Devil* shows us that the whole business of history and personality drags around behind us forever: the weight of its content produces the forms of resignation so often called "realism." This is one example of the destruction produced by the redemptive promises of desire ideology: that new instances of desire will save one from desire and that consciousness can prevent mistakes in the forging of attachment (as though knowing can protect the subject from being duped into the hope that a new good object is the end of the story of desire and the actual fulfillment of fantasy). Intervening in the pleasures of heteronormative romance and political normativity must involve dismantling their capacity to make old stories and practices look new and revolutionary while discrediting the restlessness and skepticism of the subjects who also desire them. The pleasure concept enables a postprosthetic critical engagement with those aspects of conventionality that claim to provide the better law, rule, or lexicon that will protect one from a traumatic engagement with the harsh and cutting world. In *She-Devil* the project of homeopathic cutting up involves leaving the city, coming to the United States, and becoming an individual there. Individuality, that deracinated grandiosity of being, enables Ruth to live the iconic life of the landscaped subject—but because she remembers what her body cannot show, the visible life is anchored by a melancholic one, which involves staying at home with the brilliant anger that she can only express masochistically, in the fold between the mind's wildness and the body's conventionality. To the degree that the compulsion to repeat this condition supports the romance of women's intimate public, it is this plot, the plot of optimism for the iconic *thing*, that must go in for radical surgery.

**OVERTURE/APERTURE**    *Showboat 1988—The Remake*

Sometimes politically engaged readers see in my work a decision to advance formalism over historicism because its tendency is to focus on events within the aesthetic work that interrupt the text's own modes of historicism: these are moments, gestures, phrases, episodes, and narrated scenarios that shift the terms of realism and enact "ways out" of historical embeddedness, with its narratives of struggle, defeat, and survival.[1] Its method has been called "Benjaminian" too because these flashings up of alternativity can be said to redirect historical energy toward what remains immanent in experience, and I attend to the potential for living otherwise that texts mainly make apprehensible viscerally by way of formal shifts.[2] Often, debates about formalism versus historicism locate politically good work in historical contextualization while casting formalism as merely a quietist or precious fantasy of the artwork's specialness or autonomy: but both sets of association underdescribe the dynamics of contextualization and exemplification that shape the analytic work a critical text can do.

The question should not be *whether* or not formalism can advance the analysis of history or power, as a realist analytic can do, but whether or not it is possible *not* to be a formalist.[3] Slavoj Žižek's ethics, for example, argues for an absolutely formalist fidelity to a truth claim without sacred—or any—guarantees.[4] Alain Badiou too argues for an ethical formalism, but here it is expressed in fidelity to the *whatever* point of solidarity that lets couples in love and social systems endure without assurance.[5] But what can these imperatives around formalism as ethics tell us about the conditions of the aesthetic reproduction of political inequalities and ordinary injustice?

For the purposes of this book, my claim would be that to study the kinetics of aesthetic form (as opposed to being formalist) can provide, among other things, a way to open up an analysis of the mechanisms that enable the reproduction of normativity not as a political program, but as a structure of feeling, and as an affect.[6] This may seem counterintuitive. For example, when people talk about sexual normativity they are often imagining a describable way of life and presuming that an attachment to it amounts to some version of a will to privilege, if not power. But I see normativity not only as a disciplinary operation on how people imagine the good life, but as an aspiration people have for an unshearable suturing to their social world, and as an aspiration it is an affect, a sense of something, organized by but not inhering in its conventional objects. This is why people of conflicting worldviews can agree that they are conflicting over *something*: normativity provides assurance that there is a *whatever* point for the reproduction of predictable life; that point enables the fantasies of belonging and reciprocity that we have seen magnetizing the concept and activity of the intimate public.[7]

This is also the fulcrum that allows so many critical theorists to shift between analyses of love and the social.[8] The political question is how to understand the difficulty of detaching from lives and worlds that wear out life, rather than sustain it. To interfere with the ordinary precarity of both domains requires a loss of confidence in normativity, which one can sense as the loss of a beloved object. This suggests that, whatever else it is, an object of desire is not only a thing, scene, or person, but an affect: the affect associated with the pleasure of binding or attachment itself. The loss of a world is thus not only of a singular thing, but also the loss of the capacity to keep having the feelings that were represented in the ongoingness of the thing. One might conclude from this that the hardest acts of changing are acts of breaking, even when desire is on the side of a break: they require being optimistic about loss and about the undoing of an affect world, with its promise of reciprocity. This is why so many imagined breaks end up being greenstick fractures. The female complainer's exemplarity in this book, therefore, derives not just from her skill at playing out a formally ambivalent and contradictory sexual politics in a long-term historical context, but also from the way the work expresses the formal problem of even imagining actually detaching from the disappointing object or world. To encounter this scenario, we needed to enter the impasse—each text provides its own scenarios of managing "the loss of the world"[9] with radical ambivalence.

Earlier, I traced the circuit of optimism and survival in Dorothy Parker's *A Star Is Born* through the trope of "going to an opening." On the face of it, to go to an opening is to imagine that it will be pretty fabulous to show up as a member of a public that is optimistic about a potentially transformative event that has not happened yet. But what does it mean for Parker? To adapt Nadia Seremetakis's rubric, Parker adapts the conventions of sentimental optimism not to express the "American" static nostalgia for a home in love that never existed nor to embody that "Greek" fierce nostalgia that asserts a sensually embodied communal knowledge against the political attritions of the present.[10] Parker's sentimentality is more Kafkaesque: a return to a door that is always open (to love); a self-reproaching reapproach to a scene that calls for courage despite the odds against being able to enter it and rest somewhere; and a kind of radical impassivity in her stubborn refusal to go somewhere else, to delaminate that scene of stuck potentiality from her image of having a life.[11] She stalks her optimism like it owes her money.

As a paradigm female complainer, Parker's mode is also a revolt against the kind of Žižekian realism that sees fantasy as a mechanism of disavowal that enables failed ways of life to endure, suturing a notion of the fully lived life to domains deemed nonideological.[12] Disavowal is a defense: what is startling in women's inchoate public is how much commitment there is to undefendedness. As this book has shown throughout, a view of fantasy as an affective claim, a pulse that points toward what the real ought to feel like, is a convention of women's intimate public and, I think, is at the magnetizing core of all intimate publics. Juxtapolitical, it can be open toward politics but is abundantly on the outside of it, refusing its status as determining the real of power, agency, or experience. At the same time it redirects attention to an aesthetically mediated scene of causality and experience that produces a sense of thriving in the consumer's body and sometimes in the mise-en-scène itself. In so doing it provides a sense of the better worldness that would exist if only real life would step up to the plate. Affect is formalism *avant la lettre*.

These processes of fomenting and circulating fantasy are therefore far more convoluted than in the Žižekian representation of affective self-maintenance and prevarication in liberal fantasy. First, since in the artworks of sentimental realism disavowal does not serve survival, there is an explicit aversion to the activity of disavowal: to the contrary, there is a drive for narration, explanation, and clarification of the problem-event. I realize that being committed to cognitive and emotional clarity does not vanquish the activity of disavowal: I am focusing here on the complexities of affect man-agement as a temporal process of managing being "knowing." This clarify-ing eye is what makes the women's intimate publicity critical, starting back in the 1830s. But usually the criticism comes without a program. The bargain struck in these works demands not the sacrifice of intelligence and ethical potential about the catastrophic and petty lies, violence, and disappointment with which the world proceeds without guarantees, but confirms all that while demanding the maintenance of proximity to the *promise* of affective continuity, recognition, and, metatextually, membership in the community of people constituted by *whatever* longing, the longing of the people who showed up. Nothing is hidden or unknown in this double movement: the doubleness is a commitment to maintaining contradiction and a project of making explicit the difficulties of bargaining.

Actually, the vagueness of this scenario of commonality enables a broader and more incisive critique to develop. Longing can be a political measure phrased in the idiom of the ordinary. In the intimate public it is associated with a strange mix of the community's absolute historical locatedness and its restlessness, its rage for change and its passivity, its refusal of the terms of the conventional world and its demand for the world to be reciprocal, its commitment to its own survival and to that sense of potentiality immanent in anyone. To inhabit these senses via a public approximates the feeling of reciprocity otherwise absent in the world. But the projective aspect of that sense of potentiality in affective flourishing does not equal a disavowal or foreclosure of a sense of its irreality. The intimate public modifies slightly Antonio Gramsci's assessment of ethical political subjectivity: pessimism of the intellect, optimism of the affects, realism about what can be achieved through sheer will.[13] Sentimental bargaining points explicitly to adaptation as an expression both of compromise—of being historically and materially located in a situation—and of latency, a sense that there is always a tomorrow whose different outcomes can be confirmed affectively and experienced aesthetically before they are realized.

By realism, then, I point not to philosophical projections onto the historical materiality of things, nor to the mimetic practice of transposing consensus reality into an artwork, nor to an analysis of disciplinary power: rather, I attend to a scene that Harry Shaw points to, which demonstrates realism in a mind grappling with a problem deemed to be in the world.[14] The question is how fantasies of world-making agency are different from projects of world-changing agency, and what it means that those two different registers can point to really different concepts of the political—as an imaginary, a conventional domain of contestation, or the scene of the reproduction of life as such.

As we have seen throughout *The Female Complaint*, the expansion of intimate publics mediated by commodities can help to maintain the status quo of so much structural inequality and unfreedom because the development of intelligence and related practices of survival often happen in a different affective and aesthetic register than that which would interfere with the normative instrumentalities of the reproduction of life. The sentimental realist demands on fantasy that I have been tracking situate the intimate public in its *own* scene of life; the public is a kind of mind grappling with problems in the real as it presents itself, with the processes of politics that are seen as blunt or even destructive instruments for building better worlds. So what does this entail for assigning what is political or not political in the texts of an intimate public such as this? As the political is usually a service economy for the economically and culturally elite, the intimate public's disbelief in conventional politics as a potentially rich site for all that survival energy can protect political privilege. At the same time, it means that we witness here a mass withdrawal from consent to hegemonic notions of realism, aspiration, and self-reference on behalf of fostering a rich resource for remaining actually and imaginatively undefeated.

The incommensurateness of these scenarios does not threaten the durability of the consuming community as a scene of sustaining social relation—it sustains it. At the same time this is where a Žižekian-style critique of fantasmatic disavowal of the "traumatic kernel" of the social can enter in. The traumatic kernel reveals the nonidentity or alterity among humans: the vagueness that makes an intimate public capacious and resourceful requires its scene to remain a fuzzy object. But the structuration of sentimental realism around fantasy practices is not really about the object in itself: it is about mobilizing and publicizing a process of longing for the social as a place where rest and reciprocity can be lived as something *other* than a ducking under the radar, a compromise, or a retreat. This explains why there is often a fraught transitivity or sense of identification across intimate publics: being constituted by an intense longing for a better good life looks like a likeness across different and often contradictory social positionings. A shared sense of longing as such seems to incite, even invite, belonging. The object is an opportunity for the reanimation of a critical and transformative longing in registers that include power without elevating its normative conventions of transformative fantasy over other ones.[15]

One might have predicted this account of the intimate public's tendency to route its optimism toward affects and aesthetics as against the conventionally political by tracking a shift that has taken place in cinema studies, substituting melodrama for realism as the dominant mode of "classic Hollywood cinema." Explanations for this shift point to many political, economic, and aesthetic causes: relevant here are the historical dependence of Hollywood cinematic spectacle on stage melodrama, with its shaping of spectatorial moral identification through mise-en-scène and bodily gesture; the centrality of soundtrack and music to intensifying and shaping narrative scale and impact; industry norms and codes regulating the excitement produced by scenes and performances of embodied transgression (the sexual and economic offender); conventions of narrative causality that traverse stage and novelistic adaptations of narrative drama and interest from the logics of rank to the logics of the market.[16] All of these point to a vernacular of melodramatic excess rather than mimetic realism as the industry's normative mode. Linda Williams's and Miriam Hansen's work have been crucial to this shift, which opens up a whole field of questions about how to understand the *conventionality of excess* in relation to whatever qualities stand in for normative realism. But it mainly confirms what Christine Gledhill has long argued about "the women's film"—that there one never could distinguish melodrama from realism.[17]

This is to say that addressing and historicizing conventionality in aesthetic and social terms requires a wholesale rethinking of the relation of affective intensity to realist modes of narrative causality. Genre is always a scene of potentiality, a promise of a certain affective experience. This way of thinking about it necessarily articulates realism to what Peter Brooks called "modes of excess" and excess to the intensities of mediated historical experience.[18] It also argues for a need always to focus on the difference between affect as a structure and as an experience reflected on in emotion. For instance, the conventions of women's intimate publicity focus on suffering and longing for different terms for survival. But the somatic reverb of complaint style is tonally capacious: melancholic, melodramatic, ironic, gallows humor, slapstick, camp, normative and non-normative sexual desire.[19] Therefore, I would argue, what makes a thing sentimental is the presumption of emotional clarity and affective recognition in the scene of the mediated encounter. Sometimes that *feels* sentimental in the heightened normative sense, but the key thing is that the sentimental text delivers the punctum of affective recognition.

Thus when reanimating some aspect of the woman's unfinished business with the world, the conventional female complainer is not departing from the sentimentality of the intimate public when relating, within a single work, the stark realism of a narrated stuckness or impeded survival, the event of a life worked out at melodramatic scale, the arch and comic ironies of ridiculous longing, or political opinion. What is realistic about it has nothing to do with the tone and pacing of its representational staging; nor is a given text's relation to aesthetic conventionality an allegory of its complicity or refusal of normativity as such. What makes work that is written from and for an intimate public realistic is also what makes it sentimental and juxtapolitical: its excesses and displacements are demands for recognition of the importance of a situation in terms of affectively alternate realities. The complaint's distinguishing mark is not therefore in genre or in modal tone as such, but in the way it forces in affective performance from within the ordinary a reanimation of the sense of the scene of yet unlived better survival.

While calibrating it slightly differently, this figuration of the intimate public's entertainment scene is akin to Richard Dyer's and Fredric Jameson's claims that genre films and mass culture are utopian deep freezers and incubators for the mainly impeded sense of general social membership.[20] To them, aesthetic conventionality at the scale of genre preserves the political in the absence of a world for its most just enactments. The affectivity of the elsewhere of utopia preserves, through the enactment of sentimental affective universality, a mode of general belonging not organized by hierarchies of distinction. But what I want to emphasize in all of this is that in the artifact of minor popular culture that foregrounds the comforts of genre the utopian is not some elsewhere of perfection but a sense in the here and now that thickens the present, opening it up to the way stumbling delays any moment's closure. So the presumption of displacement of the utopian or the heterotopian needs adaptation here. In mass-mediated intimate publicity, the utopian and heterotopian are adapted to a scene of bargaining not with fulfillment (that would be politics) but with sensually lived potentiality.

So what constitutes going to an opening here is different than has been previously conceived. An opening is not phrased in the genre of a full-bodied promise of a better future, but appears in any potentially transformative scene to which one can return. Adaptation, the principle of extension of the sentimental and the melodramatic and itself a figure for being undefeated, opens out its aperture whenever there is a "revival" somewhere of a previous gesture or text. Of course, after Roseanne Barr's bomb, no one remade *She-Devil*—but why bother? A tragedy that uses comedy to drive a stake deep into the heart of sentimentality, it reduces knowledge, affect, and emotion to an absolutely closeted singularity, while revealing the social energy of feminism to amount to a joke that femininity played on women. In this text, feminism just shifted the terms of femininity: while promising a creative new realism, it stripped away fantasy and left behind a kind of fierce, entropic morbidity. Neither femininity nor feminism had a shot at delivering nontragic emancipation.

Elsewhere, though, the mass cultural attachment to the sentimental opening has been dormant, but not dead, occasionally reflickering to life. Citations of *Imitation of Life* appear in the melodramas *Titanic*, *8 Mile*, and *High Heels*; of *Now, Voyager* in queer cinematic meditations such as *Love and Death on Long Island*, *The History Boys*, and *Billy's Hollywood Screen Kiss*; of *A Star Is Born* in the Streisand and Midler vehicles of the 1970s as well as their contemporary, *Play It as It Lays*, and the many porn variations thereafter (but this plot, the "price of success" plot, is endemic in Hollywood cinema and "chick-lit," too). Often, these citations are not so deep: they are gestures toward the tradition of sentimental adaptation that explain this time around why the great transformative and fulfilling love, the revolution without trauma, must remain imaginable whether or not it is impossible, discernible only in its smoldering remains.[21]

But what remains is a resource, an unfinished event. Adaptations of sentimental realism are always about splitting and bargaining to stay in the scene of the fantasy of the better good life, as atrophied and confused as the manifest content of that fantasy can be. Possessing the object of desire matters less in these texts than does the re-experience of potentiality—the "tomorrow" in today where one works with what one has in order to survive.[22] The delicate historicity of sentimental work provides pointers to the materials available for transformative opportunity. These scenarios are also archives of tactics for being undefeated, and indeed it is an attachment to this archive that also magnetizes the intimate public. To become not-something is to unlearn a way of being, to see affective and emotional recalibration not only as possible but as desirable. In other words, in the view of the intimate public, there is no politics without the sentimental aperture/overture because that promise of emotional continuity can sustain people in the social amid the flux of change.

Mostly, though, the pedagogy that we find in sentimental realism toward detaching from and unlearning what is blocking one's own and one's community's flourishing is very careful and limited: one should aspire to be interesting and creative, but not too weird or singular; one should be oneself except not when one's impulse is to be inauthentic; one should be spiritual but guided by common sense; one should use sexual agency to be emancipated without being controlling or shallow; one should be ambitious but only in the right way; one should be sensitive and alive but sensible without giving up dreaming. But all of this advice signals the unfinished business of sentimental contingency, the fact that in the intensified everyday there are always pointers to alternative experiences, even the yet unlived. It is as though common sense can never finish the sentence that would convince us to amalgamate the ordinary with the moderate.

Our final extended example of sentimentality's unfinished business is Rick Schmidt's avant-garde adaptation, *Showboat 1988—The Remake* (1977). The film's three-pronged scenario casts "Ed," a sixty-something librarian who has just received a diagnosis of fatal cancer, as the reckless impresario of a gonzo remake of *Show Boat*; this fictive plot is intercut with genuine documentary footage of a public audition for a contemporary *Show Boat* that never went further to the stage; and, finally, charged with copyright infringement, Schmidt was blocked by MGM from using the libretto, and so the film begins with an attorney's statement that all references to *Show Boat* will be x-ed out, silenced, or drowned out by a loud (quite comic) honking noise. Schmidt, an independent filmmaker from the United States, is closely associated with the Dogme 95 project, manifesting in *Showboat 1988—The Remake* the collective's commitment to filmmaking in integrated environments (all sound, lighting, and props emanating naturally from the filmed space). As we will see, one of Dogme 95's dicta is extremely pertinent here: "Genre movies are not acceptable."[23]

Yet the film's motto, repeated variously throughout, and left hanging in a card at the end, is not at all radical or ideologically anti-Hollywood: "Be the Star in Your Own Life." The narrative opens similarly, with a close-up on Ed's craggy face: "Everyone is a star. Everyone. And I want to give them the chance to show it, and to find out for themselves. I want them to write out their fantasies in celluloid. . . . The money men think that I'm out of my mind. That's what convinces me, not only that it's possible, but that it's necessary."

In this command to foment a self-loving, expansive, dramatic self-projection on behalf of social life generally Schmidt's film is quite conventional. Thus, one cannot say that this remake of *Show Boat* amounts to a refunctioning of the original work's fundamental aim to release potentiality back into historical possibility through the reanimation of fantasy. Both works aim to interrupt historical consciousness with a series of numbers that produce a momentary counterreality for individuals. That someone in Schmidt's film—one "Constance Penley"—critiques the musical for being a "bourgeois form" and charges the documentary makers with insufficient reflexivity does not distinguish it from the reflexivity of the novel, play, or Hollywood precursor, all of which are suspicious of mass culture for transposing racial and sexual violence into measures of racial and sexual melancholy while doing it anyway.

Indeed, for anyone interested in dismantling the affective props to white supremacy, it feels wrong to return to *Show Boat* as a vehicle for revived optimism. It is different than re-encountering, say, *Now, Voyager*'s racial and class privilege in Adrienne Kennedy's *A Movie Star Has to Star in Black and White* (1976). There, Kennedy's autobiography as a child and adult subject of soured and difficult love is told and projected onstage through her mother's story: they find a shared language for inhabiting their suffering in melodramatic episodes of Bette Davis's ineloquence, the overpresence of her vulnerable body in a death struggle with the potential in her words.[24] The mother/daughter projection onto Davis wants to put a clarifying rinse on something—but it is never clear what. Do they suffer because they feel ugly or sexually off-norm, or because suffering constitutes women in love and men in all domains? Does the starkness of her upper-class whiteness produce their blackness in shadow, or is her whiteness now the shadow that protects the vulnerable flesh? Does Hollywood reveal a little too beautifully or too racially the dark secret of suffering at the core of the social, or is the lure of beauty a way of pointing to the political noise without drowning it out? Kennedy cannot help but notice that Bette Davis suffers, though she has the will of lions and the wisdom of owls, and a fashion sense besides. But whatever motivates the citation, Kennedy's reanimation of *Now, Voyager* is not an incitement to reattach to the pretense of dark *victory* she embodies. Kennedy's projection onto stars, cinema, and Davis in particular opens out a sense of surviving a repetition so ordinary and so tragic that it can barely phrase itself into a critique; it takes so much work just to stage the scene. (But, then, this pattern of making an emotional opening through the intricate detailing of some structural obstacles is the a priori of women's intimate public. Kennedy manifests participation in the idiom of survival without offering the promise of optimism as a bribe.)

But Schmidt's return to *Show Boat* takes up the classic narrative's reparative motive to propel ordinary people to assume the being-such of the iconic and the important. It brackets the race and sexual politics we have examined, foregrounding class struggle at the heart of mass fantasy. Ed, the protagonist, opines, "I want a film that comes out of America; a film America gives to itself instead of buying it prefab from Hollywood; I want to give the means of production, the production of images, back to the people."

He thinks that *Show Boat* is the great vehicle for this return of the means of image production because, after all, "the greatest song in the American musical culture is sung by a stevedore" (Paul Robeson as "Jo" singing "Ol' Man River"). Taking up the precedent, he wants to stage a "sidewalk *Show Boat*" in which any nobody could become that thing, a somebody-citizen who takes up public space and has a star-sized impact, for a moment. Yet the pedagogy of *Showboat 1988—The Remake* has nothing to do with imitating particular stars' imitations of life. The narrator notes that his sister had always wanted him to make "something" of himself, but the thing that he makes is not a pedagogical primer about how to become a "somebody": "I'd like to bring the stench of death to the musical comedy." What does it mean to say such a thing? Is it, as Bataille writes, that we "are always looking to death for what life does not give us"?[25]

My claim, which I will demonstrate briefly here, is that this adaptation of *Show Boat* is an education in detaching from the world-making passivity of the sentimental subject waiting to be released from herself by an opportunity or an object. It is a master class in the importance of making intimate publics from events that might be gestural, temporary, and forgotten because even those perturbations create precedent for future informal or affective imitations. In creating precedent, a pocket of potential reciprocity on different terms is enfolded into the world. *Showboat 1988* is a rough unfinished project that reanimates the sentimental tradition because its death or attrition would be a tragic blow to the collective life drive.

The series of auditions the film stages run a gamut, affectively and generically speaking. A man mimics a garbage disposal and other sound effects from ordinary life that he says that he developed to entertain his unhappy mother; an angry punk refunctions "Ol' Man River" (which "keeps on rockin' along") to reflect contemporary conditions of structural suffering and the rage of youth at corporate homogenization; drag and bio-women perform female complaints ("I'm just a housewife, a lonely housewife"); lesbians sharing a pair of pants sing romantic vaudeville ironically; the magnificently awkward come up one by one to declaim poems about birth, death, and love; and there is tap-dancing (a father with his young daughter; a man in a turtle suit; a woman in a nun's habit who dances with her dog and strips while she taps). Little of this is expressive in any referential sense: the lyrics barely matter. The claim is in the body taking up time, space, and stage. What is important is that many versions of nobodiness are revealed in their singular and yet generic, impersonal, nonautobiographical somebodiness. This multiplication of anonymities is the opening that *Showboat 1988—The Remake* provides. One performer narrates as much: calling his dance "Direct spirit called down on emergency," he claims that it took him twenty-three years to peel away the layers of burdensome singularity laid on him by an abusive world to become this anonymous performer, an auditioner for reciprocity with a low bar, but not no bar, for recognition. The filmmaker in the diegesis and through the film lets these moments be openings to the political if the actors phrase it that way, but mainly they do not: they mix metaphors and concepts, improvising accounts of what it meant to manifest themselves. This is the political, not politics; this is affect production, not management.

Then a performer appears who would startle anyone who experienced the 1970s and beyond as the post-Stonewall era: Sylvester, a disco icon ("You Make Me Feel/Mighty Real") whose fabulous realness became a cultural touchstone for gay metropolitan exuberant uncloseting.[26] Sylvester sings "Can't Help Lovin' Dat Man," the song I have already designated as this book's most elaborate performance of racial and sexual ambivalence in the white liberal tradition of the female complaint. In *Showboat 1988—The Remake* the song is silenced, though, because of MGM's restrictions on Schmidt's use of the libretto.

What if we could hear Sylvester's rendition of the slave complaint that Julie turns into the racially pseudo-unmarked, privatized, frustrated, female complaint that she passes on to Magnolia, the exemplary being of the next generation of the intimately disappointed? The complaint has three sides: it turns a singular situation of disappointment into a blueprint for surviving what's generic about it; it translates inchoate frustrations into a convention of critique from within; and it magnifies the singular life into a version of generality in which the intensities of being an ordinary person achieve their expression in the genre of the *somebody* around whom it could be imagined that the world is organized, if for a moment.

"I am somebody" is a different message than, say, the triumphant, "I am an ordinary nobody with the sentimental dignity of having suffered privately"; it is different than the "he was a simple man" of nostalgic biography; or the "she, he, or we deserved better" of political publics whose social claims register success primarily in evaluations of how institutions change their terms of empathy and recognition. Stardom as a model of ordinary being smacks of seeking out universality, but generality is different than universality because it is normative, has qualities, and is lived sensually in a social body.

I have described this convention of transvaluing negativity (no longer loss, it is now potential) as a marketized message that shapes a historical form of American optimism; it focuses attention on the potentials released in not being defeated, in being vigilant, porous, enduring, and committed to being open to the scene in which a small complex life becomes big and simple in the revolutionary moment of its simplifying recognition. It is a mode of affect management in scenes where adjustment to loss is pragmatic but the adjustment of fantasy is not taken lightly.

One might respond to all this that I am describing a typical avant-garde or counterhegemonic "deformation" of form, to adapt Arthur Knight's phrase.[27] Much of the film feels like a 1960s "happening," after all. But I am claiming something different here, which has to do with the remake's splitting off of realism (death) from the affectivity of the *melos* or musicality (life). *Showboat 1988—The Remake* wants to break the project of universalizing transcendence in pop homogeneity, compassionate self-performance, and celebratory nationalist historicizing that is found in Ferber's and Kern's *Show Boat*s. Instead, it celebrates absolute singularity perceived through the form of intimate public generality: its intimate public is engendered by anyone who appreciates it and feels lightened by the bravado of other sentimental subjects of adaptation who make openings for themselves to be appreciated. *Showboat 1988—The Remake* directs the referent of vague sociality toward the communality of its own process, each event in which will be changed by the next act that makes its way to staging the potentialities released on impact.[28]

But can you build a transformative politics out of this, something more than citational adaptation? To "die" onstage is to perform without receiving the kudos the performer's ego needs in order to feel the reciprocity that is not in kind. But as in *Showboat 1988—The Remake*, where "dying" onstage is part of the ongoing present in which freedom is experienced even in the moment after executing the song, this death can be an opening too. Exuberantly, Sylvester covers "Blackbird" at the film's end, crowing, "You were only waiting for this moment to arrive." Which moment? Why wait? Waiting for evidence that one has not been defeated is such a different register than defeating what threatens you. *Showboat 1988—The Remake* stops waiting for the moment and makes the moment, fracturing without breaking the sentimental bond. To cite Nina Simone's magnificent aside (and the aside is another genre that stretches out the present, elasticizing its potential in an unpredictable parenthesis): "This is a show tune, but the show hasn't been written for it yet."[29]

# NOTES

## Introduction: Intimacy, Publicity, and Femininity

1. The quotation in the subhead comes from Hurst, *Today Is Ladies' Day*, 3.

2. Anonymous, *The Bride Stripped Bare*; Dowd, *Are Men Necessary?*; Hanauer, ed., *The Bitch in the House*. Often these contemporary works claim not to be feminist but to inveigh against the couple on behalf of both partners; but their complaint rhetoric comes squarely from the women's culture tradition of comic and melo-dramatic complaint while being informed by feminist and queer critiques of the couple and the family. See also the blog "True Wife Confessions," whose writers equally straddle feminist and feminine-style demands and desires for sexual and emotional recognition while demonstrating ambivalence and bitterness about their investment in the scene as such (http://truewifeconfessions.blogspot.com, accessed September 20, 2007).

3. Nancy Armstrong argues that the project of the modern novel itself is to man-age ambivalence by projecting onto women literary figures as such the respon-sibility for maintaining contradictions within liberal individuality between the model of the subject as complete, without needs, and the model of the subject as fundamentally trans-subjective and compassionate. Women never represent the subject without needs: their signification as bearers of the responsibility for managing affect, emotion, and sociality produces the *figura* of autonomy in those who have the privilege to cast their projections as truths or aspirational moral conditions. See Armstrong, *How Novels Think*, especially 3–85.

4. On the "scenario" as a genre of porous incoherence and hegemony that maintains speculation, see D. Taylor, *The Archive and the Repertoire*, especially xiii–53.

5. This is the last line of *Gone with the Wind*, declaimed by Scarlett O'Hara: "I'll go home, and I'll think of some way to get him back! After all, tomorrow is another day!"

6. Mary Ryan points out that women's entry into the political sphere as actors began in the 1840s in the United States and has a compromised, ambivalent, and fractured history of its own, including a cognate relation to the sentimental racism and class privilege I track in this book. See Ryan, *Women in Public* as well as Levander, *Voices of the Nation*.

7. This book focuses on what is conventional in "women's culture," involving mainly nonpolitical reformulations of the world in terms of the affective assurance denoted by compassionate recognition that are deemed superior to political interest. The critical literature on sentimentality has now long refused the appearance of apoliticism brandished by sentimental humanism, connecting it to racist, imperial, and exploitative alibis for control promoted by the United States and other liberal democratic nations. For examples, see essays throughout Davidson et al., *Oxford Companion to Women's Writing in the United States*; Samuels, ed., *The Culture of Sentiment*; and Stoler, ed., *Haunted by Empire*. See also the classic monographs that shaped our field and whose energies are central to this project's address to women's culture: Baym, *Woman's Fiction*; Douglas, *The Feminization of American Culture*; duCille, *The Coupling Convention*; Tompkins, *Sensational Designs*; Sanchez-Eppler, *Touching Liberty*; Hull, *Color, Sex, and Poetry*; and Wall, *Changing Our Own Words*.

These books demonstrate repeatedly that while preserving the respect for the abstract domains of recognition made possible by the circulation of love and its cognates characterizes the more conventional work of "women's culture," sentimental genres have been freely adapted as foundations for explicit political programs. For example, at the same time as the middlebrow romances this book examines were helping to expand the apolitical domains of the social into worlds of social belonging and risk-minimizing critique, Meridel LeSueur's *The Girl* (1939) provided a Popular Front redistortion of this operation. Sympathetic to the aspect of women's collaborative sentimental ordinariness that casts love as a kind of sustaining richness that the economy cannot provide, LeSueur's narrative converts this personal life energy into public agitation by way of maternalist demands on public relief funds, but it does not critique or counter the commitment to fantasies of the intimate good life that the women on the breadlines and in the bars deploy as part of their frank realism. Even in radical critique, the novel keeps a foot in the feminine economy of recognition and sympathy whose terms it wants to expand.

8. The history of feminine publicity as a mediatized market phenomenon has been flourishing in the past few decades, and saturation by that work, which focuses on women's public political impact and changes in feminine domestic ideology, provides a reinforcing background to this book's argument that while femininity has absorbed many debates and variations in what counts as realism and fantasies of happiness inside and outside of its necessities, it has had a sustained indexical presence in U.S. media culture, standing as a figure of responsibility for managing the affective, emotional, and ordinary personal lives and fantasies of Americans.

This public was first established in periodical literature. The best history of U.S. women's magazines remains Mott, *History of American Magazines*; see also Humphreys, *American Women's Magazines*; Endres and Lueck, eds., *Women's Periodicals in the United States*; and Zukerman, *A History of Women's Popular Magazines in the United States, 1792–1995*. Lots of rich thematic and institutional historicizing of women-marketed publicity has commenced in the last decade. From among these, see Aronson, *Taking Liberties*; Braithwaite, *Women's Magazines*; Damon-Moore, *Magazines for the Millions*; Farrell, *Yours in Sisterhood*; Cane and Alves, *"The Only Efficient Instrument"*; Carla Kaplan, *The Erotics of Talk*; Kitch, *The Girl on the Magazine Cover*; Lehuu, *Carnival on the Page*; Okker, *Our Sister Editors*; Scanlon, *Inarticulate Longings*; Smith, *Becoming a Woman through Romance*; and Walker, ed., *Women's Magazines 1940–1960*. Ellen Gruber Garvey, in *The Adman in the Parlor*, does an especially effective job in detailing the management of affective contradictions related to the project of stabilizing femininity as an absorptive referent for "women's culture." All of these works contribute to the literature on how feminine publicity worked through coordinating contradictory advice about how women might deal with what is overwhelming in ordinary life along with escapist drives, projects of serious and minor self-cultivation, and techniques for affect management and sexual de-repression. This range of matters, often printed right next to each other, produced an elasticity within the feminine that allowed for a normatively sanctioned range of kinds of audience absorption and browsing, exploring, and wondering.

Relatedly, there is a vital non-text-based literature on the impact of these texts on women's subjectivities whose verification of the textualist's instinct that publicity produces subjects who negotiate finding and being themselves, navigating realism and fantasy, within the world of circulation is crucial to any work on the public sphere as a space of passionate rational and irrational attachment. The ethnographic and archivally fortified works on women's book reading, cinema going, and culture-making practices that have been most influential on this book are Campbell, *Film and Cinema Spectatorship*; Feuer, *Seeing through the Eighties*; Long, *Book Clubs*; McCarthy, *Women's Culture*; Rabinovitz, *For the Love of Pleasure*; Radway, *Reading the Romance*; Spurlock and Magistro, *New and Improved*; Stacey, *Star Gazing*; and H. Taylor, *Scarlett's Women*. These and many other works on spectatorship and cultures of reading are cited throughout this and later chapters.

9. Sara Ahmed points out that the will to generality she sees in feminism is a symptom of a liberal refusal to honor the singularities and political antagonisms that must be accounted for even if one accedes that women are subordinated, dishonored, or relatively inconvenient in most political contexts. It should not be surprising that feminism emerges from sentimental culture, and that when it isn't separatist but reparative or utopian it expresses the desire for general belonging characteristic of liberalism as a political theory and sentimentality as a theory of affective assurance. Ahmed's work tends to equate universalist arguments with generalist ones, as has mine and much else: but in this book I argue that the logic of the general is quite different from that of the universal, in that the general is an experience of social belonging that is embodied and has qualities, as opposed to the universal, which has always been defined. See Ahmed, *Differences That Matter*; see also Green, *Spectacular Confessions*.

10. This genre theory is brought to us by a long conversation in my head between Fredric Jameson's brilliantly nuanced work on genre as a mediating institution in and after *The Political Unconscious* and the discussion around melodrama as aesthetic mode and site of spectatorship developed especially in feminist and queer cinema and media theory over the last few decades. These books provided the foundation for that thinking, although much debate on melodrama's role in subjectivity formation and much revisionary history of the modal and performance norms has developed since this period: Doane, *The Desire to Desire* and *Femmes Fatales*; Landy, *Imitation of Life*; Gledhill, ed., *Home Is Where the Heart Is*; Stacey, *Star Gazing*; and P. White, *Uninvited*.

11. I refer, of course, to the not identical work of Judith Butler and Eve Sedgwick on performativity as the activity of extending social being (personal and collective) into the world. This book is much more aligned with Sedgwick's emphasis on the creativity of the subject navigating identity periperformatively via nonce taxonomy (the invention of performative norms in relation to the hegemonic ones) than with Butler's more structuralist model of the subject (iterating and materializing intelligible styles of being more impermeable), although the book is deeply embedded in the enrichment of how to think about projection and mediation that both scholars have provided. See Butler, *Bodies that Matter* and *Undoing Gender*; and Sedgwick, *Epistemology of the Closet* and *Touching Feeling*.

12. David Savran suggests that middlebrow genres are about anxiety management. The relation of his formulation to mine is not at all antagonistic. All of the literary material addressed in this book is middlebrow, for example, literature that organizes anxieties about the good life as seen from an identification with middle-class aspirations for both pleasure and instruction from aesthetic transactions. Anxiety is an affective emanation of ambivalence, the latter of which I take to be more of a form or structure of relation rather than a feeling. For a longer discussion of what this distinction might mean, see chapter 7. To be clear, not all intimate publics are middlebrow, although all are marketized versions of a collective subjectivity. Some forms of aspirational normativity promoted in intimate publics include fantasies of acquiring wealth but are not about climbing up through the moral meritocracy. Being deserving is the a priori that is expressed through appetitive fantasies, of *getting out* of the bad or deadened situation and *making it* in an ongoing *now*, an intensified present. For very different takes on this phenomenon (and what follows is a stand-in for a huge literature), see the oeuvre of George Lipsitz, especially *Time Passages*; Bourdieu and Accardo, eds., *The Weight of the World*; Buckland, *Impossible Dance*; and Stewart, *Ordinary Affects*. The middlebrow designation makes greater sense for print publics and, as Savran has argued, contemporary theater than it does for the aspirations expressed in embodied scenes—even that of classic Hollywood cinema, which is muddled precisely because the logic of sensational presence rubs up against the logic of responsible affective self-management at the core of bourgeois melodrama and comedy. See Savran, *A Queer Sort of Materialism*.

13. Lee and LiPuma, "Cultures of Circulation." See also Michael McKeon's claim that the public sphere is not a bourgeois form but a seventeenth-century development of the transition from rank to class culture that generated the public sphere in the sense that there was already, by then, a public sphere of general belonging in the minds of citizens (especially city dwellers associated with incipient cosmopolitanism). See McKeon, *The Secret History of Domesticity*.

14. It was not just in the United States, as Stacey's *Star Gazing* argues. The literature on U.S. "women's culture" spans many different disciplines and genres, not just aesthetic ones. It also negotiates the racial, ethnic, religious, and age specificity of the interlocking intimate publics that make up the general space of feminine publicity. Histories of women's reform and radical movements and club cultures in the United States have been especially crucial to the verification of participation in different and overlapping (and sometimes antagonistic) spaces of gendered mediation. Some highlights from this enormous bibliography include Ginzberg, *Untidy Origins* and *Women and the Work of Benevolence*; Knupfer, *Toward a Tenderer Humanity and a Nobler Womanhood*; Rooks, *Ladies' Pages*; Taylor and

Rupp, "Women's Culture and Lesbian Feminist Activism"; and D. White, *Too Heavy a Load*. As for studies of specific marketing strategies, see M. Brown, *Television and Women's Culture*; Heide, *Television and Women's Lives*; and Press, *Women Watching Television*.

15. The original essay for this book, "The Female Complaint," along with many of the essays that comprise it, makes this argument about the ways that an image of black suffering provided a form of interiority for white women to borrow to make a legitimate social space and intimate public for their complaints. See also Berlant, "The Subject of True Feeling." For the nineteenth-century United States this argument has been taken up and enriched immeasurably by Castronovo, *Necro Citizenship*.

16. Bennett, *Poets in the Public Sphere*; Carby, *Reconstructing Womanhood*; Lowe, *Immigrant Acts*; and Wexler, *Tender Violence*.

17. Although the term "post-subculture" doesn't do much analytically itself to solve the problem of finding a way to nondominant collective social relations that express structural discriminations and ongoing dynamic practices, the debate over "subculture" is most usefully summarized in Weinzierl and Muggleton, "What Is 'Post-Subcultural Studies' Anyway?"

18. Fraser, "Rethinking the Public Sphere."

19. Moon, "Semi-Publics" and *A Small Boy and Others*.

20. Sedgwick, "Privilege of Unknowing."

21. Hansen, *Babel in Babylon*. See also Stacey, *Star Gazing*; Dyer, *Heavenly Bodies*; *Stars*; and *White*; Mayne, *Cinema and Spectatorship*; and, more recently, Farmer, *Spectacular Passions*; Campbell, *Film and Cinema Spectatorship*; and P. White, *Uninvited*. Whole literatures on collective identification through spectatorship flourished throughout the 1990s and beyond: these luminaries continue to shape that discussion.

22. Elizabeth Dillon's *The Gender of Freedom* similarly and acutely negotiates the ways the understanding of modern publicness requires an account of desire and intimacy, and not just rational criticality. But her meditations on "desire" in the public sphere are not elaborated very fully, and in the studies they become more about familial transactions than the domain of impersonal belonging on which I focus here.

23. Copjec, *Imagine There's No Woman*; and Bennett, *Poets in the Public Sphere*. Seen methodologically the perspectives of these books—one philosophical and psychoanalytic, the other historicist from feminist and literary points of view—couldn't be more different. But they share a proposition that women—as seen in the context of feminine publicity, anyway—are inevitably/invariably/mainly critical of the world in which they have to take up femininity, and that their be-

ings rage/judge against it. My counterargument is not a disagreement; rather, I argue that ambivalence is a more complex critical form than they propose.

24. Susie Orbach's book of case studies in the psychoanalytic process, *The Impossibility of Sex*, demonstrates brilliantly the articulation between closeness and distance in relations of attachment.

25. Lacan, *Le seminaire, livre VIII, Le transfert, 1960–1961*, 23. See also Vinciguerra, "The Paradoxes of Love," 46. This phrase is most famously glossed in Žižek, "Passion: Regular or Decaf?"

26. Lacan, "Feminine Sexuality"; Restuccia, *Melancholics in Love*; and Copjec, *Imagine There's No Woman*.

27. See Berlant, "Love, a Queer Feeling," 432–33, 438–39.

28. Restuccia, *Melancholics in Love*.

29. The psychoanalyst Adam Phillips is the great theorist of the foundational place of self-betrayal in the maintenance of love. See Phillips, *On Flirtation*.

30. See Probyn, "Everyday Shame"; Sedgwick, *Touching Feeling*, especially 93–151; and Sedgwick and Frank, *Shame and Its Sisters*. See also Heinz Kohut's work on the grandiose self in *The Chicago Institute Lectures 1972–1976*; as well as his essays "Forms and Transformations of Narcissism," especially 249–56; "The Psychoanalytic Treatment of Narcissistic Personality Disorders—Outline of a Systematic Approach"; and "Thoughts on Narcissism and Narcissistic Rage."

31. Fitzgerald, "Who Can Fall in Love after Thirty?," 412.

32. On overcommunication and its threat to intimacy, see Vogler, "Sex and Talk."

33. Shumway, *Modern Love*; Illouz, *Consuming the Romantic Utopia*; K. Young, *Ordinary Pleasures*; and Wexman, *Creating the Couple*. I use "middle-class" here to designate a fantasy zone of class generality in the United States—it is a status that authorizes feeling universal politically and therefore general socially.

34. See the terrific discussion of reciprocity in the context of Lacanian thought in Harari, *Lacan's Four Fundamental Concepts of Psychoanalysis*, 253–82.

35. Rose, *Sexuality in the Field of Vision*; see also Copjec, *Imagine There's No Woman*.

36. Davis, *Almost No Memory*, 134–36.

37. Ibid., 136.

38. Ibid., 27.

39. Ibid., 131.

40. Ibid., 82.

41. On the *dictée* as the genre of the law's assertion and unraveling, see Derrida, "The Law of Genre."

42. Spivak, "Subaltern Studies," 215ff. Spivak speaks of the concept/metaphor of woman as regulating scenes of transition by producing a phantasmatic or conventional continuity across change. Her phrasing of feminine figuration as

a source for creating a sense of continuity where there is actually antagonism has been crucial to this book's figuration of continuity: but importantly, Spivak does not consider what is or is not a transformative event in this piece (change is a relatively transparent term). But in the throes of sentimentality's unfinished business, the question of what *constitutes* change amid continuity (and not the other way around) is central.

43. Seltzer, "Serial Killers (II)"; and Halttunen, *Murder Most Foul*.

44. See Agamben, *The Coming Community*.

45. Berlant, "Intimacy," 286.

46. See W. Brown, "Wounded Attachments."

47. See Berlant, "The Intimate Public Sphere."

48. Berlant, *Queen of America*, 60.

49. Sedgwick, "A Poem Is Being Written," 118.

50. I am referencing here my 1988 essay, "The Female Complaint."

51. Most of this work remains imminent to *The Female Complaint*. But for a great articulation of the history of political theory in the affective world of Hollywood cinema, see Siomopoulis, "Political Theory and Melodrama Studies," and "Public Daydreams."

52. See note 14. See also the important work of duCille, *The Coupling Convention*; and Wall, *Worrying the Line*.

## Chapter 1: Poor Eliza

1. The British/Siamese/U.S. triangle is an invention of the play: the story Margaret Landon and Anna Leonowens tell is about French, not British, imperialism in the area. See Landon's *Anna and the King of Siam* and Leonowens's *The English Governess at the Siamese Court*.

2. Rodgers and Hammerstein, *The King and I*, 379.

3. See Cheah and Robbins, eds., *Cosmopolitics*; and Harvey, "Cosmopolitanism and the Banality of Geographical Evils."

4. For the longer theoretical argument, see Berlant, "The Subject of True Feeling."

5. In contrast, the contemporary version of sentimental citizenship locates the state's compassion in its promise of security for those who work and accrue private property. See Berlant, ed., *Compassion*.

6. The genre of heroic rescue is usually melodrama. To track the relation of white supremacy to melodramatic modernity in the United States, see L. Williams, *Playing the Race Card*.

7. On *Uncle Tom's Cabin* as a text that ambivalently translates regional, sexual, and racial fractures into the generic utopia of sentimentalism, see Lang, "Slavery and Sentimentalism."

8. See Merish, *Sentimental Materialism*; Staiger, *Interpreting Films*; Warhol, "Poetics and Persuasion"; Weinstein, ed., *The Cambridge Companion to Harriet Beecher Stowe*; and L., Williams, *Playing the Race Card*. Recent revelations of the novel's perdurance include T. S. Eliot's never performed ballet *Tom* and Bill T. Jones's *Uncle Tom's Cabin* (1990), the latter of which, says Jones, was explicitly committed to prying apart the violence of the novel from its demand for the liberal, visceral response. See Dent and Thompson, "Bill T. Jones."

9. On the historical novel's convention of using upheavals in love to work through historical anxieties, see Berlant, *The Anatomy of National Fantasy*; Sommer, *Foundational Fictions*; and Chakrabarty, "Domestic Cruelty and the Birth of the Subject." On the wielding of healthy heterosexuality as a cynically nationalist Cold War sign, see Corber, *In the Name of National Security*.

10. On "vernacularization," see Appadurai, "Disjuncture and Difference in the Global Cultural Economy."

11. This general conclusion about the overdetermined political story of *Uncle Tom's Cabin* in *The King and I* has also been reached in Donaldson, *Decolonizing Feminisms*, 32–51. Donaldson's focus is more on the gendering of colonial relations than on the structure of the sentimental mechanism of the play's politico-aesthetic formalism.

12. Rodgers and Hammerstein, *The King and I*, 403.

13. On the intimacy of the stereotype, the commodity form, and normal femininity in the U.S. sentimental tradition, see Berlant, "The Female Woman."

14. In the Oscar-winning film *Anna and the King of Siam* (dir. John Cromwell, 1946), there is no performance of *The Small House of Uncle Thomas*, and Tuptim is very publicly and visibly executed.

15. Rodgers and Hammerstein, *The King and I*, 429.

16. For an excellent summary of the long critical debate about sentimentality's traditional association of feminine sacrifice and feminine power, see Wexler, "Tender Violence." See also Lang, "Slavery and Sentimentalism"; and Samuels, ed., *The Culture of Sentiment*, 3–8.

17. Stowe, *Uncle Tom's Cabin or, Life Among the Lowly*, 117–18. Page references are to the 1981 edition.

18. Gossett, *"Uncle Tom's Cabin" and American Culture*, 164.

19. Atkin, *Converting America*; see also Glickman, "'Buy for the Sake of the Slave.'"

20. Here is the major archive from which I draw my conclusions about the film history of *Uncle Tom's Cabin*: Thomas A. Edison, Edwin S. Porter Production, *Uncle Tom's Cabin or Slavery Days* (1903); *Uncle Tom's Cabin*, no studio given, dir. Robert Daly (1914); United Artists, *Topsy and Eva*, dir. Del Lord (1927);

Universal, prod. Carl Laemmle, *Uncle Tom's Cabin*, dir. Harry A. Pollard (1927); E. A. Hammons, Paul Sullivan, "Felix the Cat in Uncle Tom's Crabbin'" (1927); and Tex Avery, "Uncle Tom's Cabaña" (1947). There is also a notable tradition of interpellated scenes from *Uncle Tom's Cabin* in films set in other periods, among which are the Shirley Temple vehicle *Dimples* (dir. William Seiter, 1936); Abbott and Costello, *The Gay Nineties* (n.d.); and *The King and I* (dir. Walter Lang, 1956).

21. For more on the racial soundtrack of sentimental texts in the *Uncle Tom* tradition, see chapter 2 on *Show Boat*.

22. Eckert, "Shirley Temple and the House of Rockefeller."

23. A reanimation of *Uncle Tom's Cabin* took place in Johannesburg, South Africa in 1934: Loren Kruger argues for the fundamental ambivalence of this gesture, in which a theatrical performance of U.S. slave songs, Stowe's novel, and speeches by Abraham Lincoln and Frederick Douglass circumvented strictures against antiracist publicity under the colonial regime of apartheid *and* expressed the "liberal paternalism" of the missionary curriculum. See Kruger, "Placing 'New Africans' in the 'Old' South Africa."

24. Baldwin, "Everybody's Protest Novel," 31.

25. Ibid., 29.

26. Ibid., 28.

27. Baldwin, "The Price of the Ticket," xx.

28. See, for example, Lynn Wardley's summary in her otherwise wonderful essay, "Relic, Fetish, Femmage," 206.

29. Baldwin, "Everybody's Protest Novel," 29.

30. *Uncle Tom's Children* was Richard Wright's first published book.

31. Baldwin, *The Devil Finds Work*, 565.

32. Ibid., 561.

33. Ibid., 565.

34. McLaughlin, "Post-Postmodern Discontent"; Sydney Lindauer, "Commentary," *Red Bluff Daily News*, March 9, 2005; and Jesse Green, "When Political Art Mattered," *New York Times Magazine*, December 7, 2003.

35. Frank Rich, "One-Week Stand," *New York Times Magazine*, 25 July 1993, sec. 6, 54.

36. Among the related commodities bearing the imprimatur of the novel are the film (now on video; dir. Clint Eastwood, 1996), the audiocassette, the CD *Remembering Madison County*, plus a large collection of mugs and T-shirts available on the Web. For a sampling of the related books, see Garrett, *Building Bridges*; Hemminger and Work, *The Recipes of Madison County*; Hoskinson, *Bridges in Time*;

Orleans, *The Butches of Madison County*; and Waller, *The Bridges of Madison County: Memory Book*.

37. Waller, *The Bridges of Madison County: Memory Book*, xi–xii.
38. Stowe, *Uncle Tom's Cabin or, Life Among the Lowly*, 622.
39. Žižek, *The Sublime Object of Ideology*, 29.
40. Stowe, *Uncle Tom's Cabin or, Life Among the Lowly*, 624.
41. A recent essay on the film of *The Bridges of Madison County* argues that its focus on Johnny Hartman is less soft white supremacist than it seems but adds that the presence of Hartman aims also to provide phallic ballast for Eastwood. See Gabbard, "Borrowing Black Masculinity."
42. Morrison, *Beloved*, 51.
43. Ibid., 261.

## Chapter 2: Pax Americana

1. Ferber, *Show Boat*; and Hammerstein and Kern, *Show Boat*.
2. Lott, *Love and Theft*.
3. On these minstrelsy-derived debates about the political, aesthetic, and ethical consequences of white and white ethnic caricature and stereotype of African Americans in the nineteenth and twentieth centuries in the United States, see also Kun, "The Yiddish Are Coming"; Roach, *Cities of the Dead*; and Rogin, *Blackface, White Noise*. See also Gabler, *An Empire of Their Own*; Most, *Making Americans*; and Whitfield, "Is It True What They Sing about Dixie?" See also notes 21 and 30.
4. Ferber, *A Peculiar Treasure*.
5. Julie Goldsmith Gilbert's biography of her great-aunt Edna Ferber documents that many of the incidents in *Show Boat* were indeed taken from the historical archive or hearsay evidence from her source about show boats, Charles Hunter. In particular the love story of Julie and Steve has its source in a late-nineteenth-century court case. Gilbert, *Ferber*, 378–81.
6. Ferber, *Show Boat*, 118.
7. Block, *Enchanted Evenings*.
8. I do not use the word "subalternity" casually here, nor do I seek to contribute to the emptying out of the specificity of that term for South Asia and its historiography in the work of the Subaltern Studies group. As it happens, for political progressives in proximity to socialism the articulation of the proletarian and the peasant was in force during the 1920s in the United States, providing a register in which to describe relations among different historically subordinated publics. Ferber's project is to counter the mass cultural, modernist, and cosmopolitan at-

tenuation of historical density in the United States with a brand of aesthetic historicism that secures history by iconizing race, gender, and region and bypassing the languages of class and caste. "Peasant" was the detouring term, a compromise formation from within nationalism that sought a nonracist American genealogy. As we will see, Ferber's style of evoking the peasantry as a model for all subordination opens its own questions about the desire to soften modernist realism with nostalgic memoration. Her autobiography clearly states an aversion both to "Sambo" narratives and the left-wing political rhetoric of "The Worker" (Ferber, *A Peculiar Treasure*, 254, 262), preferring instead the representation of social hierarchy to be in the rhetorical register of cliché softened by the power of emotional humanism. In this way she can traffic in caricature without feeling caricaturing. "Subaltern" stands in for the presence of peasant populations and peasantness in *Show Boat* and also marks the persistent question of how to represent the uneven economic and cultural relations of historically subordinated populations.

9. Lott argues that episodic ego diffusion in musical numbers represents a kind of utopian potential within the text of entertainment racism: I couldn't disagree more. White "ego diffusion" is the pleasure of privilege disburdened by historical self-knowledge: the conventions of diffusion in the context of white pleasures usually obstruct the kind that would destabilize the material grounds of self-extension in pleasure. See Lott, *Love and Theft*, 184.

10. Two other substantive and challenging works provide a critical interface with this one on the question of how narratives of the personal or domestic transact with the political world: Wexler's *Tender Violence* and A. Kaplan's *The Anarchy of Empire in the Making of U.S. Culture* interweave gendered, racial, and transnational forces in the privileged imaginary of U.S. national discourse in ways akin to the project of this book. But both of these books see the appearance of social relations as nonpolitical as masks for what is "really" political whereas my argument is that privileging the political as the name for important, significant, substantial life-making activity denigrates the spaces of ordinary life people live and find sustenance in, and not just because they are duped by false values or socially deprivileged.

11. Ferber, *Show Boat*, 105.

12. For the rich history of feminine upward mobility through glamour in the United States, see especially the work of Peiss, *Cheap Amusements* and *Hope in a Jar*.

13. For discussions of fantasy in its relation to seriality, see Laplanche and Pontalis, *The Language of Psycho-Analysis*, 314–19; and Laplanche and Pontalis, "Fantasy and the Origins of Sexuality," 5–34; see also Cora Kaplan, "*The Thorn Birds*."

14. Jameson, "Reification and Ideology in Mass Culture," 144.

15. For example, see Ferber, *A Peculiar Treasure*, 288, and Stanley Kaufman's review of the 1966 revival of *Show Boat*, quoted in Gilbert, *Ferber*, 68–69. See also the unsigned review, *Picture Play*, August 1936: "It begins to look as if Edna Ferber's novel had already become the modern American classic, comparable only to *Uncle Tom's Cabin* of an earlier day."

16. Dyer, *Heavenly Bodies*, 85, 89.

17. Ferber, *Show Boat*, 9, 240.

18. Ibid., 240.

19. Jameson, *Postmodernism, or, The Cultural Logic of Late Capitalism*.

20. See Jones, *Our Musicals, Ourselves*, 73, 76.

21. Gerald Mast points out that this feature of naming and remaking was a standard habit of musical writing in the 1920s and after, especially with Jewish writers writing from within black traditions and minstrel, pseudo-black traditions of music. Mast, *Can't Help Singin'*, 59.

22. For a summary of Ferber's narratives of work, see C. Wilson, *White Collar Fictions*.

23. Ferber, 522.

24. Ibid., 528–29.

25. Ferber, *Show Boat*, 153.

26. Ibid., 78.

27. I take this way of describing affective intelligence in part from Teresa Brennan's *The Transmission of Affect*. While Brennan sees affect always as a mode of judgment, Ferber associates the discerning activity of affect as special, a mode of hypervigilance shaped by the hard work of living and suffering inequality.

28. For a musicologist's take on the musical politics of racial memory in the score of *Show Boat*, and Robeson's performance in particular, see Knapp, *The American Musical and the Formation of National Identity*, especially 184–94. Knapp sees the aesthetic "weakness" of the show and the Whale film as related to the insolubility of the social problems the play engages. Geoffrey Block's more intense musical analysis leads him to think of the show more traditionally, as a masterpiece, in his *Enchanted Evenings*, 19–40.

29. The musical phrase "Ol' Man River" reverses the first three notes of the chirpy "Cotton Blossom," the first song of *Show Boat*, thus performing musically what the two songs might be said to stand for lyrically, since "Cotton Blossom" is about the show boat as "one big happy family" and "Ol' Man River" is about the labor of suffering hidden by the entertainment spectacle.

30. The *Show Boat* industry is full of stories about the gratitude and amazement African Americans express that Kern and Hammerstein could have written such

an "authentic" number. Stephen J. Whitfield writes, for example, "In rehearsing *Show Boat* in 1927, members of the black chorus went up to Jerome Kern and expressed amazement that a white man could have composed 'Ol' Man River.'" Whitfield, "Is It True What They Sing about Dixie?," 21. See also Freedland, *Jerome Kern*, 90–91; and Mast, *Can't Help Singin'*.

31. Ferber, *Show Boat*, 396.
32. Ibid., 296.
33. Ibid., 118.
34. Ibid., 120.
35. Ibid., 121–22.
36. The argument about white culture's extraction of style value from black practices is most persuasively argued by Mercer, "Black Hair/Style Politics"; and Snead, "Repetition as a Figure of Black Culture."
37. Ferber, *Show Boat*, 83, 122, 155, 291, 317, 362, and 387.
38. Ibid., 291.
39. Krueger, *Show Boat: The Story of a Classical American Musical*, 211–12.
40. Foner, *Paul Robeson Speaks*, 481–82; Duberman, *Paul Robeson*, 114, 604–5.
41. Ferber, *Show Boat*, 101.
42. It is worth noting that Ferber constantly phrases her transcendent attachments in the register of the love plot played as realism—here is her take on "Ol' Man River," for example.

> He played and sang "Ol' Man River." The music mounted and I give you my word my hair stood on end, and tears came to my eyes, I breathed like a heroine in a melodrama. This was great music. This was music that would outlast Jerome Kern's day and mine. I have never heard it since without that emotional surge. When *Show Boat* was revived at the Casino Theater in New York just four years after its original production at the Ziegfeld I saw a New York first-night audience, after Paul Robeson's singing of "Ol' Man River," shout and cheer and behave generally as I've never seen an audience behave in any theater in all my years of playgoing.

> Ferber, *A Peculiar Treasure*, 306.

43. Cf. Berlant, "The Female Complaint," 237–59.
44. Krueger, 54.
45. Ferber, *A Peculiar Treasure*, 301.
46. Ferber, *Show Boat*, 104.
47. Ibid., 83.
48. Ibid., 102.
49. Ibid., 53.

50. Ibid., 101, 104–5.

51. Ibid., 25.

52. Gramsci, *Prison Notebooks*, 246–74.

53. See, for example, John Lahr, "Mississippi Mud"; or "Facing the Music: A Revival of *Show Boat* Confronts the Production's Historical Racism," *Tucson Weekly*, April 13, 2000; http://www.tucsonweekly.com/gbase/Arts/Content?oid=42383 (accessed September 20, 2007).

54. Brion, "*Show Boat*"; Philip, *Showing Grit*.

55. Gilbert, *Ferber*, 384–85.

56. Ferber, *A Peculiar Treasure*, 288.

57. Gabler, *An Empire of Their Own*; Most, *Making Americans*; Rogin, *Blackface, White Noise*; and Whitfield, "Is It True What They Sing about Dixie?"

58. Ferber, *A Peculiar Treasure*, 9–10.

59. Ibid., 12–13.

60. The Lilly Library Script reads: "The Campbell Playhouse with Orson Welles presents *Show Boat* by Edna Ferber," March 31, 1939. Guests: Edna Ferber, Margaret Sullivan, Helen Morgan.

61. Ibid., b–e.

## Chapter 3: National Brands, National Body

My special thanks to Andy Parker for inviting me to the English Institute to deliver this essay, and to Corey Creekmur, Laura Kipnis, Bill Warner, Michael Warner, Tom Stillinger, Val Smith, Eve Sedgwick, and many others for their inspiring and challenging conversation. The epigraph to this chapter is from Presbrey, *The History and Development of Advertising*, 625.

1. Larsen, *Passing*, 149.

2. Ibid., 150.

3. Ibid., 148–49.

4. Spillers, "Mama's Baby, Papa's Maybe."

5. For an elaboration on the regimes of discipline (as concealment, as grotesque or carnivalesque display) that have expressed the bourgeois body, see Stallybrass and White, *The Politics and Poetics of Transgression*.

6. McDowell, Introduction, xxvi–xxxi.

7. I take the notion of xenophilia (and much inspiration, besides) from C. Bailey, "Nigger/Lover," 30.

8. Larsen, *Passing*, 225.

9. Ibid.

10. Elsewhere I elaborate on how American "women's culture" constructs literary "modes of containment"—notably in sentimental and melodramatic narrative—

that both testify to women's colonization within a racist/patriarchal/capitalist culture and mark the self-construed obstacles to specifically political thought and action toward social change by bourgeois-identified women. See Berlant, "The Female Complaint."

11. See, for example, Baker, "The Domestication of Politics."

12. Some major attempts to dissect masculine/Enlightenment citizenship are Bloch, "The Gendered Meanings of Virtue in Revolutionary America"; Dietz, "Citizenship with a Feminist Face"; Elshtain, *Public Man, Private Woman*; Gatens, "Towards a Feminist Theory of the Body"; Landes, *Women and the Public Sphere in the Age of the French Revolution*; MacKinnon, *Toward a Feminist Theory of the State*; Norton, *Reflections on Political Identity*; Pateman, *The Sexual Contract*; Pitkin, *Fortune Is a Woman*; and I. Young, "Polity and Group Difference."

13. Powerful arguments against these quasi-objective appearances of masculine American political culture can be found in I. Young, "Impartiality and the Civic Public"; and Fraser, "What's Critical about Critical Theory? The Case of Habermas and Gender."

14. Casting the mulatta as an ur-figure of political and rhetorical indeterminacy is the perspective of Gaines, "White Privilege and Looking Relations"; and Spillers, "Notes on an Alternative Model—Neither/Nor."

15. Spillers, "Mama's Baby, Papa's Maybe," 67.

16. Ibid.; and Scarry, *The Body in Pain*, 108–9.

17. The vast majority of critical work on *Imitation of Life*, which almost always reads the Stahl and Hurst versions through the lens of the vastly successful Sirk narrative, focuses on maternal and familial relations (to the exclusion of specifically political ones) as the central "problem" for which the narrative provides an answer. This is, in part, because of the generic (over)emphasis of film criticism, which marks this complex text as melodrama and therefore as generated by contradictions within the family. This criticism tends to denigrate Hurst's and Stahl's texts for "giving in" to sentimentality and to elevate Sirk's more explicitly critical stance toward American culture. I think each side of these valuations is extremely limited. See Christine Gledhill's (otherwise excellent) "The Melodramatic Field"; E. Kaplan, "Mothering, Feminism and Representation"; and Heung, " 'What's the Matter with Sara Jane?' " Lucy Fischer's introduction to her critical edition of Sirk's screenplay gathers the most comprehensive bibliography available on this complex text and moves beyond the auteurist and generic impasses of the criticism. See "Three Way Mirror."

18. Other crucial transformations within this "complex text" (the "work" in its three versions) also take place over time. For example, the domestic plot about the rivalry between the white daughter and the white mother finds three different reso-

lutions: in the novel, the daughter marries the mother's love interest; in Stahl's film, there is no marriage and the two women "choose" each other; in Sirk's film, the love plot works, with the older woman settling in with the man. Also, the mulatta daughter becomes progressively pathetic, insufficient, and submissive to the dominant order over the course of the complex text. The aggregate narrative fate of both daughters, unable to benefit directly from their mothers' successes, suggests some obstacles to thinking/effecting a postpatriarchal female mode of inheritance in American culture and constitutes a counternarrative to the mothers' confidence in labor and capital's liberatory possibilities. I bracket these concerns here, focusing instead on the adult women, who are already living the overembodiment into which their daughters are only emerging.

19. Hurst, *Imitation of Life*, 1, 5. The bodily cataloging to which I refer occurs throughout the chapter: this hybrid passage from its first and last sentences is its most economic formulation. Future references to the novel will be contained in the text.

20. The relation between cataloging the woman's body and national identity has been beautifully worked out, from the point of view of its service to patriarchal national cultures, by Patricia Parker in "Rhetorics of Property." Bea's strategies of female identification are ambiguously related to the patriarchal strategies of control Parker sees because her will to disembodiment and abstraction proleptically subverts the procedures she mimes.

21. The social history of women's movement into the American political public sphere follows the half-conscious Bea through the novel: Hurst not only taps the history of suffrage, of women's emergence as citizen-consumers, and of women's increased participation in the work force during World War I, but also the fear women in the Depression had that their ideological and material gains would be lost to them. The bibliography on these coterminous movements is enormous: for general histories, see Banta, *Imaging American Women*; Cott, *The Grounding of Modern Feminism*; Daniel, *American Women in the 20th Century*; and Evans, *Born for Liberty*. For Hurst's reading of the complex movement toward female "personhood" and economic and sexual legitimacy, see three Hurst titles: "Are We Coming or Going?"; *Today Is Ladies' Day*; and "A Crisis in the History of Women."

22. I describe the national public space following Simon Frith, who argues that the notion of "capitalist culture" addresses the "ideological experience" of capitalism not fully accounted for by the traditional matrix of production-consumption. Frith, "Hearing Secret Harmonies."

23. There is a story yet to be told about the way advertising appears differentially in novels and films of the 1920s and 1930s. Film historians show that very early on

the frame of the movie screen, the shop window, and the product package borrowed each other's function in the circuit of production and consumption and of creating social value. On the early history of cinematic and commodity coordination, see J. Allen, "The Film Viewer as Consumer"; Eckert, "The Carole Lombard in Macy's Window"; Ewen, "City Lights"; Doane, "The Economy of Desire"; and Gaines, "The Queen Christina Tie-Ups." Jennifer Wicke argues that literature and advertising carried on a similar (although less capital-intensive) mutual dependency earlier, at the turn of the century. See Wicke, *Advertising Fictions*.

24. P. Hall, *The Organization of American Culture, 1700–1900*, 209–81; Lears, "From Salvation to Self-Realization"; and Jowett, "The Emergence of the Mass Society."

25. Westbrook, "Politics as Consumption."

26. Levi, ed., *Atlantic City*, 28–31.

27. "H. Prynne" is really "Hiram Prynne," a Vermont businessman who uses his initial in his business dealings for "Prynne and Company." I gather that the text posits a genetic relation between Hawthorne's Hester and Hurst's Bea: Bea "inherits" from Hester the tactic of giving herself over to the name of the father (the A, the "B.") in order to "pass" through public culture in a relatively dignified way.

28. Marx, *Capital, Volume 1*, 320–21.

29. Earlier I linked Bea's tendency to link sexual desire with women (her mother), pain, and bodily abstraction: but the scary return of this form of desire in her bond with Virginia Eden may also respond to the "heterosexual revolution" that accompanied the emergence of modern consumer culture and the modern female consuming body. While capitalism made it possible to live outside of economic dependence on the nuclear family, the 1920s witnessed strong ideological pressure on women to choose heterosociality as a component of the new consumer narcissism. "Beauty culture" (and here Eden surely suggests Helena Rubenstein) was administered by women to women: but *for* men. See Featherstone, "The Body in Consumer Culture"; Rapp and Ross, "The Twenties' Backlash"; and D'Emilio, "Capitalism and Gay Identity."

30. Haug, *Critique of Commodity Aesthetics*, 50.

31. Rydell, *All the World's a Fair*, 46.

32. Presbrey, *The History and Development of Advertising*, 360.

33. Ibid., 356, 382–84.

34. Marquette, *Brands, Trademarks and Good Will*, 137–41; Boskin, *Sambo*, 139.

35. Carby, *Reconstructing Womanhood*, 3–6. See also Rydell, "The World's Columbian Exposition of 1893"; Massa, "Black Women in the 'White City'"; and Rudwick and Meier, "Black Man in the 'White City.'" For a discussion of how

African American women's particular marginality at the fair linked up to its production of the modern American woman, see Banta, *Imaging American Women*, especially 499–550.

36. Marquette, *Brands, Trademarks and Good Will*, 146.

37. This ad is taken from Atwan, McQuade, and Wright, *Edsels, Luckies, and Frigidaires*, 92.

38. While Stahl's *Imitation of Life* was vastly popular in African American communities (Cripps, *Slow Fade to Black*, 303), its depiction of the reproduction of American racist and class hegemonies in the household of Bea and Delilah has provoked a long tradition of negative criticism. The paradigm text is S. Brown, "*Imitation of Life*." Following Brown's example are Bogle, *Blacks in American Films and Television*, 113–15, and *Toms, Coons, Mullatoes, Mammies and Bucks*, 57–60; Jeremy Butler, "*Imitation of Life*"; Cripps, *Slow Fade to Black*, 301–3; Harrison, "The Negro and the Cinema"; and Noble, *The Negro in Films*, 61–63. For a brief history of the film's production and reception, see Schatz, *The Genius of the System*, 231–32.

39. Another facet to the film's cultural work in this scene is the metonymic linkage of Delilah to the body of white ethnic American immigrants. The man for whom Delilah produces her cartoon image is an Italian actor who engages in his own grotesque comic physical performance, complete with thick accent: Stahl shoots him as a direct parallel to Delilah, with Bea in the spatial center. Since Delilah is explicitly an "immigrant" from the South, her juxtaposition with him, and their equivalent service functions (helping Bea produce a business, performing slapstick comedy), signify yet another relay the film makes among social marginalities in non-melting-pot America.

40. C. Bailey, "Nigger/Lover," 40.

41. In fact, the expression "the Sirkean System" used in the subhead is Paul Willemen's phrase and idea, founding *Screen*'s revival of Sirk's reputation in the 1970s. Following this line, many cinema theorists and historians valorize Sirk's avant-garde exploitation of Hollywood's laws of genre: he is said to have worked so excessively within the melodrama as to have saturated it with irony (along with the American culture that requires its consoling release). While I don't disagree with this general reading of Sirk's political position, this section of the essay explores the limits of his irony as it circulates around the female body. Willemen, "Towards an Analysis of the Sirkean System"; see Fischer, "Three Way Mirror" for the extensive Sirk bibliography. My reading is more in line with that of Selig, "Contradiction and Reading."

42. The lyrics to this song signify that the discursive, erotic, and political space between Sarah Jane and Annie is entirely an effect of Sarah Jane's "white" skin, which can approximate for her a fantasy of racial invisibility.

The loneliest word I heard of is "empty," and anything empty is sad. An empty purse can make a good girl bad, you hear me Dad? The loneliest word I heard of is "empty," empty things make me so mad. So fill me up with what I formerly had. Now Venus, you know, was loaded with charms, and look at what happened to her. Waitin' around, she's minus two arms—could happen to me, no sir! Now is the time to fill what is empty, fill my life brim full of charms. Help me refill these empty, empty, empty arms.

The first time we see Sarah Jane dance erotically to its score is in her bedroom—where, during the dance, she not only kicks a stuffed animal (a lamb) but steps threateningly near a record of *Porgy and Bess* strewn across her floor.

43. J. Harvey, "Sirkumstantial Evidence," 55. Here is the entire passage:

> Harvey: Or the funeral scene.
> Sirk: The funeral itself is an irony. All that pomp.
> Harvey: But surely there is no irony when Mahalia Jackson sings. The emotion is large and simple and straightforward.
> Sirk: It's strange. Before shooting those scenes, I went to hear Mahalia Jackson at UCLA, where she was giving a recital. I knew nothing about her. But here on the stage was this large, homely, ungainly woman—and all those shining, beautiful young faces turned up to her, and absolutely smitten with her. It was strange and funny, and very impressive. I tried to get some of that experience into the picture. We photographed her with a three-inch lens, so that every unevenness in the face stood out.
> Harvey: You don't think the funeral scene is highly emotional?
> Sirk: I know, I know but I was surprised at that effect.

44. Dyer, "White," 49.
45. *Encyclopaedia Britannica*, 11th ed., 16: 703–10.
46. This quotation is from Stahl's film of 1934.

## Chapter 4: *Uncle Sam Needs a Wife*

Thanks so much to Russ Castronovo and Dana Nelson for their help with the first instantiation of this essay.

1. On the shift from a norm of the appetitive subject of passions to the cognitive subject with an unconscious in the U.S. middle-class imaginary of general personhood, see Stearns, *American Cool*.
2. See Berlant, "Citizenship."
3. Clarke, *Uncle Sam Needs a Wife*, hereafter cited in text. Much of the material for this book was taken from Clarke's editorials in *The Pictorial Review*, a major

middlebrow-progressive instrument of women's culture prior to World War II, previously edited by Theodore Dreiser, that was home to the first publication of *Imitation of Life* along with the works of many best-selling authors such as Kathleen Norris, Zona Gale, Edith Wharton, Booth Tarkington, and P. G. Wodehouse. Clarke's introduction thanks the magazine's publisher for courageously advancing the cause of women.

4. Boyd, *The Woman Citizen*, 7–8.

5. See, for example, the vicious and bourgeois-class-specific debates that erupted around Hirschman, *Get to Work*; Steiner, *Mommy Wars*; and Warner, *Perfect Madness*.

6. Contradictions about the impact of women's "nature," class status, and race in the formation of appropriate political solidarities and imaginaries inevitably emerge from the organization of political categories around absorptive generic identities. Explanatory swerves characterized the more manifestly committed progressive women's magazines of this era too. See the excellent summaries in Cramer, "Woman as Citizen."

7. Dionne, *Why Americans Hate Politics*; Johnson, Hayes, and Hayes, *Engaging the Public*; Cantril and Cantril, *Reading Mixed Signals*.

8. I refer here to Judith Butler's program, in *Antigone's Claim*, *Precarious Life*, and elsewhere, to advocate a performative undoing of sovereign selves in compassionate postimperial relations as a precondition for the dissolution of U.S. imperial racism and heteronormativity. For an extended critique of Butler's sentimentality, see Berlant, "Nearly Utopian, Nearly Normal."

9. The quotation in the subhead is taken from Clarke, *Uncle Sam Needs a Wife*, 75. Secondary texts on the topic of female enfranchisement that ballast my general representation of the period context and the contemporary historiography of it are Andersen, *After Suffrage*; M. Buhle, *Women and American Socialism, 1879–1920*; Cott, ed., *The History of Women in the United States*; Cott, *The Grounding of Modern Feminism*; Cramer, "Woman as Citizen"; DuBois, *Feminism and Suffrage*; Lemons, *The Woman Citizen*; Evans, *Born for Liberty*; Green, *Spectacular Confessions*; Kraditor, *The Ideas of the Woman Suffrage Movement, 1890–1920*; Lewis, *Before the Vote Was Won*; Solomon, *A Voice of Their Own*; and Marilley, *Woman Suffrage and the Origins of Liberal Feminism in the United States, 1820–1920*.

10. Branch, *Parting the Waters*.

11. Among the myriad manuals read for this essay are Austin, *The Young Woman Citizen*; Mrs. Brown, *Your Vote and How to Use It*; Baker-Crothers and Hudnut, *Problems of Citizenship*; Christ, *Teacher's Manual*; National Society, Daughters of the American Revolution, *D.A.R. Manual for Citizenship*; Dole, *The Ameri-*

*can Citizen* and *The Young Citizen*; Garrette, *A Political Handbook for Women*; Mathews, ed., *The Woman Citizen's Library*; Morey and Wilhelms, *Organizing and Conducting a Citizenship Class*; Morgan, ed., *The American Citizen's Handbook*; Mosher, ed., *Introduction to Responsible Citizenship*; Odum, *Community and Government*; Read, *Citizenship and the Vote*; Scott, *Citizenship Readers*; J. Wilson, *Woman Suffrage*; U.S. Department of Justice, *Citizenship Education and Naturalization Information*; Shurter, ed., *Woman Suffrage*; Shurter, *American Citizenship and Government* and *U.S. Army Studies in Citizenship for Recruits*.

12. This image of the subcivilized as having less capacity to abstract from the personal to the collective articulates what is often kept separate in contemporary scholarship—the relation of colonial projects of civilization and domination to intranationalist practices of citizenship formation and the relation of sentimentality to both scenes of intimate power. The condescension of Stowe, Clarke, and others toward the politically un-inculcated reproduces national citizenship along the lines we associate with the colonial model advancing civilization over barbarism up to and including contemporary U.S. relations with Iraq and Afghanistan. At the same time, the early-twentieth-century feminist view that the disenfranchised are subcivilized also produces the soft condescension of projected respect for their affective authenticity. The subcivilized are not enlightened, but they are also unimpeded by the degradations of national-capitalist civilization. As Amy Kaplan and Ann Stoler point out, this combination of condescensions reinforces the optimism of colonial citizenship projects even in the face of their contradictions, anxieties, and disciplinary improvisations. See Kaplan, *The Anarchy of Empire in the Making of U.S. Culture*; and Stoler, *Haunted by Empire*.

13. See also the discussion in Mrs. Brown, *Your Vote and How to Use It*.

14. Exemplary cases of the manuals' penchant for personality building for the nation are Dole, *The American Citizen* and *The Young Citizen*.

15. Turborg-Penn, *African-American Women in the Struggle for the Vote, 1850–1920*. For general discussions of the concept of an informed citizenry in the United States that address the relation of women's suffrage, see R. Brown, *The Strength of a People*; and Wiebe, *Self-Rule*.

16. Turborg-Penn, *African-American Women in the Struggle for the Vote, 1850–1920*, passim; Gordon et al., *African American Women and the Vote*.

17. The feminist collaboration with eugenicist thought is well-documented. See A. Allen, "German Radical Eugenics, 1900–1908" and "Feminism and Eugenics in Germany and Britain, 1900–1940"; Black, *War Against the Weak*; Kevles, *In the Name of Eugenics*; and Richardson, *Love and Eugenics in the Late Nineteenth Century*.

18. See, for example, the countless scenes of depression, lethargy, distraction, and anxiety among the unhappy women not yet bound up in politics in the pro-suffrage novel *The Sturdy Oak* (Jordan, *The Sturdy Oak*).

19. Boyd, *The Woman Citizen*, 160.

20. For a great analysis of respectability as a lever for advancing women's political participation in the United States, see Enstad, "Fashioning Political Subjects" and her extended discussion of the complex class transactions among women motivated toward politics in *Ladies of Labor, Girls of Adventure*.

21. Garrette, *A Political Handbook for Women*, 2–3. A consent-soliciting linkage between the vote and the commodity form suffused the twentieth-century suffrage and feminist movements, which made them look tactically more like mainstream politics than not. See also Anderson, "Coconsciousness and Numerical Identity of the Person."

22. D'Emilio, *Sexual Politics, Sexual Communities*.

23. Garrette, *A Political Handbook for Women*, 2.

24. On the distinction between the suffragette and the feminist, see Cott, *The Grounding of Modern Feminism*, passim. Cott argues that feminism, a more modern formation, was less focused on the vote and more broadly based politically in terms both of class and sexual activism than was suffragism.

25. Austin, *The Young Woman Citizen*, 8, 3.

26. Spivak, "Can the Subaltern Speak?"

27. Jeff Masten points out to me that the September 11 capsule obituaries by the *New York Times* present another case of juxtapolitical activity, where aspirational normativity saturates the space of imaginary porous general belonging in the United States. This is so true and so queasy-making. I bracket that information here to focus on cases that cannot confuse politics with the political. This case requires a significant shifting of the frame. See Raines and the *New York Times*, *Portraits: 9/11/01*.

28. Much thanks to Marita Sturken for this personal communication.

29. Jameson, "Reification and Ideology in Mass Culture."

30. Ross, *Fast Cars, Clean Bodies*.

31. Agamben, *Homo Sacer*; Lefort, *Democracy and Social Theory*; Marin, *Portrait of the King*; Marina Warner, *Monuments and Maidens*; Žižek, *The Sublime Object of Ideology*.

32. Taussig, *The Magic of the State*, 102.

33. Kantorowicz with Jordan, *The King's Two Bodies*.

34. Agamben, *Homo Sacer*, 106.

35. John Sartain, "Abraham Lincoln the Martyr" (1865); Dion DiMucci, "Abraham, Martin, and John" (1968). This song's remarkable staying power as a mnemonic

for national desire can be verified in any web search: thousands of hits register a vast number of usages, from memories of 1968 to personal patriotic expression to its potential classroom uses as a tool for teaching history and citizenship.

36. Meštrović, *Postemotional Society*.

37. Probyn, *Outside Belonging*.

38. Rancière, *Disagreement*, 121.

39. Rancière, *On the Shores of Politics*, 11.

40. Golding, *The Eight Technologies of Otherness*.

41. *The Island of Lost Souls* (Erle C. Kenton, 1933) is a remake of H. G. Wells's *The Island of Dr. Moreau*. I choose not to name the characters here because names humanize, and their subhumanity is the point of both the film and this anecdote.

## Chapter 5: Remembering Love

Thanks so much to "Uncle Charlotte" Corber, Jay Dickson, Eva Fernandez, Mark Miller, Jackie Stacey, Jay Schleusener, Sharif M. Youssef, and countless other auditors and interlocutors who have pushed me to see what is productive for Charlotte in bargaining with love. The first epigraph consists of passages spoken by lovers to each other: J. D. Durrance, Elliot Livingston, and Charlotte Vale, respectively, say them in the screenplay and film of *Now, Voyager* (Robinson, *Now, Voyager*, 90, 166, 294). Subsequent citations of the screenplay will appear parenthetically in the text under "Robinson," while citations of the novel will appear parenthetically under "Prouty." The second epigraph is from Phillips, "On Love," 40.

1. On the history of adjustment of heteronormative love's idealizing functions within commodity or mass culture, see Eva Illouz's wonderful *Consuming the Romantic Utopia*. Illouz distinguishes three major phases of love's circulation in the intimate public sphere: Victorian middle-class married moral friendship; early-twentieth-century transcendent romantic coupledom shaped through mass cultural consumer fantasies; and the more contemporary *combinatoire* of gender equality, economic pragmatics, and a still percolating, though weakened, romantic desire. My claim is that the core of femininity, a normative gender practice supported and tweaked in all U.S. expert cultures including popular culture, is always concerned with hoarding, protecting, and enforcing the view that romantic fantasy in whatever intensity ought, in the end, to constitute *realism*.

2. "Memory is the amnesia you like." See Berlant and Warner, "Sex in Public."

3. Eli Zaretsky distinguishes "personal life" from "private life": if the latter is really a code for the domestic, the former points to a conception of subjectivity that is experienced as a singular property of the person, something like personality that traverses stably but flexibly many spaces and locations and is not merely

an expression of institutional location or force. Personal life is thus the thing that makes it possible for the subject to experience saturation by capitalism and the dream worlds of mass society without feeling merely overcodified, instrumentalized, or defeated by the ways she is simultaneously instrumental to their reproduction. See Zaretsky, *Capitalism, the Family, and Personal Life* and *Secrets of the Soul*.

4. Keeping the lines among affect, feeling, and emotion is nigh impossible, and yet this paragraph, at least, seeks some precision on this score. Modern love adjudicates the limerance of love, the crazy, destabilizing, self-dissolving, and self-expanding effects of what is affective (nonrational, self-motored, slightly other) about love with what is emotional about it (that the feeling is a communication from someone to other people that feels grounding and authentic). For more on what it means to be constituted by an accountability to affect management involving this adjudication of possessing and being possessed by love, see chapter 1. For the baseline set of distinctions, see Shouse, "Feeling, Emotion, Affect." Terry Eagleton suggests that, in the modern novel, the contradictions outlined above as structures of modern love are effects of a capitalism that demands both identification with the instabilities of a vitalized personal life and the promise of private life as a domain of accretive, foundation-building continuity. See Eagleton, "Capitalism and Form."

5. The generalizations that follow about the conventions of modern love derive mainly from Shumway, *Modern Love*; Seidman, *Romantic Longings*; and Wexman, *Creating the Couple*; see also Illouz, *Consuming the Romantic Utopia*; and Zaretsky, *Capitalism, the Family, and Personal Life* and *Secrets of the Soul*.

6. For broad histories of the women's film, see Basinger, *A Woman's View*; Doane, *The Desire to Desire* and *Femmes Fatales*; Walsh, *Women's Film and Female Experience, 1940–1950*; and P. White, *Uninvited*.

7. See Enfield, "'A More Glittering, a Grosser Power,'" especially 140–271.

8. J. Miller, "A and *a* in Clinical Structures."

9. Prouty writes constantly about depression and shell shock throughout her early career, and her novel *Conflict*, written after her nervous breakdown but decades before *Now, Voyager*, rehearses the plot of the latter book without the complication of the child. It also rehearses the style-as-optimistic-working-class-femininity plot of *Stella Dallas*. What is striking about all of her books prior to the Vale family saga is the explicitness with which characters simultaneously manifest disrespect for and pride in their obtuseness, their unclarities, and their anxieties about what intimate attachments can provide. *Good Sports* and *The Star in the Window* politicize political depression more deliberately and openly but

depression as an outcome of social longing is never very far from the narrative surface. See especially Prouty, *The Fifth Wheel*; Bobbie, *General Manager*; *The Star in the Window*; *Good Sports*; and *Conflict*. Prouty's book of poetry, *Between the Barnacles and Bayberries*, manifests repeated scenes of hoarded or secreted depression. See *Between the Barnacles and Bayberries*, esp. 6, 25–29.

10. On the history of "queer" as anomaly, see Chauncey, *Gay New York*.

11. For ample evidence on the emerging, labile, and undertheorized category that merges bigendered with bisexual in the early-twentieth-century scientific and popular literature, see Bland and Doan, *Sexology Uncensored* and *Sexology in Culture*.

12. Balibar, "Culture and Identity (Working Notes)."

13. Prouty's suffrage novel *The Fifth Wheel* provides a beautiful instantiation of this commitment to change without loss, without a fundamental rearrangement of need.

14. Zaretsky, *Secrets of the Soul*.

15. Seidman, *Romantic Longings*, 67.

16. See Bailey, *From Front Porch to Back Seat*; and Friedman and D'Emilio, *Intimate Matters*.

17. Seidman, *Romantic Longings*, 67.

18. Haag, "In Search of 'The Real Thing.'" See also Damon-Moore, *Magazines for the Millions*; Levitt, *From Catharine Beecher to Martha Stewart*; Scanlon, *Inarticulate Longings*; Shattuc, *The Talking Cure*, 13–46; and Shumway, *Modern Love*, 63–80.

19. The locus classicus for this observation is Andreas Huyssen's "Mass Culture as Woman." See also Friedman and D'Emilio, *Intimate Matters*; Fass, *The Damned and the Beautiful*; and Armstrong, "Modernism's Iconophobia and What It Did to Gender." See also Doane, *The Desire to Desire* and *Femmes Fatales*.

20. See Shumway, *Modern Love*; Carter, "Birds, Bees, and Venereal Disease"; and Gerhard, *Desiring Revolution*.

21. See Levitt, *From Catharine Beecher to Martha Stewart*.

22. Prouty, *Pencil Shavings*, 156–57.

23. Ibid., 199; Robinson, *Now, Voyager*, 32.

24. Quite a few Stebbins family members were players in the Salem Witch Trials, serving mostly as accusers and judges. See Hall, *Witch-Hunting in Seventeenth Century New England*.

25. Austen Fox Riggs, the director of the Austen Riggs Center where Prouty convalesced from her nervous breakdowns, was well known for the therapeutic ideology the fictional Dr. Jaquith espouses, which was itself conventional for one strain of mainstream popular therapy of its time. See Cushman, *Constructing the*

*Self, Constructing America*, 116–58; Shorter, *A History of Psychiatry*, 126–44; and Lutz, *American Nervousness, 1903*. One contemporary school psychologist cites his argument that the psychoanalyst is by definition interdisciplinary (a medical doctor and a historian of the patient, the patient's family, and the larger social world) and therefore the most likely intimate of a patient to be competent in treating many different areas of her being. See Patry, "The Relationship of the Psychiatrist to the School Physician"; and Riggs, *Just Nerves*.

26. The novel and the film begin differently, with the film demonstrating the nervous breakdown in situ. Other spatial changes mark differences between the novel and its adaptation. In the novel's present the characters are taking a Mediterranean cruise to Spain and France, while the previous romance with Leslie Trotter happened on a cruise to Norway and Sweden. The film is much more racialist. In the present the characters travel to Brazil and Bolivia (Rio and Copacabana Beach); the romance with Leslie takes place on a pleasure cruise to Africa (Robinson, *Now, Voyager,* 70).

27. The nervous breakdown films most clearly adhering to the structure of heterosexual and mental healing are *The Snake Pit* (Litvak, 1948) and *Lady in the Dark* (Leisen, 1944). Both films are adaptations (from a novel and play, respectively) of works deemed revelatory and progressive in their moment. See Ward, *The Snake Pit*; and Hart and Gershwin, *Lady in the Dark*.

28. Prouty reports that Riggs forced her to read widely in contemporary psychoanalytic theory so that she would be able to understand what he was doing and what she must do to heal herself. Prouty, *Pencil Shavings*, 179–83.

29. Ann Douglas argues that Prouty's *Stella Dallas* participates in the culture of matricidal fantasy characteristic of the metropolitan middlebrow modernist elites of New York City and presumably she would say the same thing about *Now, Voyager*. See Douglas, *Terrible Honesty*, 249–50. In my view, Prouty's portrayal of mothering in these texts is far more convoluted and ambivalent than what Douglas sees. So is the binding of gender to sexuality for all of the generations.

30. P. White, *Uninvited*, 94–135; and Cavell, *Contesting Tears*. Theresa de Lauretis argues that Cavell's reading of Charlotte's homosexuality has a lot in common with Elizabeth Cowie's psychoanalytic universalization of feminine/lesbian/homosexual spectatorship. De Lauretis is quite right that what we mainly learn in these readings is the will involved in misrecognizing the heroine's experience as emotionally identical to one's own and to all universal affective structurations. See de Lauretis's excellent *The Practice of Love*. I learned to think about broken circuits of attachment from Sedgwick, *Touching Feeling*.

31. Predicting this argument is the Bugs Bunny cartoon, "Hare Ribbin," where Bugs, fleeing the threat of becoming a dog's dinner, jumps into the ocean, reappears

dressed as a chanteuse-mermaid, and sings *Now, Voyager*'s Oscar-nominated "Would It Be Wrong?" The dog then desires Lady Bugs and love's vulnerability defeats him, having dissolved his defenses and made him stupid. (Of course, the woman's film often figures men as a wholly different and emotionally limited species that needs retraining.) "Would It Be Wrong?" also appears in an episode of *Star Trek, Voyager*, sung in an alter-world fantasy café by 7 of 9 ("Killing Game, Parts 1 and 2": air date March 4, 1998; Star Date 51715.2). The lyrics of this song are a limiting caption for the *Now, Voyager* supertext—I've waited so long, so how could it be wrong?—but its reappearance as the musical index for the film in sites of in-joke fantasy says something about the sweetness of cliché and of simplification as emancipation that the figure of the film offers.

32. In the film Charlotte says "my mother's companion" but in the published screen-play it says "her" companion.

33. Prince, *The Dissociation of a Personality*. The relevant literature on Prince that also informs the following discussion includes Anderson, "Coconsciousness and Numerical Identity of the Person"; Hacking, *Rewriting the Soul*; Leys, "The Real Miss Beauchamp"; Lizza, "Multiple Personality and Personal Identity Revisited"; Nathan, "Dividing to Conquer? Women, Men, and the Making of Multiple Personality Disorder"; Schiller, "Idealism and the Dissociation of Personality"; Schwartz, *The Culture of the Copy*; and Thurschwell, *Literature, Technology and Magical Thinking, 1880–1921*.

34. Leys, "The Real Miss Beauchamp," 42–44.

35. "Bodily hexis" is Pierre Bourdieu's designation for a concept of social being enacted habitually in the performing body. See Bourdieu, *Outline of a Theory of Practice*, 72ff.

36. Prince, *The Dissociation of a Personality*, 5.

37. Ibid., 91.

38. Ibid., 444, 515.

39. Leys, "The Real Miss Beauchamp," 78ff.

40. Ibid., 78ff.

41. Hacking, *Rewriting the Soul*, 232.

42. Prince, *The Dissociation of a Personality*, 514.

43. This notion of the subject at inevitable internal war between the pre-Oedipal and symbolic projections of his body and subjectivity is classic Lacanianism. See Victor Burgin's great explication and elaboration in his "Paranoiac Space."

44. The lovers amplify this love of an absolute shared privacy in their discussions of *Sara Crewe*, a novel of 1911 by Frances Hodgson Burnett that Charlotte coveted as a child (the novel was adapted in 1939 for the Shirley Temple vehicle *The Little Princess*). In this plot a rich little girl who is suddenly fatherless and penniless is

forced to live in the garret of a posh London boarding school, Miss Minchin's. There a rich Indian gentleman who can see her suffering and kindness through her window becomes her secret benefactor, showering her with food and beautiful things (Prouty 28, 78, 306). It is also worth noting that Prouty's one book of poetry, *Between the Barnacles and Bayberries*, is full of poems about the necessity of shared secrecy to love.

45. I take the idea of the case study genre or type of personality from Vogler, "Sex and Talk."

46. Cavell, *Contesting Tears*, 183.

47. These letters are housed at the Lilly Library and are controlled by the Plath estate.

48. Rose, *The Haunting of Sylvia Plath*, 128–64.

## Chapter 6: "It's Not the Tragedies that Kill Us"

Thanks so much to Mandy Berry, Bradin Cormack, Debbie Nelson, Janet Pederson, Chicu Reddy, Amy Gentry, Jon Enfield, Candace Vogler, and Lisa Ruddick for their close attention to the work and also to the *patient* audiences at the University of Rochester, University of Chicago, and MLA, who had to bear it at different stages of incompletion. The epigraph to this chapter is Dorothy Parker, under interrogation by the FBI in 1952. Quoted in Silverstein, *Not Much Fun: The Lost Poems of Dorothy Parker*, 55.

1. Like most Hollywood films, *A Star Is Born* has a more complicated writing history than the Academy Award for Parker, Campbell, and Carson would suggest. The director, William Wellman, and Carson wrote the story. Parker and Campbell were main authors of the script. Uncredited contributors included Ben Hecht, Ring Lardner Jr., John Lee Mahin, Budd Schulberg, Adela Rogers St. Johns, and importantly David O. Selznick himself, who is said to have written the final scene. *A Star Is Born* was almost entirely rewritten for Judy Garland and James Mason in 1954 by Moss Hart: but the original final speech and the marriage proposal banter were left virtually untouched. The rock and roll readaptation of the film for Barbra Streisand and Kris Kristofferson (1976; dir. Frank Pierson) contains virtually none of the original language while maintaining the *Sister Carrie*-style plot. It was written by Pierson, Joan Didion, and John Gregory Dunne. Didion had already written her own version of *A Star Is Born* in the melodramatic realist novel *Play It as It Lays* (1970; filmed, 1973, dir. Frank Perry): there, of course, the Norman Maine figure is a woman, Maria Wyeth.

2. The original ending of *A Star Is Born* stopped with Lester's fainting spell, but audiences found it too dark. Selznick is said to have written two alternative

endings—"This is Vicki Lester" and the one that made it to the screen. That Parker is *not* the author of this ending matters not to this argument, since what made it there rhymes so perfectly with the vernacular of feminine publicity that Parker practices here and elsewhere. Likewise, even if "This is Vicki Lester" had been chosen, it would enact the same drama of feminine publicity as an adaptation of fake authenticity to intensified affect and emotion that I am tracking here throughout the chapter. The logic of feminine adaptation to love in women's intimate public is bigger than the variation of conventionality within a phrase. See Schatz, *The Genius of the System*. For a wonderful meditation on stardom, identification, and affective (in)authenticity in the Hollywood system as it pertains especially to the Judy Garland/Moss Hart remake of *A Star Is Born*, see Gallagher, "Greta Garbo Is Sad."

3. See Stacey, *Star Gazing*. See also Carla Kaplan, *The Erotics of Talk*.

4. Pettit, *A Gendered Collision*.

5. Parker, Interview with Marion Capron.

6. Agamben, *The Coming Community*.

7. Adorno, "Commitment," 89.

8. I describe the psychoanalytic bases for these observations in Berlant, "Love, a Queer Feeling."

9. Hurst, *Imitation of Life*, 42.

10. Copjec, *Imagine There's No Woman*, 126–30.

11. "Whatever optimism" tropes on Agamben's "whatever community," the potential community always coming into being, in his *The Coming Community*. It is also cognate, I think, with Stanley Cavell's argument in *Contesting Tears*, that love ideally involves a commitment to a mutual continuity without guarantees.

12. The history and continued performance of anxiety about whether and how Parker is sentimental is detailed throughout Pettit, *A Gendered Collision*.

13. Parker called her poems "whines" in her "Various Views of the Aging Miss Parker," 20.

14. Burstein, "A Few Words about Dubuque."

15. Miller, *Making Love Modern*, 146.

16. Parker, "Incredible, Fantastic . . . and True," 190.

17. Parker, Interview with Marion Capron.

18. Parker, "I Know I Have Been Happiest," in Parker, *The Portable Dorothy Parker*, 91. Subsequent citations will appear parenthetically in the text as PDP.

19. Parker and d'Usseau, *The Ladies of the Corridor*, 3.

20. Thanks to Chicu Reddy for this observation.

21. Freud, "The Economic Problem of Masochism," 160.

22. Derrida, "The Law of Genre."

23. Adorno, "Resignation," 291.

24. See Dyer, "Entertainment and Utopia" and Jameson, "Reification and Ideology in Mass Culture."

25. For the classic history of the middlebrow, brilliantly characterizing it as a space of class-based emotion that identifies with cognitive cultivation of a general, somewhat democratic, version of distinction and sensibility, see Radway, *A Feeling for Books*. Nonetheless, I think the class analysis and emotional temperature taking of middlebrow desire in David Savran's wonderful *A Queer Sort of Materialism* focuses more successfully on the incoherence and anxiety that shape middlebrow desires and defenses.

26. Bentley, *Thirty Years of Treason*, 536, 537, 722; Buhle and Wagner, *Radical Hollywood*, 78–91; Ceplair and Englund, *The Inquisition in Hollywood*, 92, 104–7; Lardner, *I'd Hate Myself in the Morning*, 100; Lichtman, "Louis Budenz, the FBI, and the 'List of 400 Concealed Communists'"; McGilligan and Buhle, *Tender Comrades*; F.B.I., Dorothy Parker Files; Meade, *Dorothy Parker*, 272–73, 343.

27. Saunders, *The Cultural Cold War*, 53.

## Chapter 7: The Compulsion to Repeat Femininity

1. *Show Boat* is an exception in Edna Ferber's *oeuvre*. Her vast amount of writing about women in sales or the service economy provides an alternative of sorts to the life-without-love-is-emptiness equation. In her corpus neither work nor love provides an antidote to loneliness, although collegiality provides a light sociality that lubricates life in the everyday. Her characters live in their heads, when they are not pleasantly going through the motions of noticing things, having conversations, reporting anecdotes, and reproducing general social intimacy. See, for example, the four Emma McChesney books (1913–15).

2. I take the notion of the metacultural concept, the unifying term linked to the universalism of liberal society, from Greg Urban's *Noumenal Community*. On the relation of metacultural norms to national sexuality in particular, see Berlant and Warner, "Sex in Public."

3. Steedman, *Landscape for a Good Woman*, 23.

4. Ibid., 27–47.

5. Ibid., 141.

6. Ibid., 7–8, 110–14.

7. See Waters, "Landscapes of Memory."

8. Steedman, *Landscape for a Good Woman*, 144.

9. Bollas, "The Transformational Object."

10. Guattari, *Soft Subversions*. Guattari's argument throughout is that "soft subversions" are a central means of pseudo-individuation provided within the capitalist project of "semiotic subjectification." "There is a microfascism of one's own body, of one's organs, the kind of bulimia that leads to anorexia, a perceptual bulimia that blinds one to the value of things, except for their exchange value, their use value, to the expense of the values of desire" (11).

11. This essay's observations on the European metropole after 1968 (especially in Britain) are largely derived from Grosz, "Bodies–Cities"; Massey, *Space, Place, and Gender*; Sassen, "Identity in the Global City"; and Thrift, *Spatial Formations*. See also S. Hall, *The Hard Road to Renewal*.

12. Morris, "Great Moments in Social Climbing."

13. See Thrift, *Spatial Formations*.

14. Žižek, "The Spectre of Ideology," 21.

15. Although *Landscape for a Good Woman* is organized around the intimate upheavals in the natal family, sexuality as a zone of upheaval, incoherence, and improvisation is much less a topic in this book than gender is. Steedman depicts her family members as aggressively isolated from each other due to the instrumental ruthlessness of their desires, and yet where mothers and daughters are concerned this atomization is experienced as a violent lack of boundaries forced on the daughters: this presumption even further isolates "gender," which happens transgenerationally, from sexuality, which happens among adults. As a result, their interrelations, institutions, practices, and contradictions are taken for granted too much by Steedman. I have written about this elsewhere: on Steedman (with Toni Morrison and Michelle Cliff) in "'68 or Something"; additionally, "Intimacy: A Special Issue," 281–88.

16. For histories of the Left and feminist conjuncture in Britain after 1968, see Bammer, *Partial Visions*; N. Black, *Social Feminism*; Caine, *English Feminism, 1780–1980*; Dworkin, *Cultural Marxism in Postwar Britain*; Epstein, *Social Protest and Cultural Revolution*; S. Hall, *The Hard Road to Renewal*; Landry and MacLean, *Materialist Feminisms*; Sares et al., eds., *The 60s without Apology*, especially Aronowitz, "When the New Left Was New," and Willis, "Radical Feminism and Feminist Radicalism"; and Rowbotham, *A Century of Women*.

17. Steedman, *Landscape for a Good Woman*, 144.

18. Adorno, *Critical Models*, 291.

19. Weldon, *The Life and Loves of a She-Devil*, 206. Subsequent citations to this work will be cited parenthetically in the text.

20. One might argue that the pronoun "she" is inappropriate for the She-Devil, who becomes a nonwoman when she delaminates herself from the love plot. She/it

would seem appropriate, since while her dramatic monologue is written from a postgendered position, Ruth's specular femaleness and sexuality serve as instruments throughout the novel. But in English "it" describes a thing whereas Ruth is simply no longer conventionally gendered. Moreover, as I will suggest, the deployment of the will against taxonomic norms does not unmake one's intelligibility within those norms (here of gender): indeed, the She-Devil's negativity and critical consciousness cannot separate her enough from the feminine. Here Weldon predicts central dicta of Judith Butler's arguments in *Gender Trouble* and *Bodies That Matter*. Both authors presume that sexual difference (as the figure of species clarity in general) is a back-formation of heterosexuality that serves its claim to emanate from nature; and both tend to see sexuality in discursive terms, which means that radical conceptual transformations of gender and sexuality tend, in their texts, to be represented as such on the body and in practice. I read this as entirely continuous with a traditional tendency to overvalue consciousness and intentional agency as sources of social change, along with a particularly feminine-identified norm that wants to literalize scenes of sexual instability and resistance in representations of them. See also Joan Copjec's argument against Butler's tendency to presume a mimesis between linguistic and practical shifts in Copjec, *Read My Desire*, 201–11.

21. In *She-Devil*, the U.S. film version of the novel, this lesbian relationship is entirely wiped out, available for reading only through the casting of the lesbian-identified actress Linda Hunt as Nurse Hopkins.

22. Here I am not arguing with the main impulse of Homi Bhabha's view of negotiation in *The Location of Culture* insofar as it sees the term as present in theoretical events that disable the compulsion to reproduce in analysis the taken for granted antinomies and contradictions one finds in practice (25–26ff.). At the same time, in Bhabha as in Butler (see note 21) there is a slippage between the theoretical commitment to change thought through the critical deployment of will and a sense that iteration in general, as an inevitable practice of making meaning, offers "opportunities" to transform the destiny of a concept or a problem.

23. Elizabeth Bronfen argues, in contrast, that Weldon's hyperbolic deployment of tautology, the uncanny, and other modes of comic repetition disconfirms what she calls the "patriarchal" norms of the compulsion to repeat femininity. See Bronfen, "'Say Your Goodbyes and Go.'" This general view about the angrily transgressive nature of "women's" comedy is detailed in Barreca, "*Untamed and Unabashed*," 11–33.

24. Common law is not prescribed by statute, but finds its shape in a jurist's reading of precedent. The juridical concept is *stare decisis* and the conventions that guide

the discovery of precedent contribute mightily to the law's conservatism, its bias toward reproducing the customary or the proper. Patricia Williams considers the effect of this process of an "undue literalism." See P. Williams, *The Alchemy of Race and Rights*, 3–14, 141–42. Fredric Jameson's work on genre in *The Political Unconscious* converges with common-law logic in its explication of genre as institution, a history of uses that refer to each other and establish conventional horizons of expectation that are frequently articulated as the proper. This characterization, in turn, articulates with Jacques Derrida's "The Law of Genre." Derrida's text works questions of counterauthority that move between the lines of the law/*récit* to talk about the inevitable agitation (or "madness") produced by juridical fantasies of broken law: this early text is realized in his more recent "Force of Law," esp. 61–63.

25. Žižek works through the nonmimetic relation between abjection and sovereignty in his *The Metastasies of Enjoyment*, 89–112.

26. Bersani, *The Freudian Body*. Bersani's argument was anticipated by Barthes in *The Pleasure of the Text*, 14, 19, 20, 26, 41–46, 55–57.

27. See note 18.

28. Bollas, "The Transformational Object."

## Overture/Aperture

1. On the scenario as an alternative to the case, see D. Taylor, *The Archive and the Repertoire*. On the potential for counterrealist forms to produce alternative tones for history, see Nealon, "The Poetic Case."

2. I cite here one of my reader's reports. But it is also worth saying that what the reader called a negative or Benjaminian historicism could also be described in terms of Fredric Jameson's shift, in *The Political Unconscious*, between a realist historicism that articulates literary genealogies with contemporary contradictions in the mode of production and a utopian historicism that opens out the text not to futures but to elsewheres.

3. Here I manifest solidarity with the claims of Richard Neer in "Connoisseurship and the Stakes of Style."

4. This is the argument throughout Žižek, *Tarrying with the Negative*, but it is repeated constantly in subsequent writing as well.

5. This version of ethical formalism comes from Badiou, *Ethics*. For its adaptation of *whatever* sociality, see note 7.

6. Famously, Raymond Williams's phrase "structure of feeling" points to the affective residue of a collective experience that mediates being historical with conditions of potentiality. See R. Williams, *The Long Revolution*.

7. The *locus classicus* for *whatever* sociality is Agamben, *The Coming Community*.

8. For example, Rose, *Why War?*; Bauman, *Liquid Love* and *Liquid Modernity*; Luhmann, *Love as Passion* and *Observations on Modernity*; Nancy, *The Inoperative Community* and *A Finite Thinking*; Giddens, *Modernity and Self-Identity* and *The Transformation of Intimacy*; and Phillips, *On Flirtation* and *Equals*.

9. This is Stanley Cavell's phrase in his "The Uncanniness of the Ordinary," 109.

10. Seremetakis, "The Memory of the Senses, Part I," 4.

11. I refer here to Kafka's classic *Before the Law*, which famously narrates a supplicant's construction *as supplicant* to the law rather than agent empowered by it or sovereign mirroring it. John Coetzee adapts this story's logic to the problem of fidelity to irrational belief in *Elizabeth Costello* and Giorgio Agamben adapts it to describe the zone of juridical indistinction that produces a radical passivity or attrition of the subject in the face and as the mirror expression of sovereignty in *Homo Sacer*, 49–52. Parker's middlebrow, modernist twist on all this articulates the stark realism of stuckness with the grand melodrama of the return to the scene of unfinished business: the suturing mechanism is the competent performance of aesthetic conventionality, with its pyrotechnic but imaginable satisfactions.

12. Žižek, *The Plague of Fantasies*.

13. The famous phrase—also emblazoned on the masthead of the newspaper edited by Gramsci, *L'ordine nuovo* (The new order)—is "Pessimism of the intellect, optimism of the will" and is part of Gramsci's critique of lazy optimism in *Prison Notebooks*. See Gramsci, *Prison Notebooks*, 172.

14. I am summarizing here the paradigms offered in Shaw, *Narrating Reality*.

15. As to what this shift says about the attrition of the political for imaginaries of collective solidaristic practice, or democracy, see Rancière, *Disagreement*.

16. I derive this collection from a reading of Bratton, Cook, and Gledhill, *Melodrama*.

17. See L. Williams, *Playing the Race Card*, "Melodrama Revisited," and "Film Bodies"; and Hansen, "The Mass Production of the Senses." See also Christine Gledhill's thoughtful "Rethinking Genre." This book's view about how to think about genre is aligned with Gledhill's understanding of the woman's film as providing a kind of realism and "modality" as that which makes genre a promise of a structure more than a delivery system for narratively enacted rules. Of course long before critics shifted to seeing melodrama as the aesthetic mode of modernity in cinema, Peter Brooks located its modes of excess within realism in nineteenth-century fiction, whose narrative norms were so important to early narrative cinema. See Brooks, *The Melodramatic Imagination*.

18. Brooks, *The Melodramatic Imagination*. Thinking about genre as an affective mediation provides one way of re-encountering Hayden White's work from *Me-*

*tahistory* to *Figural Realism*. It is worth noting that in such an encounter I would pretty seriously dispute White's overliteralized claim that there ought best be a realist-style mimesis between the event and the narrative form that points to it (so adequacy to traumatic events requires modernist tendencies toward formlessness, for example). See H. White, "The Modernist Event."

19. I figured out a way to talk about the haunting problem of tonal mixing in complaint aesthetics after reading Cynthia Morrill's discussion of gallows humor in her "Revamping the Gay Sensibility."

20. Dyer, "Entertainment and Utopia"; and Jameson, "Reification and Utopia in Mass Culture."

21. Even for Eminem, in *8 Mile*, to move beyond melodrama (the scene of the fractious, mainly African American Detroit and the white, subproletarian trailer park of his white family) toward a cowboyesque entrepreneurial virtuosity requires first trying *not* to leave it (his mother is a variation on that sweet sentimental mother who, if only she *could* have mothered, would have made everything okay). Then, when he moves through it and out, the departure is only in the plot. Meanwhile he holds on precisely to what the melodrama provides, some sense that all the eloquent lyric explanation in the world can merely point to the longing expressed in the music, the breaks, the rhythms of the subject who refuses to be defeated, at least in his own mind.

22. This is, again, a reference to the last line of the film and the novel of *Gone with the Wind*.

23. King, "Danish for Digital Film."

24. Kennedy, *A Movie Star Has to Star in Black and White*. For background, see Kennedy, *People Who Led to My Plays*. Davis's dazzlingly ugly face and white patrician embodiment has magnetized so much varied identification. See also James Baldwin's heart-rending description of being menaced and relieved by Davis's "pop-eyed" face on the screen—but here it is not her whiteness or melodrama that provides the suturing material, but her ugliness:

> Here, after all, was a *movie star: white*; and if she was white and a movie star, she was *rich*; and she was *ugly*. . . . I gave Davis's skin the dead-white greenish cast of something crawling from under a rock, but I was held, just the same, by the tense intelligence of the forehead, the disaster of the lips; and when she moved she moved just like a nigger. . . . I discovered that my infirmity might not be my doom; my infirmity, or infirmities, might be forged into weapons.

See Morrison, ed., *James Baldwin, Collected Essays*, 482–83. Judith Mayne and Patricia White track the queer trajectory of Davis's feminine address: Mayne, *Cinema and Spectatorship*; and P. White, *Uninvited*.

25. Bataille, *The Unfinished System of Nonknowledge*, 128.

26. It is worth noting that Sylvester's entree into *The Cockettes* and what would be a legendary career was marked early on by a *Cockettes* performance of *Gone with the Showboat to Oklahoma*, "a promiscuous mix of musical Americana that included a Mammy drag queen in a bandana who was a servant to Scarlett O'Hara." See Gamson, *The Fabulous Sylvester*, 45. Schmidt notes that his footage of Sylvester taken in 1975 was also included in Tim Smith's *Sylvester/Mighty Real* (2002); Schmidt's Cannes Film Festival diary commenting on this can be found at http://www.filmfederation.net/schmidtdiary.html (accessed September 20, 2007).

27. Knight, *Disintegrating the Musical*.

28. I learned to think this way about the distribution of awareness from Stewart, *Ordinary Affects*.

29. "Mississippi Goddamn" from *Nina Simone in Concert* (1964; Phillips Records).

# BIBLIOGRAPHY

Adorno, Theodor. "Commitment." Trans. Frances McDonagh. *New Left Review* (September–December 1974): 75–89.

————. *Critical Models: Interventions and Catchwords*. Trans. Henry R. Pickford. New York: Columbia University Press, 1998.

————. "Resignation." Trans. Wes Blomster. *Telos* 35 (1978): 165–68. Reprinted in Adorno, *Critical Models*, 289–93.

Agamben, Giorgio. *The Coming Community*. Trans. Michael Hardt. Minneapolis: University of Minnesota Press, 1993.

————. *Homo Sacer: Sovereignty and Bare Life*. Trans. Daniel Heller Roazen. Palo Alto, Calif.: Stanford University Press, 1998.

Ahmed, Sara. *Differences That Matter: Feminist Theory and Postmodernism*. Cambridge: Cambridge University Press, 1998.

Allen, Ann Taylor. "Feminism and Eugenics in Germany and Britain, 1900–1940: A Comparative Perspective." *German Studies Review* 23, no. 3 (October 2000): 477–505.

————. "German Radical Eugenics, 1900–1908." *German Studies Review* 11, no. 1 (February 1988): 31–56.

Allen, Jeanne. "The Film Viewer as Consumer." *Quarterly Review of Film Studies* 5, no. 4 (fall 1980): 481–99.

Andersen, Kristi. *After Suffrage: Women in Partisan and Electoral Politics before the New Deal*. Chicago: University of Chicago Press, 1996.

Anderson, Susan Leigh. "Coconsciousness and Numerical Identity of the Person." *Philosophical Studies* 30 (1976): 1–10.

Anonymous. *The Bride Stripped Bare*. London: Perennial, 2004.

Appadurai, Arjun. "Disjuncture and Difference in the Global Cultural Economy." In *Modernity at Large: Cultural Dimensions of Globalization*, 27–47. Minneapolis: University of Minnesota Press, 1996.

Armstrong, Nancy. *How Novels Think: The Limits of Individualism from 1719–1900*. New York: Columbia University Press, 2005.

———. "Modernism's Iconophobia and What It Did to Gender." *Modernism/Modernity* 5, no. 2 (1998): 47–75.

Aronowitz, Stanley. "When the New Left Was New." In *The 60s Without Apology*, ed. Sohnya Sares, Anders Stephanson, Stanley Aronowitz, and Fredric Jameson, 10–43. Minneapolis: University of Minnesota Press, 1984.

Aronson, Amy Beth. *Taking Liberties: Early American Women's Magazines and Their Readers*. Westport, Conn.: Praeger, 2002.

Atkin, Andrea. "Converting America: The Rhetoric of Abolitionist Literature." Ph.D. dissertation, University of Chicago. 1995. Abstract in AAT 9530712.

Atwan, Robert, Donald McQuade, and John W. Wright. *Edsels, Luckies, and Frigidaires: Advertising the American Way*. New York: Delta, 1979.

Austin, Mary. *The Young Woman Citizen*. New York: Woman's Press, 1920.

Badiou, Alain. *Ethics: An Essay on the Understanding of Evil*. London: Verso, 2002.

Bailey, Beth. *From Front Porch to Back Seat: Courtship in Twentieth-Century America*. Baltimore: Johns Hopkins University Press, 1988.

Bailey, Cameron. "Nigger/Lover: The Thin Sheen of Race in *Something Wild*." *Screen* 29, no. 4 (fall 1988): 28–42.

Baker, Paula. "The Domestication of Politics: Women and American Political Society, 1780–1920." *American Historical Review* 89, no. 3 (June 1984): 620–47.

Baker-Crothers, Hayes, and Ruth A. Hudnut. *Problems of Citizenship*. New York: Henry Holt, 1924.

Baldwin, James. *The Devil Finds Work*. New York: Dial, 1976.

———. "Everybody's Protest Novel." In *The Price of the Ticket: Collected Nonfiction, 1948–1985*, 27–34. New York: St. Martin's, 1985.

———. "The Price of the Ticket." In *The Price of the Ticket: Collected Nonfiction, 1948–1985*, i–xx. New York: St. Martin's, 1985.

Balibar, Etienne. "Culture and Identity (Working Notes)." In *The Identity in Question*, trans. J. Swenson, ed. John Rajchman, 147–72. New York: Routledge, 1995.

Bammer, Angelica. *Partial Visions: Feminism and Utopianism in the 1970s*. New York: Routledge, 1991.

Banta, Martha. *Imaging American Women: Idea and Ideals in Cultural History*. New York: Columbia University Press, 1987.

Barnes, Elizabeth. *States of Sympathy: Seduction and Democracy in the American Novel*. New York: Columbia University Press, 1997.

Barreca, Regina. *"Untamed and Unabashed": Essays on Women and Humor in British Literature*. Detroit: Wayne State University Press, 1994.

Barthes, Roland. *The Pleasure of the Text*. Trans. Richard Miller. Intro. Richard Howard. New York: Hill and Wang, 1975.

Basinger, Jeanne. *A Woman's View: How Hollywood Spoke to Women, 1930–1960*. Middletown, Conn.: Wesleyan University Press, 1993.

Bataille, Georges. *The Unfinished System of Nonknowledge*. Trans. Michelle Kendall and Stuart Kendall. Ed. and intro. Stuart Kendall. Minneapolis: University of Minnesota Press, 2001.

Bauman, Zygmunt. *Liquid Love: On the Frailty of Human Bonds*. Cambridge: Polity Press, 2003.

———. *Liquid Modernity*. Cambridge: Polity Press, 2000.

Baym, Nina. *Woman's Fiction: A Guide to Novels by and about Women in America, 1820–70*. Ithaca, N.Y.: Cornell University Press, 1978.

———. "Women's Novels and Women's Minds: An Unsentimental View of Nineteenth-Century American Women's Fiction." *Novel* 31, no. 3 (summer 1998): 335–50.

Bennett, Paula Bernat. *Poets in the Public Sphere: The Emancipatory Project of American Women's Poetry, 1800–1900*. Princeton, N.J.: Princeton University Press, 2002.

Bentley, Eric, ed. *Thirty Years of Treason: Excerpts from Hearings before the House Committee on Un-American Activities, 1938–1968*. Intro. Frank Rich. 1971. Reprint, New York: Nation Books, 2002.

Berlant, Lauren. *The Anatomy of National Fantasy: Hawthorne, Utopia, and Everyday Life*. Chicago: University of Chicago Press, 1991.

———. "Citizenship." In *Keywords of American Cultural Studies*, ed. Glenn Hendler and Bruce Burgett. New York: New York University Press, 2007.

———. "The Female Complaint." *Social Text* 19/20 (fall 1988): 237–59.

———. "The Female Woman: Fanny Fern and the Form of Sentiment." In *The Culture of Sentiment: Race, Gender, and Sentimentality in Nineteenth-Century America*, ed. Shirley Samuels, 265–81. New York: Oxford University Press, 1992.

———. "Intimacy: A Special Issue." *Critical Inquiry* 24, no. 2 (winter 1998).

———. "The Intimate Public Sphere." In *The Queen of America Goes to Washington City: Essays on Sex and Citizenship*, 1–22. Durham, N.C.: Duke University Press, 1997.

———. "Love, a Queer Feeling." In *Homosexuality and Psychoanalysis*, ed. Tim Dean and Christopher Lane, 432–51. Chicago: University of Chicago Press, 2001.

———. "Nearly Utopian, Nearly Normal: Post-Fordist Affect in *La Promesse* and *Rosetta*." *Public Culture* 19, no. 2 (2007): 273–302.

———. *The Queen of America Goes to Washington City: Essays on Sex and Citizenship*. Durham, N.C.: Duke University Press, 1997.

———. "'68 or Something." *Critical Inquiry* 21 (fall 1994): 124–55.

———. "The Subject of True Feeling: Pain, Privacy, and Politics." In *Cultural Pluralism, Identity Politics, and the Law*, ed. Austin Sarat and Thomas Kearns, 49–84. Ann Arbor: University of Michigan Press, 1998.

———, ed. *Compassion: The Culture and Politics of an Emotion*. Oxford: Routledge, 2004.

Berlant, Lauren, and Michael Warner. "Sex in Public." *Critical Inquiry* 24 (winter 1998): 547–66.

Bersani, Leo. *The Freudian Body: Psychoanalysis and Art*. New York: Columbia University Press, 1986.

Bhabha, Homi. *The Location of Culture*. New York: Routledge, 1994.

Black, Edwin. *War Against the Weak: Eugenics and America's Campaign to Create a Master Race*. New York: Four Walls Eight Windows Press, 2003.

Black, Naomi. *Social Feminism*. Ithaca, N.Y.: Cornell University Press, 1989.

Blanchot, Maurice. *The Madness of the Day*. Barrytown, N.Y.: Station Hill Press, 1984.

Bland, Lucy, and Laura Doan. *Sexology in Culture: Labeling Bodies and Desires*. Chicago: University of Chicago Press, 1998.

———. *Sexology Uncensored: The Documents of Sexual Science*. Chicago: University of Chicago Press, 1999.

Bloch, Ruth H. "The Gendered Meanings of Virtue in Revolutionary America." *Signs* 13, no. 1 (1987): 37–58.

Block, Geoffrey. *Enchanted Evenings: The Broadway Musical from Show Boat to Sondheim*. New York: Oxford University Press, 1997.

Bogle, Donald. *Blacks in American Films and Television: An Encyclopedia*. New York: Garland, 1988.

———. *Toms, Coons, Mulattoes, Mammies and Bucks: An Interpretive History of Blacks in American Film*. New York: Viking, 1973.

Bollas, Christopher. "The Transformational Object." In *The Shadow of the Object: Psychoanalysis of the Unthought Known*, 13–29. New York: Columbia University Press, 1987.

Boskin, Joseph. *Sambo: The Rise and Demise of an American Jester*. New York: Oxford University Press, 1986.

Bourdieu, Pierre. *Outline of a Theory of Practice*. Trans. Richard Nice. Cambridge: Cambridge University Press, 1977.

Bourdieu, Pierre, and Alain Accardo, eds. *The Weight of the World: Social Suffering in Contemporary Societies*. Trans. Susan Emanuel, Priscilla Parkhurst Ferguson, Joe Johnson, and Shoggy T. Waryn. Palo Alto, Calif.: Stanford University Press, 1999.

Boyd, Mary Sumner. *The Woman Citizen: A General Handbook of Civics, with Special Consideration of Women's Citizenship*. Intro. Carrie Chapman Catt. New York: Frederick A. Stokes Co., 1918.

Braithwaite, Brian. *Women's Magazines: The First 300 Years*. London: Peter Owen, 1995.

Branch, Taylor. *Parting the Waters: America in the King Years, 1954–63*. New York: Simon and Schuster, 1988.

Bratton, Jacky, Jim Cook, and Christine Gledhill, eds. *Melodrama: Stage, Picture, Screen*. London: BFI, 1994.

Brennan, Teresa. *The Transmission of Affect*. Ithaca, N.Y.: Cornell University Press, 2004.

Brion, Robin. "*Show Boat*: The Revival, the Racism." *The Drama Review* 39, no. 22 (summer 1995): 86–105.

Bronfen, Elizabeth. " 'Say Your Goodbyes and Go': Death and Women's Power in Fay Weldon's Fiction." In *Fay Weldon's Wicked Fictions*, ed. Regina Barreca, 69–82. Hanover, N.H.: University Press of New England, 1994.

Brooks, Peter. *The Melodramatic Imagination: Balzac, Henry James, Melodrama, and the Mode of Excess*. New Haven, Conn.: Yale University Press, 1995.

Brown, M. E. *Television and Women's Culture: The Politics of the Popular*. London: Sage Publications, 1990.

Brown, Mrs. Raymond. *Your Vote and How to Use It*. New York: Harper and Brothers, 1918.

Brown, Richard D. *The Strength of a People: The Idea of an Informed Citizenry in America, 1650–1870*. Chapel Hill: University of North Carolina Press, 1996.

Brown, Sterling. "*Imitation of Life*: Once a Pancake." *Opportunity* 13 (March 1935): 87–88.

Brown, Wendy. "Wounded Attachments: Late Modern Oppositional Political Formations." In *The Identity in Question*, ed. John Rajchman, 199–227. New York: Routledge, 1995.

Buckland, Fiona. *Impossible Dance: Club Culture and Queer World-Making*. Middletown, Conn.: Wesleyan University Press, 2002.

Buhle, Mary Jo. *Women and American Socialism, 1879–1920*. Urbana: University of Illinois Press, 1981.

Buhle, Paul, and Dave Wagner. *Radical Hollywood: The Untold Story Behind America's Favorite Movies*. New York: The New Press, 2002.

Burgin, Victor. "Paranoiac Space." In *In/Different Spaces: Place and Memory in Visual Culture*, 117–38. Berkeley: University of California Press, 1996.

Burstein, Jessica. "A Few Words about Dubuque: Modernism, Sentimentalism, and the Blasé." *American Literary History* 14, no. 2 (summer 2002): 227–54.

Butler, Jeremy G. "*Imitation of Life*: Style and the Domestic Melodrama." *Jump Cut* 32 (1987): 25–28.

Butler, Judith P. *Antigone's Claim: Kinship between Life and Death*. New York: Columbia University Press, 2000.

———. *Bodies That Matter: On the Discursive Limits of Sex*. London: Routledge, 1993.

———. *Gender Trouble: Feminism and the Subversion of Identity*. New York: Routledge, 1990.

———. *Precarious Life: The Power of Mourning and Violence*. New York: Verso, 2004.

———. *Undoing Gender*. London: Taylor and Francis, 2004.

Caine, Barbara. *English Feminism, 1780–1980*. New York: Oxford University Press, 1997.

Campbell, Jan. *Film and Cinema Spectatorship: Melodrama and Mimesis*. Cambridge: Polity Press, 2004.

Cane, Aleta Feinsod, and Susan Alves. *"The Only Efficient Instrument": American Women Writers and the Periodical, 1837–1916*. Iowa City: University of Iowa Press, 2001.

Cantril, Albert H., and Susan Davis Cantril. *Reading Mixed Signals: Ambivalence in American Public Opinion about Government*. Baltimore: Johns Hopkins University Press, 1999.

Carby, Hazel. *Reconstructing Womanhood: The Emergence of the Afro-American Woman Novelist*. New York: Oxford University Press, 1987.

Carter, Julian B. "Birds, Bees, and Venereal Disease: Toward an Intellectual History of Sex Education." *Journal of the History of Sexuality* 10, no. 2 (2001): 213–49.

Castronovo, Russ. *Necro Citizenship: Death, Eroticism, and the Public Sphere in the Nineteenth-Century United States*. Durham, N.C.: Duke University Press, 2001.

Cavell, Stanley. *Contesting Tears: The Hollywood Melodrama of the Unknown Woman*. Chicago: University of Chicago Press, 1996.

———. "The Uncanniness of the Ordinary." Tanner Lecture on Human Values, delivered at Stanford University, April 3 and 8, 1986. Available online at http://www.tannerlectures.utah.edu/lectures/documents/cavell88.pdf (accessed September 20, 2007).

Ceplair, Larry, and Steven Englund. *The Inquisition in Hollywood: Politics in the Film Community, 1930–1960*. Urbana: University of Illinois Press, 2003.

Chakrabarty, Dipesh. "Domestic Cruelty and the Birth of the Subject." In *Provincializing Europe: Postcolonial Thought and Historical Difference*, 117–48. Princeton, N.J.: Princeton University Press, 2000.

Chauncey, George. *Gay New York: Gender, Urban Culture, and the Making of the Gay Male World 1890–1940*. New York: Basic Books, 1994.

Cheah, Peng, and Bruce Robbins, eds. *Cosmopolitics: Thinking and Feeling Beyond the Nation*. Minneapolis: University of Minnesota Press, 1998.

Christ, Raymond F. *Teacher's Manual. Arranged for the Guidance of Public-School Teachers of the United States for Use with the Students Textbook to Create a Standard Course of Instruction for the Preparation of the Candidate for the Responsibilities of Citizenship*. U.S. Bureau of Naturalization, 1918.

Clarke, Ida Clyde. *Uncle Sam Needs a Wife*. Philadelphia: John C. Winston Co., 1925.

Coetzee, J.M. *Elizabeth Costello*. New York: Viking, 2003.

Copjec, Joan. *Imagine There's No Woman: Ethics and Sublimation*. Cambridge, Mass.: MIT Press, 2004.

———. *Read My Desire: Lacan Against the Historicists*. Cambridge, Mass.: MIT Press, 1994.

Corber, Robert. *In the Name of National Security: Hitchcock, Homophobia, and the Political Construction of Gender in Counterwar America*. Durham, N.C.: Duke University Press, 1993.

Cott, Nancy F. *The Grounding of Modern Feminism*. New Haven, Conn.: Yale University Press, 1987.

———, ed. *The History of Women in the United States*. Vols. 19 and 20. Munich: K. G. Saur, 1994.

Cramer, Janet M. "Woman as Citizen: Race, Class, and the Discourse of Women's Citizenship, 1894–1901." *Journalism and Mass Communication* 165 (March 1998): 1–39.

Cripps, Thomas. *Slow Fade to Black: The Negro in American Film, 1900–1942*. New York: Oxford University Press, 1977.

Cushman, Richard. *Constructing the Self, Constructing America: A Cultural History of Psychotherapy*. Reading, Mass.: Addison-Wesley, 1995.

Damon-Moore, Helen. *Magazines for the Millions: Gender and Commerce in the "Ladies' Home Journal" and the "Saturday Evening Post," 1880–1910*. Albany: State University of New York Press, 1994.

Daniel, Robert L. *American Women in the 20th Century*. New York: Harcourt Brace Jovanovich, 1987.

Davidson, Cathy N., Linda Wagner-Martin, Elizabeth Ammons, Trudier Harris, Ann Kibbey, Amy Ling, and Janice Radway. *The Oxford Companion to Women's Writing in the United States*. New York: Oxford University Press, 1995.

Davis, Lydia. *Almost No Memory*. New York: Picador, 2001.

de Lauretis, Theresa. *The Practice of Love: Lesbian Sexuality and Perverse Desire*. Bloomington: Indiana University Press, 1994.

Deleuze, Gilles, and Félix Guattari. "What Is a Minor Literature?" In *Kafka: Toward a Minor Literature*, trans. Dana Polan, 16–27. Minneapolis: University of Minnesota Press, 1986.

D'Emilio, John. "Capitalism and Gay Identity." In *Powers of Desire: The Politics of Sexuality*, eds. Ann Snitow, Christine Stansell, and Sharon Thompson, 100–13. New York: Monthly Review Press, 1983.

———. *Sexual Politics, Sexual Communities: The Making of a Homosexual Minority in the United States, 1940–1970*. 2nd ed. Chicago: University of Chicago Press, 1998.

Dent, Michelle, and M. J. Thompson. "Bill T. Jones: Moving, Writing, Speaking." *The Drama Review* 49, no. 2 (T 186) (summer 2005): 48–63.

Derrida, Jacques. "Force of Law: The 'Mystical Foundations of Authority.'" In *Deconstruction and the Possibility of Justice*, ed. Drucilla Cornell, Michel Rosenfeld, and David Grey Carlson, 3–67. New York: Routledge, 1992.

———. "The Law of Genre." Trans. Avital Ronell. *Critical Inquiry* 7, no. 1 (fall 1980): 55–81.

Dietz, Mary G. "Citizenship with a Feminist Face: The Problem with Maternal Thinking." *Political Theory* 13, no. 1 (February 1985): 19–37.

Dillon, Elizabeth. *The Gender of Freedom: Fictions of Liberalism and the Literary Public Sphere*. Stanford, Calif.: Stanford University Press, 2004.

Dionne, E. J., Jr. *Why Americans Hate Politics*. New York: Touchstone, 1992.

Doane, Mary Ann. *The Desire to Desire: The Woman's Film of the 1940's*. Bloomington: Indiana University Press, 1987.

———. "The Economy of Desire: The Commodity Form in/of the Cinema." *Quarterly Review of Film and Video* 11, no. 1 (1989): 23–33.

———. *Femmes Fatales: Feminism, Film Theory and Psychoanalysis*. London: Routledge, 1991.

Dole, C. F. *The American Citizen*. Boston: D. C. Heath, 1895.

———. *The Young Citizen*. Boston: D. C. Heath, 1899.

Donaldson, Laura. *Decolonizing Feminisms: Race, Gender, and Empire-Building*. Chapel Hill: University of North Carolina Press, 1992.

Douglas, Ann. *The Feminization of American Culture*. New York: Knopf, 1977.

———. *Terrible Honesty: Mongrel Manhattan in the 1920s*. New York: Farrar, Strauss, and Giroux, 1995.

Dowd, Maureen. *Are Men Necessary? When Sexes Collide*. New York: Putnam, 2005.

Duberman, Martin. *Paul Robeson: A Biography*. New York: New Press, 1995.

DuBois, Ellen Carol. *Feminism and Suffrage: The Emergence of an Independent Women's Movement in America, 1848–1869*. Ithaca, N.Y.: Cornell University Press, 1978.

duCille, Ann. *The Coupling Convention: Sex, Text, and Tradition in Black Women's Fiction*. New York: Oxford University Press, 1993.

Dworkin, Dennis. *Cultural Marxism in Postwar Britain*. Durham, N.C.: Duke University Press, 1997.

Dyer, Richard. "Entertainment and Utopia." In *Only Entertainment*, 19–35. London: Routledge, 1992.

———. *Heavenly Bodies*. New York: Macmillan, 1986.

———. *Stars*. London: BFI, 1998.

———. "White." *Screen* 29, no. 4 (fall 1988): 44–64.

———. *White: Essays on Race and Culture*. London: Routledge, 1997.

Eagleton, Terry. "Capitalism and Form." *New Left Review* 14 (March/April 2002): 119–31.

Eckert, Charles. "The Carole Lombard in Macy's Window." *Quarterly Review of Film Studies* 3, no. 1 (winter 1978): 1–21.

———. "Shirley Temple and the House of Rockefeller." In *American Media and Mass Culture: Left Perspectives*, ed. Donald Lazere, 164–77. Berkeley: University of California Press, 1987.

Ellison, Julie. *Cato's Tears*. Chicago: University of Chicago Press, 1999.

Elshtain, Jean Bethke. *Public Man, Private Woman*. Princeton, N.J.: Princeton University Press, 1981.

Emerson, Ralph Waldo. "The Tragic." In *Uncollected Prose*, 120–25. Whitefish, Mont.: Kessinger, 2004.

Endres, Kathleen L., and Therese L. Lueck, eds. *Women's Periodicals in the United States: Consumer Magazines*. Westport, Conn.: Greenwood Press, 1995.

Enfield, Jonathan A. "'A More Glittering, a Grosser Power': American Film and Fiction 1915–1941." Ph.D. diss., University of Chicago, 2005. Abstract in AAT 3168339.

Enstad, Nan. "Fashioning Political Subjects: Cultural Studies and the Historical Construction of Political Subjects." *American Quarterly* 50, no. 4 (1998): 745–82.

———. *Ladies of Labor, Girls of Adventure*. New York: Columbia University Press, 1999.

Epstein, Barbara. *Social Protest and Cultural Revolution: Nonviolent Direct Action in the 1970s and 1980s*. Berkeley: University of California Press, 1991.

Evans, Sara M. *Born for Liberty: A History of Women in America*. New York: The Free Press, 1989.

Ewen, Elizabeth. "City Lights: Immigrant Women and the Rise of the Movies." *Signs* 5, no. 3, supplement (spring 1980): S45–S65.

Farmer, Brett. *Spectacular Passions: Cinema, Fantasy, and Gay Male Spectatorship*. Durham, N.C.: Duke University Press, 2000.

Farrell, Amy Erdman. *Yours in Sisterhood: "Ms. Magazine" and the Promise of Popular Feminism*. Chapel Hill: University of North Carolina Press, 1998.

Fass, Paula. *The Damned and the Beautiful: American Youth in the 1920's*. New York: Oxford University Press, 1977.

F.B.I. Dorothy Parker Files. Available online at http://foia.fbi.gov/foiaindex/parker_dorothy.htm (accessed September 20, 2007).

Featherstone, Mike. "The Body in Consumer Culture." *Theory, Culture and Society* 1, no. 2 (September 1982): 18–33.

Ferber, Edna. *A Peculiar Treasure*. New York: Doubleday, 1939.

———. *Show Boat*. New York: Doubleday, 1926.

———. "You're Not the Type." In *One Basket*, 522–43. Chicago: People's Book Club, 1947.

Feuer, Jane. *Seeing through the Eighties*. London: BFI, 1996.

Fischer, Lucy. "Three Way Mirror: *Imitation of Life*." In *Imitation of Life*, ed. Lucy Fischer, 3–28. New Brunswick, N.J.: Rutgers University Press, 1991.

Fisher, Philip. *Hard Facts: Setting and Form in the American Novel*. New York: Oxford University Press, 1987.

Fitzgerald, Zelda. "Who Can Fall in Love after Thirty?" In *The Collected Writings of Zelda Fitzgerald*, ed. Matthew J. Bruccoli, 411–14. New York: Macmillan, 1991.

Foner, Philip S., ed. *Paul Robeson Speaks: Writings, Speeches, Interviews, 1918–1974*. New York: Brunner/Mazel, 1978.

Fraser, Nancy. "Rethinking the Public Sphere: A Contribution to the Critique of Actually Existing Democracy." *Social Text* 25/26 (1990): 56–80.

———. "What's Critical about Critical Theory? The Case of Habermas and Gender." In *Feminism as Critique*, ed. and intro. Selya Benhabib and Drucilla Cornell, 31–56. Minneapolis: University of Minnesota Press, 1987.

Freedland, Michael. *Jerome Kern: A Biography*. New York: Stein and Day, 1978.

Freud, Sigmund. "The Economic Problem of Masochism." In *The Standard Edition of the Complete Psychological Works of Sigmund Freud* (1923–25), trans. and ed. James Strachey, 19, 155–70. London: Hogarth Press, 1961.

Friedman, Estelle, and John D'Emilio. *Intimate Matters: A History of Sexuality in America*. New York: Harper and Row, 1988.

Frith, Simon. "Hearing Secret Harmonies." In *High Theory/Low Culture: Analyzing Popular Television and Film*, ed. Colin MacCabe, 53–70. New York: St. Martin's Press, 1986.

Gabbard, Krin. "Borrowing Black Masculinity: The Role of Johnny Hartman in *The Bridges of Madison County*." In *Soundtrack Available: Essays on Film and Popular Music*, ed. Pamela Robertson Wojcik and Arthur Knight, 295–318. Durham, N.C.: Duke University Press, 2001.

Gabler, Neal. *An Empire of Their Own: How the Jews Invented Hollywood*. New York: Doubleday, 1988.

Gaines, Jane. "The Queen Christina Tie-Ups: Convergence of Show Window and Screen." *Quarterly Review of Film and Video* 11, no. 1 (1989): 35–60.

———. "White Privilege and Looking Relations: Race and Gender in Feminist Film Theory." *Screen* 8, no. 4 (fall 1988): 12–27.

Gallagher, Brian. "Greta Garbo Is Sad: Some Historical Reflections on the Paradoxes of Stardom in the American Film Industry, 1910–1960." *Images* 3 (May 1997). Available online at http://www.imagesjournal.com/issue03/infocus/stars1.htm (accessed September 20, 2007).

Gamson, Joshua. *The Fabulous Sylvester: The Legend, the Music, the Seventies*. New York: Henry Holt, 2005.

Garrett, Thomas. *Building Bridges: The Phenomena and Making of "The Bridges of Madison County."* Boston: Commonwealth, 1996.

Garrette, Eve. *A Political Handbook for Women*. Garden City, N.Y.: Doubleday, Doran, and Co., 1944.

Garvey, Ellen Gruber. *The Adman in the Parlor: Magazines and the Gendering of Consumer Culture, 1880s to 1910s*. New York: Oxford University Press, 1996.

Gatens, Moira. "Towards a Feminist Theory of the Body." In *Crossing Boundaries: Feminisms and the Critique of Knowledges*, ed. Barbara Caine, E. A. Grosz, and Marie de Lepervanche, 59–70. Winchester, Mass.: Allen and Unwin, 1988.

Gerhard, Jane. *Desiring Revolution: Second-Wave Feminism and the Rewriting of American Sexual Thought, 1920 to 1982*. New York: Columbia University Press, 2001.

Giddens, Anthony. *Modernity and Self-Identity: Self and Society in the Late Modern Age*. Cambridge: Polity Press, 1991.

———. *The Transformation of Intimacy: Sexuality, Love and Eroticism in Modern Societies*. Cambridge: Polity Press, 1992.

Gilbert, Julia Goldsmith. *Ferber: A Biography of Edna Ferber and Her Circle*. New York: Doubleday, 1978.

Ginzberg, Lori. *Untidy Origins: A Story of Women's Rights in Antebellum New York*. Chapel Hill: University of North Carolina Press, 2005.

———. *Women and the Work of Benevolence: Morality, Politics, and Class in the Nineteenth-Century United States*. New Haven, Conn.: Yale University Press, 1990.

Gledhill, Christine. "The Melodramatic Field: An Investigation." In *Home Is Where the Heart Is: Studies in Melodrama and the Woman's Film*, ed. Christine Gledhill, 5–39. London: BFI, 1987.

———. "Rethinking Genre." In *Reinventing Film Studies*, ed. Christine Gledhill and Linda Williams, 221–44. London: Edward Arnold, 2000.

———, ed. *Home Is Where the Heart Is: Studies in Melodrama and the Woman's Film*. London: BFI, 1987.

Glickman, Lawrence B. "'Buy for the Sake of the Slave': Abolitionism and the Origins of American Consumer Activism." *American Quarterly* 56, no. 4 (2004): 889–912.

Golding, Sue. *The Eight Technologies of Otherness*. New York: Routledge, 1997.

Gordon, Ann D., Bettye Collier-Thomas, John H. Bracey, Arlene Voski Avakian, and Joyce Avrech Berkman, eds. *African American Women and the Vote: 1937–1965*. Amherst: University of Massachusetts Press, 1997.

Gossett, Thomas. *"Uncle Tom's Cabin" and American Culture*. Dallas, Tex.: Southern Methodist University Press, 1985.

Gramsci, Antonio. *Prison Notebooks: Selections*. Ed. Joseph A. Buttigieg. New York: Columbia University Press, 1975.

———. *Selections from the Prison Notebooks of Antonio Gramsci*. Trans. and ed. Quintin Hoare and Geoffrey Nowell-Smith, 289–311. London: Lawrence and Wishart, 1971.

Green, Barbara. *Spectacular Confessions: Autobiography, Performative Activism, and the Sites of Suffrage*. New York: St. Martin's Press, 1997.

Grosz, Elizabeth. "Bodies–Cities." In *Sexuality and Space*, ed. Beatriz Colomina, 241–53. Princeton, N.J.: Princeton Architectural Press, 1992.

Guattari, Félix. *Soft Subversions*. Trans. David L. Sweet and Chet Wiener. Ed. Sylvère Lotringer. New York: Semiotexte, 1996.

Haag, Pamela S. "In Search of 'The Real Thing': Ideologies of Love, Modern Romance, and Women's Sexual Subjectivity in the United States, 1920–1940." *Journal of the History of Sexuality* 2, no. 4 (April 1992): 547–77.

Hacking, Ian. *Rewriting the Soul: Multiple Personality and the Sciences of Memory*. Princeton, N.J.: Princeton University Press, 1995.

Hall, David D. *Witch-Hunting in Seventeenth Century New England: A Documentary History, 1638–1693*. Boston: Northeastern University Press, 1991.

Hall, Peter Dobkin. *The Organization of American Culture, 1700–1900: Private Institutions, Elites, and the Origins of American Nationality*. New York: New York University Press, 1984.

Hall, Stuart. *The Hard Road to Renewal: Thatcherism and the Crisis of the Left*. London: Verso, 1990.

Halttunen, Karen. *Murder Most Foul: The Killer and the American Gothic Imagination*. Cambridge, Mass.: Harvard University Press, 1998.

Hammerstein, Oscar, II, and Jerome Kern. *Show Boat*, libretto and lyrics. Available online at http://libretto.musicals.ru/text.php?textid=303&language=1 (accessed September 20, 2007).

Hanauer, Cathi, ed. *The Bitch in the House: 26 Women Tell the Truth about Sex, Solitude, Work, Motherhood, and Marriage*. London: Perennial, 2003.

Hansen, Miriam. *Babel in Babylon: Spectatorship in American Silent Film*. Cambridge, Mass.: Harvard University Press, 1991.

———. "The Mass Production of the Senses: Classical Cinema as Vernacular Modernism." In *Reinventing Film Studies*, ed. Christine Gledhill and Linda Williams, 332–50. London: Edward Arnold, 2000.

Harari, Roberto. *Lacan's Four Fundamental Concepts of Psychoanalysis: An Introduction*. Trans. Judith Filc. New York: Other Press, 2004.

Harrison, William. "The Negro and the Cinema." *Sight and Sound* 8, no. 29 (spring 1939): 17.

Hart, Moss, and Ira Gershwin. *Lady in the Dark*. New York: Random House, 1941.

Harvey, David. "Cosmopolitanism and the Banality of Geographical Evils." *Public Culture* 12, no. 2 (spring 2000): 529–64.

Harvey, James. "Sirkumstantial Evidence." *Film Comment* 14, no. 4 (July-August 1978): 52–59.

Haug, W. F. *Critique of Commodity Aesthetics: Appearance, Sexuality and Advertising in Capitalist Society*. Trans. Robert Bock. Intro. Stuart Hall. Minneapolis: University of Minnesota Press, 1986.

Heide, Margaret J. *Television and Women's Lives: "Thirtysomething" and the Contradictions of Gender*. Philadelphia: University of Pennsylvania Press, 1995.

Hemminger, Jane M., and Courtney A. Work. *The Recipes of Madison County*. Birmingham, Ala.: Oxmoor House, 1995.

Heung, Marina. "'What's the Matter with Sara Jane?': Daughters and Mothers in Douglas Sirk's *Imitation of Life*." *Cinema Journal* 26, no. 3 (spring 1987): 21–43.

Hirschman, Linda. *Get to Work: A Manifesto for Women of the World*. New York: Viking, 2006.

Hoskinson, Rob. *Bridges in Time: Keepsakes Celebrating the Covered Bridges of Madison County*. Cambridge, Minn.: Adventure Publications, 1995.

Hull, Gloria T. *Color, Sex, and Poetry: Three Women Writers of the Harlem Renaissance*. Bloomington: Indiana University Press, 1987.

Humphreys, Nancy K. *American Women's Magazines: An Annotated Historical Guide*. New York: Garland, 1989.

Hurst, Fannie. "Are We Coming or Going?" *Vital Speeches of the Day* (December 3, 1934): 82–83.

———. "A Crisis in the History of Women: Let Us Have Action Instead of Lip-Service." *Vital Speeches of the Day* (May 15, 1943): 479–80.

———. *Imitation of Life*. New York: Harper and Brothers, 1933.

———. *Today Is Ladies' Day*. Rochester, N.Y.: Home Institute, 1939.

Huyssen, Andreas. "Mass Culture as Woman." In *After the Great Divide: Modernism, Mass Culture, Postmodernism*, 22–62. Bloomington: University of Indiana Press, 1986.

Illouz, Eva. *Consuming the Romantic Utopia: Love and the Cultural Contradictions of Capitalism*. Berkeley: University of California Press, 1997.

Jameson, Fredric. *The Political Unconscious: Narrative as a Socially Symbolic Act*. Ithaca, N.Y.: Cornell University Press, 1981.

———. *Postmodernism, or, The Cultural Logic of Late Capitalism*. Durham, N.C.: Duke University Press, 1991.

———. "Reification and Ideology in Mass Culture." *Social Text* 1 (1979): 130–48.

Johnson, Thomas J., Carol E. Hayes, and Scott P. Hayes, eds. *Engaging the Public: How Government and the Media Can Reinvigorate American Democracy*. London: Sage, 1999.

Jones, John Bush. *Our Musicals, Ourselves: A Social History of the American Musical Theatre*. Hanover, N.H.: Brandeis University Press, 2003.

Jordan, Elizabeth Garver, ed. *The Sturdy Oak*: *A Composite Novel of American Politics by Fourteen American Authors*. 1917. Reprint, Whitefish, Mont.: Kessinger, 2004.

Jowett, Garth S. "The Emergence of the Mass Society: The Standardization of American Culture, 1830–1920." *Prospects* 7 (1982): 207–28.

Kafka, Franz. "Before the Law." In *The Trial*, 268–271. 1925. Trans. Willa and Edwin Muir. New York: Alfred A. Knopf, 1937.

Kantorowicz, Ernst H., with William Chester Jordan. *The King's Two Bodies: A Study in Mediaeval Political Theology*. Princeton, N.J.: Princeton University Press, 1997.

Kaplan, Amy. *The Anarchy of Empire in the Making of U.S. Culture*. Cambridge, Mass.: Harvard University Press, 2002.

Kaplan, Carla. *The Erotics of Talk: Women's Writing and Feminist Paradigms*. Oxford: Oxford University Press, 1996.

Kaplan, Cora. "*The Thorn Birds*: Fiction, Fantasy, Femininity." In *Formations of Fantasy*, ed. Victor Burgin, James Donald, and Cora Kaplan, 142–66. New York: Methuen, 1986.

Kaplan, E. Ann. "Mothering, Feminism and Representation: The Maternal in Melodrama and the Woman's Film, 1910–40." In *Home Is Where the Heart Is: Studies in Melodrama and the Woman's Film,* ed. Christine Gledhill, 113–37. London: BFI, 1987.

Kelves, Daniel J. *In the Name of Eugenics: Genetics and the Uses of Human Heredity.* Cambridge, Mass.: Harvard University Press, 1998.

Kennedy, Adrienne. *A Movie Star Has to Star in Black and White.* 1976. Reprinted in *Adrienne Kennedy in One Act,* 79–103. Minneapolis: University of Minnesota Press, 1985.

———. *People Who Led to My Plays.* New York: Alfred A. Knopf, 1987.

King, Brad. "Danish for Digital Film: *Dogme.*" *Wired,* February 19, 2002.

Kitch, Carolyn. *The Girl on the Magazine Cover: The Origins of Visual Stereotypes in American Mass Media.* Chapel Hill: University of North Carolina Press, 2001.

Knapp, Raymond. *The American Musical and the Formation of National Identity.* Princeton, N.J.: Princeton University Press, 2005.

Knight, Arthur. *Disintegrating the Musical: Black Performance and the American Musical Film.* Durham, N.C.: Duke University Press, 2002.

Knupfer, Anne Meis. *Toward a Tenderer Humanity and a Nobler Womanhood: African American Women's Clubs in Turn-of-the-Century Chicago.* New York: New York University Press, 1996.

Kohut, Heinz. *The Chicago Institute Lectures 1972–1976.* Ed. Marian Tolpin and Paul Tolpin. Hillsdale, N.J.: The Analytic Press, 1996.

———. "Forms and Transformations of Narcissism." *Journal of the American Psychoanalytic Association* 14 (1966): 243–72.

———. "The Psychoanalytic Treatment of Narcissistic Personality Disorders— Outline of a Systematic Approach." *Psychoanalytic Study of the Child* 23 (1968): 26–113.

———. "Thoughts on Narcissism and Narcissistic Rage." *Psychoanalytic Study of the Child* 27 (1972): 360–400.

Kraditor, Aileen. *The Ideas of the Woman Suffrage Movement, 1890–1920.* Garden City, N.Y.: Anchor, 1971.

Krueger, Miles. *Show Boat: The Story of a Classic American Musical.* Oxford: Oxford University Press, 1977.

Kruger, Loren. "Placing 'New Africans' in the 'Old' South Africa: Drama, Modernity, and Racial Identities in Johannesburg, circa 1935." *Modernism/Modernity* 1, no. 2 (1994): 113–31.

Kun, Josh. "The Yiddish Are Coming: Mickey Katz, Anti-Semitism, and the Sound of Jewish Difference." *American Jewish History* 87, no. 4 (1999): 343–74.

Lacan, Jacques. "Feminine Sexuality." In *Feminine Sexuality: Jacques Lacan and the École Freudienne,* ed. Juliet Mitchell and Jacqueline Rose. New York: W. W. Norton and Co., 1985.

————. *Le seminaire, Livre VIII, Le transfert, 1960–1961*. Paris: Le Seuil, 2002.

Lahr, John. "Mississippi Mud." *New Yorker*, October 25, 1993, 123–26.

Landes, Joan B. *Women and the Public Sphere in the Age of the French Revolution*. Ithaca, N.Y.: Cornell University Press, 1988.

Landon, Margaret. *Anna and the King of Siam*. New York: John Day, 1944.

Landry, Donna, and Gerard MacLean. *Materialist Feminisms*. Cambridge, Mass.: Blackwell, 1993.

Landy, Marcia. *Imitation of Life: A Reader in Film and Television Melodrama*. Detroit: Wayne State University Press, 1991.

Lang, Amy Schrager. "Slavery and Sentimentalism: The Strange Career of Augustine St. Clare." *Women's Studies* 12 (1986): 31–54.

Laplanche, Jean, and Jean-Bertrand Pontalis. "Fantasy and the Origins of Sexuality." In *Formations of Fantasy*, ed. Victor Burgin, James Donald, and Cora Kaplan, 5–34. London: Methuen, 1986.

————. *The Language of Psycho-Analysis*. Trans. Donald Nicholson-Smith. New York: W. W. Norton and Co., 1967.

Lardner, Ring, Jr. *I'd Hate Myself in the Morning: A Memoir*. New York: Thunder's Mouth Press/Nation Books, 2000.

Larsen, Nella. *Passing*. In *Quicksand and Passing*, ed. and intro. Deborah E. McDowell, 143–242. New Brunswick, N.J.: Rutgers University Press, 1986.

Lears, T. J. Jackson. "From Salvation to Self-Realization: Advertising and the Therapeutic Roots of the Consumer Culture, 1880–1930." In *The Culture of Consumption: Critical Essays in American History, 1880–1980*, ed. Richard Wightman Fox and T. J. Jackson Lears, 1–38. New York: Pantheon Books, 1983.

Lee, Ben, and Edward LiPuma. "Cultures of Circulation: The Imaginations of Modernity." *Public Culture* 14, no. 1 (2002): 191–213.

Lefort, Claude. *Democracy and Social Theory*. Trans. David Macey. Cambridge: Polity Press, 1988.

Lehuu, Isabelle. *Carnival on the Page: Popular Print Media in Antebellum America*. Chapel Hill: University of North Carolina Press, 2000.

Lemons, J. Stanley. *The Woman Citizen: Social Feminism in the 1920s*. Urbana: University of Illinois Press, 1973.

Leonowens, Anna. *The English Governess at the Siamese Court: Being Recollections of Six Years in the Royal Palace at Bangkok*. Boston: Fields, Osgood, and Co., 1870.

LeSueur, Meridel. *The Girl* (1939). Albuquerque, N.M., 1978.

Levander, Caroline Field. *Voices of the Nation: Women and Public Speech in Nineteenth-Century American Literature and Culture*. New York: Cambridge University Press, 1998.

Levi, Vicki Gold, ed. *Atlantic City: 125 Years of Ocean Madness*. Text by Lee Eisenberg. New York: Clarkson N. Potter, Inc., 1979.

Levitt, Sara. *From Catharine Beecher to Martha Stewart: A Cultural History of Domestic Advice*. Chapel Hill: University of North Carolina Press, 2002.

Lewis, Janet. *Before the Vote Was Won: Arguments For and Against Woman's Suffrage*. New York: Routledge, 1987.

Leys, Ruth. "The Real Miss Beauchamp: An Early Case of Traumatic Dissociation." In *Trauma: A Genealogy*, 41–82. Chicago: University of Chicago Press, 2000.

Lichtman, Robert M. "Louis Budenz, the FBI, and the 'List of 400 Concealed Communists': An Extended Tale of McCarthy-Era Informing." *American Communist History* 3, no. 1 (June 2004): 25–54.

Lipsitz, George. *Time Passages: Collective Memory and American Popular Culture*. Minneapolis: University of Minnesota Press, 2001.

Lizza, John P. "Multiple Personality and Personal Identity Revisited." *The British Journal for the Philosophy of Science* 44, no. 2 (June 1993): 263–74.

Long, Elizabeth. *Book Clubs: Women and the Uses of Reading in Everyday Life*. Chicago: University of Chicago Press, 2003.

Lott, Eric. *Love and Theft: Blackface Minstrelsy and the American Working Class*. New York: Oxford University Press, 1995.

Lowe, Lisa. *Immigrant Acts: On Asian-American Cultural Politics*. Durham, N.C.: Duke University Press, 1996.

Luhmann, Niklas. *Love as Passion: The Codification of Intimacy*. Trans. Jeremy Gaines and Doris L. Jones. Palo Alto, Calif.: Stanford University Press, 1998.

———. *Observations on Modernity*. Trans. William Whobrey. Palo Alto, Calif.: Stanford University Press, 1998.

Lutz, Tom. *American Nervousness, 1903: An Anecdotal History*. Ithaca, N.Y.: Cornell University Press, 1993.

MacKinnon, Catherine A. *Toward a Feminist Theory of the State*. Cambridge, Mass.: Harvard University Press, 1989.

Marilley, Suzanne M. *Woman Suffrage and the Origins of Liberal Feminism in the United States, 1820–1920*. Cambridge, Mass.: Harvard University Press, 1996.

Marin, Louis. *Portrait of the King*. Trans. Martha M. Houle. Foreword by Tom Conley. Minneapolis: University of Minnesota Press, 1988.

Marquette, Arthur F. *Brands, Trademarks and Good Will: The Story of the Quaker Oats Company*. New York: McGraw-Hill Book Company, 1967.

Marx, Karl. *Capital, Volume 1*. In *The Marx-Engels Reader*, ed. Robert C. Tucker, 294–438. New York: W. W. Norton and Co., 1978.

Massa, Ann. "Black Women in the 'White City.'" *Journal of American Studies* 8, no. 3 (December 1974): 319–37.

Massey, Doreen. *Space, Place, and Gender*. Minneapolis: University of Minnesota Press, 1994.

Mast, Gerald. *Can't Help Singin': The American Musical on Stage and Screen*. Woodstock, N.Y.: Overlook Press, 1987.

Mathews, Shaler, ed. *The Woman Citizen's Library*. Vols. 1–12. Chicago: The Civics Library, 1914.

Mayne, Judith. *Cinema and Spectatorship*. London: Routledge, 1993.

McCarthy, K. D. *Women's Culture: American Philanthropy and Art, 1830–1930*. Chicago: University of Chicago Press, 1991.

McDowell, Deborah E. Introduction to *Quicksand and Passing*, by Nella Larsen, ix–xxxv. New Brunswick, N.J.: Rutgers University Press, 1986.

McGilligan, Patrick, and Paul Buhle. *Tender Comrades: A Backstory of the Hollywood Blacklist*. New York: St. Martin's Press, 1997.

McKeon, Michael. *The Secret History of Domesticity: Public, Private, and the Division of Knowledge*. Baltimore: Johns Hopkins University Press, 2005.

McLaughlin, Robert L. "Post-Postmodern Discontent: Contemporary Fiction and the Social World." *symplokē* 12, nos. 1–2 (2001): 53–68.

Meade, Marion. *Dorothy Parker: What Fresh Hell Is This?* New York: Penguin Press, 1987.

Mercer, Kobena. "Black Hair/Style Politics." In *Out There: Marginalization and Contemporary Cultures*, ed. Russell Fergusson, Martha Gever, Trinh T. Minh-ha, and Cornel West, 247–64. Cambridge, Mass.: MIT Press, 1990.

Merish, Lori. *Sentimental Materialism: Gender, Commodity Culture, and Nineteenth-Century American Literature*. Durham, N.C.: Duke University Press, 2000.

Meštrović, Stjepan. *Postemotional Society*. London: Sage, 1997.

Miller, Jacques-Alain. "A and *a* in Clinical Structures." *The Symptom*. Available online at http://www.lacan.com/symptom6_articles/miller.html (accessed September 20, 2007).

Miller, Nina. *Making Love Modern: The Intimate Public Worlds of New York's Literary Women*. New York: Oxford, 1999.

Mitchell, Margaret. *Gone with the Wind*. New York: Macmillan, 1936.

Moon, Michael. "Semi-publics." Keynote address, Cornell University Humanities Center Conference, "Publics and Privates," May 1994.

———. *A Small Boy and Others: Imitation and Initiation in American Culture from Henry James to Andy Warhol*. Durham, N.C.: Duke University Press, 1998.

Morey, Victor P., and Fred T. Wilhelms. *Organizing and Conducting a Citizenship Class: A Guide for Use in the Public Schools by Teachers of Candidates for Naturalization*. U.S. Government Printing Office, 1945.

Morgan, Joy Elmer, ed. *The American Citizen's Handbook*. 1941. Reprint, Washington D.C.: National Council for Social Studies, 1968.

Morrill, Cynthia. "Revamping the Gay Sensibility: Queer Camp and *Dyke Noir*." In *The Poetics and Politics of Camp*, ed. Moe Meyer, 110–29. London: Routledge, 1994.

Morris, Meaghan. "Great Moments in Social Climbing: King Kong and the Human Fly." In *Sexuality and Space*, ed. Beatriz Colomina, 1–51. Princeton, N.J.: Princeton Architectural Press, 1992.

Morrison, Toni. *Beloved*. New York: Penguin, 1987.

———, ed. *James Baldwin, Collected Essays: Notes of a Native Son / Nobody Knows My Name / The Fire Next Time / No Name in the Street / The Devil Finds Work / Other Essays*. New York: Library of America, 1998.

Mosher, William E., ed. *Introduction to Responsible Citizenship*. New York: Henry Holt, 1941.

Most, Andrea. *Making Americans: Jews and the Broadway Musical*. Cambridge, Mass.: Harvard University Press, 2004.

Mott, Frank Luther. *History of American Magazines*. Cambridge, Mass.: Harvard University Press, 1968.

Nancy, Jean-Luc. *A Finite Thinking*. Trans. Simon Sparks. Palo Alto, Calif.: Stanford University Press, 2003.

———. *The Inoperative Community*. Trans. Peter Connor. Foreword by Christopher Fynsk. Minneapolis: University of Minnesota Press, 1991.

Nathan, Debbie. "Dividing to Conquer? Women, Men, and the Making of Multiple Personality Disorder." *Social Text* 40 (1994): 77–114.

National Society, Daughters of the American Revolution. *D.A.R. Manual for Citizenship*. Washington, D.C.: National Society, Daughters of the American Revolution, 1981.

Nealon, Chris. "The Poetic Case." *Critical Inquiry* (summer 2007).

Neer, Richard. "Connoisseurship and the Stakes of Style." *Critical Inquiry* 32 (2005): 1–26.

Noble, Peter. *The Negro in Films*. London: Skelton Robinson, 1948.

Norton, Anne. *Reflections on Political Identity*. Baltimore: Johns Hopkins University Press, 1988.

Odum, Howard Washington. *Community and Government: A Manual of Discussion and Study of the Newer Ideals of Citizenship*. Extension leaflet. Chapel Hill: University of North Carolina, 1921.

Okker, Patricia. *Our Sister Editors: Sarah J. Hale and the Tradition of Nineteenth-Century Women Editors*. Athens: University of Georgia Press, 1995.

Orbach, Susie. *The Impossibility of Sex: Stories of the Intimate Relationship between Therapist and Patient*. New York: Scribner, 2000.

Orleans, Ellen. *The Butches of Madison County*. Bala Cynwyd, Pa.: Laugh Lines Press, 1995.

Parker, Dorothy. "Incredible, Fantastic . . . and True." 1937. Reprinted in *The New Masses: An Anthology of the Rebel Thirties*, ed. Joseph North, intro. Maxwell Geismar, 190. New York: International Publishers, 1969.

———. Interview with Marion Capron. *The Paris Review: The Art of Fiction* 13 (summer 1956–57): 86.

———. *The Portable Dorothy Parker*. Intro. Brendan Gill. New York: Penguin, 1976.

———. "Various Views of the Aging Miss Parker." *New York Herald Tribune*, October 13, 1963.

Parker, Dorothy, and Arnaud d'Usseau. *The Ladies of the Corridor*. 1952. Reprint, New York: Viking, 1954.

Parker, Patricia. "Rhetorics of Property: Exploration, Inventory, Blazon." In *Literary Fat Ladies: Rhetoric, Gender, Property*, 126–54. New York: Methuen, 1987.

Pateman, Carole. *The Sexual Contract*. Stanford, Calif.: Stanford University Press, 1988.

Patry, Frederick L. "The Relationship of the Psychiatrist to the School Physician." *Psychoanalytic Quarterly* 6, no. 1 (March 1932): 107–20.

Peiss, Kathy. *Cheap Amusements: Working Women and Leisure in Turn-of-the-Century New York*. Philadelphia: Temple University Press, 1987.

———. *Hope in a Jar: The Making of America's Beauty Culture*. New York: Owl Books, 1999.

Pettit, Rhonda S. *A Gendered Collision: Sentimentalism and Modernism in Dorothy Parker's Poetry and Fiction*. Teaneck, N.J.: Fairleigh Dickinson University Press, 2000.

Philip, M. Nourbese. *Showing Grit: Showboating North of the 44th Parallel*. Toronto: Poui Publications, 1993.

Phillips, Adam. *Equals*. New York: Basic Books, 2003.

———. *On Flirtation: Psychoanalytic Essays on the Uncommitted Life*. Cambridge, Mass.: Harvard University Press, 1994.

———. "On Love." In *On Flirtation: Psychoanalytic Essays on the Uncommitted Life*, 39–41. Cambridge, Mass.: Harvard University Press, 1994.

Pitkin, Hanna Fenichel. *Fortune Is a Woman: Gender and Politics in the Thought of Niccolò Machiavelli*. Berkeley: University of California Press, 1984.

Presbrey, Frank. *The History and Development of Advertising*. New York: Doubleday, Doran and Company, 1929.

Press, Andrea L. *Women Watching Television: Gender, Class, and Generation in the American Television Experience*. Philadelphia: University of Pennsylvania Press, 1991.

Prince, Morton. *The Dissociation of a Personality: A Biographical Study in Abnormal Psychology*. 1906. Reprint, New York: Greenwood Press, 1969.

Probyn, Elspeth. "Everyday Shame." *Cultural Studies* 18, nos. 2–3 (March/May 2004): 328–49.

———. *Outside Belonging*. New York: Routledge, 1996.

Prouty, Olive Higgins. *Between the Barnacles and Bayberries*. Worcester, Mass.: Friends of the Goddard Library and the Olive Higgins Prouty Foundation, 1997.

———. *Bobbie, General Manager*. New York: Grosset and Dunlap, 1913.

———. *Conflict*. New York: Houghton Mifflin, 1927.

———. *The Fifth Wheel*. 1915. Reprint, New York: Frederick A. Stokes Co., 1916.

———. *Good Sports*. New York: Frederick A. Stokes Co., 1919.

———. *Now, Voyager*. Boston: Houghton Mifflin, 1941.

———. *Pencil Shavings: Memoirs*. 1961. Reprint, Worcester, Mass.: Friends of the Goddard Library, Clark University, 1985.

———. *The Star in the Window*. New York: Grosset and Dunlap, 1918.

Rabinovitz, Lauren. *For the Love of Pleasure: Women, Movies, and Culture in Turn-of-the-Century Chicago*. New Brunswick, N.J.: Rutgers University Press, 1998.

Radway, Janice. *A Feeling for Books: The Book-of-the-Month Club, Literary Taste, and Middle Class Desire*. Chapel Hill: University of North Carolina Press, 1997.

———. *Reading the Romance*. Chapel Hill: University of North Carolina Press, 1984.

Raines, Howell, and *The New York Times*. *Portraits: 9/11/01: The Collected "Portraits of Grief" from the New York Times*. Rev. ed. New York: Times Books, 2003.

Rancière, Jacques. *Disagreement*. Minneapolis: University of Minnesota Press, 1998.

———. *On the Shores of Politics*. London: Verso, 1995.

Rapp, Rayna, and Ellen Ross. "The Twenties' Backlash: Compulsory Heterosexuality, the Consumer Family, and the Waning of Feminism." In *Class, Race, and Sex: The Dynamics of Control*, ed. Amy Swerdlow and Hanna Lesinger, 93–107. Boston: G. K. Hall, 1983.

Read, Elizabeth Fisher. *Citizenship and the Vote: A Statement for the Women Citizens of the State of New York*. New York: Americanization Committee of the New York State Woman Suffrage Party and the New York City Woman Suffrage Party, 1918.

Restuccia, Frances. *Melancholics in Love: Representing Women's Depression and Domestic Abuse*. Lanham, Md.: Rowman and Littlefield, 2000.

Richardson, Angelique. *Love and Eugenics in the Late Nineteenth Century: Rational Reproduction and the New Woman*. London: Oxford University Press, 2003.

Riggs, Austen Fox. *Just Nerves*. Boston: Houghton Mifflin Co., 1922.

Roach, Joseph. *Cities of the Dead: Circum-Atlantic Performance*. New York: Columbia University Press, 1996.

Robinson, Casey. *Now, Voyager*. Ed. and intro. Jeanne Allen. Madison: University of Wisconsin Press, 1984.

Rodgers, Richard, and Oscar Hammerstein II. *The King and I*. In *Six Plays by Rodgers and Hammerstein*, 371–456. New York: The Modern Library, 1953.

Rogin, Michael. *Blackface, White Noise: Jewish Immigrants in the Hollywood Melting Pot*. Berkeley: University of California Press, 1996.

Rooks, Nowlie M. *Ladies' Pages: African American Women's Magazines and the Culture That Made Them*. New Brunswick, N.J.: Rutgers University Press, 2004.

Rose, Jacqueline. *The Haunting of Sylvia Plath*. Cambridge, Mass.: Harvard University Press, 1991.

———. *Sexuality in the Field of Vision*. London: Verso, 1986.

———. *Why War?: Psychoanalysis, Politics, and the Return to Melanie Klein*. Ed. Harold Schweizer. Oxford: Blackwell Publishers, 1993.

Ross, Kristin. *Fast Cars, Clean Bodies: Decolonization and the Reordering of French Culture*. Cambridge, Mass.: MIT Press, 1995.

Rowbotham, Sheila. *A Century of Women: The History of Women in Britain and the United States*. New York: Viking, 1997.

Rudwick, Elliott M., and August Meier. "Black Man in the 'White City': Negroes and the Columbia Exposition, 1893." *Phylon* 26, no. 4 (winter 1965): 354–61.

Ryan, Mary. *Women in Public: Between Banners and Ballots, 1825–1880*. Baltimore: Johns Hopkins University Press, 1990.

Rydell, Robert W. *All the World's a Fair: Visions of Empire at American International Expositions, 1876–1916*. Chicago: University of Chicago Press, 1984.

———. "The World's Columbian Exposition of 1893: Racist Underpinnings of a Utopian Artifact." *Journal of American Culture* 1, no. 2 (summer 1978): 253–75.

Samuels, Shirley, ed. *The Culture of Sentiment: Race, Gender, and Sentimentality in Nineteenth-Century America*. New York: Oxford University Press, 1992.

Sanchez-Eppler, Karen. *Touching Liberty: Abolition, Feminism, and the Politics of the Body*. Berkeley: University of California Press, 1993.

Sares, Sohnya, Anders Stephanson, Stanley Aronowitz, and Fredric Jameson, eds. *The 60s without Apology*. Minneapolis: University of Minnesota Press, 1984.

Sassen, Saskia. "Identity in the Global City: Structural and Economic Encasements." In *The Geography of Identity*, ed. Patricia Yaeger, 131–51. Ann Arbor: University of Michigan Press, 1996.

Saunders, Frances Stonor. *The Cultural Cold War: The CIA and the World of Arts and Letters*. New York: New Press, 2001.

Savran, David. *A Queer Sort of Materialism: Recontextualizing American Theater*. Ann Arbor: University of Michigan Press, 2003.

Scanlon, Jennifer. *Inarticulate Longings: "The Ladies' Home Journal," Gender, and the Promises of Consumer Culture*. London: Routledge, 1995.

Scarry, Elaine. *The Body in Pain: The Making and Unmaking of the World*. New York: Oxford University Press, 1985.

Schatz, Thomas. *The Genius of the System: Hollywood Filmmaking in the Studio Era*. New York: Pantheon Books, 1988.

Schiller, F. C. S. "Idealism and the Dissociation of Personality." *The Journal of Philosophy, Psychology, and Scientific Methods* 3, no. 18 (August 1906): 477–82.

Schwartz, Hillel. *The Culture of the Copy: Striking Likenesses, Unreasonable Facsimiles*. New York: Zone Books, 1996.

Scott, Benjamin D. *Citizenship Readers: Notable Events in the Making of America*. Philadelphia: Lippincott, 1930.

Sedgwick, Eve Kosofsky. *Epistemology of the Closet*. Berkeley: University of California Press, 1990.

———. "A Poem Is Being Written." *Representations* 17 (winter 1987): 110–43.

———. "Privilege of Unknowing: Diderot's *The Nun*." In *Tendencies*, 23–51. Durham, N.C.: Duke University Press, 1993.

———. *Touching Feeling: Affect, Pedagogy, Performativity*. Durham, N.C.: Duke University Press, 2003.

Sedgwick, Eve Kosofsky, and Adam Frank, eds. *Shame and Its Sisters: A Sylvan Tomkins Reader*. Durham, N.C.: Duke University Press, 1995.

Seidman, Steven. *Romantic Longings: Love in America, 1830–1980*. London: Routledge, 1991.

Selig, Michael E. "Contradiction and Reading: Social Class and Sex Class in *Imitation of Life*." *Wide Angle* 10, no. 4 (1988): 14–23.

Seltzer, Mark. "Serial Killers (II): The Pathological Public Sphere." *Critical Inquiry* 22, no.1 (fall 1995): 122–49.

Seremetakis, C. Nadia. "The Memory of the Senses, Part I: Marks of the Transitory." In *The Senses Still: Perception and Memory as Material Culture in Modernity*, 1–18. Chicago: University of Chicago Press, 1994.

Shattuc, Jane. *The Talking Cure: TV Talk Shows and Women*. New York: Routledge, 1997.

Shaw, Harry E. *Narrating Reality: Austen, Scott, Eliot*. Ithaca, N.Y.: Cornell University Press, 1999.

Shorter, Edward. *A History of Psychiatry: From the Era of the Asylum to the Age of Prozac*. New York: John Wiley and Sons, 1997.

Shouse, Eric. "Feeling, Emotion, Affect." *M/C Journal* 8, no. 6 (2005). Available online at http://journal.media-culture.org.au/0512/03-shouse.php (accessed September 20, 2007).

Shumway, David. *Modern Love: Romance, Intimacy and the Marriage Crisis*. New York: New York University Press, 2003.

Shurter, Edwin DuBois. *American Government and Citizenship*. Chicago: Lippincott, 1930.

———. U.S. Adjunct-General's Office. *Studies in Citizenship for Recruits*. Washington, D.C.: War Department, U.S. Army, 1922. Available online at http://1a350609 .us.archive.org/1/items/studiesincitizenoounitiala/studiesincitizenoounitiala .pdf (accessed September 20, 2007).

———, ed. *Woman Suffrage: Bibliography and Selected Arguments June 1, 1912*. Bulletin of the University of Texas, no. 31. Austin: University of Texas, 1915.

Silverstein, Stuart Y. *Not Much Fun: The Lost Poems of Dorothy Parker*. New York: Scribner, 1996.

Siomopoulis, Anna. "Political Theory and Melodrama Studies." *Camera Obscura: Feminism, Culture, and Media Studies* 21, no. 2 (summer 2006): 178–83.

———. "Public Daydreams: Consumer Citizenship and Hollywood Cinema of the 1930s." Ph.D. diss., University of Chicago, 2003. Abstract in AAT 3097160.

Smith, Linda K. Christian. *Becoming a Woman through Romance*. London: Routledge, 1990.

Snead, James. "Repetition as a Figure of Black Culture." In *Out There: Marginalization and Contemporary Cultures*, ed. Russell Fergusson, Martha Gever, Trinh T. Minh-ha, and Cornel West, 213–30. Cambridge, Mass.: MIT Press, 1990.

Solomon, Martha M., ed. *A Voice of Their Own: The Woman Suffrage Press, 1840–1910*. Tuscaloosa: University of Alabama Press, 1991.

Sommer, Doris. *Foundational Fictions: The National Romances of Latin America*. Berkeley: University of California Press, 1993.

Spillers, Hortense J. "Mama's Baby, Papa's Maybe: An American Grammar Book." *Diacritics* 17, no. 2 (summer 1987): 67–80.

———. "Notes on an Alternative Model—Neither/Nor." In *The Difference Within: Feminism and Critical Theory*, ed. Elizabeth Meese and Alice Parker, 165–87. Philadelphia: John Benjamins Publishing Company, 1989.

Spivak, Gayatri Chakravorty. "Can the Subaltern Speak?" In *Marxism and the Interpretation of Culture*, ed. and intro. Cary Nelson and Lawrence Grossberg, 271–313. Urbana: University of Illinois Press, 1988.

———. "Subaltern Studies: Deconstructing Historiography." In *In Other Worlds: Essays in Cultural Politics*, 197–221. London: Routledge, 1987.

Spurlock, John C., and Cynthia A. Magistro. *New and Improved: The Transformation of American Women's Emotional Culture*. New York: New York University Press, 1998.

Stacey, Jackie. *Star Gazing: Hollywood Cinema and Female Spectatorship*. London: Routledge, 1994.

Staiger, Janet. *Interpreting Films: Studies in the Historical Reception of American Cinema*. Princeton, N.J.: Princeton University Press, 1992.

Stallybrass, Peter, and Allon White. *The Politics and Poetics of Transgression*. Ithaca, N.Y.: Cornell University Press, 1986.

Stearns, Peter N. *American Cool: Constructing a Twentieth-Century Emotional Style*. New York: New York University Press, 1994.

Steedman, Carolyn Kay. *Landscape for a Good Woman: A Story of Two Lives*. Newark, N.J.: Rutgers University Press, 1986.

Steiner, Leslie Morgan. *Mommy Wars: Stay-at-Home and Career Moms Face Off on Their Choices, Their Lives, and Their Families*. New York: Random House, 2006.

Stern, Julia. *The Plight of Feeling: Sympathy and Dissent in the Early American Novel*. Chicago: University of Chicago Press, 1997.

Stewart, Kathleen. *Ordinary Affects*. Durham, N.C.: Duke University Press, 2007.

Stoler, Ann Laura, ed. *Haunted by Empire: Geographies of Intimacy in North American History*. Durham, N.C.: Duke University Press, 2006.

Stowe, Harriet Beecher. *Uncle Tom's Cabin or, Life Among the Lowly*. 1852. Reprinted with editing and introduction by Ann Douglas. New York: Penguin, 1981.

Taussig, Michael. *The Magic of the State*. New York: Routledge, 1997.

Taylor, Diana. *The Archive and the Repertoire: Performing Cultural Memory in the Americas*. Durham, N.C.: Duke University Press, 2003.

Taylor, Helen. *Scarlett's Women: "Gone with the Wind" and Its Female Fans*. New Brunswick, N.J.: Rutgers University Press, 1989.

Taylor, Verta, and Leila J. Rupp. "Women's Culture and Lesbian Feminist Activism: A Reconsideration of Cultural Feminism." *Signs* 19, no. 1 (1993): 32–61.

Thrift, Nigel. *Spatial Formations*. London: Sage, 1996.

Thurschwell, Pamela. *Literature, Technology and Magical Thinking, 1880–1921*. Cambridge: Cambridge University Press, 2001.

Tompkins, Jane. *Sensational Designs: The Cultural Work of American Fiction, 1790–1860*. Oxford: Oxford University Press, 1985.

Turborg-Penn, Rosalind. *African-American Women in the Struggle for the Vote, 1850–1920*. Bloomington: Indiana University Press, 1998.

Urban, Greg. *Noumenal Community: Myth and Reality in an Amerindian Brazilian Society*. Austin: University of Texas Press, 1996.

U.S. Department of Justice. *Citizenship Education and Naturalization Information*. Washington, D.C.: Immigration and Naturalization Service, 1987.

Vinciguerra, Rose-Paule. "The Paradoxes of Love." *Psychoanalytical Notebooks* 3 (1999). Available online at http://www.londonsociety-nls.org.uk/Vinciguerra_paradoxes.htm (accessed September 20, 2007).

Vogler, Candace. "Sex and Talk." *Critical Inquiry* 24, no. 2 (winter 1998): 328–65.

Walker, Nancy, ed. *Women's Magazines, 1940–1960: Gender Roles and the Popular Press*. Boston: Bedford/St. Martin's, 1998.

Wall, Cheryl A. *Changing Our Own Words: Essays on Criticism, Theory, and Writing by Black Women*. New Brunswick, N.J.: Rutgers University Press, 1990.

————. *Worrying the Line: Black Women Writers, Lineage, and Literary Tradition*. Chapel Hill: University of North Carolina Press, 2005.

Waller, Robert James. *The Bridges of Madison County: Memory Book*. New York: Warner Books, 1995.

Walsh, Andrea S. *Women's Film and Female Experience, 1940–1950*. New York: Praeger, 1984.

Ward, Mary Jane. *The Snake Pit*. New York: Random House, 1946.

Wardley, Lynn. "Relic, Fetish, Femmage: The Aesthetics of Sentiment in the Work of Stowe." In *The Culture of Sentiment: Race, Gender and Sentimentality in Nineteenth-Century America*, ed. Shirley Samuels, 203–20. New York: Oxford University Press, 1992.

Warhol, Robyn. "Poetics and Persuasion: *Uncle Tom's Cabin* as a Realist Novel." *Essays in Literature* 13, no. 2 (fall 1988): 283–98.

Warner, Judith. *Perfect Madness: Motherhood in the Age of Anxiety*. New York: Riverhead Press, 2005.

Warner, Marina. *Monuments and Maidens: The Allegory of the Female Form*. New York: Atheneum, 1985.

Warner, Michael. *Publics and Counterpublics*. New York: Zone Books, 2002.

Waters, Chris. "Landscapes of Memory: Art and Everyday Life in Postwar Britain." *Ideas* 5, no.1 (1997): n.p.

Weinstein, Cindy, ed. *The Cambridge Companion to Harriet Beecher Stowe*. Cambridge: Cambridge University Press, 2004.

Weinzierl, Rupert, and David Muggleton. "What Is 'Post-Subcultural Studies' Anyway?" In *The Post-Subcultures Reader*, ed. David Muggleton and Rupert Weinzierl, 3–23. Oxford: Berg, 2003.

Weldon, Fay. *The Life and Loves of a She-Devil*. New York: Pantheon Books, 1983.

Westbrook, Robert B. "Politics as Consumption: Managing the Modern American Election." In *The Culture of Consumption: Critical Essays in American History, 1880–1980*, ed. Richard Wightman Fox and T. J. Jackson Lears, 1–38. New York: Pantheon Books, 1983.

Wexler, Laura. *Tender Violence: Domestic Visions in an Age of U.S. Imperialism*. Chapel Hill: University of North Carolina Press, 2000.

————. "Tender Violence: Literary Eavesdropping, Domestic Fiction, and Educational Reform." In *The Culture of Sentiment: Race, Gender and Sentimentality in Nineteenth-Century America*, ed. Shirley Samuels, 9–38. New York: Oxford University Press, 1992.

Wexman, Virginia. *Creating the Couple: Love, Marriage, and Hollywood Performance.* Princeton, N.J.: Princeton University Press, 1993.

White, Deborah Gray. *Too Heavy a Load: Black Women in Defense of Themselves.* New York: W. W. Norton and Co., 1999.

White, Hayden. *Figural Realism: Studies in the Mimesis Effect.* Baltimore: Johns Hopkins University Press, 1999.

———. *Metahistory: The Historical Imagination in Nineteenth-Century Europe.* Baltimore: Johns Hopkins University Press, 1975.

———. "The Modernist Event." In *Figural Realism: Studies in the Mimesis Effect,* 66–86. Baltimore: Johns Hopkins University Press, 1999.

White, Patricia. *Uninvited: Classical Hollywood Cinema and Lesbian Representability.* Bloomington: Indiana University Press, 1999.

Whitfield, Stephen J. "Is It True What They Sing about Dixie?" *Southern Cultures* (summer 2002): 9–37.

Wicke, Jennifer. *Advertising Fictions: Literature, Advertisement, and Social Reading.* New York: Columbia University Press, 1988.

Wiebe, Robert. *Self-Rule: A Cultural History of American Democracy.* Chicago: University of Chicago Press, 1995.

Willemen, Paul. "Towards an Analysis of the Sirkean System." *Screen* 13, no. 4 (winter 1972/73): 128–34.

Williams, Linda. "Film Bodies: Gender, Genre, and Excess." *Film Quarterly* 44, no. 4 (summer): 2–13.

———. "Melodrama Revisited." In *Reconfiguring American Film Genres: Theory and History,* ed. Nick Browne, 42–88. Berkeley: University of California Press, 1998.

———. *Playing the Race Card: Melodramas of Black and White from Uncle Tom to O. J. Simpson.* Princeton, N.J.: Princeton University Press, 2002.

Williams, Patricia. *The Alchemy of Race and Rights: Diary of a Law Professor.* Cambridge, Mass.: Harvard University Press, 1991.

Williams, Raymond. *The Long Revolution.* 1961. Reprint, Peterborough, Ont.: Broadview Press, 2001.

Willis, Ellen. "Radical Feminism and Feminist Radicalism." In *The 60s without Apology,* eds. Sohnya Sares, Anders Stephanson, Stanley Aronowitz, and Fredric Jameson, 91–118. Minneapolis: University of Minnesota Press, 1984.

Wilson, Christopher P. *White Collar Fictions: Class and Social Representation in American Literature, 1885–1925.* Athens: University of Georgia Press, 1992.

Wilson, Justina Leavitt. *Woman Suffrage: A Study Outline.* White Plains, N.Y.: The H. W. Wilson Co., 1916.

Wright, Richard. *Uncle Tom's Children.* 1940. Reprint, New York: Harper Collins, 1993.

Young, Iris Marion. "Impartiality and the Civic Public: Some Implications of Feminist Critique of Moral and Political Theory." *Feminism as Critique*, ed. and intro. Selya Benhabib and Drucilla Cornell, 57–76. Minneapolis: University of Minnesota Press, 1987.

———. "Polity and Group Difference: A Critique of the Ideal of Universal Citizenship." *Ethics* 99, no. 2 (January 1989): 250–74.

Young, Kay. *Ordinary Pleasures: Couples, Conversation, and Comedy*. Columbus: Ohio State University Press, 2001.

Zaretsky, Eli. *Capitalism, the Family, and Personal Life*. New York: Harper, Collins, 1982.

———. *Secrets of the Soul: A Social and Cultural History of Psychoanalysis*. New York: Knopf, 2004.

Žižek, Slavoj. *The Metastasies of Enjoyment: Six Essays on Women and Causality*. New York: Verso, 1994.

———. "Passion: Regular or Decaf?" *In These Times*, February 27, 2004. Available online at www.lacan.com/zizek-passion.htm (accessed September 20, 2007).

———. *The Plague of Fantasies*. London: Verso, 1997.

———. "The Spectre of Ideology." In *Mapping Ideology*, ed. Slavoj Žižek, 1–33. London: Verso, 1994.

———. *The Sublime Object of Ideology*. New York: Verso, 1989.

———. *Tarrying with the Negative: Kant, Hegel, and the Critique of Ideology*. Durham, N.C.: Duke University Press, 1993.

Zukerman, Mary Ellen. *A History of Women's Popular Magazines in the United States, 1792–1995*. Westport, Conn.: Greenwood Press, 1998.

# INDEX

Acting: fantasies of, 52; in *Imitation of Life*, 136, 138–40; in *Show Boat*, 71, 81–83, 92, 97, 103; in *A Star is Born*, 208, 224–26. *See also* Imitation

Adaptation, 12, 23, 26, 269, 272, 278; in *Show Boat*, 69, 76; in the *Uncle Tom's Cabin* tradition, 32, 39–40, 44–47

Adorno, Theodor, 213, 224

Aesthetics. *See* Convention; Genre; Mediation; Sentimentality; Situation

Affect, 2, 4, 12, 14, 170, 266–68, 271. *See also* Bargaining

Affect management, 3, 17, 268, 278. *See also* Emotion

Agamben, Giorgio, 27, 162–63, 211, 315 n. 11

Ambivalence, xi, 2, 5–6, 11, 21, 25, 234, 261–62, 267, 281 n. 3, 285 n. 12; in *Landscape for a Good Woman*, 238–43; of Parker, 215–16, 218–21, 223, 228; in *Poor Eliza*, 36, 55–58; in Prouty, 173–74, 179; in *Uncle Sam Needs a Wife*, 148–49. *See also* Bargaining; Female complaint

Amnesia: historical, 9, 29; in *Imitation of Life*, 122; in *Now, Voyager*, 170–71, 179–80; in *Show Boat*, 72–74, 89, 92, 98. *See also* Memory

Anxiety, 13, 15–16, 21, 23, 146,179. 210, 224, 247, 285 n. 12. *See also* Bargaining; Female complaint; Love

Attachment, 10–11, 13–15, 20, 32, 266

Autobiography, vii–x, 250

Badiou, Alain, 266

Baldwin, James, 28, 33, 35, 57–60, 66, 316–17 n. 24

Bargaining, viii, 2, 9–10, 12–13, 16, 20–22, 32, 44, 170, 233, 268–69; Baldwin's critique of, 57; in *Landscape for A Good Woman*, 249, 255; in Parker, 213–15, 218, 223–24; in Prouty, 173, 177, 182, 184, 198; in *Show Boat*, 80–81, 99; in *Uncle Sam Needs a Wife*, 149, 156, 159. *See also* Affect; Ambivalence; Optimism

Belonging, viii–x, 10, 25, 28, 35, 266; citizenship as, 150–67; vague, 3–7, 9,

Belonging (*cont.*)

11, 22, 24, 30, 37, 106, 145, 172, 258, 270, 278–79

*Beloved* (Morrison), 28, 36, 66–67

Biopower, 8–9

*Bluest Eye, The* (Morrison), 54, 66

Bollas, Christopher, 27, 25, 239–40, 262

*Bridges of Madison County, The* (Waller), 36, 60–65

Brooks, Peter, 271, 316 n. 17

Bugs Bunny, 308 n. 31

Capitalism. *See* Adaptation; Commodity; Fantasy; Mass culture; Women's culture

Cavell, Stanley, 189, 204, 308 n. 30, 310 n. 11, 315 n. 9

Citizenship, xi, 8, 20, 29, 35, 39, 54, 76, 89, 109–12, 116, 140, 166, 216, 241; cities and, 235; "educated," 152–54; manuals, 151–58. *See also* Belonging; Female complaint; Nationality; Publics; Suffrage

Cliché, 30, 35–36, 58, 202–4, 226–27, 247

Commodity, viii, 7, 10, 42, 46, 52, 96. *See also* Identification

Compassion, 6, 28, 34, 41, 55–58, 99–100, 106, 146, 170

Complaint. *See* Female complaint

Consumption and identity, 5–13, 20, 30, 45–46, 51–54, 89–90, 94–97, 109, 116–18, 150, 237–38

Convention, 4, 36; aesthetic, 13–14, 19–20, 215, 271–72. *See also* Cliché; Form, formalism

Conventionality, xi, 2–4, 18, 210, 230, 270; literary, xii, 12, 19, 27, 158–59; normative, xii, 3, 6, 7, 12, 19, 21, 27, 219–21, 235–36. *See also* Cliché; Genre; Mass culture; Normativity; Stereotype

Davis, Lydia, 16–19

Deleuze, Gilles, ix–x

Democracy, 28, 52–54

Depression: economic, 50–54, 73, 81, 131–32, 297 n. 21; emotional, 15, 175, 185–94, 198, 306 n. 9; political, 151, 154–55, 230, 303 n. 18, 306 n. 9

Derrida, Jacques, 18, 222

*Dimples*, 36, 49–54

Dyer, Richard, 227

Eckert, Charles, 53

Edison, Thomas A., 45, 49

Emotion, 160–67; women's emotional labor, xi–xii, 2, 5, 17–20, 82, 170–71. *See also* Affect management; Sentimentality

Empathy, 55, 165–66, 229

Episodes, 4, 16, 211. *See also* Situation

"Everybody's Protest Novel," 33, 58

Fantasy, 5–12, 25–32, 35–36, 47–48, 55, 74–75, 85–90, 234–36; of "being somebody," 3, 24, 98, 207–10, 215, 224, 226, 228, 230–31, 276–78

Female complaint, 1–2, 13, 15, 19, 51, 60, 90, 150, 154, 228, 230, 267, 271, 276–77

Femininity, 210–11, 215, 218, 222; conventions of, viii–ix, 2–4, 11, 17–19. *See also* Female complaint; Genre

Feminism, xii, 1, 28–30, 110–12, 149, 178, 233–37, 243–46, 256, 261, 281 n. 2, 286–87 n. 23

Ferber, Edna, 23; "Old Man Minnick," 100–101; *A Peculiar Treasure*, 104; "You're Not the Type," 80–83

Fetchit, Stepin, 50–51

Form, formalism, 4, 28, 210–12, 215–16, 220–22, 224, 226, 228, 230–31, 268; historicism vs., 265–67; normative, 60, 192, 241, 254; placeholder, 3, 27, 30, 99, 160, 184, 203, 207, 214, 217, 259. *See also* Cliché; Convention; Genre

Fraser, Nancy, 7–8
Freud, Sigmund: "The Economic Problem of Masochism," 221–22; opponents of, 154, 185–86, 195

Genre, ix–x, 3–4, 13, 18–19, 21, 24, 210–13, 215–16, 219–22, 226–28; of intimacy, 25, 37, 259–60, 271–72. *See also* Conventionality; Form, formalism; Identity
Gledhill, Christine, 271, 316 n. 17
Goulding, Sue, 166
*Gone with the Wind*, 282 n. 5, 316 n. 22
Gramsci, Antonio, 98, 268
Guattari, Félix, ix–x, 240, 312 n.10

Halttunen, Karen, 20
Hansen, Miriam, 10
Hurst, Fannie, 23

Identification, viii, 29, 160–63, 170. *See also* Commodity; Fantasy; Identity
Identity: through celebrity, 29, 71, 78, 88–91, 97, 160–66, 208–9; general, viii, 4–7, 26, 28, 30, 219, 223, 244, 255, 277–78; singular, x, 4, 11, 214, 217, 231, 272, 277–78; universal, 6, 12–13, 25, 75. *See also* Genre; Mass culture
Imitation, 12, 29, 80–83, 88–89; in *Imitation of Life*, 119, 127, 129, 136–41; in *Now, Voyager*, 183, 188–91, 193, 196–97 199–200, 202; Parker and, 208, 216, 226; in *She-Devil*, 252–55, 258–59, 262–63; in *Showboat 1988*, 276
*Imitation of Life*: 1933 (Fannie Hurst), 113–23, 142–44; 1934 (John Stahl), 123–31; 1956 (Douglas Sirk), 131–41; abstraction and embodiment in, 107–12, 118–22, 132–39; capitalist public in, 116–17; com-

modities and trademarks in, 117–22, 132–39; feminine solidarity and, 112, 117, 120, 123–31, 139; labor in, 112, 116–17, 133, 138–39, 234; leisure and consumption in, 116, 121–23, 130–40; motherhood in, 117, 119, 123; national fantasy and, 115–16, 122, 141–44; racialized publicity and, 117–29; sexuality and fantasy in, 114–20
Imperialism, 34, 39–40, 43, 157, 159, 176. *See also* Nationality
Intimacy, 25, 27–28, 39, 70, 169, 181–90
*Island of Lost Souls*, 167

Jameson, Fredric, 75, 78–79, 161, 227, 271, 284 n. 10

Kennedy, Adrienne, 275
*King and I, The*, 33–34, 37–44
Knight, Arthur, 278

Lacan, Jacques, 14, 26, 239
*Landscape for a Good Woman* (Steedman), 30–31, 235, 244–45, 249, 255, 258; anonymity and misrecognition in, 240–41; class and fantasy in, 236, 241; feminine bodies and fantasy in, 236–43; love as fantasy in, 239–40, 242; politics in, 241, 243; space and fantasy in, 236, 238–41; things and fantasy in, 236–37
Larsen, Nella, 107–10
Lefort, Claude, 162–63
LeSueur, Meridel, 282 n. 7
Leys, Ruth, 194–95
Liberalism: as fantasy of sovereign universality, 110–11, 146, 166–67, 204, 256–62, 268; as post-racist fantasy, 6, 8, 29, 35–37, 46, 52–67, 69–72, 99–102, 121; as sentimental ideology of "true feeling," xi, 22–25, 8, 150. *See also* True feeling; White supremacy

*Life and Loves of a She-Devil*, 30–31,
    235–36; affect and emotion in, 247,
    257, 261–63; capitalism in, 247–51,
    253–56, 262; cities in, 249–51, 255;
    extreme embodiment in, 246–47,
    252–54, 257–59, 262; feminism in,
    245–46, 248, 250, 260–61; formal-
    ism in, 245–47, 252–58, 259–60, 263;
    heterofemininity in, 245–48, 254–56,
    258–59; lesbianism in, 250, 253; love
    and romance in, 245–48, 251–53, 259,
    263; nation in, 252, 255, 258
Lott, Eric, 60
Love, 1, 11, 13–15, 28, 61–62, 164, 216–21;
    aesthetic conventions of, 7, 16–19,
    37–43, 70, 74–94, 171–77, 203, 219,
    228, 231, 245, 257–60, 294 n. 42

Masochism, 221–22, 240
Mass culture, viii, 5–13, 24–25, 30–32,
    112, 176–79; in *Imitation of Life*,
    116–29, 131–41; in *Show Boat*,
    72–73, 92–98; therapy culture and,
    29, 154–55, 204–5, 307 n. 25; in *Uncle
    Tom* lineage, 17, 35, 46. *See also* Con-
    ventionality; Depression; Fantasy;
    Identification; Mediation
Mediation, viii, xii, 4–5, 12, 25, 37, 42, 47,
    160–67, 190, 267. *See also* Mass culture
Melodrama, xi–x, 6, 13, 173, 272; in *Now,
    Voyager*, 171, 172, 180, 184–85, 197,
    202; in Parker, 211, 218, 229–30; in
    *Show Boat*, 71, 82–83, 89, 92–97, 101,
    104–5, 158, 171–72, 184–85, 197, 202,
    211, 230, 260, 270–71; in *Uncle Tom's
    Cabin* and cognates, 40, 48, 60. *See
    also* Conventionality; Nationality;
    Realism; Sentimentality
Memory, 6, 64–65, 179, 182, 185–86;
    citizenship and, 28–29; collective, 122,
    131, 161–66; love and, 7, 16, 169–72,

191, 202, 205; sentimentality and, 21; in
    *Show Boat*, 72–74, 80, 83, 88–89, 94–106;
    in *Uncle Tom* tradition, 52–59. *See also*
    Amnesia; Cliché; Love; Nationality
Middlebrow genres, 4, 30; Parker and,
    211–13, 224, 227–28, 234, 285 n. 12,
    311 n. 25; *Show Boat* as, 70, 98, 102
Misrecognition, 18, 40, 47, 169–70,
    196–97. *See also* Recognition
Moon, Michael, 9
*Movie Star Has to Star in Black and
    White, A* (Kennedy), 275

Nationality, xi, 21–22, 25, 34, 38, 40, 43, 49,
    53, 60–63, 72, 78, 109, 122, 161, 235–36
Normativity, 5, 9, 18, 22, 25, 28, 266. *See
    also* Cliché; Conventionality; Fantasy;
    Love; Optimism
*Now, Voyager*, 16, 24–25, 30, 197–204,
    207, 272; class in, 171–72, 175–77;
    cliché in, 184–90, 192–93, 203;
    Davis in, 180, 275; heteronormativ-
    ity in, 170–74, 177–93, 205; love in,
    169–79; memory in, 169, 179–82,
    185–86, 191, 202, 205; psychoanalysis
    in, 183–87, 192–96, 198–200, 205;
    queerness in, 174–77, 181, 189; sexual
    desire in, 182–84, 188–91; therapy
    culture in, 171, 179, 181–82, 193, 202,
    205; white racial and imperial fantasy
    in, 175–77, 180–81

Optimism, xi–xii, 2, 15, 28, 40, 70,
    169–74, 180–82, 205, 214–15, 223, 267

Parker, Dorothy, 4, 23, 214, 267; aesthetic
    form and, 209–12, 220–31, 216–25,
    227; "Ballade at Thirty-Five," 219–20;
    "Big Blonde," 216–17, 223; feminine
    norm and, 209, 211–13, 216, 225, 227;
    Garland and, 224, 226; inanity and,

213, 215, 226, 226–30; intellectualism and, 215–16, 223, 226; *It's a Wonderful Life*, 229; *Ladies of the Corridor*, 218; love and, 210–12, 222, 225–28; politics and, 228–31; *Smash-Up*, 217; "Sonnet for the End of a Sequence," 220–21; *A Star is Born*, 30, 207–10, 224–26, 234, 236, 309–10 nn. 1–2

*Passing*, 70, 83

Performativity, 4, 81, 183, 284

Philip, M. Nourbese, 100

Plath, Sylvia, 205

Prince, Morton, 193–202, 308 n. 33, 36–38, 309 n. 42

Probyn, Elspeth, 166

Prouty, Olive Higgins, 23, 30, 172–78, 186; *Pencil Shavings*, 181; *Stella Dallas*, 24–25, 175, 180; *White Fawn*, 174

Psychoanalysis, 14–20, 30, 212, 239–40, 255, 262. *See also* Fantasy; Love

Publics, viii; affective, x–xi, 25, 171–73; counterpublics, 7–8, 24, 35; intimate, vii, 2–3, 5–13, 19–20, 25, 41, 44, 70, 146, 160, 167, 170, 173, 212, 215, 233–34, 267–73, 275, 278; juxtapolitical, x, 2, 10, 24–25, 29, 164, 267, 269–70; mass, 69, 72, 96, 113, 166, 170; pathological, 20; political, 7–9, 20–22, 41, 46, 64, 77, 110, 116, 150–67, 275, 278, 297 n. 21; racialized, 6, 26, 73–75, 99, 121, 125, 153, 176; semi-, 9; strong and weak, 8; women's, 6, 12, 19–20, 26, 67, 170, 196, 233–34, 242, 267, 283 n. 8

Racism, 6, 28, 46, 53, 65, 69, 72, 245. *See also* Liberalism; Publics; Sentimentality; White supremacy

Rancière, Jacques, 166

Realism, viii, ix, 17, 40, 44, 265–71; *Life and Loves of a She-Devil*, 246, 262; *Now, Voyager*, 173; *Show Boat*, 73, 92,

95. *See also* Melodrama; Sentimentality

Reciprocity: love and, 15–20, 174, 179, 212–22; social, xi, 5–11, 22–23, 35, 238, 244, 266–79. *See also* Belonging; Love

Recognition, viii–xi, 4, 6, 10–15, 19–21, 34–35, 100, 146, 165–67, 173, 179, 210, 231, 239 256, 268, 271, 278. *See also* Love; Misrecognition; Publics

Repetition, 14–15, 56, 136–37, 218–19, 222–23, 243–44, 254, 257–61. *See also* Love

Riggs, Austin, 181, 186–87, 307 n. 25

Robeson, Paul, 85, 89, 276

Rose, Jacqueline, 16, 205

Ross, Kristin, 161

Secrets: open, 1, 22, 82, 211, 226, 228, 239; secret life, 139, 182–93, 196–204, 238, 242, 251–53

Sedgwick, Eve, 9, 23, 284 n. 11, 286 n. 20, 288 n. 49, 308 n. 30

Seltzer, Mark, 20

Sentimentality: aesthetics of, 1, 17, 20, 36–37, 44–48, 73–80, 100–106, 230–31, 265, 268–69, 272–73; comic modes and, 37, 45, 47–52, 70, 77, 90, 125, 128, 158–59, 171, 211, 271, 281 n. 2, 299 n. 39, 314 n. 23; countersentimental modes and, 55–67, 89; as ideology, 2–3, 20, 34, 46–47, 65–66, 145–46; liberal and national modes of, x–xii, 22, 26; in normative femininity, 2–3, 19, 36; pedagogy and, 63–67; in politics, 2–3, 21, 34–6, 145–46; in rhetoric, 20–21, 141; tragicomic modes and, 16, 31, 34, 171, 174; "unfinished business" of, 2, 32, 34, 44–45, 46, 99, 145, 149, 271, 273

Sexuality, 146, 167; heteronormative, 74–75, 80, 84, 90–92, 158–59, 166–67,

True feeling: culture of, 12, 34–35, 43, 65, 106; rhetoric of, 42, 54, 56, 145–46. *See also* Liberalism; Sentimentality

*Uncle Sam Needs a Wife*, 29, 147–59
*Uncle Tom's Cabin*, 28, 36–40, 42, 44, 55–67, 69, 76–78, 86; contemporary remakes of, 45, 48–49; history and modernity in, 45–54; music and, 49; souvenirs of, 47–48
Utopian fantasy, 98, 123, 213, 220, 227, 271–72

Waller, Robert James, 36, 60–65
Warner, Michael, 7
Whale, James, 86

White supremacy, 6, 28–29, 30; in *Life and Loves of a She-Devil*, 245; in *Now, Voyager*, 175–77; in *Show Boat* and remakes, 69–70, 72, 76, 80, 83, 122, 275; in *Uncle Tom's Cabin* and remakes, 46, 53, 58, 65. *See also* Liberalism; Racism; Sentimentality
Whitman, Walt, 180
Women's culture, viii, xii, 2, 5–13, 16, 19, 35–36, 81, 170–71, 178–82, 202–5, 213–15, 225–26, 281 n. 2, 282 n. 6, 282 n. 7, 283 n. 8, 285 n. 14, 295 n. 10, 301 n. 3; as culture industry, x; as fantasy zone, ix–x. *See also* Belonging: vague; Capitalism

Žižek, Slavoj, 265–70

Lauren Berlant is the George M. Pullman Professor of English at the University of Chicago.

Library of Congress Cataloging-in-Publication Data
Berlant, Lauren Gail, 1957–
The female complaint : the unfinished business of sentimentality in American culture / Lauren Berlant.
p. cm.
Includes bibliographical references and index.
ISBN 978-0-8223-4184-0 (cloth : alk. paper)
ISBN 978-0-8223-4202-1 (pbk. : alk. paper)
1. Sentimentalism. 2. Sentimentalism in literature. 3. Sentimentalism in motion pictures. 4. Mass media and women. 5. Women—Psychology. 6. Emotions (Psychology). 7. Women in literature. 8. Women in motion pictures. I. Title.
BH301.E45B47 2008
305.420973—dc22    2007043974